# MEDIA MESSAGES IN THE 2022 MIDTERM ELECTION

The 2022 midterms marked a transformative moment in American politics, as the combined influence of legacy media and social platforms reached new heights. Traditional outlets like television news and print journalism set the stage, while a vast digital ecosystem—spanning Facebook, TikTok, YouTube, and more—enabled campaigns to amplify messages on issues like abortion rights, the economy, and immigration. As these platforms shaped the voter experience in a fragmented and often-polarized media environment, campaigns and citizens harnessed their power to reach diverse audiences and build momentum across both established and emerging channels.

This book offers a compelling, scholarly exploration of these dynamics, revealing how communication across traditional and digital media shaped an election forecasted as a Republican "red wave" but instead delivered unexpected, narrower results. Through detailed analyses, data-driven research, and case studies from high-profile races, this book uncovers how media strategies influenced voter behavior, shaped public discourse, and framed electoral outcomes. Essential for academics, political analysts, and media professionals, this work provides crucial insights into the evolving role of media in U.S. elections and the weighty implications for future democratic engagement.

**John Allen Hendricks** is Chair of the Department of Media & Communication and Professor at Stephen F. Austin State University, a member of the University of Texas System, where he teaches courses in communication theory, research methods, First Amendment law, and media and politics. He is the recipient of book awards from the National Communication Association (NCA) and the Broadcast Education Association (BEA).

**Dan Schill** is Professor in the School of Communication Studies and Affiliate Professor in Political Science at James Madison University, where he teaches courses in advocacy, political communication, research methods, and media and politics. His research focuses on communication, politics, media, and technology.

# MEDIA MESSAGES IN THE 2022 MIDTERM ELECTION

Division, Deniers, Dobbs, and the Donald

*Edited by John Allen Hendricks and Dan Schill*

NEW YORK AND LONDON

Designed cover image: Getty Images

First published 2025
by Routledge
605 Third Avenue, New York, NY 10158

and by Routledge
4 Park Square, Milton Park, Abingdon, Oxon, OX14 4RN

*Routledge is an imprint of the Taylor & Francis Group, an informa business*

© 2025 selection and editorial matter, John Allen Hendricks and Dan Schill;
individual chapters, the contributors

The right of John Allen Hendricks and Dan Schill to be identified as the authors
of the editorial material, and of the authors for their individual chapters,
has been asserted in accordance with sections 77 and 78 of the Copyright,
Designs and Patents Act 1988.

All rights reserved. No part of this book may be reprinted or reproduced or utilised
in any form or by any electronic, mechanical, or other means, now known or
hereafter invented, including photocopying and recording, or in any information
storage or retrieval system, without permission in writing from the publishers.

*Trademark notice*: Product or corporate names may be trademarks or registered trademarks,
and are used only for identification and explanation without intent to infringe.

ISBN: 978-1-032-57755-5 (hbk)
ISBN: 978-1-032-57754-8 (pbk)
ISBN: 978-1-003-44083-3 (ebk)

DOI: 10.4324/9781003440833

Typeset in Times New Roman
by Newgen Publishing UK

# CONTENTS

| | |
|---|---|
| *List of Figures* | *viii* |
| *List of Tables* | *ix* |
| *About the Editors* | *xi* |
| *About the Contributors* | *xiii* |
| *Acknowledgments* | *xxi* |

1    Media, Messaging, and the Midterms: Communication
Dynamics in the 2022 U.S. Elections      1
*Dan Schill and John Allen Hendricks*

## SECTION I
## Amplified Doubts: Conspiracy Theories, Communication, and the 2022 Midterm Elections      25

2    Conspiratorial Ideation, Election Denial, and Voter Choice      27
*Diana Owen, Thom Crockett, Arjun Chawla,
Kelton Miller, Kyle Kim, Haydyn Hendricks,
Parisa Bruce, and Brenda Zhong*

3    *2000 Mules*: A Story of Consequence and Conspiracy      48
*Stephen D. Caldes, Zach Justus, and
Jennifer A. Malkowski*

**vi** Contents

**SECTION II**
**Framing the Debate: How issues Shaped 2022
Candidate Communication**      67

4   Post-*Roe* Politics: Priming, Framing, and the Dynamics
of Abortion Discourse in Congressional Campaigns      69
*Christopher Chapp, India Bock, and Cali Goulet*

5   Winning Stories Amid Partisanship: Narratives in
Political Advertisements and Overperforming Candidates
in the 2022 U.S. Midterm Election      91
*B. Theo Mazumdar*

6   How Congress Managed Social Media Agenda Fracture
and Inversion during the 2022 Election      125
*Jason B. Reineke, Kenneth R. Blake, and Jun Zhang*

**SECTION III**
**News Narratives: 2022 Media Coverage and Public
Perception**      147

7   The Impact of Digital Partisan News Algorithms in the
2022 Midterm Election      149
*Hyun Jung Yun and Jae Hee Park*

8   Reply "STOP": Dominant Media Frames of SMS-Based
Political Communication as a Consumer Problem      166
*Ryan Cheek and Samuel Allen*

9   Of Red Waves, Election Deniers, Candidate Quality
and Other Issues: Political Cartoons during the 2022
Midterm Elections      191
*Jody C Baumgartner and Hanna Kassab*

Contents **vii**

SECTION IV
**Midterm Communication in the States: Case Studies
from Arizona, Nevada, Florida, Texas, and Kansas**    **211**

10 The Limits of Being "100% Pro-life": Rhetorical
Trajectory and Abortion in the American Southwest    213
*Calvin R. Coker and Desmond J. McCarthy*

11 Florida's 2022 Senate Race: Social Media, Social
Justice, and Partisanship    233
*David Lynn Painter, Tanja Vierrether, and Fiona Bown*

12 The Centrality of Citizen-as-Consumer: A Study of the
2022 Texas Midterms and the Failing Concept of the
Marketplace of Ideas in a Digital Era    252
*Zoë Hess Carney and Rita Kirk*

13 Gendered Treatment in the Communication Strategy
of a Female Gubernatorial Candidate    266
*Joyce H. Glasscock*

*Index*    *288*

# FIGURES

| | | |
|---|---|---|
| 1.1 | The Party that Controls the White House Almost Always Loses Seats in the House During Midterms | 2 |
| 1.2 | The Party that Controls the White House Often Loses Senate Seats in Midterms, but Less Commonly than in the House | 2 |
| 4.1 | Congressional Candidate Abortion Statements, 2008–2022 | 76 |
| 4.2 | Republican Frames 2008–2022 | 83 |
| 4.3 | Democratic Frames 2008–2022 | 83 |
| 4.4 | Predicting Candidates' Abortion Framing | 85 |
| 6.1 | Total Topic Volume by Week | 134 |
| 6.2 | Immigration Topic Volume, by Week and Source | 135 |
| 6.3 | Abortion Topic Volume, by Week and Source | 136 |
| 6.4 | Economy Topic Volume, by Week and Source | 138 |
| 6.5 | "Trump" Topic Volume, by Week and Source | 139 |
| 6.6 | "Biden" Topic Volume, by Week and Source | 140 |
| 8.1 | Four Phases of the Research Process | 168 |
| 8.2 | Frequency of Codes | 176 |
| 8.3 | Example of "Annoying, but Legal" Media Coverage | 182 |
| 9.1 | Number of Cartoons and Stories about "Midterm Elections" Per Week | 197 |

# TABLES

| | | |
|---|---|---|
| 2.1 | Conspiracy Theory Items and Labels | 35 |
| 2.2 | Correlations (Pearson's *R*) between Belief in the Big Lie and Fringe Conspiracies | 37 |
| 2.3 | Correlations (Pearson's *R*) between Conspiracy-Related Items | 37 |
| 2.4 | OLS Regression of Conspiracy Variables, Media Variables, and Party Identification on Engagement (Beta Coefficients) | 38 |
| 2.5 | OLS Regression of Conspiracy Variables, Media Variables, and Party Identification on Vote Choice (Beta Coefficients) | 40 |
| 4.1 | Top Frames by Party | 79 |
| 5.1 | Overperforming Winning Candidates in the 2022 U.S. Midterm Election, by District Partisan Lean and Victory Margin | 101 |
| 5.2 | Analysis of Narratives: Winning 2022 Republican Candidates Who Overperformed in Republican-Leaning Districts | 102 |
| 5.3 | Analysis of Narratives: Winning 2022 Republican Candidates Who Overperformed in Democratic-Leaning Districts | 107 |
| 5.4 | Analysis of Narratives: Winning 2022 Democratic Candidates Who Overperformed in Democratic-Leaning Districts | 109 |
| 5.5 | Analysis of Narratives: Winning 2022 Democratic Candidates Who Overperformed in Republican-Leaning Districts | 115 |
| 6.1 | Congressional and Preferred Media Outlet Twitter Data Descriptives | 133 |
| 7.1 | Partisan News Framing in Digital Partisan News Algorithms | 157 |
| 7.2 | Partisan News Appeals in Digital Partisan News Algorithms | 157 |
| 7.3 | Partisan News Properties in Digital Partisan News Algorithms | 159 |

**x** List of Tables

| | | |
|---|---|---|
| 7.4 | Partisan News Comments in Digital Partisan News Algorithms | 160 |
| 8.1 | Truncated Codebook Containing All Codes Found Relevant to the Study | 170 |
| 8.2 | Significant Co-Occurrence (c/o) Relationships | 175 |
| 9.1 | GDELT Project Television Comparer Values for News Stories, by Category | 196 |
| 9.2 | Number and Percentage of Cartoons in Each Category | 198 |
| 11.1 | Candidate Evaluation Changes by Condition | 242 |
| 11.2 | Candidate Evaluation Changes by Party | 242 |
| 11.3 | Evaluation Changes by Party and Condition | 244 |
| 13.1 | Chi-square Test for Kelly Traits, Feminine and Masculine, by Platform | 275 |
| 13.2 | Chi-square Test for Kelly Issues, Feminine and Masculine, by Platform | 276 |
| 13.3 | Kelly's Top-Ranked Feminine and Masculine Issues, Platforms Combined | 276 |
| 13.4 | Schmidt Attacks, Acclaims, and Defenses by Platform | 277 |
| 13.5 | Schmidt's Campaign Attacks on Kelly Traits by Gender and Platform | 277 |
| 13.6 | Schmidt's Campaign Attacks on Kelly Issues by Gender and Platform | 278 |
| 13.7 | Kelly Tweet Agenda Versus Schmidt Tweet Attack Agenda | 279 |
| 13.8 | Kelly TV Ad Agenda Versus Schmidt TV Ad Agenda | 279 |
| 13.9 | Kelly Debate Statement Agenda Versus Schmidt Debate Statement Agenda | 280 |

# ABOUT THE EDITORS

**John Allen Hendricks** (Ph.D., The University of Southern Mississippi) is Chair and Professor of the Department of Media & Communication at Stephen F. Austin State University in Nacogdoches, Texas. He has held the department leadership role since 2009.

He has published numerous books on the topics of media/politics, social media/new media technologies, and the media industry, including: *Social Media Politics: Digital Discord in the 2020 Presidential Election* (with Dan Schill, Routledge, 2024), *The Presidency and Social Media* (with Dan Schill, Routledge, 2016), *Presidential Campaigning and Social Media* (with Dan Schill, Oxford University Press, 2014), *Social Media and Strategic Communications* (with Hana Noor Al-Deen, Palgrave MacMillan, 2013), *Social Media: Usage and Impact* (with Hana Noor Al-Deen; Lexington Books, 2012), *Techno Politics in Presidential Campaigning* (with Lynda Lee Kaid; Routledge, 2011), and *Communicator-in-Chief: How Barack Obama Used New Media Technology to Win the White House* (with Robert E. Denton, Jr.; Lexington Books, 2009).

He has received book awards from the National Communication Association and the Broadcast Education Association. Dr. Hendricks is founding editor of the book series, "Studies in New Media," for Lexington Books/Rowman & Littlefield.

**Dan Schill** (Ph.D., University of Kansas) is Professor in the School of Communication Studies and Affiliate Professor in Political Science at James Madison University (JMU), where he teaches courses in advocacy, political communication, research methods, and media and politics. He holds numerous teaching awards, including the Carl Harter Distinguished Teacher Award, JMU's

**xii** About the Editors

top award for teaching excellence, and the School of Communication Top Teacher Award from the JMU student body. Schill previously worked on Capitol Hill as an American Political Science Association (APSA) Congressional Fellow and often conducts dial focus groups for news organizations.

His research focuses on communication, politics, media, and technology. He has published five books on political communication topics, including *Social Media Politics: Digital Discord in the 2020 Presidential Election* (with John Allen Hendricks, Routledge, 2024), *The Presidency and Social Media* (with John Allen Hendricks, Routledge, 2018), *Political Communication in Real Time* (with Rita Kirk and Amy Jasperson; Routledge, 2017), *Communication and Midterm Elections* (with John Allen Hendricks; Palgrave Macmillan, 2015), *Presidential Campaigning and Social Media* (with John Allen Hendricks; Oxford University Press, 2014), and *Stagecraft and Statecraft: Advance and Media Events in Political Communication* (Lexington Books, 2009). Other work has appeared in the *Journal of Political Marketing*, *American Behavioral Scientist*, *Mass Communication & Society*, *Argumentation and Advocacy*, *Review of Communication*, and *PS: Political Science & Politics*.

He has also received top paper awards from the Political communication Divisions of the International Communication Association, National Communication Association, and the Central States Communication Association.

# ABOUT THE CONTRIBUTORS

**Samuel Allen** (Ph.D., University of Pittsburgh) is the author of "Donald Trump Doesn't Laugh: Laughter, Affect, and Angry White Male Victimization" in Todd Reeser (ed.) *The Routledge Companion to Gender and Affect*. His research interests include U.S. political communication, contemporary argumentation, and political humor.

**Jody C Baumgartner** (Ph.D., Miami University) is the Thomas Harriot College of Arts and Sciences Distinguished Professor in the Department of Political Science at East Carolina University. He teaches various courses in American politics and writing for political science. He has authored or edited numerous books, journal articles, and book chapters, individually or in collaboration with others, on political humor, the vice presidency, and other subjects.

**Kenneth R. Blake** (Ph.D., The University of North Carolina at Chapel Hill) is a professor in the School of Journalism and Strategic Media at Middle Tennessee State University (MTSU). He teaches courses in media and society, news writing, reporting, data journalism, and empirical media theory and research. He directs the Office of Communication Research at MTSU and has been Director of the MTSU Poll, a statewide survey of public opinion in Tennessee regarding a variety of political and social issues. He has published in the areas of public opinion, journalism education, and data analysis methods.

**India Bock** (B.A., St. Olaf College) received bachelor's degrees in Political Science, History, and Gender and Sexuality Studies at St. Olaf College in

**xiv** About the Contributors

Minnesota. She currently works at Hennepin County District Court as a court operations associate.

**Fiona Bown** (A.B., Rollins College) is an Alfond scholar who has authored several conference presentations and publications. Fiona's academic background includes a wide range of honors, and her research interests focus on social and political marketing, particularly in relation to racial justice issues.

**Parisa Bruce** (M.A., Georgetown University) is a graduate of Georgetown University's Communications, Culture & Technology Master's Program. She works in the communications field with a focus on public relations, corporate social responsibility, and social and digital media strategy.

**Stephen D. Caldes** (MFA, New Mexico State University) is an associate professor in the Department of Journalism & Public Relations at California State University, Chico, where he teaches writing intensive courses on narrative nonfiction, propaganda, and digital media literacy. His most recent work can be found in the edited collection *Discordant Pandemic Narrative in the U.S.* and the *International Journal of Multidisciplinary Perspectives in High Education.*

**Zoë Hess Carney** (Ph.D., Georgia State University) is a Professor of Practice of Corporate Communication and Public Affairs at Southern Methodist University. She is a rhetorical scholar who focuses on contemporary politics and democracy, publishing articles and book chapters on the presidency in a global era, including the use of presidential speech as a transnational rhetorical resource and Nixon's opening to China. She won the Rose B. Johnson Award (with Mary Stuckey) for their essay, "The World as the American Frontier: Racialized Presidential War Rhetoric." She teaches courses in political communication, free speech and the first amendment, and communication theory.

**Christopher Chapp** (Ph.D., University of Minnesota) is a professor in the Department of Political Science at St. Olaf College and the Morrison Family Director of the Institute for Freedom and Community. He teaches courses on American politics, parties and elections, and research methodology. He is author of numerous works on public opinion and political communication, including *Religious Rhetoric and American Politics: The Endurance of Civil Religion in Electoral Campaigns* (2012) and *Moral Issues: How Public Opinion on Abortion and Gay Rights Affects American Religion and Politics* (2024).

**Arjun Chawla** (M.A., Georgetown University) is a research associate at the Civic Education Research Lab. He is interested in studying political communication and political behavior.

About the Contributors **xv**

**Ryan Cheek** (Ph.D., Utah State University) is the author of "Making a Case for Political Technical Communication (PxTC)" published in 2022 by *Technical Communication Quarterly* and "Political Technical Communication and Ideographic Communication Design in a Pre-digital Congressional Campaign" published in 2020 by *Communication Design Quarterly*. His research interests center on the role that political communication technologies and apocalyptic rhetoric play in shaping democratic norms, outcomes, and institutions in the United States.

**Calvin R. Coker** (Ph.D., University of Missouri) is an assistant professor in the Department of Communication at the University of Louisville. Dr. Coker's research is animated by the following question: "When marginality and exclusion are discussed in the United States through publicly available channels of communication, what constraints are placed on, or liberties taken by, non-dominant groups?" The contemporary issues discussed in his published scholarship include **economic policy** and **abortion access** and can be found in academic journals such as *Rhetoric & Public Affairs, Communication and Critical/Cultural Studies,* and *Women's Studies in Communication.* Though Dr. Coker has published articles featuring multiple methodologies (including survey and experimental work), his core interest and expertise is in rhetorical criticism. Following the overturn of *Roe*, Dr. Coker's attention turned toward integrating and advancing frameworks of reproductive justice into political communication and rhetorical scholarship.

**Thom Crockett** (M.A., Georgetown University) manages the Technology & International Affairs program at the Carnegie Endowment for International Peace. His work centers on questions surrounding the geopolitics and international governance of artificial intelligence.

**Joyce H. Glasscock** (M.S., Kansas State University) serves as Executive Director for the Kansas Alliance of Boys & Girls Clubs. Joyce's prior experience spans work in government and politics, including in government relations roles with Boys & Girls Clubs of America, as chief of staff to former Kansas Governor Bill Graves, and in Washington, D.C., as press secretary to a member of Congress, legislative correspondent for a U.S. Senator, and communications director at the U.S. Department of Commerce/Economic Development Administration. Joyce's political campaign experience includes leading a successful gubernatorial campaign, staffing a presidential campaign, and serving as press secretary for a U.S. Senate campaign. She recently published an article examining former President Trump's appeals to populism in his treatment of immigrants during the 2018 and 2020 general elections.

**xvi** About the Contributors

**Cali Goulet** (B.A., St. Olaf College) received bachelor's degrees in Political Science and Race and Ethnic Studies at St. Olaf College in Minnesota. She currently works at St. Olaf College as a Student Financial Services Specialist.

**Haydyn Hendricks** (M.A., Georgetown University) is a Government Relations Analyst for the Porter Group in Washington, D.C. where he focuses on bipartisan government affairs and business consulting. He has worked extensively on the intersection of public policy, politics, and the evolving role of technology in governance. He also has experience in the U.S. House of Representatives.

**Zach Justus** (Ph.D., Arizona State University) is Professor of Communication Arts and Sciences at California State University, Chico. He currently serves as the Director of Faculty Development. His research is on extremist rhetoric, including gun-rights and anti-immigration advocacy and educational strategies for improving dialogue. His work can be found in *Argumentation and Advocacy* and *Communication Teacher* as well as other edited volumes and journals.

**Hanna Kassab** (Ph.D., University of Miami) is Assistant Professor of Political Science and Security Studies at East Carolina University. He teaches courses in national security, foreign policy and global politics. His most recent book *Post-Cold War Predictions: Politicism in Practice* is published by Routledge. He has published articles and books on great power competition, nationalism, and terrorism. He is the recipient of the Department of Defense's Minerva Grant conducting a study called *Food Fights: War Narratives and Identity Reproduction in Evolving Conflicts.'*

**Kyle Kim** (M.A., Georgetown University) is a Management and Program Analyst at the Department of Justice Office of the Inspector General. He works on congressional affairs, A.I. legislation and implementation, agency budgeting, and data visualization and analysis.

**Rita Kirk** (Ph.D., University of Missouri) is Professor of Corporate Communication and Public Affairs at Southern Methodist University. Concurrently, she holds the William F May Endowed Chair as the Director of the Maguire Center for Ethics & Public Responsibility. Her passions for aligning resources with innovation, empowering ideas, and building coalitions to successfully implement strategic initiatives is a hallmark of her work. A frequent news commentator and featured speaker, she excels as a communication strategist who specializes in the analysis of public arguments and the successful (and ethical) implementation of communication campaigns. Kirk has served as an analyst for CNN during presidential elections and major political events for 16 years. She continues to consult with national and multinational corporations on public policy and leadership. The author of five books and numerous articles, Kirk's current research focuses on public integrity and the politics of trust. In 2023–2024, she was a visiting fellow at Harvard University's Edmond & Lily Safra Center for Ethics researching System Trust, that part of the social contract where organizations are given custody of the public's trust as an element of governance. Kirk has been recognized as Altshuler Distinguished Teaching Professor and Meadows Distinguished Professor by her peers and the prestigious *"M" Award* and the *Outstanding Faculty Teaching Award* by the SMU student body.

**Jennifer A. Malkowski** (Ph.D., University of Colorado, Boulder) is Associate Professor of Communication Arts and Sciences at California State University, Chico, who researches the rhetorics of public health, risk management, and biomedical controversy. Her co-edited collection, *Covid and...How to do Rhetoric in a Pandemic* (2023, Michigan University Press) interrogates the intersections of health politics, social justice, and everyday democratic life and is the recipient of the Association for the Rhetoric of Science, Technology and Medicine's Book of the Year Award.

**B. Theo Mazumdar** (Ph.D., University of Southern California) is an assistant professor in the Department of Communication and Media at California State University, San Bernardino. He teaches courses in strategic communication, communication theory, persuasion, and media studies. He has published articles on public and digital diplomacy, media framing of the 2011 Egyptian Revolution, and the public relations of the Israel Defense Forces. His current research centers on narrative approaches to political communication and on non-normative strategic political communication.

**Desmond J. McCarthy** (B.S., University of Louisville) is an independent scholar working in the Communication field. He is interested in the study of political and interpersonal communication.

**Kelton Miller** (B.A., Georgetown University) is a paralegal at Cadwalader, Wickersham & Taft LLP in New York City. He is planning on attending law school to pursue a career in either employment law or human rights law.

**Diana Owen** (Ph.D., University of Wisconsin-Madison) is Professor of Political Science teaching in the Communication, Culture, and Technology graduate program. She is the Director and Principal Investigator of the Civic Education Research Lab at Georgetown University (https://cerl.georgetown.edu/). She served as Director of Georgetown's American Studies Program for almost a decade. She is the author of *Media Messages in American Presidential Elections*

**xviii** About the Contributors

(Greenwood, 1991), *New Media and American Politics* (with Richard Davis, Oxford, 1998), and *American Government and Politics in the Information Age* (with David Paletz and Timothy Cook, 6th edition, 2024). She is the co-editor of *The Internet and Politics: Citizens, Voters, and Activists* (with Sarah Oates and Rachel Gibson, Routledge, 2006); *Making a Difference: The Internet and Elections in Comparative Perspective* (with Richard Davis, Stephen Ward, and David Taras, Lexington, 2009); and *Internet Election Campaigns in the United States, Japan, South Korea, and Taiwan* (with Shoko Kiyohara and Kazuhiro Maeshima, 2019). She is the author of numerous journal articles and book chapters in the fields of civic education and engagement, media and politics, political socialization, elections and voting behavior, and political psychology/sociology. She has conducted studies funded by the Pew Charitable Trusts, the Center for Civic Education, the Bill of Rights Institute, The Clinton Foundation, Google, Storyful, and others. She is the recipient of multiple competitive grants from the U.S. Department of Education that fund programs and research on civic education for elementary and secondary school high-need students nationwide. Her current research explores the relationship between civic education and political engagement over the life course and new media's role in politics. She has been an American Political Science Association Congressional Media Fellow. She is the recipient of the Daniel Roselle Award of the Middle States Council on the Social Studies and the APSA Established Leader Award in Civic Engagement.

**David Lynn Painter** (Ph.D., University of Florida) is an associate professor in the Communication Department and Co-director of the Master's in Strategic Communication program at Rollins College. David's teaching career has been distinguished by extensive service-learning involvement, integrating community engagement in more than 20 courses with about 500 students serving 12 local nonprofit organizations. David's research agenda focuses on political communication, with particular expertise in social media and advertising. David has authored more than 30 scholarly publications, and his research has been competitively selected for presentation at more than 40 national and international conferences. His work on political communication, media responsibility, and social issues has also garnered numerous media appearances on outlets like NBC News, NPR, local Orlando channels, and Spectrum News.

**Jae Hee Park** (Ph.D., University of Tennessee) is an associate professor in the School of Communication at the University of North Florida. He teaches courses in principles of media planning, social media for communication, and integrated marketing communication. His research interests are online brand communities, online consumer behaviors, online political communication, inter-cultural studies, and online marketing communication. His work has appeared in *the Journal of Promotion Management, Public Relations Review, Journal of International Consumer Marketing, Quarterly Review of Business Disciplines,* and *Online Journal of Communication and Media Technologies.* He has served on the international board of directors for *Korea Entertainment Association* and the editorial board of *Korean Journal of Out of Home Advertising Research.*

**Jason B. Reineke** (Ph.D., The Ohio State University) is an associate professor in the School of Journalism and Strategic Media at Middle Tennessee State University (MTSU). He teaches courses in freedom of expression, media law, social science research methods and statistics, public opinion, and environmental communication. He has been the Graduate Director of the school's Master of Science in Media and Communication program and Associate Director of the MTSU Poll, a statewide survey of public opinion in Tennessee regarding a variety of political and social issues. He has published articles on public opinion regarding freedom of expression, the effects of entertainment media on public opinion, and news coverage of cancer and its effects.

**Tanja Vierrether** (Ph.D., Bowling Green State University) is a visiting assistant professor in Communication at Rollins College. Tanja's research focuses on narrative persuasion and attitude change. Tanja's work has been selected for presentation at national and international conferences and published in the *International Journal of Communication, Media Psychology,* and the *Iowa Journal of Communication.*

**Hyun Jung Yun** (Ph.D., University of Florida) is a professor in the Department of Political Science at Texas State University. Along with her two doctoral degrees in Political Science and in Journalism and Communications, she teaches courses in media and public opinion, campaigns and elections, and American political discourse. Her research has been dedicated to interdisciplinary approaches across political communication, public opinion, geopolitics, and applied methodology, focusing on e-government, political ads and debates, ethno-politics, social capital, and social media. Her publications in several leading journals, such as *American Behavioral Scientist, Journalism Studies,* and *The American Review of Politics,* and several book chapters in edited books by prestigious publishers, such as *Oxford University Press*, demonstrate how individuals' political perceptions, attitudes, and behaviors are influenced by political predispositions within a group and by political resources within a geopolitical and media system at the aggregate level. She has served on international and national academic journal editorial boards and government advisory boards, including *the International Interdisciplinary Advisory and Editorial Board, the Korean Congress Advisory Council, the National Unification Advisory Council, the Korea Advertising*

*Society Executive Board, and the Journal of Cybercommunication Academic Society Editorial Board.*

**Jun Zhang** (Ph.D., Syracuse University) is an assistant professor in the School of Journalism and Strategic Media at Middle Tennessee State University (MTSU). She teaches courses in public relations, social media, and research methods. Her research focuses on crisis spillover effects, CSR/CSA legitimacy, organizational adoption of innovative technologies, and health misinformation. Her work has been published in leading academic journals, including *Public Relations Review*, *Asian Journal of Communication, Computers in Human Behavior*, *Journal of Broadcasting and Electronic Media, Health Communication*, and *Journal of Brand Management*, among others. She also serves as the Co-director of the Social Media Insights Lab at MTSU.

**Brenda Zhong** (BSFS, Georgetown University) is an International Arbitration Legal Assistant at Gaillard Banifatemi Shelbaya Disputes in Paris, France. As a graduate from Georgetown University's Edmund A. Walsh School of Foreign Service, her research interests include the role of digital media on political coalition building, civic education, and elections in the United States and internationally.

# ACKNOWLEDGMENTS

The 2022 midterm election was as polarized and divisive as recent elections have been in the United States. Murray (2022) explained: "Eighty-one percent of Democrats say they believe the Republican Party's agenda poses a threat that, if it isn't stopped, will destroy America as we know it. An almost identical share of Republicans—79%—believe the same of the Democratic Party's agenda" (para. 36). The scholars who contributed to this book were motivated by a genuine interest to better understand the electorate and the influence of social and digital media in the electoral process. The editors are indebted to each author for their diligent work to create a clearer understanding of how a grand experiment in democracy continues to work in the 21st century with technology playing a role, social and digital media technology to be more specific.

Routledge/Taylor & Francis Group has been our primary publishing "home" for more than a decade, and we sincerely value the assistance and mentorship of Natalja Mortensen. She is the Senior Editor for Politics at Routledge and has always been helpful and supportive of our interests in the role social and digital media play in the American political process. Indeed, Natalja guided us through the acquisition process with this book. Routledge was founded in 1836 and is a global juggernaut in today's academic publishing world, and we're honored to have our work continue to be a part of that respected history.

The editors are beholden to Natalja Mortensen, Charlotte Christie, Charlie Baker, and Devon Harvey at Routledge/Taylor & Francis for their assistance with the project through all stages of publication from initial concept to completed work. They played a pivotal role in bringing this book to life and we are sincerely thankful for their collaboration.

**xxii** Acknowledgments

The editors also wish to acknowledge Rajathi Ramakrishnan and the production team at Newgen Knowledge Works for their work in copy editing and page setting this book. Their professionalism and expertise have significantly contributed to the book's polished presentation.

Importantly, the editors wish to express gratitude to those individuals who provided peer-review input on ways in which to improve the final project. The external feedback received during the blind review process at the beginning of this project was very helpful to us as we molded and shaped this book's final contents. Each reviewer's insightful input improved this book.

John Allen Hendricks is indebted to his wife, Dr. Stacy Hendricks—Associate Dean and Professor of the James I. Perkins College of Education. He wishes to recognize the support of Stephen F. Austin State University (SFA), a member of the University of Texas System. SFA's beautiful campus in rural, deep East Texas has been a wonderful academic home to pursue intellectual pursuits.

Dan Schill remains deeply thankful for Jessica, Ellie, and Bennett. He would also like to recognize his colleagues at James Madison University for their continued collegiality, encouragement, and strong support for research and teaching.

## Reference

Murray, M. (2022, October 23). 'Anger on their minds': NBC news poll finds sky-high interest and polarization ahead of midterms. *NBC News*. www.nbcnews.com/meet-the-press/first-read/anger-minds-nbc-news-poll-finds-sky-high-interest-polarization-ahead-m-rcna53512

# 1

# MEDIA, MESSAGING, AND THE MIDTERMS

## Communication Dynamics in the 2022 U.S. Elections

*Dan Schill and John Allen Hendricks*

As mandated by Article I of the United States Constitution, members of the United States House of Representatives serve two-year terms, while Senators serve six-year terms. Senate terms are staggered, with one-third of the Senate up for election every two years. As a result, elections are held every two years for both the House of Representatives and the Senate. These elections are referred to as "midterm" elections because they occur between presidential election years— halfway through a president's four-year term. Importantly, in addition to federal elections, state and local elections are also held every two years, including races for offices such as governor and other important state and local positions. Notably, 36 states hold their gubernatorial elections during midterms.

Frequently, midterm elections are setbacks for the president, as scholars and election observers frequently note. Phillips (2022) pointed out that "one of the surest trends in American politics is that the party that holds the White House loses seats in midterm elections" (para. 7). Owen (2023) further explained: "Midterm elections traditionally are viewed as a referendum on the sitting president and the party in power" (p. 204). For context, Hartman (2022) underscored: "If that is the case, then voters over the past 80 years have generally not been impressed with their elected presidents, as results of past midterm elections show the party in power almost always loses seats in either the House of Representatives or Senate (and usually both)" (para. 1). Inman (2022) added: "Since the end of World War II, the commander in chief's party has gained seats in the House of Representatives only twice" (para. 1). Jacobson (2022) highlighted the trend further: "There have been 19 midterm elections since the end of World War II in 1945. In 17 of those elections, the president's party has lost seats in the House. The average loss has been 27 House seats" (para. 5) (see Figures 1.1 and 1.2).

DOI: 10.4324/9781003440833-1

**2** Media Messages in the 2022 Midterm Election

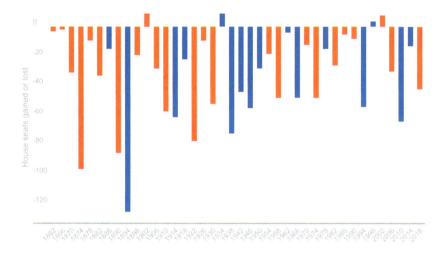

Midterm elections in which Republicans held the White House are shown in **red**, and elections when Democrats held the White House are shown in **blue**.

**FIGURE 1.1** The Party that Controls the White House Almost Always Loses Seats in the House During Midterms.

Midterm elections in which Republicans held the White House are shown in **red**, and elections when Democrats held the White House are shown in **blue**.

**FIGURE 1.2** The Party that Controls the White House Often Loses Senate Seats in Midterms, but Less Commonly than in the House.

To say the least, the stakes are very high for the president and their party during midterm elections.

Among other reasons, midterm elections are important in American politics because they have the ability to shift power in the legislative branch, influencing which laws get passed and the oversight process. Hence, it's important to the individual who occupies the Oval Office that their political party stays in control of the legislative branch in order to facilitate and advance their legislative and political agenda. Moreover, midterm elections are a way for the electorate to communicate approval or disapproval of the president's performance. Hartman (2022) explained: "In the United States, midterm congressional elections take place every two years, dividing each president's four-year term, and are often thought of as a referendum on the current administration's performance" (para. 1). Because the sitting president's political party, more often than not, loses seats in the legislative branch, midterm elections are colloquially known as the "midterm curse" (Inman, 2022). Voters whose candidate lost the White House in the previous election are particularly motivated in the next election. Inman (2022) observed: "The theory is that once voters win the White House, they tend to sit out the lower profile midterms, while the losers are mad and motivated" (para. 9). This trend is especially evident when the president's approval ratings are low, as was the case for President Biden in 2022.

Leading up to the midterm election, a *Pew Research Center* (2022) survey found that a majority of U.S. adults (59%) disapproved of the way Biden was handling his job as president, with 40% expressing strong disapproval. Similarly, a CNN (2002) poll conducted in September and October 2022 indicated that only 38% of Americans approved of President Biden's job performance. This low approval led CNN, along with many other media outlets, to make the following assessment: "History suggests that the single biggest predictor of how a midterm election is going to go is the popularity (or unpopularity) of the sitting president. If history repeats itself in 13 days, that's a very bad thing for Democrats" (Cillizza, 2022, para. 1). Furthermore, Biden's approval rating among members of his own political party were troubling, leading Goldmacher (2022a) to assert: "President Biden is facing an alarming level of doubt from inside his own party, with 64 percent of Democratic voters saying they would prefer a new standard-bearer in the 2024 presidential campaign" (para. 1). The same poll revealed that Biden's job approval rating dropped to only 33%, with only 13% of Americans believing that the country was headed in the right direction (Goldmacher, 2022a). As the midterms approached, Biden's low approval ratings intensified the media narrative of an anticipated Republican surge, widely characterized as the red wave.

Economic factors also suggested 2022 would be a good year for Republican congressional and gubernatorial candidates. Sievert and Garand (2024) wrote that the relatively weak state of the economy should have resulted in large

**4** Media Messages in the 2022 Midterm Election

Republican gains: "While unemployment in the months leading up to the election was low, inflation was high (particularly in consumer-visible goods like groceries and gasoline), interest rates were up, and there was quite a bit of economic disruption due to unfilled jobs in the labor force" (p. 207). With high inflation and interest rates, the argument for change should have been an easy sell. As Carson and Ulrich (2024) surmised: "By all the traditional metrics, this election should have been a slam dunk for Republicans, the party out of power" (p. 13). Economic uncertainty influenced general voter sentiment, but specific issues like reproductive rights and voting access emerged as core motivators, particularly among younger and more progressive voters.

Based on all of these factors, the predictions for the election outcome were dire for the Democratic Party (Sabato et al., 2023). "The expectation that the Republicans would make major gains in the midterms, characterized as a 'red wave' or more dramatically as a 'red tsunami,' was the dominant narrative of mainstream media coverage for months leading up to the elections," wrote Georgetown professor Diana Owen (2023, p. 202). For instance, on the eve of the election, Henry Olsen (2022) of *The Washington Post* forecasted:

> Inflation, crime, progressive attempts at overreach and a general sense that President Biden is not up to the job will likely deliver a surprisingly large victory to Republicans. I predict the GOP will win the national popular vote by about 5.5 points, likely gaining between 31 and 40 House seats in the process. I also expect it will retake control of the Senate, gaining two to four seats.
>
> *(para. 2)*

Olsen predicted that Republicans would seize control of the Senate with 54 seats and the House of Representatives with 246 seats. Similarly, in mid-October 2022, Pollster Mark Penn predicted a Republican "red wave," saying: "Republicans are inching closer towards a wave election as they connect with voters on their key issues of inflation, crime, and immigration. The GOP is now winning the generic Congressional ballot 53–47 among likely voters" (Penn & Cusack, 2022, para. 3). On November 2, 2022, *Axios* ran a headline declaring: "The Tide is Turning for Republicans." In the article, Josh Kraushaar (2022) wrote: "With less than a week left to go before the midterms, just about everything is breaking in the Republicans' favor" (para. 1). Even *The New York Times* had an October 25, 2022, headline declaring: "Democrats, on Defense in Blue States, Brace for a Red Wave in the House" (Goldmacher, 2022b). According to Goldmacher (2022b), "Strategists and officials in both parties said they were seeing the trend of both Democratic weakness and Republican overperformance in states that are fully ruled by Democrats" (para. 22). Social media platforms amplified these legacy media narratives through news apps and social media sharing, underscoring the powerful role of digital media in modern campaigns. Despite the polling results and widespread predictions of a "red wave," it did not unfold that way on election night in 2022.

After all of the votes were counted, the results were not even close to being a "red wave." Campbell (2023) summarized the outcome:

Several observers predicted Republicans to win more House seats than at any time since the 1920s. A Republican red wave was anticipated. The only serious question was how big it would be. But what hit shore on Election Day was more of a weak ripple than a powerful wave.

*(para. 2)*

National news headlines had to backtrack from their earlier, headline "red wave" declarations. For example, *The New York Times* called it a "red wave washout" (Rutenberg et al., 2022), while a *U.S. News & World Report* headline declared it was "the red wave that wasn't" (Milligan, 2022). Scholar Alan Abramowitz (2023) labeled the election as "the worst results for the opposition party in the past seventy years" (p. 36). The results of the election were a surprising disappointment to the Republican party. Milligan wrote:

Republicans were gleefully anticipating a big night Tuesday, predicting a "red wave" – even a "red tsunami" – that would give the GOP control of the House and Senate, plus pickups in statehouses across the country. With the polls starting to close, Donald Trump Jr. tweeted out "bloodbath!" in expectation of a brutal night for Democrats. House GOP leader Kevin McCarthy, with a measuring-the-drapes tone to his voice, confidently talked to supporters about the plans to undermine Democrats once he took the speaker's gavel. Within hours, that storyline began to unravel, along with GOP hopes of delivering devastating losses that would repudiate the Biden presidency and send Democrats into despair. While outstanding races could still give the GOP control of one or both chambers of Congress, their majorities would be paltry, undermining the Republican argument that American voters would deliver a loud message against Biden and his agenda.

*(para. 1)*

As votes were tallied on election night, the Republicans realized there would be no "bloodbath" for Democrats, and many election observers were surprised by the unexpected outcome. Balz and Keating (2022) summarized the results:

The 2022 elections will be remembered for Republican exuberance colliding with Democratic resistance to produce an unexpected outcome that, while potentially shifting the balance of power in Congress, suggests no call for a dramatic change in direction nor a mandate for the GOP.

*(para. 1)*

**6** Media Messages in the 2022 Midterm Election

The 2022 midterm elections were notable not only for their outcome but also for their record-breaking cost. According to Open Secrets (n.d.), approximately $9.5 billion dollars was spent on all federal elections by Senate and House candidates, political parties, and interest groups. Nearly $2 billion was spent by candidates ($612,986 per candidate) in House races and about $1.8 billion was spent by candidates (about $3 million per candidate) in Senate races. This financial surge, particularly in high-stakes Senate races like Pennsylvania and Georgia, reflected the nationalized and highly competitive nature of the election.

A majority of this spending was on advertising. Broadcast television advertising remained an important communication vehicle in the midterms. In fact, there was a record volume of television advertising for a midterm election in 2022 with 4.8 million total ad airings across gubernatorial, U.S. Senate, and U.S. House contests (Franz et al., 2023). Outside groups played a significant role in House and Senate elections in the 2022 cycle, sponsoring over 35% of all advertisements (Franz et al., 2023).

Advertising was also forefront on digital platforms. While campaign spending on traditional media hit record highs, digital advertising and social media enabled targeted, cost-effective outreach, allowing campaigns to connect with specific voter groups at unprecedented levels. In 2022, Meta (including Facebook and Instagram) and Google (including YouTube, search ads, and display and banner advertising) were the most important platforms for election advertising. Despite the overall increase in digital ad spending across political campaigns in recent years, Fowler et al. (2023) found a decline in the share of media spending allocated to Meta and Google by federal candidates in 2022 compared to 2020. This may reflect the increased use of other digital platforms, such as streaming services like Hulu, for which systematic ad tracking isn't available. In particular, Meta saw a notable decrease in spending, while Google's share of digital ad spending increased, especially in U.S. Senate races. High turnout marked the 2022 midterms, with social media platforms playing a crucial role in energizing specific voter bases, particularly younger voters concerned about issues like reproductive rights. Abortion and inflation were among the most discussed issues in advertising, although notably, abortion and inflation were less frequently mentioned in digital ads compared to television ads. For example, only 18.3% of Democratic digital ads on Meta mentioned abortion, compared to 26% of their TV ads. Similarly, Republicans mentioned inflation in 19.2% of their Meta digital ads compared to 45.4% of their TV ads (Fowler et al., 2023).

Across both U.S. Senate and competitive U.S. House races, Democratic candidates consistently outspent their Republican counterparts on digital advertising (Fowler et al., 2023). Notably, a significant portion of digital advertising was devoted to fundraising. For instance, nearly half (47%) of the

U.S. Senate candidates' spending on Meta platforms was aimed at donation appeals. Candidates often directed these appeals to out-of-state audiences, suggesting that digital platforms were used not just for voter persuasion but also to raise campaign funds nationally (Fowler et al., 2023). Furthermore, the 2022 midterms highlighted shifting voter demographics, with targeted digital ad strategies focusing on younger, suburban, and ethnically diverse voters who are redefining political alignments.

Despite all of the ads, debates, social media posts, and news stories, the results of the 2022 midterms were more about continuity than change. All incumbent Senators successfully secured re-election, resulting in minimal changes to the Senate's party composition. The only shift came from the Democrats gaining one seat in Pennsylvania. Meanwhile, Republicans narrowly took control of the U.S. House, claiming a slim majority with 222 seats, a change that significantly impacted future policymaking. In the gubernatorial races, Democrats gained three governorships in Arizona, Maryland, and Massachusetts, but lost one in Nevada. Despite media and polling predictions of a Republican red wave, the actual election results revealed a more complex picture, with Republicans securing only modest gains.

Voter turnout was also high for a non-presidential election, with over 112 million voters participating (McDonald, 2023). The U.S. Census Bureau (2023) reported:

Voter turnout for the 2022 U.S. congressional elections was the second highest for a nonpresidential election year since 2000, with 52.2% of the citizen voting-age population participating. And registration rates were the highest for a midterm election since 2000, with 69.1% of the citizen voting-age population registered to vote, up 2.2 percentage points from 66.9% in 2018.

*(para. 1)*

Indeed, high voter turnout was one factor in averting the Republican "red wave." Debusmann and Sherman (2022) suggested that high voter turnout was, in part, due to a "Democratic base that was driven by young people motivated by issues like reproductive rights" (para. 13). Indeed, turnout was high among younger voters. The Center for Information & Research on Civic Learning and Engagement (CIRCLE, 2022a) asserted:

27% of young people (ages 18–29) turned out to vote in the 2022 midterm election and helped decide critical races, wielding the growing power of a generation that is increasingly engaged even as many remain disillusioned about U.S. politics. This 2022 youth turnout is likely the second-highest youth turnout rate for a midterm election in the past 30 years, behind only the historic 31% turnout in 2018. Votes cast by young people made up 12% of all votes in this election, nearly matching the 13% youth share of the vote from the 2014 and 2018 midterms.

*(para. 2)*

*TIME* magazine's Ashley Aylward (2022) summarized the impact of younger voters this way: "Many were expecting a red wave to crash on Tuesday, Nov. 8—instead, an earthquake of young voters shook up the political world" (para. 1). Furthermore, Aylward (2022) astutely observed: "When young people's rights are on the ballot and championed by the candidate, they show up" (para. 2). On issues important to voters, the younger voters preferred the Democratic Party by a 28-point margin (CIRCLE, 2022b). Similarly, the *Pew Research Center* found: "Nearly seven-in-ten voters under 30 (68%) supported Democratic candidates in 2022 – much higher than the shares of voters ages 30 to 49 (52%), 50 to 64 (44%) and 65 and older (42%) who did so" (Hartig et al., 2023, para. 21).

There were a number of important issues discussed by the candidates during the 2022 election, including: 1) inflation and the economy, 2) abortion rights (due to the Supreme Court's decision to overturn *Roe v. Wade* in the *Dobbs* case), 3) voting rights and election integrity, 4) public safety and crime, 5) healthcare, 6) immigration, and 7) climate change and environmental policy. Trzcińska (2024) content analyzed over 6,000 articles on the 2022 midterm elections that appeared in 70 of the most popular American newspapers and digital media in the final weeks of the campaign and found that abortion and inflation were the most frequently mentioned topics. As one of the most debated issues, abortion was a determinative issue for many voters. Exit polls indicated that a substantial number of voters were driven to the polls specifically by this issue, particularly among women and Democrats which helped Democrats maintain control of the Senate (Carson & Hitefield, 2023). Notably, even though they had essentially no formal role in the midterm elections, Joe Biden and Donald Trump were among the most popular topics of news coverage, while the individual candidates running were mentioned very rarely.

Former President Donald Trump also played a key role in 2022. Research (Carson & Hitefield, 2023) found that Trump's presence in the election, particularly his endorsements of candidates who supported his claims of a stolen 2020 election, harmed Republican chances in competitive Senate and House races. Many Trump-endorsed candidates underperformed, especially in key states like Pennsylvania, where the GOP lost a Senate seat. In contrast to the general election, Trump was an asset to Republican candidates in the primaries. Blum et al. (2024) studied the factors that lead to success in the 2022 Republican primaries and identified that Trump endorsements, Fox News appearances, campaign funds, and Twitter mentions all had large and statistically significant relationships with vote share, showing that, although intra-party divisions persist, the media ecosystem around Trump exerted substantial control over the party's 2022 nomination processes.

Another reason the red wave didn't materialize in 2022 is the shifting political dynamics have led to notable changes in voter behavior with suburban voters. Democrats performed well in America's suburbs in 2022, particularly among college-educated white voters, driven by reactions to Trump's presidency and the increasing polarization based on education and social attitudes (Schaffner & Gaus, 2023). These voters viewed Trump and the Republican Party as increasingly ideologically extreme and responded by moving away from the GOP, perceiving Trump's policies and rhetoric as incompatible with their more moderate or progressive values.

Like past elections, social and digital media campaign strategies were front and center in the 2022 election. Owen (2023) observed: "Voters were bombarded with social media and text messages in the months leading up to the midterms. The volume of election-related content disseminated via all digital channels defies measurement" (p. 205). Mitch Mansfield (2022), a political reporter for the *BBC*, pondered the role of social media in the midterm election and whether it could influence the outcome with the following article headline: "Could social media swing it?"

Undeniably, social media platforms during the midterm elections were a juggernaut and tens of millions of voters were consuming political content across social networking platforms, including Twitter, Facebook, Instagram, YouTube, and TikTok. Specifically, social media platforms were used for 1) rapid information dissemination, 2) grassroots mobilization, 3) targeted advertising, 4) direct communication with the electorate, 5) influencer and community engagement, 6) countering misinformation, and 7) voter turnout initiatives. In November 2022, Mansfield highlighted TikTok's pervasiveness in the election by sharing: "Videos about this month's U.S. midterms have been viewed hundreds of millions of times. There are concerns about the spread of misinformation on the platform, but young influencers insist it can be a force for good" (para. 3). Furthermore, Neal and McGrath (2023) found

> the outcome of the 2022 United States Midterm Elections was heavily influenced by the power of progressive young voters. With the increased use of social media in recent years, many young activists have adopted online platforms as spaces for political conversation.
>
> *(para. 1)*

During the 2022 midterm elections, news articles sparked significant discussion on social media, with stories spreading beyond traditional news websites and apps to platforms like Facebook, Twitter, and Reddit. Using data from over 1.3 million social media posts, Lepird, Ng, Wu, and Carley (2024) analyzed news during the 2022 midterm elections and discovered several platform-specific trends. Reddit had the highest proportion of real news, while Facebook led in the sharing of local news. Twitter, on the other hand, had the highest proportion of low-credibility news or so-called "pink slime" news. Pink slime news—partisan and often misleading news posing as local journalism—received the highest relative engagement across platforms, especially on Facebook. These sites are designed to mimic local news, which makes them more appealing to regional audiences. This suggests that localized, partisan content can generate substantial public interaction, even if the credibility is questionable. Despite being the most credible source, real news received the lowest levels of engagement across the platforms (Lepird et al., 2024). The study also found that news sharing on social media typically occurred within political echo chambers. Users tended to share news that aligned with their political ideologies, creating isolated information spheres.

The 2022 political media ecosystem was fragmented. Social media platforms, with their tightly knit online communities, significantly impacted midterm electoral outcomes by reinforcing political beliefs and amplifying support for candidates within these networks. Independent media platforms, such as podcasts, Substack newsletters, and YouTube channels, became crucial sources for political analysis and discussion, offering voters perspectives outside the mainstream media narratives. Through long-form conversations on podcasts, political analysts and candidates alike could explore topics in depth, creating a counterpoint to the often soundbite-focused narratives of cable news. Content creators encouraged active discussions around the elections, creating online communities where followers could discuss issues and share information, amplifying the impact of these independent sources on voter perspectives. For instance, using a large dataset from Twitter, Panagopoulos and Lore (2024) found that "embeddedness," or how tightly connected Republican Twitter users are within their social networks, impacted the vote share for Republican Senate candidates. Specifically, in counties where Republican Twitter users had higher levels of embeddedness, there was a significant increase in support for Republican Senate candidates, establishing how social reinforcement within tight-knit online communities can bolster electoral support. Twitter users in this study, particularly Republicans, tended to form highly homogenous social networks, reinforcing political beliefs within their communities. For many voters disillusioned with traditional media, alternative news sources provided a sense of authenticity, fostering communities around shared political ideals and sometimes shifting perspectives on mainstream political narratives. Influencers and independent content creators, particularly on platforms like TikTok and Instagram, were pivotal in reaching younger voters, blending entertainment with political messaging to drive engagement on key issues like climate change and reproductive rights.

Social media content, particularly when it was polarizing or emotionally charged, tended to generate higher levels of engagement from users in the midterms. Rafail, O'Connell, and Sager (2024) investigated over 134,000 tweets from 527 U.S. congressional representatives during the 2022 midterms and confirmed that all types of polarizing content—whether ideological, affective, or issue-based—receive significantly more engagement from users in the form of both favorites and retweets. Negative, emotionally charged tweets generated the highest levels of engagement, illustrating the attention-grabbing power of divisive rhetoric online. Tweets posted by Republicans, especially those containing affective polarization (i.e., language that stirs emotions like anger or distrust toward the opposing party), received stronger user reactions than those posted by Democrats. The study shows how polarizing rhetoric on Twitter can create feedback loops, where politicians post divisive content that generates public engagement, which in turn incentivizes further polarization. Relatedly, Evans and Parton (2024) studied Twitter content from 2022 congressional candidates in Virginia and found that candidates were significantly more likely to "go negative" during the general election compared to the primary, and that challengers, particularly those facing incumbents, sent more tweets overall and were much more likely to tweet negatively about their opponents. The study also documented that candidates' social media behavior mirrored traditional campaign strategies: they started the election season with positive messages to build their profiles during the primaries but shifted to more aggressive, negative tactics closer to Election Day.

Social media platforms faced significant criticism for their role in perpetuating misinformation about the integrity of American elections. Disinformation surged on social media leading up to the 2022 midterms, with false claims about voting procedures, mail-in ballots, and election security circulating widely across platforms like Facebook and Twitter. The Center for American Progress, an independent nonpartisan policy institute, issued a scathing rebuke of social media companies' actions during the 2022 election, as well as their potential impact on future elections: "Social media companies are choosing again to abdicate their public responsibilities rather than accept accountability for how their tools are being used to destroy the public institutions that maintain the free society in which they operate" (Simpson et al., 2022, para. 41). Indeed, the spread of misinformation on social media in 2022 was a major concern. Klepper (2022) highlighted the issue, observing: "With less than three weeks before the polls close, misinformation about voting and elections abounds on social media despite promises by tech companies to address a problem blamed for increasing polarization and distrust" (paras. 3–4).

False claims about voter fraud and rigged elections contributed to a wave of online harassment directed at election officials, with many facing threats and accusations that cast doubt on the legitimacy of their work. Rozo et al. (2024)

focused on the role of hate speech and harassment on social media, particularly Twitter, during the 2022 U.S. midterm elections and identified that Chief Election Officials were the primary targets of hate speech, especially in key battleground states like Arizona and Michigan. Twitter data revealed widespread hostility toward these officials, including threats and accusations based on misinformation and conspiracy theories. This finding aligns with the broader trend of increasing online harassment of election officials in the U.S. after the 2020 elections.

Aware of the criticism from organizations and voters, social media companies made efforts to combat the misinformation that was posted on their sites during the election. For instance, TikTok launched an election center earlier in 2022 to help U.S. voters with registration and ballot information in multiple languages (Klepper, 2022). Meta, the parent company of Facebook and Instagram, also opened an election center in 2022. Nick Clegg (2022), Meta's President of Global Affairs stated: "We're focused on preventing voter interference, connecting people with reliable information and providing industry-leading transparency for ads about social issues, elections and politics" (para 3). Given the influence of social media, it's crucial for platforms to provide accurate information. The Pew Research Center found that "younger adults – including both Democrats and Republicans – are more trusting than older adults of information from social media" (Eddy, 2024, para. 13), underscoring the responsibility social media companies have to ensure the integrity of the information they distribute. Social media companies attempted to address disinformation through fact-checking labels and election information centers, but the volume of misleading content in 2022 revealed the limitations of these measures.

The 2022 U.S. midterm elections underscored the profound impact of media in shaping public opinion, mobilizing voters, and framing political discourse. From traditional broadcast ads to the influence of social media and digital platforms, the election demonstrated how intertwined media and electoral outcomes have become. This volume aims to explore the multifaceted role of media and communication in shaping the dynamics of the 2022 U.S. midterm elections. As previewed in the next section, the proceeding chapters present and discuss empirical findings regarding the 2022 midterms and 1) conspiracy theory discourse, 2) issues and candidate communication, 3) media framing, and 4) election-specific communication. Through quantitative analyses, qualitative case studies, and mixed-methods approaches, the chapters provide detailed insights into how various effects of communication strategies in the 2022 midterms advance broader discussions about the implications for future U.S. elections.

## Amplified Doubts: Conspiracy Theories, Communication, and the 2022 Midterm Elections

In contemporary politics, the intertwining of media, conspiratorial beliefs, and social media use has reshaped how voters engage with electoral processes.

Due to an increasingly fragmented digital media ecosystem and pervasive distrust of information and political leaders, conspiracy theories gain traction on social media platforms, fueled by the algorithms that prioritize attitudinal reinforcement and attention-grabbing, sensational content. The first section of this book explores the ways in which conspiratorial thinking not only reflects societal anxieties but also drives voter mobilization and engagement.

Conspiracy theories were prevalent in American political discourse during the 2022 midterm elections and social media played a role in amplifying conspiratorial beliefs, such as the Big Lie and QAnon. In Chapter 2, Diana Owen, Thom Crockett, Arjun Chawla, Kelton Miller, Kyle Kim, Haydyn Hendricks, Parisa Bruce, and Brenda Zhong examine the relationship between conspiratorial ideation and voter engagement in the 2022 midterms. Based on a national survey of nearly 2000 respondents, the chapter reveals a significant link between conspiratorial beliefs and electoral engagement, with implications for the upcoming electoral cycle. It highlights concerns regarding the impact of conspiracy theories on democratic processes, especially in the context of increased media proliferation.

One cultural artifact that tapped into and reflected the broader conspiracy culture that has become more prevalent with the rise of social media is the film 2000 Mules, a 2022 documentary by Dinesh D'Souza, which claims to present evidence of coordinated voter fraud in the 2020 U.S. Presidential Election. The film represents a significant moment in American political culture, as it builds on and propagates conspiracy theories that question the legitimacy of democratic processes. In Chapter 3, Stephen D. Caldes, Zach Justus, and Jennifer A. Malkowski use a rhetorical analysis framework to dissect the storytelling techniques employed by D'Souza. The chapter concludes that 2000 Mules exemplifies how documentary-style presentations can be used to lend credibility to conspiracy theories, especially when supported by strategic storytelling and aesthetics that mimic scientific inquiry. The findings suggest that mainstream media responses, often limited to fact-checking, may be insufficient to counteract such narratives. Instead, the chapter advocates for a more nuanced approach that considers the emotional and narrative appeal of these films in order to more effectively engage audiences in constructive dialogue about misinformation and media literacy.

## Framing the Debate: How Issues Shaped 2022 Candidate Communication

In the wake of the Supreme Court's decision to overturn Roe v. Wade, the 2022 midterm elections highlighted the crucial role of issue framing in political campaigns. As candidates navigated an environment marked by heightened polarization and strategic issue ownership, abortion emerged as a defining topic that reshaped electoral dynamics. This section delves into how candidates

**14** Media Messages in the 2022 Midterm Election

communicated their positions on abortion and other issues on websites, in advertisements, and on social media, analyzing shifts in narrative strategies employed by both parties in response to changing public sentiment and regulatory frameworks. By examining the strategic management of these critical issues on social media, these chapters unpack the ways in which political actors not only respond to but also shape public discourse.

After the Dobbs v. Jackson Women's Health Organization decision in June 2022, the U.S. Supreme Court overturned Roe v. Wade, ending nearly 50 years of federally protected abortion rights. This landmark ruling returned the authority to regulate abortion to individual states, leading to a swift and dramatic reshaping of abortion policy across the country. In the aftermath, several states with conservative legislatures enacted "trigger laws" that immediately restricted or banned abortion, while other states moved to reinforce and expand access to abortion services. This shift resulted in a patchwork of abortion laws, with significant disparities in access based on geographic location. The decision also intensified political debates around reproductive rights and made abortion a top issue across the country in the 2022 midterms. With abortion rights no longer federally guaranteed, candidates faced a new political situation in 2022, where they had to explicitly communicate their stance on abortion. Employing a content analysis of congressional candidates' campaign websites from 2008 to 2022, in Chapter 4, Christopher Chapp, India Bock, and Cali Goulet examine how often candidates mentioned abortion, in what contexts, and whether their framing varied by party affiliation, gender, and incumbency status. Among other conclusions, Chapp, Bock, and Goulet find that Democratic candidates, especially those in competitive districts, increasingly mentioned abortion on their campaign websites, with a marked rise in 2022. This trend suggests that Democrats are positioning abortion as a "core issue" in their campaigns, particularly post-Dobbs. Additionally, Democrats primarily framed abortion in terms of "women's rights" and "healthcare," while Republicans emphasized "unborn rights" and "religion/morality." There was a notable lack of middle ground, with fewer candidates in either party acknowledging exceptions or nuanced positions. The chapter suggests that abortion has become a more prominent and polarized issue in U.S. politics, with Democrats increasingly owning the issue as a key component of their campaigns. The findings indicate that abortion is not just a policy debate but a strategic tool in electoral politics, influenced by candidate risk assessments and district competitiveness. This research emphasizes the changing context of issue ownership in American politics and underscores the potential long-term effects of judicial decisions on campaign strategies and voter mobilization.

As previously discussed, the predicted Republican "red wave" did not materialize despite factors such as President Biden's low approval ratings and historical precedents of midterm losses for the president's party. In an attempt to

Media, Messaging, and the Midterms **15**

understand 2022 unexpected outcomes, in Chapter 5, B. Theo Mazumdar studies both Republicans and Democrats who outperformed in competitive districts for the U.S. House of Representatives to understand how narrative-based strategies in political ads helped some candidates win. Mazumdar suggests that emotional engagement through narrative persuasion was a key to the success of overperforming candidates. Specifically, successful Republican narratives focused on themes of Democrats ruining America through failed policies on the economy, crime, and immigration. This narrative conveyed fear and anxiety about the future of the American Dream and positioned the Republican candidates as action-oriented protectors. Across the aisle, winning Democratic narratives emphasized establishing trust through shared values, local priorities, and their personal backgrounds. They portrayed themselves as credible, bipartisan leaders who would hold President Biden accountable when necessary and their Republican opponents as a dangerous alternative to stability. This chapter has broader implications for understanding how political communication shapes electoral outcomes in a polarized environment, particularly in midterm elections where local dynamics and candidate qualities play significant roles.

One of the classic theories in political communication is agenda setting, which suggests that media do not dictate what the public thinks, but instead influence which issues the public deems important. The 2022 midterms, marked by economic concerns, inflation, and debates on abortion following the Supreme Court's Dobbs ruling, provided a rich backdrop to explore how political actors strategically managed these issues on social media in Chapter 6. In this chapter, Jason B. Reineke, Kenneth R. Blake, and Jun Zhang analyze how members of the U.S. Congress and media outlets interacted with social media agendas leading up to and during the 2022 U.S. midterm elections. Using Twitter's API and social media analytics tool Brandwatch, the chapter collected and analyzed all tweets from members of the 117th U.S. Congress between January 2021 and January 2023. The study also examined tweets from 15 prominent media outlets, divided into those preferred by Democratic and Republican members, to track how political and media actors engaged with key issues, including immigration, abortion, and the economy. The chapter discovered that political agendas on social media were deeply fractured along partisan lines. While issues like the economy, immigration, and abortion were discussed by both parties, the emphasis and framing differed significantly. Republicans, for instance, dominated conversations around immigration, while Democrats surged in abortion-related discussions following the Dobbs ruling. Another notable finding was the shift in issue ownership over abortion. Prior to Dobbs, Republicans led the discussion on abortion, but after the ruling, Democrats took over, using abortion as a central mobilizing issue for the midterms. In contrast, Republicans maintained control over discussions about the economy and inflation, despite Democratic efforts to shift attention through the Inflation Reduction Act. The study sheds light on the

## 16 Media Messages in the 2022 Midterm Election

fractured nature of political agendas in the U.S. and emphasizes the importance of strategic issue management in elections. Furthermore, the chapter contributes to our understanding of how external events, like Supreme Court rulings or economic shifts, can reshape the political landscape and force parties to adapt their communication strategies.

### News Narratives: 2022 Media Coverage and Public Perception

Political campaigns in the United States have undergone a dramatic transformation with the rise of social and digital media. The significant role played by the media in American political campaigns extends beyond mere information dissemination— media platforms act as both amplifiers and moderators of political discourse, framing the issues and narratives that dominate public attention. This section studies media coverage during the 2022 midterm elections, focusing on digital news algorithms, media framing of political texting, and narratives in political cartoons. Together, these chapters illustrate the complex interplay between various media formats and electoral processes in the 2022 midterms.

Digital news algorithms, often used by social media platforms and news aggregators to curate and prioritize content based on user preferences, past behavior, and engagement metrics, play a role in shaping political information, voter behavior, and overall election dynamics. Algorithmic filtering can reinforce existing viewpoints and create echo chambers, where users are predominantly exposed to news and perspectives that align with their beliefs and can obscure diverse viewpoints and limit exposure to opposing perspectives. During election periods, these algorithms can amplify certain political narratives and shape public discourse by giving more visibility to specific topics or candidates, thereby influencing the agenda and framing of issues that voters consider important. In Chapter 7, Hyun Jung Yun and Jae Hee Park explore these news algorithms in the context of the 2022 midterm elections and concluded that digital news algorithms are significant drivers of political polarization by funneling ideologically congruent content to users, reinforcing existing political biases. Particularly, conservative-leaning articles were more likely to feature pro-Republican and anti-Democratic statements, while liberal algorithms promoted pro-Democratic and anti-Republican content. The chapter also uncovered that partisan news sources favored emotional and source credibility appeals, using emotional triggers to mobilize audiences, while politically neutral news aggregators, by contrast, relied more on logical appeals. As digital platforms continue to dominate the media landscape, these digital ecosystems amplify the fragmentation of political discourse and a complex, divided media structure.

In 2022, Americans received 15 billion political texts, a 158% increase from 2021, indicating that political texting is a primary campaign strategy for politicians and campaigners because it is a relatively inexpensive direct line to potential voters for donation requests and requests for support at the polls (Robokiller, n.d.). In Chapter 8, Ryan Cheek and Samuel Allen assess how media portray political text messaging as an annoying, intrusive, and legally unregulated practice to understand how media coverage shapes public perceptions of political texting. The chapter shows how media coverage primarily frames political texting as a consumer nuisance, portraying it as an "annoying but legal" intrusion, a framing that emphasizes individual responsibility to block political texts, rather than calling for regulatory solutions. Moreover, the chapter documents how the anti-spam industry is frequently included as a solution, suggesting that private, market-based solutions are the most viable path forward. The chapter submits that media framing of political text messaging contributes to the commodification of political communication problems, stressing individual responsibility over collective action, and that by framing political texting as an unregulated nuisance, the media may inadvertently reduce pressure on lawmakers and campaigns to seek regulatory solutions.

Editorial cartoons have long been a medium for political critique, using satire to expose societal and political issues, and the 2022 midterm elections were no exception. In Chapter 9, Jody C Baumgartner and Hanna Kassab content analyze online political cartoons to argue that cartoons serve as a mirror to daily news coverage, where cartoons reflect and magnify the themes dominating news coverage and influencing public perception. This chapter demonstrates that editorial cartoons, though often dismissed as mere satire, serve as a significant barometer of political sentiment and media narratives. By reflecting and amplifying news themes, rather than challenging or reframing them, cartoons contribute to shaping public perception, particularly during politically charged periods like elections.

## Midterm Communication in the States: Case Studies from Arizona, Nevada, Florida, Texas, and Kansas

Most of the national media coverage of the 2022 midterms focused on a few high-stakes races, including in Pennsylvania, Georgia, Florida, and Michigan. The Pennsylvania Senate race between Republican Dr. Mehmet Oz and Democrat John Fetterman was a clash of Oz's celebrity doctor television personality and Fetterman's progressive populist, working-class image. Meanwhile, the Georgia Senate contest between incumbent Democrat Raphael Warnock and Republican Herschel Walker was notable for controversies and personal attacks. Warnock, a Senior Pastor at Atlanta's Ebenezer Baptist Church and the first Black U.S. Senator from Georgia, was running for a full term after winning a 2021 special election runoff. Walker, a former University of Georgia college football star and Heisman Trophy winner, was endorsed by former President Donald Trump and used his fame to appeal to Georgia's conservative voters. Walker's campaign was

**18** Media Messages in the 2022 Midterm Election

hit with allegations of domestic violence, claims that he had paid for a former partner's abortion, and questions about his fitness for office due to his limited political experience and inconsistent public statements, issues that dominated media coverage. In neighboring Florida, the governor's race where incumbent Republican Ron DeSantis faced former Governor Charlie Crist, a Democrat who previously served as a Republican governor, was closely watched as it served as a bellwether for DeSantis's status as a potential 2024 presidential candidate. DeSantis's handling of contentious issues such as COVID-19 policies, education reform, and his combative stance against what he termed "woke" culture drew intense national attention and made the race a key indicator of conservative momentum. Another potential 2024 presidential candidate was on the ballot in the Michigan governor's race. Incumbent Democratic Governor Gretchen Whitmer faced Republican challenger Tudor Dixon, a conservative commentator backed by former President Trump. Whitmer's re-election bid was seen as a crucial test of voter sentiment regarding her leadership during the COVID-19 pandemic, where she implemented strict public health measures that drew both praise and intense criticism. As these examples demonstrate, while influenced by national dynamics, each midterm election is unique with provincial issues, audiences, and constraints. Researching lower ballot races can help us understand political communication in situ and also use these races as barometers of national political trends. The final four chapters in this book are such in-depth case studies of 2022 political communication in Arizona and Nevada, Florida, Texas, and Kansas.

Two of the 2022 key Senate contests were in the southwest states of Arizona and Nevada. Arizona's race between Democrat Mark Kelly and Republican Blake Masters brought immigration and economic policy to the forefront and featured contrasting campaign styles and rhetoric. Kelly, a former astronaut and Navy veteran, ran on his bipartisan approach and focus on pragmatic solutions, while Masters, a venture capitalist and political newcomer, positioned himself as a strong conservative voice aligned with Donald Trump's America First agenda. Meanwhile, in Nevada, incumbent Democratic Senator Catherine Cortez Masto, the first Latina elected to the Senate, faced a formidable challenge from Republican Adam Laxalt, a former Nevada Attorney General with strong ties to the Trump wing of the GOP. In Chapter 10, Calvin R. Coker and Desmond J. McCarthy examine the shifting rhetoric surrounding abortion in the wake of the Dobbs decision through an analysis of the 2022 midterm Senate races in Arizona and Nevada. Coker and McCarthy argue that, prior to Dobbs, public debate had largely stagnated within a "choice vs. life" binary, which limited rhetorical strategies to entrenched positions. However, the changing abortion framework created new opportunities for political candidates to employ innovative rhetorical strategies that addressed the outcomes of the Dobbs decision, especially for states like Arizona and Nevada, where abortion access was immediately threatened. This new rhetorical trajectory signals a more expansive stance on reproductive rights that could influence both state and national politics, positioning abortion as a pivotal issue in American politics for years to come.

Chapter 11 explores how different types of social media content influenced voter perceptions in Florida's 2022 Senate race between incumbent Republican Marco Rubio and Democratic challenger Val Demings. Using an online experiment with a pretest-posttest design, David Lynn Painter, Tanja Vierrether, and Fiona Bown expose participants to one of three types of social media content (i.e., image-focused, issue-focused, or negative) from both Rubio and Demings to gauge their impact on candidate evaluations. The chapter determined that image-focused content led to the most significant increases in candidate evaluations for Demings, while issue-focused content had the greatest impact on Rubio's evaluations. Regarding partisanship, independents in the study reported greater changes in candidate evaluations compared to Republicans and Democrats, showing that independents may be more influenced by political social media content. Finally, racial justice and gender equity attitudes were significantly related to evaluations of Demings, but not Rubio, and participants with strong social justice attitudes responded more positively to Demings, reflecting the racial and gender dynamics at play in the race. Like all communication, the chapter suggests that social media strategies should be tailored to the candidate and audience because lesser-known candidates like Demings may benefit most from image-based content, while policy-oriented content may help established figures like Rubio. This research also highlights the growing influence of social justice attitudes on voter behavior, particularly in races involving candidates from diverse backgrounds.

In Chapter 12, Zoë Hess Carney and Rita Kirk use the 2022 Texas gubernatorial race between incumbent Republican Greg Abbott and Democratic challenger Beto O'Rourke as a case study to critique the concept of the "marketplace of ideas" in the digital era, arguing that the metaphor, which suggests that truth will emerge from a free exchange of ideas, falls short in today's digital system. Carney and Kirk assert that digital media's commercial incentives undermine civic discourse and participation, with campaign messages increasingly tailored to profit-driven algorithms over fostering genuine public debate and digital advertising transforming citizens into consumers. Instead of promoting diverse viewpoints, microtargeting and algorithmically driven content placement exacerbate echo chambers and limit citizens' exposure to opposing perspectives, thus undermining democratic ideals. The chapter calls for a reevaluation of the marketplace of ideas metaphor in the context of digital platforms, proposing that new frameworks are needed to address the role of private companies in shaping political discourse.

In Chapter 13, Joyce H. Glasscock scrutinizes gendered communication strategies in the 2022 Kansas gubernatorial race between incumbent Democrat Laura Kelly and Republican challenger Derek Schmidt. As a rare Democratic

**20** Media Messages in the 2022 Midterm Election

governor in a predominantly Republican state, Kelly's re-election campaign offers a unique opportunity to analyze how gendered traits and issues were used by both candidates. Using a mixed-methods approach that combines quantitative content analysis and qualitative interviews with Kelly and her campaign staff, Glasscock finds Kelly strategically balanced masculine and feminine traits across platforms, using masculine traits like competence and strength in debates while emphasizing feminine traits like collaboration in TV ads. Although abortion was a contentious issue in the campaign, Kelly minimized its presence in her messaging, framing abortion as a private matter rather than a political one, an approach that aligned with her overall strategy of avoiding divisive topics and focusing on a centrist, bipartisan image. Schmidt, on the other hand, predominantly used attack strategies by targeting Kelly's honesty and effectiveness, traits typically seen as essential in masculine leadership. The chapter stresses the complexities of gendered communication in mixed-gender political races, showing how female candidates like Kelly must navigate stereotypes by balancing traits and issues.

## Conclusion

Celebrated scholar Richard Perloff (2023) has called for researchers to study congressional and midterm elections, writing:

> scholars examining political marketing in U.S. elections need to redirect their energies to exploring the multitude of non-presidential electoral contests, applying political marketing principles, harnessing communication and psychological theories to appreciate underlying mechanisms, and considering broader implications for normative democratic theory.
>
> *(p. 88)*

This book answers Perloff's appeal by applying communication theories to the 2022 midterms. There is a pressing need for more research on the role of communication and media in midterm elections, as the landscape of political discourse is increasingly shaped by digital platforms, social media, and the rapid spread of information. With voters relying more heavily on social media for political news, understanding how information—both accurate and misleading—circulates is crucial for assessing its impact on voter behavior and election outcomes. Studies of how candidates use social media to engage with voters, the influence of partisan echo chambers, and the growing phenomenon of misinformation are essential to understand how media can affect electoral processes. Additionally, the polarization of media coverage, particularly how different platforms frame issues and candidates, may influence public opinion and voter turnout. By deepening our understanding of these dynamics, we can better address the challenges posed by these issues, while also strengthening the democratic process by ensuring a well-informed electorate. As midterm elections continue to grow in importance, especially with their potential to shift power in Congress, further research into the intersection of media, communication, and electoral outcomes is critical for shaping future election policies and strategies.

The surprising results of the 2022 midterms revealed the limits of polling and media narratives, showing how voters defied expectations of a "red wave" despite widespread media projections. This election illustrated that while media outlets continue to shape voter perceptions, it is not the sole driver of electoral outcomes. Looking ahead, candidates and campaigns will need to adapt to a fragmented media landscape where traditional media, social platforms, and emerging technologies compete for influence. With the rise of artificial intelligence, predictive algorithms, and even more targeted advertising, future campaigns may navigate an environment where voter engagement is increasingly customized and complex, raising questions about the balance between influence and democratic integrity. As we look toward 2024 and beyond, understanding media's power to inform—or misinform—voters will be crucial for a healthy democracy.

## References

Abramowitz, A. (2023). Donald Trump and the vanishing red wave. In L. J. Sabato, K. Kondik, C. O. Whaley, & J. M. Coleman (Eds.), *The red ripple: The 2022 midterm elections and what they mean for 2024* (pp. 27–38). Rowman & Littlefield.

Aylward, A. (2022, November 10). How Gen Z held off the red wave. *TIME*. https://time.com/6232272/generation-z-voters-midterm-elections/

Balz, D., & Keating, D. (2022, November 9). GOP exuberance crashed into Democratic resistance to defy midterm expectations. *The Washington Post*. www.washingtonpost.com/politics/2022/11/09/gop-exuberance-crashed-into-democratic-resistance-defy-midterm-expectations/

Blum, R. M., Cowburn, M., & Masket, S. (2024). Who decides? Media, MAGA, money, and mentions in the 2022 Republican primaries. *Political Research Quarterly*. https://doi.org/10.1177/10659129241268820

Campbell, J. E. (2023, May 16). Mystery at the midterm: What happened to the red wave? *Real Clear Politics*. www.realclearpolitics.com/articles/2023/05/16/mystery at the_midterm_what_happened_to_the_red_wave_149208.html

Carson, J. L., & Hitefield, A. A. (2023). A red wave or a ripple? Nationalized politics and the 2022 midterm elections. *The Forum, 21*(1), 3–25. https://doi.org/10.1515/for-2023-2002

Carson, J. L., & Ulrich, S. (2024). In the shadow of Trump: The 2022 midterm elections. *Journal of Political Marketing, 23*(3), 211–226. https://doi.org/10.1080/15377857.2024.2359241

**22** Media Messages in the 2022 Midterm Election

Center for Information & Research on Civic Learning and Engagement (CIRCLE). (2022a, November 9). Millions of youth cast ballots, decide key 2022 races. https://circle.tufts.edu/latest-research/millions-youth-cast-ballots-decide-key-2022-races

Center for Information & Research on Civic Learning and Engagement (CIRCLE). (2022b). The Youth Vote in 2022. https://circle.tufts.edu/2022-election-center#youth-prefer-democrats-by-28-point-margin

Cillizza, C. (2022, October 26). Joe Biden's poll numbers are in a very bad place for Democrats. CNN. www.cnn.com/2022/10/26/politics/joe-biden-gallup-poll-midterm-elections/index.html

Clegg, N. (2022, August 16). How Meta is planning for the 2022 U.S. midterms. *Meta Fact Sheet.* https://about.fb.com/news/2022/08/meta-plans-for-2022-us-midterms/

CNN. (2022). CNN poll of polls: Biden approval rating. www.cnn.com/polling/approval-rating-poll-of-polls

Debusmann, Jr., B., & Sherman, N. (2022, November 9). U.S. midterms: Why a Republican 'wave' never happened. *British Broadcasting Corporation.* www.bbc.com/news/world-us-canada-63569850

Eddy, K. (2024, October 16). Republicans, young adults now nearly as likely to trust info from social media as from national news outlets. *Pew Research Center.* www.pewresearch.org/short-reads/2024/10/16/republicans-young-adults-now-nearly-as-likely-to-trust-info-from-social-media-as-from-national-news-outlets/

Evans, H. K., & Parton, K. (2024). A tale of two elections: Changes in candidates' tweets during the 2022 midterm elections in Virginia. *Journal of Political Marketing.* https://doi.org/10.1080/15377857.2024.2383142

Fowler, E. F., Franz, M. M., Neumann, M., Ridout, T. N., & Yao, J. (2023). Digital advertising in the 2022 midterms. *The Forum, 21*(1), 53–73. https://doi.org/10.1515/for-2023-2006

Franz, M. M., Ridout, T. N., & Fowler, E. F. (2023). Television advertising in the 2022 midterms. *The Forum, 21*(1), 27–51. https://doi.org/10.1515/for-2023-2005

Goldmacher, S. (2022a, July 11). Most Democrats don't want Biden in 2024, new poll shows. *The New York Times.* www.nytimes.com/2022/07/11/us/politics/biden-approval-polling-2024.html

Goldmacher, S. (2022b, October 25). Democrats, on defense in blue states, brace for a red wave in the house. *The New York Times.* www.nytimes.com/2022/10/25/politics/blue-states-midterm-landscape.html

Hartig, H., Daniller, A., Keeter, S., & Van Green, T. (2023, July 12). Voting patterns in the 2022 elections. *Pew Research Center.* www.pewresearch.org/politics/2023/07/12/voting-patterns-in-the-2022-elections/#Age-and-the-2022-election

Hartman, T. (2022, November 7). How does the president's party fare in the midterms? *Reuters.* www.reuters.com/graphics/USA-ELECTION/MIDTERMS/gdpzyzowgvw/

Inman, W. J. (2022, October 25). Why does the President's party typically lose midterms? *Scripps News.* www.scrippsnews.com/politics/midterm-elections/why-does-the-president-s-party-typically-lose-midterms

Jacobson, L. (2022, September 15). The party that controls the White House usually loses in midterm elections. Here's what could make 2022 different. *Poynter.* www.poynter.org/fact-checking/2022/which-party-control-congress-midterm-election-2022/

Klepper, D. (2022, October 21). As 2022 midterms approach, disinformation on social media platforms continues. *Associated Press*. www.pbs.org/newshour/politics/as-2022-midterms-approach-disinformation-on-social-media-platforms-continues

Kraushaar, J. (2022, November 2). The tide is turning for Republicans. *Axios*. www.axios.com/2022/11/02/midterm-elections-2022-crime-hispanics-abortion

Lepird, C. S., Ng, L. H. X., Wu, A., & Carley, K. M. (2024). What news is shared where and how: A multi-platform analysis of news shared during the 2022 U.S. midterm elections. *Social Media + Society, 10*(2). https://doi.org/10.1177/20563051241245950

Mansfield, M. (2022, November 7). U.S. midterms: Could social media swing it? *British Broadcasting Corporation*. www.bbc.com/news/newsbeat-63509041

McDonald, M. P. (2023). 2022 general election. *United States Elections Project*. www.electproject.org/2022g

Milligan, S. (2022, November 9). The red wave that wasn't. *U.S. News & World Report*. www.usnews.com/news/elections/articles/2022-11-09/the-red-wave-that-wasnt

Neal, A., & McGrath, S. (2023). Political bias on Instagram: Generation Z and the 2022 midterm elections. *Journal of Student Research, 12*(3). https://doi.org/10.47611/jsrhs.v12i3.4837

Olsen, H. (2022, November 7). Opinion: My predictions for the 2022 midterm elections. *The Washington Post*. www.washingtonpost.com/opinions/2022/11/07/midterm-elections-2022-prediction-house-senate-forecast/

Open Secrets. (n.d.). *Elections overview*. www.opensecrets.org/elections-overview?cycle=2022

Owen, D. (2023). Mainstream and social media in the midterm elections. In L. J. Sabato, K. Kondik, C. O. Whaley, & J. M. Coleman (Eds.), *The red ripple: The 2022 midterm elections and what they mean for 2024* (pp. 197–211). Rowman & Littlefield.

Panagopoulos, C., & Lore, N. (2024). Embeddedness, social contagion, and vote choice in the 2022 U.S. Senate elections. *Journal of Political Marketing*. https://doi.org/10.1080/15377857.2024.2383138

Penn, M., & Cusack, B. (Hosts). (2022, October 17). Mark Penn predicts red wave in 2022 midterm elections [Audio podcast episode]. In *Mark Penn polls*. www.markpennpolls.com/episodes/mark-penn-predicts-red-wave-in-2022-midterm-elections

Perloff, R. M. (2023). A cri de coeur for political marketing research in U.S. midterm and off-year elections. *Journal of Political Marketing, 22*(2), 87–91. https://doi.org/10.1080/15377857.2023.2192594

Pew Research Center. (2022, October 20). Midterm voting intentions are divided, economic gloom persists. www.pewresearch.org/politics/2022/10/20/the-midterm-elections-and-views-of-biden/

Phillips, A. (2022, November 1). What are midterm elections and why are they important? *The Washington Post*. www.washingtonpost.com/politics/2022/10/03/what-are-midterm-elections/

Rafail, P., O'Connell, W. E., & Sager, E. (2024). Polarizing feedback loops on Twitter: Congressional tweets during the 2022 midterm elections. *Socius, 10*, https://doi.org/10.1177/23780231241228924

Robokiller. (n.d.). The state of political messages in 2022. www.robokiller.com/reports/robokiller-2022-political-message-report

Rozo, A. Z., Campo-Archbold, A., Díaz-López, D., Gray, I., Pastor-Galindo, J., Nespoli, P., Mármol, F. G., & McCoy, D. (2024). Cyber democracy in the digital age: Characterizing hate networks in the 2022 US midterm elections. *Information Fusion*, 110, Article 102459. https://doi.org/10.1016/j.inffus.2024.102459

Rutenberg, J., Bensinger, K., & Eder, S. (2022, December 31). The 'red wave' washout: How skewed polls fed a false election narrative. *The New York Times*. www.nytimes.com/2022/12/31/us/politics/polling-election-2022-red-wave.html

Sabato, L. J., Kondik, K., Whaley, C. O., & Coleman, J. M. (Eds.). (2023). *The red ripple: The 2022 midterm elections and what they mean for 2024*. Rowman & Littlefield.

Schaffner, B. F., & Gaus, K. (2023). Donald Trump and the Democratic shift among college-educated suburban White voters. *The Forum, 21*(1), 75–96. https://doi.org/10.1515/for-2023-2004

Sievert, J., & Garand, J. C. (2024). Editor's introduction: Special issue on the 2022 midterm congressional election. *Journal of Political Marketing*. https://doi.org/10.1080/15377857.2024.2359234

Simpson, E., Conner, A., & Maciolek, A. (2022, November 3). Social media and the 2022 midterm elections: Anticipating online threats to democratic legitimacy. *The Center for American Progress*. www.americanprogress.org/article/social-media-and-the-2022-midterm-elections-anticipating-online-threats-to-democratic-legitimacy/

Trzcińska, J. (2024). Media coverage of the 2022 campaign. In R. Duda & M. Turek (Eds.), *The crossroads elections: European perspectives on the 2022 U.S. midterm elections* (pp. 192–203). Routledge.

United States Census Bureau. (2023, May 2). 2022 voting and registration data now available. www.census.gov/newsroom/press-releases/2023/2022-voting-registration.html

## SECTION I

# Amplified Doubts

Conspiracy Theories, Communication, and the 2022 Midterm Elections

# 2

# CONSPIRATORIAL IDEATION, ELECTION DENIAL, AND VOTER CHOICE

*Diana Owen, Thom Crockett, Arjun Chawla, Kelton Miller, Kyle Kim, Haydyn Hendricks, Parisa Bruce, and Brenda Zhong*

Conspiratorial beliefs attributing events and power relations to secret manipulation by individuals, groups, and organizations gained prominence in the discourse surrounding the 2022 midterm elections. Election denial, epitomized by the "Big Lie"—the false claim that the 2020 presidential election was stolen from Donald Trump—received significant media coverage and was promoted by candidates during the midterms. QAnon conspiracies—a set of unfounded beliefs that allege a secret cabal of powerful individuals, often linked to political elites and celebrities, is involved in human trafficking, political corruption, and other nefarious activities—moved beyond the shadows of alt-right social media platforms to become mainstream media obsessions. In prior research that provides a context for this study, we found that in 2022, belief in the Big Lie and support for fringe conspiracy theories was significantly correlated with conservative political ideology, strength of party identification, and holding authoritarian populist attitudes. Voters who exhibited conspiratorial ideation were more likely to feel isolated, distrust those in positions of authority, and feel threatened by people outside their social groups. Lastly, alternative media use was strongly related to belief in conspiracies (Owen et al., 2023).

People drawn to conspiracies share a complex set of intersecting political, social, and psychological traits that have been researched extensively (Bowes et al., 2023; Goreis & Voracek, 2019). However, academic studies examining whether belief in conspiracies predicts voter engagement in elections is lacking. Thus, the following question is addressed in this chapter: Were election denialism and belief in conspiracy theories related to voters' engagement in the 2022 midterm elections? Similarly, there is speculation but little empirical research examining the relationship of conspiratorial beliefs to candidate preference. Was

DOI: 10.4324/9781003440833-3

**28** Media Messages in the 2022 Midterm Election

conspiratorial ideation a factor in voters' partisan candidate choices? An original post-midterm survey was employed to examine these questions empirically.

Conspiratorial thinking was abundant among voters in the 2022 midterms. In this study, we found a connection between conspiratorial ideation and voters' campaign participation and vote choice. Voters who exhibited greater belief in conspiracies were more likely than other voters to engage in higher-threshold forms of online campaign activity, such as donating to a candidate and posting campaign information online. Party identification was, unsurprisingly, the strongest predictor of vote choice. However, belief in the Big Lie and adherence to authoritarian populist beliefs were significantly related to voting for Republican candidates.

## Conspiracy Theories

Conspiracies are "explanatory beliefs about a group of actors that collude in secret to reach malevolent goals" (Bales, 2007, p. 65). They predate the country's founding and are deeply embedded in American culture (Hofstadter, 1964). Belief in conspiracy theories is widespread, and cuts across political, social, and demographic lines. The term conspiracy theory has a negative connotation and often is used to discredit those who challenge authority. Plausible conspiracies, such as the Watergate scandal or the fear that the National Security Administration (NSA) is spying on Americans, involve conflicting interpretations of events that have been addressed by the government and are at least partially true. However, the present study focuses on fringe conspiracies. These theories are far-fetched, often racist and antisemitic, and have little to no evidence supporting them. They are detached from reality, vague, and inaccurate. Examples include the extended QAnon universe of beliefs and the "birther" conspiracy alleging Barack Obama is not a natural-born U.S. citizen.

An anonymous online figure known as QAnon (or Q) is a source of many baseless conspiracies. Core QAnon beliefs are antisemitism, denial of election results, and the pursuit of exposing a cabal of prominent "pedophilic, satanic" global elites (Wendling, 2021). QAnon has endorsed the Great Replacement Theory which suggests that nonwhite citizens are being brought to the U.S. to replace white voters (Jones, 2022). Q's followers are awaiting The Storm, an uprising in which former President Donald Trump would arrest and exile Democratic leaders to a U.S. military prison located in Guantanamo Bay (Domonoske, 2021). Most of the specific QAnon-based conspiracy theories build upon the ideas encompassed by the Great Replacement Theory and The Storm. Persistent QAnon conspiracies examined in this study are that 9/11 was an inside job and that the U.S. government was complicit in the attacks on the World Trade Center ("9/11"), Satan-worshipping pedophiles are plotting to run the world ("Satan"), a small group of religious elites are taking over government institutions ("Elites"), the birther conspiracy ("Birther"), and that the COVID-19 pandemic was planned by Bill Gates who wants to reduce the world's population by three billion people by administering deadly vaccines ("Gates"). A conspiracy that emerged during the 2022 campaign purports that John F. Kennedy, Jr. is still alive and will reinstate Donald Trump as president ("JFK, Jr.") (Anglesey, 2021).

QAnon promoted Trump's Big Lie, the empty accusations of the 2020 presidential election being stolen from him (Block, 2021; Farivar, 2021). When waiting to cast their ballots, voters were urged by QAnon influencers to "fight," "hold the line," and "trust the plan," commands that were used to incite unrest on January 6. Purported evidence of widespread voter fraud supporting the Big Lie went viral on social media. Fake videos depicted voting machines blocking voters from casting a ballot for Trump and switching votes to Democratic candidates, ballots being burned or discarded in ditches, and Republican voters being turned away at the polls (CNN Staff, 2022).

Belief in the Big Lie went far beyond the QAnon adherents and created a core constituency of voters (Norris, 2024; Jacobson, 2023). Approximately 70% of Republicans did not believe that Joe Biden legitimately won the 2020 presidential election at the time of the 2022 midterms (Greenberg, 2022). Nearly 60% of voters had an election denier on their 2022 midterm ballots. In fact, well over 100 candidates in state races promoting the Big Lie won Republican primary victories and ran for office in the 2022 midterms (Oladipo, 2022). Nearly 50 of these candidates won elections for governor, U.S. House, U.S. Senate, secretary of state, and attorney general (Beard, 2022). High-profile election deniers included Marjorie Taylor Greene (R-GA), who regularly posted QAnon conspiracies along with anti-Muslim and antisemitic comments, won her House reelection bid. Ron Johnson (R-WI), who called for a federal commission to investigate voter fraud in the 2020 presidential contest, prevailed in a tight race. However, some high-profile election deniers, such as gubernatorial candidates Tudor Dixon (R-MI) and Geoff Diehl (R-MA) lost their campaigns. The majority of gubernatorial and secretary of state candidates who spread false claims about election fraud and refused to certify the 2020 presidential election also were not successful (Bedekovics & Maciolek, 2022).

## Conspiratorial Ideation

Conspiratorial ideation, or a conspiracy mentality, is a well-established construct in psychological research (Pilch et al., 2023). It refers to a generalized, fundamental tendency "to believe that events and power relations are secretly manipulated by clandestine groups and organizations" with nefarious intentions (Grimes, 2016, p. 1). Individuals exhibiting a conspiracy mentality adhere to a monological belief system associated with acceptance of a range of conspiracies, including those that are unrelated (Brotherton et al., 2013; Goertzel, 1994), contradictory (Wood et al., 2012), and completely fictitious (Swami et al., 2011). Conspiratorial ideation is aligned with pathological tendencies, such as paranoia, antagonism, and suspicion toward others. It is central to antisemitic and authoritarian belief systems (Center for Antisemitism Research, 2023; Groh, 1987; Hofstadter, 1964; Lipset & Raab, 1978) and is linked to socio-political factors, including perceived powerlessness, interpersonal and political distrust, and anomie (Goreis & Voracek, 2019). The prevalence of online communities that incubate misinformation combined with sustained engagement with social media can feed a conspiratorial mindset, especially among people who seek to justify their worldview (Foley & Wagner, 2020). A period of national stress can lead to an upward trend in belief in conspiracy theories as a confused population looks for answers. The COVID-19 pandemic coupled with the rise of politicians who elevated fear appeals through divisive rhetoric created an environment where more than half of the American public accepts a conspiratorial narrative related to political affairs (Miller et al., 2015; Moyer, 2019).

Scholars have pointed to a rise in authoritarianism in the U.S. in recent years coinciding with an increase in populist political discontent and upheaval (Waller, 2022). Populism has been described as a political logic (Judis, 2016) or a thinly centered ideology loosely tied to a political agency that lacks a coherent policy focus (Mudde & Kaltwasser, 2017). High levels of authoritarianism have been linked to belief in conspiracies (Abalakina-Paap et al., 1999; Imhoff et al., 2022; Thielmann & Hilbig, 2023). This study examines authoritarian populism associated with support for Donald Trump. In addition to perpetuating the Big Lie, Trump and his adherents ratcheted up the QAnon conspiracy rhetoric throughout the campaign. A cluster of three values defines authoritarianism as it relates to Trumpian populism: "1) the importance of security against risks of instability and disorder, 2) the value of conformity to preserve conventional traditions and guard our way of life, and 3) the need for loyal obedience toward strong champions who protect the group" (Norris & Inglehart, 2019, p. 8). Trump's brand of authoritarian populism is infused with strong nativist and nationalist themes. It is a populism of exclusionary politics that emphasizes a perceived threat that is posed by out-groups, especially immigrants and racial/ ethnic minorities. Anyone who disagrees with Trump is cast as a member of the corrupt elite establishment which encompasses the mainstream press, political opponents, government institutions, interest groups, and international organizations.

Populism and conspiratorial ideation, while related, are distinct constructs. Populism is a broad political movement or program premised upon the perception that society is being destroyed by self-serving elites. Conspiracy theories are attempts to explain actions and events that are rooted in suspicions about powerful actors secretly plotting to achieve malicious goals. Populism and conspiratorial beliefs share the same core underpinnings anchored in

Conspiratorial Ideation, Election Denial, and Voter Choice **31**

an us-versus-them, good-versus-evil disposition. Both concepts also share a generalized distrust of political and societal institutions (Imhoff & Bruder, 2014; Thielman & Hilbig, 2023).

Most studies of the political correlates of conspiratorial ideation focus on its connection to ideology and partisanship. Findings are not entirely settled about the nature of the relationships between political identities and belief in conspiracies. A long-standing perspective holds that people who are most susceptible to believing conspiracy theories are more conservative and likely to identify as Republican (Hofstadter, 1964). Large-scale studies in the Trump era revealed that conservatives were more likely to embrace conspiracies than moderates or liberals (Imhoff et al., 2022; van der Linden et al., 2021). The relentless espousal of fringe conspiracy rhetoric by prominent right-wing political figures, such as Donald Trump, Steve Bannon, and Joe Rogan, prompted more widespread acceptance of conspiracies among mainstream members of the Republican Party (Garrett & Bond, 2021; Sawyer, 2022). They accept conspiracies congruent with Republican aims to derail the implementation of liberal policies and programs (Frazier, 2013; Muirhead & Rosenblum, 2016; Public Policy Polling, 2013). Other research indicates that the partisan-conspiracy relationship is quadratic in form. Strong Democrats are as likely as strong Republicans to exhibit conspiratorial tendencies (Imhoff et al., 2022; Uscinski et al., 2022). Strong partisans on both sides have been shown to be more rigid in their processing of information than moderates or independents. They are more likely to hold negative views about politics and society and to be receptive to information that casts out-groups in a negative light (Zmigrod et al., 2020). Finally, belief in specific conspiracies may evoke different responses based on partisan predispositions. Liberals may be more willing to believe theories critical of conservatives, while Republicans may be more likely to believe in theories critical of Democrats (Garrett & Bond, 2021; Uscinski et al., 2022).

## Media Use and the Proliferation of Conspiracies

Conspiracy theories proliferated long before the advent of online platforms and social media (Uscinski & Enders, 2020). As misinformation has proliferated exponentially and become more easily spreadable across channels, the likelihood of people being exposed repeatedly to conspiratorial ideas has increased markedly (Enders et al., 2023; Rose, 2021). There is a connection between news media consumption and conspiratorial ideation among people who are high in political knowledge, lack trust in political institutions, have populist tendencies, and have been on the losing side of an election (Stempel et al., 2007). People who avoid mainstream news, but gain information through social media and personal networks, are prone to conspiratorial thinking (Enders, et al., 2023; Stecula & Pickup, 2021). Individuals who have strong distrust in the mainstream

**32** Media Messages in the 2022 Midterm Election

media and rely on social media almost exclusively for political information are especially susceptible to conspiratorial appeals (Mari et al., 2021).

Niche social media platforms are pivotal in the dissemination and acceptance of conspiracy theories. Conspiratorial messaging that initiates on alt-social media platforms can create a special bond between users that can spread to "echo platforms," mainstream social media sites, such as Facebook, Twitter, YouTube, and Reddit, colonized by users within ideological echo chambers (Cinelli et al., 2022, p. 1). QAnon conspiracies are uniquely associated with social media. They often begin as a "Q Drop" or "breadcrumb," a cryptic message written in coded language featuring slogans and pro-Trump themes (Iacobuzio, 2021, para.6). They appear first on alternative social media sites like 4chan and its spinoff 8kun (Iacobuzio, 2021) where anonymous users post pictures and memes to image boards that generate discussion. These sites have a reputation for disseminating far-right, racist, and misogynist content (Zheng et al., 2024). The initial posts are collected and filtered to QAnon-based social media groups and posters who adapt them for dissemination on "echo platforms" and more mainstream conservative and right-wing social media platforms (Iacobuzio, 2021).

## Conspiracy Theories and Elections

Conspiracy theories are more prevalent during election years, especially presidential campaigns (Brown, 2020). The 2022 midterms were no exception. Candidates openly pushed the Big Lie and fringe conspiracies in their platforms and stump speeches that were amplified by the press and spread through social media. Campaign strategies incorporating conspiracies are most effective in periods of uncertainty. Conspiracies that are built upon established assumptions that are repeated, embellished, and widely disseminated. QAnon disciples ascribe to the unfounded conspiratorial assumptions that a globally active "Deep State" cabal of satanic pedophile elites, such as former Secretary of State Hillary Clinton, are perpetuating evil which is not specifically defined. Donald Trump has secret knowledge of the cabal, and is dismantling it from within. Trump will have the evildoers arrested during a major event known as "The Storm," which will be followed by the "Great Awakening," the creation of a new society free of evil (Robertson & Amarasingam, 2022). Conspiratorial campaign strategies can convey a sense of control to voters. Politicians who promote conspiracies are perceived to be outsiders and change-agents, even as conspiratorial language is designed to cultivate fear and uncertainty (Dow et al., 2022). Wang (2022) describes a self-perpetuating cycle of "epistemic junk food" (Schmalz, 2022, para. 9) where candidates prime audiences to be increasingly receptive to conspiracies that can justify winning and losing elections. Conspiracies appeal to voters because they are novel and relatively simple, requiring little analytical thinking. Motivated partisan reasoning contributes to the proliferation of conspiracies as voters seek to reinforce their candidate choices and political beliefs (Edelson et al., 2017).

The bulk of research on conspiracies and elections has focused on the effects on voters' perceptions of election legitimacy. For example, despite a lack of evidence, almost 80% of Trump voters in 2020 believed that election fraud was widespread and systemic and 65% were convinced that their candidate had won the election (Pennycook & Rand, 2021). Conspiracies weaken voters' trust in the election information environment (Invernizzi & Mohamed, 2022). Research into conspiratorial ideation and electoral engagement is limited and focuses primarily on the connection to broader right-wing mobilization. Believers in QAnon conspiracies have been found to engage in protest behavior during and after elections that are aligned with street movements, such as "Save Our Children" (Kishi et al., 2020, p. 8).

## Hypotheses

While there is a paucity of scholarly literature on the relationship between conspiratorial ideation and voter engagement in elections, observational evidence suggests that voters who believed in the Big Lie and QAnon conspiracies were mobilized during the 2022 midterms. The January 6th insurrection at the U.S. Capitol was motivated by the Big Lie, a notion that was documented over 100 times in the January 6th Committee's Final Report (Select Committee, 2022). Voters espousing conspiracies were active on social media and attended rallies for conspiracy-friendly candidates. Thus, the following hypotheses were tested:

$H_1$: Voters who believed in the Big Lie and fringe conspiracies were more likely to engage online in the 2022 midterm elections than those who did not.

$H_2$: The greater the use of social media and alternative media, the more likely voters were to engage online in the midterms.

Republican candidates widely embraced conspiracy theories during the midterms (Milbank, 2022). The relationship between conspiratorial ideation to partisan candidate preference was examined:

$H_3$: Voters who believed in the Big Lie and conspiracy theories were more likely to vote for Republican candidates than those who did not.

## Data

The study uses data from an original national survey of voters designed by the Media and American Elections graduate seminar sponsored by the Civic Education Research Lab (CERL) at Georgetown University. Respondents were recruited via Mechanical Turk (Mturk) based on their status as eligible voters

**34** Media Messages in the 2022 Midterm Election

and received a stipend for their participation. The survey was in the field on November 9, 2022—the day after Election Day—until November 12. Data were collected on a total of 1,958 respondents of which 1,579 were voters who are included in this study.

Participants were recruited based on a variety of characteristics, including their party identification, gender, and racial and ethnic identities for an additional fee. The percentage of Republicans in the sample (36%) matched the percentage of voters in the election based on exit polls (Chen et al., 2022). Democrats were slightly overrepresented in the sample (38% in the sample compared to 33% of voters in the election). Independents were underrepresented in the sample (26% compared to 31% of voters in the election). The gender composition of the sample was 48% male, 51% female, and 1% nonbinary. The racial/ethnic makeup of the sample closely resembled their representation in the electorate (see Bloomberg Government, 2022). 70% of the sample was White compared to 73% in the electorate. Blacks constituted 13% of the sample as opposed to 11% of voters. Latine respondents made up 11% of the sample which is the same percentage as in the electorate. 5% of the sample were Asian American Pacific Islanders (AAPIs) who compose 4% of voters. The recruitment strategy employed here of using validated respondents largely mitigated concerns with oversampling liberals which has plagued MTurk samples (Alkhatib et al., 2021). The personality and value-based motivations of MTurk respondents are associated with ideologies from across the political spectrum (Clifford et al., 2015).

### *Measures*

Voters' online engagement in the midterms was conceptualized as a continuum. Respondents were asked how often they engaged in a list of activities online. While some of these activities also can take place offline, the focus here is on online behavior. Low-threshold online activities are primarily associated with monitoring and consuming digital information and require a relatively small commitment of time, effort, and skills. The Low-Threshold Activities Index consisted of variables measuring how often respondents consumed content (e.g., read articles, viewed videos), looked for information about candidates and issues, and "liked" or "favorited" political content. It was reliable (Cronbach's $\alpha$ = .782) and ranged from 1 to 10. Medium-threshold activities involve digital expression. A Medium-Threshold Activities Index was constructed of items measuring how often voters participated online in political discussions, commented on or responded to political content, shared or reposted information about a candidate, and shared or reported a political video or picture. It ranged from 1 to 13 (Cronbach's $\alpha$ = .874). High-Threshold activities encompass active behaviors that respondents took part in online that can have expressly political outcomes. Respondents indicated how often they had donated to a campaign or political organization, created and posted a political video or picture, organized a political event, and tried to convince others to vote for or against a candidate. The index was reliable (Cronbach's $\alpha$ = .879) and ranged from 1 to 13.

Voters were asked if they cast their ballot for Republican, Democrat, or third-party candidates in the 2022 contests for U.S. House, U.S. Senate, and governor. We created a variable of voters' 2022 partisan candidate preference that was scored: 1 = all Democratic candidates, 2 = two Democrats and one Republican, 3 = two Republicans and one Democrat, and 4 = all Republican candidates. Nonvoters and voters who cast their ballots for third-party candidates (109 respondents/5.6% of the sample) were excluded.

Respondents were asked about their belief in the Big Lie and six fringe conspiracies that were prevalent during the midterms (see Table 2.1.) A dichotomous variable measured acceptance of the Big Lie: Do you believe that the 2020 presidential election was stolen? (0 = no, 1 = yes). Six fringe theories on the survey consisted of "JFK, Jr.," "Satan," "9/11," "Birther," "Gates," and "Elites" (see previous definition of these theories). An additive Fringe Conspiracy Index ranged from 1 = definitely not true to 25 = definitely true and had a Cronbach's $\alpha$ of .910.). The Index was scored so that the higher the score, the greater the belief in conspiracy theories. A score of 1 indicated that the respondent did not believe that any of the conspiracies were true, while a score of 25 meant the respondent believed that all of the conspiracies were definitely true.

Survey participants were asked how much they knew about two core QAnon beliefs—The Storm and the Great Awakening (see previous definition of these conspiracies). These variables were coded so that higher values were equated with greater QAnon knowledge. An additive QAnon Knowledge Index combined these items (Cronbach's $\alpha$ =. 794) and ranged from 1 = no knowledge to 7 = a great deal of knowledge.

An index of authoritarian populism was constructed from six measures asking respondents how much they agreed with the statements: 1) Politics is ultimately a struggle between good and evil, 2) Diversity limits my freedom,

**TABLE 2.1** Conspiracy Theory Items and Labels

| Conspiracy Theory | Label |
| --- | --- |
| The 2020 presidential election was stolen. | Big Lie |
| JFK, Jr. is alive and planning a return to politics. | JFK, Jr. |
| Satan-worshipping pedophiles are plotting to run the world. | Satan |
| 9/11 was an inside job. | 9/11 |
| A small group of religious elites are taking over government institutions. | Elites |
| Barack Obama is not a natural-born U.S. citizen. | Birther |
| Bill Gates wants to control people through vaccines. | Gates |

3) What people call 'compromise' in politics is really just selling out one's principles, 4) When Congress hinders the work of our government, we should govern without the Congress, 5) Politicians representing the people should adopt a more confrontational attitude in order to make their voice heard and influence decision-making, and 6) Our government would run better if decisions were left up to successful business people (see Owen, 2019). The variables were coded: 1 = strongly disagree to 5 = strongly agree. The additive index of Authoritarian Populism had a range of 1–25 (Cronbach's $\alpha$ = .887).

Respondents were asked how often they used traditional and social media, including alternative right-wing media sources, cable television news, and mainstream social media. These variables measured how often a respondent used the source on a five-point scale. The original variables were coded so that higher values were equated with greater frequency of use. For each index created from these items, the higher the score, the more frequent the media use. Two measures of online right-leaning alternative media—Breitbart News and The Daily Caller—were chosen because they were among the most popular conservative and far-right websites (Statista, 2023) that prominently promoted false election narratives and conspiracy theories favored by the right in 2022 (Center for an Informed Public, 2022). Three social media platforms that regularly host alternative right-wing content—4Chan/8Chan, Parler, and Truth Social, Donald Trump's social media platform—were combined to form the Alt-Media Index, with a range of 1–26 and reliability (Cronbach's $\alpha$) of .902. Cable TV news measured how often voters tuned into CNN, MSNBC, and Fox News. Americans consider all three of these sources to be established mainstream media outlets (Shearer & Mitchell, 2021). The three cable news variables were added to form a TV News Index which ranged from 1 to 14 (Cronbach's $\alpha$ = .849). Respondents use of seven types of mainstream social media were included in the analysis: Facebook, Twitter, YouTube, Instagram, Snapchat, Tumblr, and TikTok. These items were added to form a Social Media Index which ranged from 1 to 36 (Cronbach's $\alpha$ = .926).

Party identification was measured on a five-point scale (1 = strong Democrat, 2 = moderate Democrat, 3 = independent, 4 = moderate Republican, 5 = strong Republican). Dummy variables were created for each of the categories. The original variable was collapsed into a three-point scale. Partisan identification was included as a control variable in the models estimated in this study to test the hypotheses. It had a much stronger association with election engagement and vote choice than ideology, which we dropped from the analysis.

## Analysis

Belief in the Big Lie and fringe conspiracies was substantial during the midterms (Owen et al., 2023). Consistent with the notion of conspiratorial ideation, people who believed one conspiracy theory were likely to accept others. The

Pearson's R correlation between the Big Lie and the Fringe Index was positive and moderately high (.430). The bivariate correlations between the individual conspiracy measures provide evidence that a monological belief system underpins a conspiratorial mindset (see Table 2.2). The Big Lie's correlation with specific fringe conspiracy theories was greatest for "Gates" (.417), "Birther" (.407), and "Satan" (.399), followed by "JFK, Jr." (.332), "9/11" (.327), and "Elites" (.266). The associations among the individual fringe conspiracy measures were strongest for "Birther"/"Satan" (.684), "Birther"/"Gates" (.683), and "Gates"/ "Satan" (.682). All but four of the fifteen correlations were above .600. Every coefficient was statistically significant at the .01 level.

To test the first hypothesis that conspiratorial ideation was related to campaign participation, ordinary least squares regression (OLS) analyses were run for the conspiracy-related variables (Big Lie, Fringe Index, QAnon Knowledge Index, and Authoritarian Populism Index), media variables, and party identification on the three engagement indexes. Moderate to high correlations existed between the conspiracy items (see Table 2.3). Four separate models were computed for each of the conspiracy variables on each of the dependent engagement measures to deal with multicollinearity. Alt-media, TV news, and social media use along with dummy variables for party identification (reference group = independent) were included in the models.

The analysis provided support for Hypothesis 1. The relationship between the conspiracy-related variables generally increased with the level of campaign engagement (see Table 2.4). The beta coefficients for the Big Lie and fringe

**TABLE 2.2** Correlations (Pearson's *R*) between Belief in the Big Lie and Fringe Conspiracies

|  | Big Lie | JFK, Jr. | Satan | 9/11 | Birther | Gates |
|---|---|---|---|---|---|---|
| **JFK, Jr.** | .332[a] | -- | -- | -- | -- | -- |
| **Satan** | .339[a] | .663[a] | -- | -- | -- | -- |
| **9/11** | .327[a] | .654[a] | .651[a] | -- | -- | -- |
| **Birther** | .407[a] | .605[a] | .684[a] | .622[a] | -- | -- |
| **Gates** | .417[a] | .648[a] | .682[a] | .640[a] | .683[a] | -- |
| **Elites** | .266[a] | .587[a] | .640[a] | .572[a] | .542[a] | .570[a] |

[a] $p \leq .01$.

**TABLE 2.3** Correlations (Pearson's *R*) between Conspiracy-Related Items

|  | Big Lie | Fringe Index | QAnon Know |
|---|---|---|---|
| **Fringe Index** | .430 | -- | -- |
| **QAnon Know** | .403 | .351 | -- |
| **Authoritarian Populism** | .512 | .530 | .542 |

Note: All coefficients statistically significant at $p \leq .01$.

**38** Media Messages in the 2022 Midterm Election

**TABLE 2.4** OLS Regression of Conspiracy Variables, Media Variables, and Party Identification on Engagement (Beta Coefficients)

| *LOW-THRESHOLD ENGAGEMENT* | *Model 1 Big Lie* | *Model 2 Fringe Conspiracies* | *Model 3 QAnon Knowledge* | *Model 4 Authoritarian Populism* |
|---|---|---|---|---|
| ***Conspiracy Variables*** | .027 | .020 | .181[a] | .155[a] |
| ***Media Variables*** | | | | |
| Alt-Media | -.361[a] | -.340[a] | -.427[a] | -.383[a] |
| TV News | .297[a] | .279[a] | .275[a] | .293[a] |
| Social Media | .585[a] | .582[a] | .573[a] | .525[a] |
| ***Party Identification*** | | | | |
| Strong Republican | .133[a] | .114[a] | .128[a] | .113[a] |
| Moderate Republican | -.042 | -.035 | -.032 | -.043 |
| Moderate Democrat | .047[b] | .022 | .042 | .053[b] |
| Strong Democrat | .125[a] | .091[a] | .116[a] | .112[a] |
| Model $R^2$ | .406[a] | .369[a] | .427[a] | .423[a] |

| *MODERATE-THRESHOLD ENGAGEMENT* | *Model 1 Big Lie* | *Model 2 Fringe Conspiracies* | *Model 3 QAnon Knowledge* | *Model 4 Authoritarian Populism* |
|---|---|---|---|---|
| ***Conspiracy Variables*** | .100[a] | .116[a] | .151[a] | .193[a] |
| ***Media Variables*** | | | | |
| Alt-Media | -.057[b] | -.052 | -.061[a] | -.046 |
| TV News | .206[a] | .195[a] | .178[a] | .186[a] |
| Social Media | .503[a] | .492[a] | .488[a] | .432[a] |
| ***Party Identification*** | | | | |
| Strong Republican | .149[a] | .136[a] | .160[a] | .125[a] |
| Moderate Republican | -.006 | -.023 | .006 | -.011 |
| Moderate Democrat | .068[a] | .055[b] | .062[a] | .068[a] |
| Strong Democrat | .142[a] | .114[a] | .132[a] | .122[a] |
| Model $R^2$ | .560[a] | .543[a] | .567[a] | .575[a] |

| *HIGH-THRESHOLD ENGAGEMENT* | *Big Lie* | *Fringe Conspiracies* | *QAnon Knowledge* | *Authoritarian Populism* |
|---|---|---|---|---|
| ***Conspiracy Variables*** | .123[a] | .184[a] | .161[a] | .273[a] |
| ***Media Variables*** | | | | |
| Alt-Media | .233[a] | .246[a] | .239[a] | .242[a] |
| TV News | .142[a] | .114[a] | .104[a] | .109[a] |
| Social Media | .334[a] | .313[a] | .322[a] | .239[a] |
| ***Party Identification*** | | | | |
| Strong Republican | .113[a] | .093[a] | .127[a] | .075[a] |
| Moderate Republican | -.032 | -.021 | -.017 | -.036[b] |
| Moderate Democrat | .066[a] | .054[a] | .060[a] | -.062[a] |
| Strong Democrat | .125[a] | .094[a] | .117[a] | .093[a] |
| Model $R^2$ | .638[a] | .633[a] | .645[a] | .668[a] |

[a] $p \leq .01$; [b] $p \leq .05$; $n = 1,579$.

conspiracies were near zero in the low-threshold engagement model. The coefficients increased and were significant for the Big Lie and moderate-threshold engagement (.100) and high-threshold engagement (.123). A similar pattern was evident for fringe conspiracies, as the strength of the relationship increased for moderate engagement (.116) and high engagement (.184). The relationship between QAnon knowledge and engagement was relatively consistent and statistically significant across low (.181), moderate (.151), and high (.161) threshold engagement. The beta coefficients for authoritarian populism increased notably from .155 for low-threshold, .193 for moderate-threshold, and .273 for high-threshold engagement.

The alt-media, TV news, and social media variables had different relational patterns to the three engagement levels. The alt-media variables had a strong negative relationship to low-threshold activities which involve surveillance of mainstream media across all four models. The association between alt-media and moderate-threshold engagement related to discussion and opinion expression was weak and negative. However, the relationship of alt-media to high-threshold engagement was moderate and positive in support of the second hypothesis. The beta coefficient was highest for the authoritarian populism model at .273. Model 1 (Big Lie) exemplifies the trend for alt-media, as the coefficients were -.361 for low, -.057 for moderate, and .123 for high engagement levels. The association between TV news use and engagement decreased as the level of activity increased. The beta coefficients indicated a moderate positive correspondence with low-threshold engagement and the weakest relationship with high-threshold engagement. The trend in Model 1 (Big Lie) was apparent across equations, with beta coefficients of .297 for low, .206 for moderate, and .142 for high levels of engagement. Social media had a more robust relationship to all three types of engagement than alt-media and TV news. The strongest relationship was between social media use and low-level engagement followed by moderate and high levels of engagement. High-threshold engagement was associated with active election participation via social media, so a strong correspondence with mainstream social media engagement was expected. Again, the findings for Model 1 (Big Lie) illustrated the trend across the four models, with beta coefficients of .585 for low, .503 for moderate, and .334 for high levels of engagement.

Strong partisan identification on either end of the spectrum was a better predictor of engagement than moderate affiliation. Both strong Republicans and strong Democrats had significant, positive relationships to all engagement measures. The association was slightly higher for moderate-threshold than for low- or high-level engagement. For Model 1 (Big Lie), the beta coefficients for strong Republican were .133 for low, .149 for moderate, and .113 for high-threshold engagement. For strong Democrat they were .125 for low, .142 for moderate, and .125 for high-level engagement. All coefficients across models for strong partisans were statistically significant. For moderate Republicans, most

# Media Messages in the 2022 Midterm Election

**TABLE 2.5** OLS Regression of Conspiracy Variables, Media Variables, and Party Identification on Vote Choice (Beta Coefficients)

| VOTE CHOICE 2022 | Model 1 Big Lie | Model 2 Fringe Conspiracies | Model 3 QAnon Knowledge | Model 4 Authoritarian Populism |
|---|---|---|---|---|
| Conspiracy Variables | .251[a] | .027 | .031 | .082[a] |
| Party Identification | .613[a] | .649[a] | .622[a] | .613[a] |
| Model $R^2$ | .443[a] | .421[a] | .383[a] | .383[a] |

[a] $p \leq .01$; $n = 1,579$.

of the beta coefficients were near zero and nonsignificant. The relationships for moderate Democrats were slightly higher than for moderate Republicans but were still weak.

Hypothesis 3—that conspiratorial ideation predicted Republican candidate preference—was tested through separate OLS regression models predicting vote choice. A low score on vote choice indicated consistent support for Democratic candidates and a high score indicate voting for all Republican candidates in the midterm contests. Each model included one of the conspiracy-related variables, and the three-point party identification scale (Democrat, Independent, Republican) (see Table 2.5). Support for the hypothesis was mixed. The Big Lie was the strongest predictor of voting for Republican candidates of the conspiracy-related variables (.251), followed by authoritarian populism (.082). Both variables were statistically significant. There was no relationship between belief in fringe conspiracies or QAnon knowledge and vote choice even in bivariate analyses. Party identification was by far the strongest predictor of vote choice in each model, with beta coefficients of .613 for the Big Lie (Model 1), .649 for fringe conspiracies (Model 2), .622 for QAnon knowledge (Model 3), and .613 for authoritarian populism (Model 4). Party identification was the only significant predictor in the Big Lie and QAnon Knowledge models.

## Conclusion

This study corroborates decades-long research findings of a proclivity toward conspiratorial thinking in the American population. About half of the public consistently endorses at least one political conspiracy theory (Oliver & Wood, 2014). This research breaks new ground by exploring empirically the relationship between conspiratorial ideation and electoral behavior during the 2022 midterm elections. The most compelling revelation was the link between voters' conspiratorial ideation and electoral engagement. Voters who believed in the Big Lie and fringe conspiracies, who conformed to Trumpian authoritarian populism, and who were well-acquainted with core QAnon theories were the most likely to engage online in the midterm election at moderate and high levels. Coinciding with this finding, use of right-wing alternative media, where conspiracy theories flourish, predicted active campaign engagement online. While unsurprisingly party identification had by far the greatest association with candidate preference, there was a notable amount of ticket-splitting in 2022. Voters who believed the Big Lie were more likely to vote Republican along with authoritarian populists, although acceptance of QAnon conspiracies was not a significant factor.

Studies of conspiratorial ideation to date have focused heavily on the characteristics of those who ascribe to conspiracies (Uscinski et al., 2022; Moyer, 2019; Swami et al., 2011) and the extent to which conspiracy theories can change attitudes about democratic norms and practices, such as faith in the voting system (Schnaudt, 2024; Albertson & Guiller, 2020). Research on the connection between belief and conspiracy theories and engagement has been limited, and centers on people's intention to participate (Kim, 2019). This work goes beyond prior studies by establishing a link between belief in conspiracy theories and actual engagement online. It demonstrates that voters who ascribed to the Big Lie and fringe QAnon conspiracies engaged in moderate and high-threshold forms of online engagement during the 2022 midterm elections more often than people who did not ascribe to conspiracy theories.

There are limitations to our study that are related to the use of survey research. The study relied on self-reports of voters' beliefs in specific conspiracy theories. We provided brief descriptions of each conspiracy and respondents could indicate that they had no familiarity with the item. Still, these questions may have been difficult for some people to answer accurately due to lack of familiarity with the conspiracies. Respondents also reported on the frequency of their media use and the extent to which they engaged in activities online. While these concepts are distinct and have been used in prior research (e.g., Chan & Yi, 2024; Oden & Porter, 2023), it is possible that they can be conflated by some respondents.

The present era has been referred to as the "Golden Age of Conspiracies" (Stanton, 2020; Uscinski & Parent, 2014). In a time of political upheaval, the proliferation and amplification of conspiratorial beliefs has intensified alongside the increased availability of mainstream, social, and alternative media communication. The dominant conspiracies at the time of the 2022 midterms were unsubstantiated alt-right fringe theories that were publicly promulgated by highly visible political and media figures. Many originated in the shadowy spaces of alternative social media platforms and emerged to populate the media mainstream. Scholars' and political observers' concern that conspiratorial beliefs have the potential to undermine attitudes and behaviors at the heart of the democratic process (Ardevol-Abreu et al., 2020) deserve careful consideration, especially as QAnon conspiracy theories and the Big Lie 2024 remained prominent in the 2024 presidential election.

## References

Abalakina-Paap, M., Stephan, W. G., Craig, T., & Gregory, W. L. (1999). Beliefs in conspiracies. *Political Psychology*, *20*(3), 637–647. https://doi.org/10.1111/0162-895X.00160

Albertson, B., & Guiler, K. (2020). Conspiracy theories, election rigging, and support for democratic norms." *Research & Politics, 7*(3). https://doi.org/10.1177/2053168020959859

Alkhatib, A., DellaVigna, S., Lenz, G., & Chen, S. (2021, October 14). Doing academic research with Amazon Mechanical Turk. *U.C. Berkeley Social Science Matrix*. https://matrix.berkeley.edu/research-article/doing-academic-research-with-amazon-mechanical-turk/

Anglesey, A. (2021, November 2). QAnon believers claim JFK Jr. will 'reappear' in Dallas, declare Donald Trump President. *Newsweek*. www.newsweek.com/qanon-claim-jfk-jr-reappear-dallas-texas-announce-donald-trump-president-1644851

Ardevol-Abreu, A., Gil de Zuniga, H., & Gamez, E. (2020). The influence of conspiracy beliefs on conventional and unconventional forms of political participation: The mediating role of political efficacy. *British Journal of Social Psychology*, *59*(2), 549–569. https://doi.org/10.1111/bjso.12366

Bales, J. M. (2007). Political paranoia v. political realism: On distinguishing between bogus conspiracy theories and genuine conspiratorial politics. *Patterns of Prejudice*, *41*(1), 45–60. https://doi.org/10.1080/00313220601118751

Beard, S. J. (2022, November 11). How many election deniers won? Where 'the big lie' paid off (and didn't) in the midterms. *USA Today*. www.usatoday.com/in-depth/graphics/2022/11/11/how-election-deniers-fared-in-midterm-election/8314254001/

Bedekovics, G., & Maciolek, A. (2022). Election deniers lost key races for federal and state offices in the 2022 midterm elections. *Center for American Progress*. www.americanprogress.org/article/election-deniers-lost-key-races-for-federal-and-state-offices-in-the-2022-midterm-elections/

Block, M. (2021, December 23). *The clear and present danger of Trump's enduring 'Big Lie'*. NPR. www.npr.org/2021/12/23/1065277246/trump-big-lie-jan-6-election

Bloomberg Government. (2022). *Voter demographics and redistricting*. https://assets.bbhub.io/bna/sites/3/2022/07/Voter-Demographics-and-Redistricting.pdf

Bowes, S. M., Costello, T. H., & Tasimi, A. (2023). The conspiratorial mind: A meta-analytic review of motivational and personological correlates. *Psychological Bulletin*, *149*(5-6), 259–293. https://doi.org/10.1037/bul0000392

Brotherton, R., French, C. C., & Pickering, A. D. (2013). Measuring belief in conspiracy theories: The generic conspiracist beliefs scale. *Frontiers in Psychology*, *4*(279), 1–14. https://doi.org/10.3389%2Ffpsyg.2013.00279

Brown, S. (2020, October 5). *MIT Sloan research about social media, misinformation, and elections*. MIT Sloan School of Management. https://mitsloan.mit.edu/ideas-made-to-matter/mit-sloan-research-about-social-media-misinformation-and-elections

Center for an Informed Public. (2022, July 1). Examining how an influential 'repeat spreader' account sowed doubt in the 2020 U.S. elections. University of Washington. www.cip.uw.edu/2022/07/01/2020-election-misinformation-repeat-spreader-breitbart

Center for Antisemitism Research. (2023). *Antisemitic attitudes in America: Conspiracy theories, holocaust education and other predictors of antisemitic belief.*

Anti-Defamation League. www.adl.org/resources/report/antisemitic-attitudes-amer ica-conspiracy-theories-holocaust-education-and-other

Chan, M., & Yi, J. (2024). Social media use and political engagement in polarized times. Examining the contextual roles of issue and affective polarization in developed democracies. *Political Communication, 41*, 743–762. https://doi.org/10.1080/10584 609.2024.2325423

Chen, J. K., Alcantara, C., & Guskin, E. (2022, November 10). How different groups voted according to exit polls and AP VoteCast. *The Washington Post*. www.washing tonpost.com/politics/2022/11/08/exit-polls-2022-elections/

Cinelli, M., Etta, G., Avalle, M., Quattrociocchi, A., Di Marco, N., Valensise, C., Galeazzi, A., & Quattrociocchi, W. (2022). Conspiracy theories and social media platforms. *Current Opinions in Psychology, 47*, Article 101407. https://doi.org/10.1016/j.cop syc.2022.101407

Clifford, S., Jewell, R. M., & Waggoner, P. D. (2015). Are samples drawn from Mechanical Turk valid for research on political ideology, *Research and Politics, 2*(4), 1–9. https:// doi.org/10.1177/2053168015622072

CNN Staff. (2022). *Five baseless 2022 election conspiracy theories, fact-checked.* CNN. www.cnn.com/2022/11/08/politics/fact-check-election-voter-fraud-conspiracies/ index.html

Domonoske, C. (2021, January 20). *The QAnon 'storm' never struck. Some supporters are wavering, others steadfast.* NPR. www.npr.org/sections/inauguration-day-live-updates/2021/01/20/958907699/the-qanon-storm-never-struck-some-supporters-are-wavering-others-steadfast

Dow, B. J., Menon, T., Wang, C. S., & Whitson, J. A. (2022). Sense of control and conspiracy perceptions: Generative directions on a well-worn path. *Current Opinion in Psychology, 47*, Article 101389. https://doi.org/10.1016/j.copsyc.2022.101389

Edelson, J., Alduncin, A., Krewson, C., Sieja, J. A., & Uscinski, J. E. (2017). The effect of conspiratorial thinking and motivated reasoning on belief in election fraud. *Political Research Quarterly, 70*(4), 933–946. https://doi.org/10.1177/106591291 7721061

Enders, A., Uscinski, J. E., Seelig, M. I., Klofstad, C. A., Wuchty, S., Funchion, J. R., Murthi, M. N., Premaratne, K., & Stoler, J. (2023). The relationship between social media use and beliefs in conspiracy theories and misinformation. *Political Behavior, 45*, 781–804. https://doi.org/10.1007/s11109-021-09734-6

Farivar, M. (2021, March 31). *Capitol riot exposed QAnon's violent potential.* Voice of America. www.voanews.com/a/usa_capitol-riot-exposed-qanons-violent-potential/ 6203967.html

Foley, J. M., & Wagner, M. W. (2020, May 26). How media consumption patterns fuel conspiratorial thinking. *Brookings Tech Stream*. www.brookings.edu/techstream/how-media-consumption-patterns-fuel-conspiratorial-thinking/

Frazier, K. (2013). Do you believe that? Poll zeroes in on conspiracy beliefs. *Skeptical Inquirer, 37*(4), 5–8. https://cdn.centerforinquiry.org/wp-content/uploads/sites/29/ 2013/07/22164216/p05.pdf

Garrett, K. R., & Bond, R. M. (2021). Conservatives' susceptibility to political misperceptions. *Science Advances, 7*(23), 1–9. https://doi.org/10.1126/sciadv. abf1234

Goertzel, T. (1994). Belief in conspiracy theories. *Political Psychology, 15*(4), 731–742. https://doi.org/10.2307/3791630

González-Bailón, S., Lazer, D., Barberá, P., Zhang, M., Allcott, H., Brown, T.,... & Tucker, J. A. (2023). Asymmetric ideological segregation in exposure to political news on Facebook. *Science*, *381*(6656), 392–398. https://doi.org/10.1126/science.ade7138

Goreis, A., & Voracek, M. (2019). A systematic review and meta-analysis of psychological research on conspiracy beliefs: Field characteristics, measurement instruments, and associations with personality traits. *Frontiers in Psychology*, *10*(205), 1–13. https://doi.org/10.3389/fpsyg.2019.00205

Greenberg, J. (2022, June 14). Most Republicans still believe Trump's false election claims. *PolitiFact*. www.politifact.com/article/2022/jun/14/most-republicans-falsely-believe-trumps-stolen-ele/

Grimes, D. R. (2016). On the viability of conspiratorial beliefs. *PloS One*, *11*(1), 1–17. https://doi.org/10.1371/journal.pone.0147905

Groh, D. (1987). The temptation of conspiracy theory, or: Why do bad things happen to good people? Part I: Preliminary draft of a theory of conspiracy theories. In C. F. Graumann, & S. Moscovici (Eds.), *Changing conceptions of conspiracy* (pp. 1–38). Springer-Verlag.

Hofstadter, R. (1964). *The paranoid style in American politics, and other essays*. Knopf.

Iacobuzio, N. (2021, January 7). *A breeding ground for conspiracies: How QAnon helped bring about the U.S. Capitol assault*. U.S. Foreign Policy and National Security Program, American University. www.american.edu/sis/centers/security-technology/how-qanon-helped-bring-about-the-us-capitol-assault.cfm

Imhoff, R., & Bruder, M. (2014). Speaking (un-)truth to power: Conspiracy mentality as a generalized political attitude. *European Journal of Personality*, *28*(1), 25–43. https://doi.org/10.1002/per.1930

Imhoff, R., Zimmer, F., Klein, O., Antonio, J. H., Babinska, M., Bangerter, A., Bilewicz, M., Blanuša, N., Bovan, K., Bužarovoska, R., Cichocka, A., Delouvée, S., Douglas, K. M., Dyrendal, A., Etienne, T., Gjoneska, B., Graf, S., Gualda, E., Hirschberger, G.,...van Prooijen, J. (2022). Conspiracy mentality and political orientations across 26 countries. *Nature Human Behavior*, *6*, 392–403. https://doi.org/10.1038/s41562-021-01258-7

Invernizzi, G. M., & Mohamed, A. E. (2022). Trust nobody: How voters react to conspiracytheories. *Journal of Experimental Political Science*, 1–8. https://doi.org/10.1017/XPS.2022.11

Jacobson, J. C. (2023). The dimensions, origins, and consequences of belief in Donald Trump's big lie. *Political Science Quarterly*, *138*(2), 133–166. https://doi.org/10.1093/psquar/qqac030

Jones, D. (2022, May 16). *What is the 'great replacement' and how is it tied to the Buffalo shooting suspect?* NPR. www.npr.org/2022/05/16/1099034094/what-is-the-great-replacement-theory

Judis, J. B. (2016, October 13). Us v them: The birth of populism. *The Guardian*. www.theguardian.com/politics/2016/oct/13/birth-of-populism-donald-trump

Kim, Y. (2019). How conspiracy theories can stimulate political engagement. *Journal of Elections, Public Opinion, and Parties*, *32*(1), 1–21. https://doi.org/10.1080/17457289.2019.1651321

Kishi, R., Stall, H., & Jones, S. (2020). The future of 'stop the steal': Post-election trajectories for right-wing mobilization in the United States. Armed Conflict Location & Event Data Project.

Lipset, S. M., & Raab, E. (1978). *The politics of unreason: Right wing extremism in America 1790-1977* (2nd ed.). University of Chicago Press.

Mari, S., Gil de Zúñiga, H., Suerdem, A., Hanke, K., Brown, G., Vilar, R., Boer, D., & Bilewicz, M. (2021). Conspiracy theories and institutional trust: Examining the role of uncertainty avoidance and active social media use. *Political Psychology, 43*(2), 278–296. https://doi.org/10.1111/pops.12754

Milbank, D. (2022). *The deconstructionists: The twenty-five year crack-up of the Republican party.* Doubleday.

Miller, J. M., Saunders, K. L., & Farhart, C. E. (2015). Conspiracy endorsement as motivated reasoning: The moderating roles of political knowledge and trust. *American Journal of Political Science, 60*(4), 824–844. https://doi.org/10.1111/ajps.12234

Moyer, M. W. (2019, March 1). People drawn to conspiracy theories share a cluster of psychological features. *Scientific American.* www.scientificamerican.com/article/peo ple-drawn-to-conspiracy-theories-share-a-cluster-of-psychological-features/

Mudde, C., & Kaltwasser, C. R. (2017). *Populism: A very short introduction.* Oxford University Press.

Muirhead, R., & Rosenblum, N. L. (2016). Speaking truth to conspiracy: Partisanship and trust. *Journal of Politics and Society, 28*(1), 63–88. https://doi.org/10.1080/08913 811.2016.1173981

Norris, P. (2024). Big little election lies: Cynical and credulous evaluations of electoral fraud. *Parliamentary Affairs, 77*(1), 1–24. https://doi.org/10.1093/pa/gsad022

Norris, P., & Inglehart, R. (2019). *Cultural backlash: Trump, Brexit, and Authoritarian populism.* Cambridge University Press. https://doi.org/10.1017/9781108595841

Oden, A., & Porter, L. (2023). The kids are online: Teen social media use, civic engagement, and affective polarization. *Social Media + Society, 9*(3), 1–12. https://doi.org/10.1177/20563051231186364

Oladipo, G. (2022, June 14). More than 100 Republican primary winners support Trump's baseless election claim. *The Guardian.* www.theguardian.com/us-news/2022/jun/14/trump-big-lie-support-republican-primary-winners-gop

Oliver, J. E., & Wood, T. J. (2014). Conspiracy theories and the paranoid style(s) of mass opinion. *American Journal of Political Science, 58*(4), 952–966.

Owen, D. (2019, August 30). *Populist attitudes and political media use.* Paper prepared for presentation at the Annual Meeting of the American Political Science Association, Washington, D.C.

Owen, D., Chawla, A., Crockett, T., Kim, K, Miller, K, Bruce, P., Hendricks, H., & Zhong, B. (2023, April 14). Conspiratorial ideation, election denial, and voter choice. Presented at the Annual Meeting of the Midwest Political Science Association, Chicago, IL.

Pennycook, G., & Rand, D. G. (2021). The psychology of fake news. *Trends in Cognitive Science, 25*(5), 388–402. https://psycnet.apa.org/doi/10.1016/j.tics.2021.02.007

Pilch, I., Turska-Kawa, A., Wardawy, P., Olszanecka-Marmola, A., & Smotkowska-Jedo, W. (2023). Contemporary trends in psychological research on conspiracy beliefs. A systematic review. *Frontiers in Psychology, 14*, 1–19. https://doi.org/10.3389/fpsyg.2023.1075779

Public Policy Polling. (2013, April 2). *Democrats and Republicans differ on conspiracy theory beliefs* [Press Release]. www.publicpolicypolling.com/wp-content/uploads/2017/09/PPP_Release_National_ConspiracyTheories_040213.pdf

## 46 Media Messages in the 2022 Midterm Election

Robertson, D. G., & Amarasingam, A. (2022). How conspiracy theorists argue: Epistemic capital in the QAnon social media sphere. *Popular Communication, 20*(3), 193–207. https://doi.org/10.1080/15405702.2022.2050238

Rose, J. (2021, March 2). 'More dangerous and more widespread': Conspiracy theories spread faster than ever. *NPR*. www.npr.org/2021/03/02/971289977/through-the-looking-glass-conspiracy-theories-spread-faster-and-wider-than-ever

Sawyer, P. S. (2002). Conspiracism in populist radical right candidates: Rallying the base or mainstreaming the fringe. *International Journal of Politics, Culture, and Society, 35*, 305–340. https://doi.org/10.1007/s10767-021-09398-4

Schmalz, F. (2022, October 28). *Why are so many politicians embracing conspiracy theories?* Kellogg Insight. https://insight.kellogg.northwestern.edu/article/why-are-so-many-politicians-embracing-conspiracy-theories

Schnaudt, C. (2024). Conspiracy beliefs and perceptions of electoral integrity: Cross-national evidence from 29 countries. *Public Opinion Quarterly, 88*(SI), 814–827. https://doi.org/10.1093/poq/nfae027

Select Committee to Investigate the January 6th Attack on the United States Capitol (Select Committee). (2022, December 22). *Final Report of the Select Committee to Investigate the January 6th Attack on the United States Capitol.*

Shearer, E., & Mitchell, A. (2021, May 7). Broad agreement in U.S.—even among partisans—on which news outlets are part of the 'mainstream media'. *Pew Research Center*. www.pewresearch.org/short-reads/2021/05/07/broad-agreement-in-u-s--even-among-partisans--on-which-news-outlets-are-part-of-the-mainstream-media/

Stanton, Z. (2020, June 16). You're living in the Golden Age of conspiracy theories. *Politico Magazine*. www.politico.com/news/magazine/2020/06/17/conspiracy-theories-pandemic-trump-2020-election-coronavirus-326530

Statista. (2023). *Most popular conservative and far-right websites in the United States based on number of unique visitors.* www.statista.com/statistics/1340485/usa-most-visited-conservative-websites

Stecula, D. A., & Pickup, M. (2021). Social media, cognitive reflection, and conspiracy beliefs. *Frontiers in Political Science, 3*, Article 647957, 1–8. https://doi.org/10.3389/fpos.2021.647957

Stempel, C., Hargrove, T., & Stempel, G. H. (2007). Media use, social structure, and belief in 9/11 conspiracy theories. *Journalism & Mass Communication Quarterly, 84*(2), 353–372. https://doi.org/10.1177/107769900708400210

Swami, V., Coles, R., Stiger, S., Pietschnig, J., Furnham, A., Rehim, S., & Voracek, M. (2011). Conspiracist ideation in Britain and Austria: Evidence of a monological belief system and associations between individual psychological differences and real-world and fictitious conspiracy theories. *British Journal of Psychology, 102*(3), 443–463. https://doi.org/10.1111/j.2044-8295.2010.02004.x

Thielmann, I., & Hilbig, B. E. (2023). Generalized dispositional distrust as the common core of populism and conspiracy mentality. *Political Psychology, 44*(4), 789–805. https://doi.org/10.1111/pops.12886

Uscinski, J., Enders, A., Diekman, A., Funchion, J., Klofstad, C., Kuebler, S., Murthi, M., Premaratne, K., Seelig, M., Verdear, D., & Wuchty, S. (2022). The psychological and political correlates of conspiracy theory beliefs. *Scientific Reports, 12*(21672), 1–12. https://doi.org/10.1038/s41598-022-25617-0

Uscinski, J. E., & Enders, A. M. (2020, June 18). *Don't blame social media for conspiracy theories—They would still flourish without it*. The Conversation. https://theconversation.com/dont-blame-social-media-for-conspiracy-theories-they-would-still-flourish-without-it-138635

Uscinski, J. E, & Parent, J. M. (2014). Ages of conspiracy. In J. E. Uscinski & J. M. Parent (Eds.), *American conspiracy theories* (pp. 105–129). Oxford University Press.

van der Linden, S., Panagopoulos, C., Azevedo, F., & Jost, J. T. (2021). The paranoid style in American politics revisited: An ideological asymmetry in conspiratorial thinking. *Political Psychology, 42*(1), 23–51. https://doi.org/10.1111/pops.12681

Waller, J. G. (2022). Authoritarianism here? *American Affairs, 6*(1), 158–178. https://americanaffairsjournal.org/2022/02/authoritarianism-here/

Wang, C. S. (2022, October 28). Why are so many politicians embracing conspiracy theories? *KelloggInsight*. Kellogg School of Management at Northwestern University. https://insight.kellogg.northwestern.edu/article/why-are-so-many-politicians-embracing-conspiracy-theories

Wendling, M. (2021, January 6). *QAnon: What is it and where did it come from?* BBC News. /www.bbc.com/news/53498434

Wood, M. J., Douglas, K. M., & Sutton, R. M. (2012). Dead and alive: Beliefs in contradictory conspiracy theories. *Social Psychological and Personality Science, 3*(6), 767–773.

Zheng, M., Sear, R. F., Illari, L., Restrepo, N. J., & Johnson, N. F. (2024). Adaptive link dynamics drive online hate networks and their mainstream influence." *npj Complexity, 1*(2), 1–8. https://doi.org/10.1038/s44260-024-00002-2

Zmigrod, L., Rentfrow, P. J., & Robbins, T. W. (2020). The partisan mind: Is extreme political partisanship related to cognitive inflexibility? *Journal of Experimental Psychology, 149*(3), 407–418. https://doi.org/10.1037/xge0000661

# 3

## *2000 MULES*

## A Story of Consequence and Conspiracy

*Stephen D. Caldes, Zach Justus, and
Jennifer A. Malkowski*

After Joe Biden's victory in the 2020 presidential election, many Donald Trump supporters embraced conspiracy theories to explain the election outcome. Conspiracies involving Dominion Voting Systems, Hugo Chavez, Italian spy satellites, and a host of other fragments circulated in media ecosystems (The Daily Show, 2022). The appetite for fantastic explanations for President Biden's victory was substantial and unfulfilled. The principal issue with these conspiracies is that they are fragmentary. "Dominion Voting Systems" is not a theory in and of itself, instead it is a catchphrase that alludes to a larger web of corruption without explaining it. Similar to the allegations of voter fraud that have animated right-wing concerns for decades, these more recent conspiracies have little explanatory power because they are not cohered into a story. The 2022 release of *2000 Mules* by well-known conservative commentator and filmmaker Dinesh D'Souza changed that by pulling pieces together to create a coherent, if deeply flawed, narrative.

Dinesh D'Souza is an influential and prominent figure in right-wing circles. He is the author of several best-selling books (Victor, 2018) and the director of some of the most financially successful political documentaries in the last decade (*Business Wire*, 2022). For years he has been a regular guest on Fox News and in the broader right-wing ecosystem. He is currently a podcast host and content producer for Salem Media, the group which helped to produce and fund *2000 Mules* (D'Souza, 2022a), a feature length conspiracy theory political film. The film and associated book were pulled from distribution after one of the figures in the film who had been subjected to extensive harassment, filed suit

DOI: 10.4324/9781003440833-4

(Dreisbach, 2024). Pulling the film was perhaps a bit too late; *2000 Mules* has established itself as fact within the ecosystem (Farley et al., 2023).

The online documentary-style film *2000 Mules* tells the purported story of voter fraud wherein a shadowy group of non-profit organizations harvest votes to secure a victory for Joe Biden. The film was released during an odd time in American politics, late Spring 2022. President Trump was still banned from Twitter and the fervor of election conspiracies following the 2020 election had subsided as attention had shifted to the 2022 midterms. Major conservative media outlets were under increased scrutiny about their coverage of election conspiracies, in fact the $1.6 billion defamation suit from Dominion Voting Systems against Fox News had just been filed two months prior (Izadi & Farhi, 2021). In some ways this vacuum created space for D'Souza's documentary, but in other ways it tempered the embrace of normally friendly media outlets as they were dealing with the fallout from a previous round of spreading election lies.

The film had a limited release in theaters and also circumvented normal streaming services to offer it on the right-wing alternative to YouTube, Rumble. com and on the website for the media production company, Salem Media. It was warmly received by former President Trump who went so far as to call it "the greatest [and] most impactful documentary of our time" (Huseman, 2024) in a TruthSocial post and screened it at Mar-a-Lago, his private club and residence (Palmer, 2022). The film provided a bridge between the conspiracies embraced by former President Trump that inspired the January 6, 2021, U.S. Capitol attack to the 2022 midterm elections. In doing so it inspired a new round of election suspicion that resulted in vigilante activity in Arizona (Neugeboren, 2022) and other states (Bond, 2022). For example, the film was screened three separate times at the 2022 Texas Republican National Convention where attendees voted affirmatively on a resolution characterizing Biden's 2020 win as fraudulent (Neugeboren, 2022). The documentary reanimated concerns about election integrity heading into the 2022 election and moved the conversation in far-right circles away from the future and back to disputing the 2020 election. In Arizona, figureheads like gubernatorial candidate Kari Lake, extremist representative Paul Gosar, and Secretary of State nominee Mark Finchem adopted the talking points from the film while not always referencing it by name (Jones, 2022). Despite its atypical circulation pattern, the film generated $10 million in revenue in just a few weeks making it the most financially successful political documentary since a previous D'Souza release, *2016: Obama's America,* 10 years earlier (*Business Wire*, 2022).

This chapter unpacks the story told by *2000 Mules* to understand why it is so compelling for specific audiences. We also examine the mainstream reaction to the film to understand how academics and journalists typically engage with conspiracy culture to consider how we might augment and improve that engagement moving forward.

## Conspiracy and Theory

Conspiracy theories as a way to explain life and politics are not new (Uscinski & Parent, 2014). Some of the same themes of antisemitism and anti-science have existed for thousands of years. European villagers in the Middle Ages facing an unknown pathogen and concluding that Jews were poisoning the well relied on the same tropes as the white-supremacists marching in Charlottesville in 2017 (Lindemann & Levy, 2010). However, a few things have changed in recent years that have altered the spread and reach of conspiracy theories.

First, the internet and social media have expanded the reach of conspiracy theories and engaged consumers as co-creators of theories. This move uncouples the term "conspiracy" from "theory." Rosenblum and Muirhead (2019) concluded that the presence of evidence is no longer required to popularize a conspiracy and, in this way, the "theory" part of the phrase is no longer necessary. Second, the election of Donald Trump in 2016 placed an overt conspiracy enthusiast in the most powerful office in the world. Trump adhered to and promoted a wide range of conspiracies from being the primary proponent of birtherism (Warner & Neville-Shepard, 2014), to linking windmills with cancer (Plumer, 2019), and also suggesting Joe Biden had Seal Team 6 killed to cover up the fact that Osama bin Laden was still alive (Fichera & Spencer, 2020). His ascension to the White House gave new life and new platforms to unhinged theories and helped to spawn QAnon, a meta-conspiracy and movement that led to bloodshed, broken families, and an insurrection (Sommer, 2023).

Scholars across fields have sought to understand the rhetoric of conspiracy theories (see Reyes & Smith [2014] for a review). Two areas of work shore up our approach to unpacking the narrative and persuasive dimensions of *2000 Mules*. Warner and Neville-Shepard's (2014) work on conspiracy theories and media relationships helps to explain the spread of these ideas while also providing a ray of hope. The authors used experimental analysis to understand the relationships between media intake and propensity to believe conspiracy theories ("9/11 truth," for instance). They found a strong relationship between echo-chamber media and belief in conspiracy theories. These conclusions are reinforced by Kim and Cao (2016) in their study of government conspiracy theory videos. This is not a particularly surprising outcome and, given the increasingly siloed media landscape, likely worse now than when the research was conducted. However, Warner and Neville-Shepard also concluded that in cases where alternative information is allowed into a conspiracy ecosystem there is hope and people can move out of these destructive cycles. This reinforces the power of efforts like fact-checking or rebuttal, but only if they find their way into the conspiracy ecosystems.

In their recent work examining the COVID conspiracy video, *Plandemic,* which posited a range of conspiracies about the pandemic spanning from the

*2000 Mules*: A Story of Consequence and Conspiracy **51**

danger of masks to the idea that the virus was a designed bioweapon, Caldes, Justus, and Malkowski (2022) argued that the slick packaging of the video, specifically its employment of documentary tropes, helped the audience engage with the material as truthful rather than contested. In addition, the somewhat cohesive narrative tells a story with familiar components (e.g., distrust of authority, a whistleblower, etc.) that resonate with audiences. Reyes and Smith (2014) also dove into the trappings of conspiracy theories, and also in video form. They concluded, "Aesthetically, the best conspiracy theories are not measured by their truth claims or persuasiveness…but by their ability to set and keep in motion a labyrinthine argument that is itself the mark and measure of conspiracy rhetoric" (p. 413). There is power in story and presentation that go beyond tables, graphs, and facts. With these background pieces of modern conspiracy theories and responses, we now move to an analysis of the story told in *2000 Mules* and how it bridges the divide between the 2020 presidential election and the 2022 midterm elections.

### *2000 Mules*: A Storied Account

The film opens with a creative retelling of the events leading to and on January 6, 2021. According to D'Souza (2022a), "January 6th was not an insurrection. It was a primal scream" (6:40). He goes on to state that the participants simply wanted lawmakers to evaluate election fraud claims. This is somewhat undercut by video in the documentary wherein participants are confronting police and have overrun the actual Capitol. Nonetheless the documentary moves on to a series of round table discussions where the audience is invited to identify with D'Souza's journey of discovery.

First, D'Souza is joined by fellow conservative Salem Media podcast hosts Sebastian Gorka, Charlie Kirk, Dennis Prager, Eric Metaxas and Larry Elder for a discussion about whether they believed the results of the 2020 election. Broadly, the group is suspicious of the election, but also of the voter fraud claims that have been put forward following the election. In a promotional interview on the Dave Rubin show, D'Souza explained the desired function of this first act was to allow the audience to see themselves in the personas of the podcast hosts. In this way they could find an avatar for their own journey of discovery (Rubin, 2022).

In the second act, D'Souza meets with leadership from the "True the Vote" election monitoring group. This is the core of the film. The group acquired a large volume of cell phone data from cities in swing states and used the data to weave an elaborate plot of vote manipulation. The theory is that ballots were acquired by unnamed non-profit organizations from illicit sources like nursing homes, where some residents were not capable of voting, or other unnamed locations. The ballots are then picked up by "mules" and deposited in drop boxes

## 52 Media Messages in the 2022 Midterm Election

all over the city. They provide evidence in the form of movement patterns of individual people near non-profits and ballot drop boxes. Later they interview a front office worker from a non-profit who remains anonymous and speculates about ballot payment without providing any evidence. D'Souza concludes that this process swung the election for Joe Biden. Critically, no other part of this elaborate conspiracy is evidenced other than people traveling adjacent to non-profits and drop boxes.

The final act of the film is a return to the roundtable discussion with the other Salem Media hosts, now joined by representatives from "True the Vote." There is no additional evidence here, just D'Souza presenting the material from the second act to his colleagues and having them respond. The third act is basically a reaction video. The group is thoroughly convinced of fraud in the election showing varying levels of outrage. Connecting back to the Dave Rubin interview, the viewer of *2000 Mules* can now watch the hosts—who initially represented a voter fraud critic—model the response of a now fully converted believer. On camera, the group speculates about foreseeable mainstream outlet reactions to the film and then proceeds to get visibly angry about those imagined reactions. Ironically, D'Souza closes *2000 Mules* with a call for viewers to vote in the midterms, which seemingly undercuts the film's central concern that the election system and its results ought not be trusted.

Reactions to and reviews of the film were generally warm from right-wing outlets and critical from mainstream sources, however, there were some deviations from this typical pattern. Most notably, the film and D'Souza were not present on Fox News and had an appearance canceled on Newsmax despite D'Souza having a historically strong presence with the networks (Weaver, 2022). This became a source of frustration for D'Souza and former President Trump, who posted on TruthSocial in relation to the film, "Fox News is no longer Fox News" (Trump, 2022). There is widespread and reasonable speculation that many outlets distanced themselves from D'Souza and the documentary given the pending lawsuits from Dominion Voting Systems, also related to election conspiracy theories (Dreisbach, 2022a). This is further evidenced by an odd development with D'Souza's book, also entitled *2000 Mules* (2022b). In the book D'Souza names several non-profits he alleges were hubs for ballot trafficking and upon initial reads of the book, lawsuits seemed likely. The publishing house, Regnery Publishing, quickly pulled copies of the book from shelves and took the costly step of reprinting the book without the specific non-profit names in an attempt to avoid litigation (Dreisbach, 2022b). Beyond this sordid tale, reactions were more predictable.

Mainstream outlets like FactCheck.org (Farley, 2022) and the Associated Press (Swenson, 2022) assessed the accuracy of the film. Journalists focused on the flawed analysis in the film which relies heavily on the accuracy of cell phone geolocation data and fills in gaps with speculation. *The Associated Press*'s check goes into significant detail on the limits of the data and the pieces in the film in particular noting, "experts say cellphone location data, even at its most advanced, can only reliably track a smartphone within a few meters—not close enough to know whether someone actually dropped off a ballot or just walked or drove nearby" (para. 12).

The film received a much warmer reception among far-right podcast hosts and commentators. D'Souza made a series of appearances on cross-platform programs hosted by right-wing influencers including Megyn Kelly, Dave Rubin, Glenn Beck, Candace Owens, Charlie Kirk, and Sebastian Gorka, and his work was featured on shows hosted by Ben Shapiro and David Deace. Shapiro (2022) raised concerns about the shortcomings of the film and Megyn Kelly (2022) asked some probing questions of D'Souza. Most other hosts summarized the film and then proceeded to attack the fact-checking responses from mainstream media outlets.

Our analysis of *2000 Mules* focuses on dual rhetorical strategies that make the film simultaneously impactful for predisposed audiences and dismissible by mainstream groups. Specifically, we focus on the aesthetics of science and the structural dimensions of the story told to gain a clearer understanding of how the narrative was received and how critics might better engage and ideally offset similar conspiracy rhetoric.

## Strategy 1: Scientific Rationalism

Scientific rationalism—an epistemological approach that emphasizes the use of deductive reasoning and empirical evidence as the primary means of understanding the world—supplies a framework for understanding the *2000 Mules* story. Scientific rationalism values skepticism and encourages questioning established beliefs in favor of evidence-based conclusions wherein the scientific method—hypothesis formulation, experimentation, observation, and analysis—is understood as the most valid way to acquire knowledge. D'Souza makes a number of rhetorical choices throughout his film that speak to this underlying epistemology; choices that allow him to align with and borrow from the ethos of scientific rationalism as an established means of reliable knowledge production.

In the first act of *2000 Mules*, we are presented with various Salem Media hosts who showcase different degrees of skepticism about voter fraud claims. Podcast host and former California gubernatorial candidate Larry Elder best summarizes the skeptic perspective when, at the 13-minute mark, he tells D'Souza: "bold accusations require bold evidence and they [Republican voters] haven't seen it" (D'Souza, 2022a, 13:08). This early set-up assures the audience that it is okay if they also have unanswered questions about the 2020 election and establishes a standard for the type of evidence required to convince skeptics. Several hosts comment that the election didn't 'feel right' with Turning Point

USA CEO Charlie Kirk saying, "I think millions of Americans know something went wrong and they have little pieces and no one's really put it together. They know there was injustice, they know it in their gut" (D'Souza, 2022a, 11:00). The commenters ultimately coalesce around the idea that evidence is required and so far, it has not been presented. D'Souza is clearer about his intention in a subsequent interview with Glenn Beck when he called into question early fraud claims, referring to them as "sincerely meant, but unsubstantiated" (Beck, 2022, 34:55). There was a clear effort to separate this work from those earlier efforts through the performance of scientific investigation.

With the frames of objectivity and skepticism established, viewers move to the heart of the film in Act 2, where D'Souza meets with representatives from "True the Vote." Collectively, the group's credibility gets established through a listing of shared connections and experiences and overt references to their technical acumen, such as when collaborator Gregg Phillips says, in reference to the 2020 election, "no one has more data than we do" (D'Souza, 2022a, 16:55). Most critically, their objectivity is foregrounded by featuring work they did to overturn a North Carolina election where a Republican candidate was paying for ballots. The framework of scientific rationalism is further set up through argument and evidence in Act 2 using aesthetics. In the transition between acts, D'Souza is on the phone with "True the Vote" leader Catherine Engelbrecht, who suggests they need to meet in person, saying, "probably best not to discuss it over the phone" (D'Souza, 2022a, 15:11), because the information they have is so critical. The setting for Act 2 is an amalgamation of an electronics workshop and a staged display of computer equipment. This is never explained, but the aesthetic is one of high-tech surveillance, data collection, and analysis. In panning shots around the table, the viewer sees electrical equipment, toolboxes, and servers with cycling lights. The background ambiance connects the filmmakers to a world where high-tech tools convey precise metrics and verifiable evidence, two mechanisms used to draw trustworthy conclusions per the scientific method.

In the context of this initial conversation with "True the Vote" representatives, the theme of objectivity comes up repeatedly. In this conversation Engelbrecht sets the stage for the remainder of the documentary by speculating about how voter fraud may have happened and then going in search of evidence for this story. Obviously, this is not how any ethical investigation proceeds, but in the film the investigative approach is portrayed as rational through the adoption of scientific terminology. Engelbrecht summarizes her initial approach to investigating voter fraud this way: "The hypothesis was: if you were going to cheat, how might one go about this that would be provable? Trackable? Traceable?" (D'Souza, 2022a, 20:05). Notably, this question and statement combination does not reflect the denotative meaning of hypothesis at all; in fact, the combination may be its opposite. Nonetheless, deploying the term "hypothesis" here effectively mobilizes its connotative meaning, that is, its culturally significant gesture to the objective scientific method that begins with a question for which an inquirer has no certain answer but must, instead, rely on a systematic equation for observing and reasoning that intentionally displaces the biases of any curious questioner. Importantly, a scientist sets out to *disprove* their hypothesis ala the scientific method, not—as Engelbrecht revealingly purports— prove their hypothesis. Engelbrecht's misappropriation of scientific jargon echoes how right-wing influencers often use the phrase, "do your own research," to encourage individuals to seek information outside mainstream media or established sources. As a rhetorical strategy, this slogan typically promotes a sense of personal empowerment and skepticism toward traditional institutions, suggesting that individuals should question official narratives. However, this call-to-action can also lead followers to adopt unverified or fringe theories, as it implies that credible sources are biased or untrustworthy and, therefore, require a more individualistic approach to information gathering, often aligned with their ideological perspectives.

Act 2 culminates in D'Souza posing a question about the flourishment of conspiracies following the election and Engelbrecht explaining that their approach was to "let the data tell the tale" (D'Souza, 2022a, 20:35). This is of course absurd given they have already admitted to inventing a story and then searching for evidence to corroborate it, but the language and aesthetics of scientific rationality give the viewer the distinct impression that everyone is dutifully and ethically following the facts to see where they lead.

The documentary now turns to an explanation of the geo-tracking technology they use to test their hypothesis. This mix of interviews and b-roll is reminiscent of a Jason Bourne movie as we see graphics of satellites flying by cut with aerial footage of cities and a soundtrack of voice over and technical sounding beeps. The reliability of geo-tracking is further enhanced with a mix of anecdotes and traditional appeals to authority ranging from references to the tracking of Osama bin Laden to a trip to the Apple store. D'Souza compares the reliability of geo-tracking to "the reliability of a fingerprint or the reliability of DNA" (D'Souza, 2022a, 22:35), a refrain he often repeats in promotional interviews. In aggregate, the viewer is awash in the aesthetics and verbiage of science and technology. Whether it is understood or accurate is beside the point. D'Souza is an experienced filmmaker, and this project had significant funding behind it, which becomes evident at moments like this. A casual or friendly viewing of this scene would easily lead a viewer to conclude our protagonists are simply following the data.

As Act 2 progresses the aesthetics and argument construction of the film continue to flow through the framework of scientific rationalism. The bulk of the film is at this roundtable surrounded by computer and electronics equipment with occasional splicing to workers viewing large monitors and looking concerned. Phillips goes into detail about their methodology and specifics about how they acquired "10 trillion signals" which amounts to "more than a petabyte of data" to do the tracking. D'Souza refers to this as "a lot of data" (D'Souza, 2022a, 25:05) but without mentioning anything for comparison. The explanations are sober and reasonable sounding, but ultimately entirely unscientific. For instance, at one point Phillips explains their criteria for identifying a mule as someone who traveled near "10 or more drop boxes...and five or more visits to one or more of these organizations" to "absolutely insure we don't have false positives" (D'Souza, 2022a, 26:05). There is extensive labor done here to make this seem reasonable and scientific, but there is no actual explanation for why these are reasonable thresholds or preferable to other criteria. That said, a transparent synopsis of their scientific mode of inquiry (like you would find in a methods section of a scientific journal, for instance) does not appear to be the goal here; the *appearance* of science-based rationality is paramount.

With the scientific basis of geo-tracking established for the audience, the documentary takes an awkward turn to loop in right-wing hobby horses. Phillips and Engelbrecht link the signals of their set of "mules" to people who participated in the summer 2020 George Floyd protests through a dataset of an unnamed organization. Then they introduce a theme that will run through the rest of the film and D'Souza's post-release media tour—the suspicious nature of anyone who looks or acts differently regarding elections. The "mules" themselves are referred to as people with "bad backgrounds, bad reputations" (D'Souza, 2022a, 27:22) including "transients motivated by money." Furthermore, anyone who would use a ballot box at night is regularly disparaged as if being out at night is an admission of guilt. The media is also implicated as complicit in fraud by going along with voter protection bills. Engelbrecht remarks that national voter laws indicate "all the pieces are in place for our election system to be in permanent lockdown. And it will be done under the watchful eye of a media that will tell you it's all just fine" (D'Souza, 2022a, 45:15). Here the phrase "permanent lockdown" links perceived efforts to control the election system to previous COVID-19 lockdowns. Insinuating that media is complicit and will similarly portray this situation as "just fine," D'Souza feeds distrust in mainstream sources and reinforces the idea of a hidden agenda. This combination of fear, distrust, and the notion of a powerful elite controlling the narrative aligns with common themes in conspiratorial thinking, making it resonate with those who already harbor skepticism about authority and established institutions.

The documentary also starts to weave in video footage to triangulate the geo-tracking data. An incongruity emerges here that is glossed over. The group drops an impressive statement that they have over "4 million minutes of footage" (D'Souza, 2022a, 35:10) and yet does not produce any video proof of anyone visiting more than one drop box. There is an attempt to explain this away with stonewalling from some states, but if there is video from certain states there would be video of a person visiting more than one box. Instead, there is video of people engaging in pretty typical behavior (e.g., casually walking by a drop box, sitting on a public bench near a drop box, or glancing at a cellphone in the proximity of a drop box) while a voiceover from Phillips narrates extreme, ominous possible interpretation accompanied by tense music. Later, D'Souza voices over video of a black man depositing ballots and says, "what you are seeing is a crime" (D'Souza, 2022a, 48:01). However, in this scene there was no crime, the ballots were legitimate, and D'Souza was sued for defamation (Brumback, 2022).

About halfway through the documentary D'Souza recaps "what we know" to concretize the speculation and half-explained ideas from the film as scientific facts which can then be referenced in the future. D'Souza asks Phillips and Engelbrecht: "Do we know for a fact that there was coordinated, systematic fraud, in all the key states where the election was decided?" To which they respond: "Yes." (D'Souza, 2022a, 46:27). D'Souza then does some careful pandering to the audience, who he knows were already suspicious of the election results by telling them their instincts were correct even if they did not have the proof. This is the end of the evidence portion of the documentary, but not the aesthetic work of scientific rationalism.

The next section mashes up some data from the now-established "facts" from the first half of the documentary to recalculate the 2020 election. Crucially missing from this calculus is a reason why all of the trafficked votes were for Biden, relying instead on the audiences' ideas about the racial and political make-up of large cities where they did their analysis. Even granting this race- and class-tainted assumption, this is the only evidence of mules in these locations because this is the only place "True the Vote" decided to look for fraud. They simply did not examine areas where Trump did well because they were only looking for one kind of voter fraud. D'Souza tabulates their results, initially concluding Trump won the electoral college, but narrowly. Of course, this is insufficient, so they arbitrarily change the criteria they had painstakingly established earlier to conclude that Trump won a landslide victory in 2020. No rationale is given for this change, but it is delivered amid a flurry of math calculations while Phillips and Engelbrecht engage in an intense conversation in front of an illuminated electoral map—once again maximizing the aesthetics of math and science.

The third act of the documentary presents no new evidence, but instead shows the viewer a roadmap of how they should be reacting. D'Souza gathers his Salem Media colleagues with Phillips and Engelbrecht to show them the evidence they collected, which involves watching all the same video clips again (for a third time in one instance). There are some implied gaps filled in here. At one point Elder asks the group if they have video of the same person going to multiple drop boxes and they respond affirmatively—even though we never see the video. Again, this leans back on the aesthetics of scientific evidence throughout the film. Regardless of their starting point, the panelists are now

**58** Media Messages in the 2022 Midterm Election

on-board commenting: "extraordinary criminal activity," "case closed," and "jaw dropping" (D'Souza, 2022a, 56:00–57:00). Panel reactions like these model behavior for viewers and can lead viewers to adopt similar attitudes or reactions. Seeing others react can validate viewers' own beliefs, reinforcing their viewpoints and encouraging them to express those beliefs in their own interactions. If the viewer had questions about the science and technology in Act 2, those are swept aside as now they have validation from people who may have shared their skepticism to start the journey. There are some odd asides to further triangulate the data spliced into the third act including a few interviews with anonymous insiders sharing stories from poll watching or non-profit organizations. D'Souza also talks with lawyers about voter integrity and tax law allowing him to trot out other conspiratorial tropes including George Soros and Big Tech (embodied in Mark Zuckerberg) as role players. Linking election fraud to other prominent conspiracy theories creates a narrative that insinuates a much larger scheme. Tapping into confirmation bias, the documentary reinforces the worldview of conspiracy theorists who may already believe in a web of interconnected conspiracies. For these viewers, the film provides them with additional "evidence" that supports their beliefs, creating a more cohesive narrative of manipulation by Big Tech, mass news media, and political elites.

### Strategy 2: Inverted Storytelling

In addition to the perspective of scientific rationalism already explained, *2000 Mules* is told using a familiar format that adds to the fidelity and probability of the story told. As pointed out in their analysis of the popular piece of anti-vax propaganda, *Plandemic*, Caldes, Justus, and Malkowski (2022) echo the sentiments of narrative critic Walter Fisher and conclude: "If a story is told in the right way"—meaning in a familiar and recognizable way—and "rings true"—we are more likely to believe it, even if it presents questionable information, incredible coincidences, or logical fallacies (1984, p. 8). Like *Plandemic*, *2000 Mules* is presented using a recognizable narrative "shape." Whereas *Plandemic* used a "redemption story" format to structure and deliver information, *2000 Mules* adopts a "detective story" formula, a format that is recognizable and appealing to anyone who's ever watched a popular television police procedural or whoever has read the denouement of an Agatha Christie type fiction mystery. This story shape—one that creates an important role for the audience itself—invites readers to "let down [their] guard," and in so doing offers up a "powerful tool of deception" (Konnikova, 2015, para 12).

Opposed to the traditional "whodunnit" detective story formulation that aims to tell a story through the pursuit and discovery of *who* perpetrates a crime, *2000 Mules* adopts a "howcatchem" configuration, one that identifies the "who"/perpetrator early on (usually along with their motive) and spends the rest of the time investigating *how* the known perpetrator committed the crime. As an inverted detective story, the "howcatchem" narrative formula typically places the viewer/audience alongside the "detective" as they overcome obstacles and puzzles on the road to solving what often appears, at first blush, to be the "perfect crime." One of the most popular uses of the inverted detective story was the popular television series *Columbo* where each episode began by revealing both the crime and the perpetrator, therefore, no "whodunnit" was required, and instead the show focused on how this perpetrator known to the viewer will eventually be caught and exposed.

*2000 Mules'* narrative shape is quite similar to a *Columbo* episode. By the end of Act I, the crime (a stolen presidential election), the perpetrator(s) (the "left"), and the why ("no president more hated by the left than Trump") are established. To develop the idea of an unbiased and fair investigation, and set the "howcatchem" in motion, this information is communicated to viewers using a documentarian's usual bag of tricks: we get a series of out-of-context clips and soundbites from mainstream television news sources (CBS, ABC, CNN, NBC, Fox News, Newsmax) asking questions about the security of the 2020 election, we get the previously mentioned roundtable of panelists, we get clever rhetorical questions ("Was it a big lie? Was it a lie at all?") and opinions masquerading as facts ("January 6th wasn't an insurrection") from our director-narrator-"detective" Dinesh D'Souza. Ultimately, the table-setting introduction concludes with nearly all panelists demanding a magic bullet. To fully believe, they must know how this crime was executed. They have "crumbs" of "evidence here and there," bits of proof, but the "picture is far from complete." What they say they need is definitive proof, undeniable hard evidence, a play-by-play explaining the crime's methodology. These panelists—stand-ins for the viewer—are finally going to get what they've been demanding and are perfectly primed for D'Souza's attestation: video evidence and technology-laden data. That it never arrives is beside the point. We've been told it's coming and, later, will be told how incriminating it is, even if we, the viewer, didn't really see it for ourselves. This, again, is textbook "inverted detective" story methodology.

Imperative to many inverted detective stories is "suspension of disbelief," a concept first observed by Aristotle in regard to theater-goers ignoring the "unreality" of fiction in order to experience the "catharsis" of the story. Suspension of disbelief asks for and requires the viewer's avoidance of critical thinking and logic for the sake of enjoyment. When we already know who did it, we can just sit back and watch the process of *how* unfold. And for that we need our "detective" to explain it, for not just anyone can solve this perfect crime. In this way, the suspension of disbelief allows individuals to embrace conspiracy theories, fostering an environment where extraordinary claims can be accepted without the usual demands for evidence or logical coherence.

**60** Media Messages in the 2022 Midterm Election

In stories, as is the case in arguments as well, the audience is of great import and thus is heavily considered by the storyteller. This is especially true of inverted detective stories because the detective must explain the how, but cannot risk breaking the fourth wall, and so "audience surrogates" (e.g., supporting characters) must be provided. Since the who (perpetrator) and the why (motive) are already made clear in inverted stories like *2000 Mules*, everything hinges on the audience to clearly understand the how (the evidence). However, like most mysteries, even though the audience is following along and seeing everything the detective is seeing, oftentimes the audience cannot make sense of the evidence like the wily detective can, and thus need conclusions clearly spelled out for them. Which brings us back to the roundtable panelists—the audience surrogates—and their reemergence in the second half of *2000 Mules*.

Near the conclusion of nearly every one of genre novelist Agatha Christie's 33 detective mysteries featuring Inspector Hercule Poirot, the Inspector provides his "detective denouement," a literary device commonly used in the mystery and true-crime genres to explain who did what, why, and how. The device assumes that although the audience and supporting characters/audience surrogates have been paying close attention, they haven't surmised as much from the "evidence" presented as the "detective," and so they must have the conclusions explained to them slowly and in detail. Traditionally, as originally described by Aristotle in *Poetics*, this explanation is preceded by "anagnorisis," a discovery that "produces a change from ignorance to knowledge." In their "detective denouement," a detective thoroughly reveals the evidence and connects-the-dots in a manner that surprises the audience. Although the audience surrogates in *2000 Mules* have seen exactly the same "evidence" that we've seen (or not), as they reconvene in Act 3 for D'Souza's denouement, they appear to be flabbergasted by what's been presented. Indeed, through the detective's lead, they now see the magic bullet they've so desperately been waiting for.

As nearly all serious reviews of *2000 Mules* have claimed, this "documentary" is mostly an exercise in confirmation bias. There is obviously one audience and one audience only for *2000 Mules* and it is 2020 "election truthers," and our audience surrogates most definitely fall into this category. As Bump (2022) points out in his *Washington Post* review, "the point [of the film] …is that the viewers come away from the movie believing that they were right all along about the election being stolen" (para. 35). They already knew who did what anyway, and now, presented with if not evidence but a detailed explanation of "evidence," they're even more emboldened to accept the conspiracy as fact.

The documentary is deeply flawed throughout with an over-reliance on the aesthetics of science and technology, numerous unsubstantiated claims, and a methodology that is designed to produce a specific result. Yet it is also cohesive in that it tells a story of voter fraud that has to this point been incomplete. In some ways this returns to a world of conspiracy theory where there is an attempt at proof and validation as opposed to the unhinged trajectory charted by Rosenblum and Muirhead (2019). For an audience seeking validation of their gut instincts that the election was stolen, this story rings true. In fact, conspiracy theorists don't even have to connect those dots because D'Souza and his other hosts repeatedly validate those basic feelings of betrayal by the election system saying, "you were right all along." Ultimately, *2000 Mules* is about validation, not persuasion.

D'Souza ends the documentary with a somewhat odd call to vote and participate. There is the standard idea that more voting is good, which undercuts the message of the film, but it also closes with a general, chilling call to explicitly "Do what is necessary to save this great country." This was taken literally by vigilantes in Arizona who were overtly inspired by D'Souza's film and showed up armed and in tactical gear to closely monitor drop boxes during the 2022 midterm elections (Fifield, 2022).

Misinformation surrounding the 2020 election cycle continues to impact public perceptions of democracy (Sanchez & Middlemass, 2022). We have woven some of D'Souza's media tour into this analysis to remove speculation about his intentions and just hear from him directly. Next we trace reactions to the film in a broader media environment to explore more viable ways to have conversations about similar media products.

## Mainstream Responses: A Partial Engagement

Major media outlets primarily engaged with *2000 Mules* through fact-checks. *The Associated Press* (Swenson, 2022), *Politifact* (Greenberg & Sherman, 2022), and *FactCheck.org* (Farley, 2022) produced the most widely circulated responses. The articles focused on the gaping holes in the film and the litany of unverified claims. Several fact-checks spent a lot of time unpacking the specifics of cell phone tracking data which quickly gets technical. The more compelling checks pointed out the complete lack of evidence for several links in the conspiracy chain, for instance *The Associated Press* article by Swenson (2022) noted, "The group hasn't offered any evidence of any sort of paid ballot harvesting scheme" as one of many holes in D'Souza's narrative. The *Politifact* response even incorporated testimony by former Attorney General William Barr in rebutting claims made in *2000 Mules*. Several of the checks pointed out that local law enforcement followed up on claims made in the documentary and found no evidence of fraud.

These fact-checks were somewhat typical of the mainstream engagement with right-wing conspiracies and media products. *The Associated Press* produced 19 articles that referenced the documentary. Most of these articles covered the vigilante drop box monitoring mentioned earlier, or they focused on various figures like Texas Attorney General Ken Paxton's staff supporting the film (Bleiberg, 2022). The film was always associated with terms like "widely debunked" or "flawed analysis." In this way, subsequent reporting on the film relied on the credibility and acceptance of the fact-check as a reasonable and effective means to confront conspiratorial claims.

Despite fears of backfire or entrenchment, research regularly shows that fact-checking can be effective in countering disinformation (Boukes & Hameleers, 2022; Walter & Tukachinsky, 2020). In this particular case, D'Souza spent a lot of time in promotional interviews answering fact-checking questions from Megyn Kelly, Glenn Beck, and others. It's possible this was just a mechanism for the host and guest to team up and complain about mainstream media, but there was a defensiveness in the conversations that would lead one to believe they take criticism seriously and want to respond. In the Beck (2022) interview, D'Souza specifically and convincingly responded to a *Washington Post* article by Phillip Bump (2022) by diving into the weeds on "ballot harvesting" versus "ballot trafficking." This is just to note that the people involved seem willing to engage with fact-checking rather than dismissing all claims as liberal media bias. Nonetheless, as a defense strategy, fact-checking alone has failed; "creators of debunked '2000 Mules' haven't stopped selling [the] movie, or its false premise" (Huseman, 2024).

Though fact-checking may prove a reasonable way to challenge disinformation, among journalists and academics alike, it too often gets treated as the end of a conversation rather than a beginning. *The Associated Press* example is instructive here as subsequent coverage of the film fell back on the fact-checking done earlier to assess and dismiss the film. What remains missing across mainstream media coverage is a substantive engagement with the story told in the film. Though media outlets should be addressing the factual inaccuracies of the film, effectively confronting conspiratorial thinking will require that they also help readers understand why the story told becomes so compelling to friendly audiences. Often left-leaning outlets and podcast hosts will review material— "so you don't have to," as the trope goes. This pattern leaves mainstream and progressive audiences ill-equipped to understand other perspectives and engage in meaningful dialogue. Insofar as rhetoric is "equipment of living" (Burke, 1941/1973), the fact-check is incomplete equipment.

Returning to the distinction between conspiracy and conspiracy theory (Rosenblum & Muirhead, 2019), we can see fact-checking as a response to the theory—the attempt to prove a point through logic and evidence. What this approach leaves out is engagement *with* the conspiracy—the story that is told to resonate with receptive audiences. A more effective response from mainstream outlets would be to include fact-checking alongside guiding audiences through the scaffolding of the story that encases those facts. This would equip friendly and dismissive audiences alike to better understand why—*even when we know the facts are wrong*—a story can still ring true in ways that captivate and mobilize viewers, especially those politically predisposed to receive them well.

## Conclusion

The chaotic aftermath of the 2020 election left the American right fragmented and dissatisfied. Their champion was no longer in the White House, which was beyond belief for the voters who rarely ventured outside a sealed media ecosystem. The insurrection on January 6th was not even clear, as some claimed it was great and wore participation as a badge of honor, while others insisted it was peaceful and the violence was perpetrated by the FBI or left-wing agitators. Regardless, they did not like the outcome of the election and admitting legitimate defeat would mean introspection and admitting fault in Donald Trump. *2000 Mules* was a cohesive narrative that explained such a disappointing moment for them without cognitive dissonance. It is a narrative of fraud involving their favorite foils—Big Tech, Democratic elites, transients, and mainstream media—woven together in a pleasing tapestry. Beyond that, it was wrapped in the aesthetics and reasoning of a scientific rationalism reminiscent of a CSI episode or a true-crime podcast. There were charts, maps, testimony, and math leading to the inevitable conclusion that Trump actually won and they were right all along.

There is no doubt the story is profoundly incomplete. Fact-checkers from major organizations have done dutiful work pointing out inconsistencies and missing evidence in the story. Here, we have expanded that work with special emphasis on the vast majority of the conspiracy which is entirely unevidenced. However, we have to do better in our mainstream engagement with similarly themed material. It is necessary, but not sufficient, to point out the ways a piece of media is factually inaccurate. We need to understand that these products are not just compelling because they portend accuracy, but because they present as a story—and often one that is quite familiar and enthralling. In understanding how to cover and report on this kind of material, major media outlets need to equip readers to engage with the narrative, not just with the facts. While this won't always be possible, it is an aspiration for deepening the conversation and genuinely engaging people in honest disagreement.

## References

Beck, G. (Host). (2022, May 5). Best of the program. *The Glenn Beck Program*. Blaze TV.

Bleiberg, J. (2022, September 30). Dysfunction in Texas AG's office as Paxton seeks third term. *The Associate Press*. https://apnews.com/article/elections-texas-president ial-election-2020-ken-paxton-a1bdcfd0a9d25bd6aa3666b70f74f2b2

Bond, S. (2022, November 3). Debunked film causes Republicans to mobilize, raising concerns of voter intimidation. *NPR*. www.npr.org/2022/11/03/1134079077/debun ked-film-causes-republicans-to-mobilize-raising-concerns-of-voter-intimidat

**64** Media Messages in the 2022 Midterm Election

Boukes, M., & Hameleers, M. (2022). Fighting lies with facts or humor: Comparing the effectiveness of satirical and regular fact-checks in response to misinformation and disinformation. *Communication Monographs*, *90*(1), 69–91. https://doi.org/10.1080/03637751.2022.2097284

Brumback, K. (2022, October 28). Georgia man sues over false ballot fraud claim in Dinesh D'Souza film '2000 Mules.' *Fox 5 Atlanta.* www.fox5atlanta.com/news/georgia-false-ballot-fraud-dinesh-dsouza-film-2000-mules-lawsuit

Bump, P. (2022, May 11). '2000 Mules' offers least convincing election fraud theory yet. *The Washington Post.* www.washingtonpost.com/politics/2022/05/11/2000-mules-offers-least-convincing-election-fraud-theory-yet/

Burke, K. (1941/1973). *The philosophy of literary form.* University of California Press.

*Business Wire.* (2022, May 12). *2000 Mules* becomes the most successful political documentary in a decade, seen by 1 million. www.businesswire.com/news/home/20220511006114/en/2000-Mules-Becomes-the-Most-Successful-Political-Documentary-in-a-Decade-Seen-by-1-Million

Caldes, S. D., Justus, Z., & Malkowski, J. A. (2022). Manufacturing disinformation: The story of *Plandemic.* In S.-L. S. Chen & N. Allaire (Eds.), *Discordant pandemic narratives in the U. S.* (pp. 157–173). Lexington Books.

Dreisbach, T. (2022a, October 5). Prominent election deniers are facing growing legal trouble. *NPR.* www.npr.org/2022/09/20/1123898736/prominent-election-deniers-are-facing-growing-legal-trouble

Dreisbach, T. (2022b, September 8). A publisher abruptly recalled the '*2,000 Mules*' election denial book. NPR got a copy. *NPR.* www.npr.org/2022/09/08/1121648290/a-publisher-abruptly-recalled-the-2-00 0-mules-election-denial-book-npr-got-a-cop

Dreisbach, T. (2024). Publisher of '2,000 Mules' election conspiracy theory film issues apology. *NPR.* www.npr.org/2024/05/31/g-s1-2298/publisher-of-2000-mules-election-conspiracy-theory-film-issues-apology

D'Souza, D. (2022a). *2000 Mules.* Salem Media. https://node-1.2000mules.com/

D'Souza, D. (2022b). *2000 Mules: They thought we'd never find out. They were wrong.* Regnery.

Farley, R. (2022, June 10). Evidence gaps in '2000 Mules.' *FactCheck.org.* www.factcheck.org/2022/06/evidence-gaps-in-2000-mules/

Farley, R., Gore, D., Robertson, L., Kiely, E., & Christensen, S. (2023, May 11). FactChecking Trump's CNN town hall. *FactCheck.org.* www.factcheck.org/2023/05/factchecking-trumps-cnn-town-hall/

Fichera, A., & Spencer, S. H. (2020, October 15). Debunking viral claims: Conspiracy theory baselessly claims Biden had Navy SEALs killed. *FactCheck.org.* www.factcheck.org/2020/10/conspiracy-theory-baselessly-claims-biden-had-navy-seals-killed/

Fifield, J. (2022, October 27). Dropbox watchers in Arizona connected to national effort from "2000 Mules" creators. *Votebeat Arizona.* www.votebeat.org/arizona/2022/10/27/23427525/clean-elections-usa-drop-box-watchers-voter-intimidation/

Fisher, W. R. (1984). Narration as a human communication paradigm: The case of public moral argument. *Communication Monographs*, *51*(1), 1–22. https://doi.org/10.1080/03637758409390180

Greenberg, J., & Sherman, A. (2022, October 28). The documentary "2,000 Mules proves" Democrats "cheated on the 2020 elections." *PolitiFact.* www.politifact.com/factchecks/2022/oct/28/instagram-posts/instagram-post-falsel y-says-2000-mules-proves-demo/

Huseman, J. (2024, June 10). Some creators of debunked '2000 Mules' haven't stopped selling movie, or its false premise. *Votebeat* [Opinion]. www.tucsonsentinel.com/opinion/report/061024_2000_mules/some-creators-debunked-2000-mules-havent-stopped-selling-movie-or-its-false-premise/

Izadi, E., & Farhi, P. (2021, March 26). Fox News sued by Dominion in $1.6 Billion defamation case that could set new guardrails for broadcasters. *The Washington Post*. www.washingtonpost.com/media/2021/03/26/fox-dominion-lawsuit-defamation/

Jones, J. (2022, October 17). Right-wing group behind '*2000 Mules*' could face federal scrutiny. *MSNBC*. www.msnbc.com/the-reidout/reidout-blog/arizona-fraud-investigation-2000-mules-rcna52549

Kelly, M. (Host). (2022, May 20). Dinesh D'Souza on ballot trafficking, "election integrity," and his movie, "2000 Mules". *The Megyn Kelly Show*. www.youtube.com/watch?v=2tQ5uLtA8QQ

Kim, M., & Cao, X. (2016). The impact of exposure to media messages promoting government conspiracy theories on distrust in the government: Evidence form a two-stage randomized experiment. *International Journal of Communication*, *10*, 3808–3827. https://ijoc.org/index.php/ijoc/article/view/5127

Konnikova, M. (2015, December 29). How stories deceive. *The New Yorker*. www.newyorker.com/science/maria-konnikova/how-stories-deceive

Lindemann, A. S., & Levy, R. S. (Eds.). (2010). *Antisemitism: A history*. Oxford University Press.

Neugeboren, E. (2022, June 18). Fed up and fired up: Texas Republicans meet in a climate of mistrust, conspiracy and victimhood. *The Texas Tribune*. www.texastribune.org/2022/06/18/texas-state-republican-convention/

Palmer, E. (2022, May 5). Donald Trump holds screening of '2,000 Mules' documentary at Mar-a-Lago. *Newsweek*. www.newsweek.com/donald-trump-2000-mules-film-election-fraud-dsouza-ritten house-1703680

Plumer, B. (2019, April 3). We fact-checked President Trump's dubious claims on the perils of wind power. *The New York Times*. www.nytimes.com/2019/04/03/climate/fact-check-trump-windmills.html

Reyes, I., & Smith, J. K. (2014). What they don't want you to know about Planet X: *Surviving 2012* and the aesthetics of conspiracy rhetoric. *Communication Quarterly*, *62*(4), 399–415. https://doi.org/10.1080/01463373.2014.922483

Rosenblum, N. L., & Muirhead, R. (2019). *A lot of people are saying: The new conspiracism and the assault on democracy*. Princeton University Press.

Rubin, D. (Host). (2022, June 5). *2000 Mules*: Why I changed my mind about the 2020 election. *The Rubin Report*. www.youtube.com/watch?v=IHqk3Pq9oSg

Sanchez, G. R., & Middlemass, K. (2022, July 26). Misinformation is eroding the public's confidence in democracy. *Brookings*. www.brookings.edu/articles/misinformation-is-eroding-the-publics-confidence-in-democracy/

Shapiro, B. (Host). (2022). Examining *2000 Mules* and the 2020 election (Ep. 1491) [Audio Podcast]. *The Ben Shapiro Show*. https://soundcloud.com/benshapiroshow/ep1491

Sommer, W. (2023). *Trust the plan: The rise of QAnon and the conspiracy that unhinged America*. Harper Collins.

Swenson, A. (2022, May 3). Fact focus: Gaping holes in the claim of 2k ballot 'mules.' *The Associated Press.* https://apnews.com/article/2022-midterm-elections-covid-tec hnology-health-arizona-e1b49d2311bf900f44fa5c6dac406762

The Daily Show. (2022, December 14). *Voter fraud, Italian satellites and...Marla Maples? -Jordan Klepper fingers the conspiracy* [Video]. YouTube. www.youtube.com/watch?v=CMwk8HzRrKg

Trump, D. [@realDonaldTrump]. (2022, May 14). *Fox News is no longer Fox News.* [Truth]. TruthSocial. https://truthsocial.com/@realDonaldTrump/posts/10830164357 7625757

Uscinski, J. E., & Parent, J. M. (Eds.). (2014). *American conspiracy theories.* Oxford University Press.

Victor, D. (2018, May 31). A look at Dinesh D'Souza, pardoned by Trump. *The New York Times.* www.nytimes.com/2018/05/31/us/politics/dinesh-dsouza-facts-history.html

Walter, N., & Tukachinsky, R. (2020). A meta-analytic examination of the continued influence of misinformation in the face of correction: How powerful is it, why does it happen, and how to stop it? *Communication Research, 47*(2), 155–177. https://doi.org/10.1177/0093650219854600

Warner, B. R., & Neville-Shepard, R. (2014). Echoes of a conspiracy: Birthers, truthers, and the cultivation of extremism. *Communication Quarterly, 62*(1), 1–17. https://doi.org/10.1080/01463373.2013.822407

Weaver, M. (2022, May 14). Donald Trump slams Fox News, echoes Dinesh D'Souza's '2000 Mules' complaint. *Newsweek.* www.newsweek.com/donald-trump-slams-fox-news-echoes-dinesh-dsouzas-2000-mules-complaint-1706723

## SECTION II

# Framing the Debate

How Issues Shaped 2022 Candidate Communication

# 4

# POST-*ROE* POLITICS

## Priming, Framing, and the Dynamics of Abortion Discourse in Congressional Campaigns

*Christopher Chapp, India Bock, and Cali Goulet*

The *Dobbs* v. *Jackson Women's Health,* 597 U.S. 215 (2022), decision dramatically altered the scope of legal access to abortion and women's reproductive health in the United States. The decision also altered the 2022 midterm elections in non-trivial ways, with 2022 campaigns representing the first opportunity in fifty years for candidates to communicate to their prospective constituents exactly how they would govern in an America where abortion is not a guaranteed right. In short, the 2022 midterms became voters' first chance to see what abortion representation would look like in a post-*Roe* America.

Political strategists expressed conflicting views about how candidates should message in this altered landscape. A memorandum from KAConsulting, the Tarrance Group, and the Republican National Committee (2022) urged candidates to "go on offense and expose their opponents as having extreme views" (p. 4). Other Republicans were less sanguine. "If you're debating abortion at this point, you're losing" asserted former Virginia Representative Tom Davis (as cited in Messerly & Ollstein, 2022, para. 22). Strategists like James Carville worried that Democrats were too focused on abortion: "A lot of these consultants think if all we do is run abortion spots that will win for us. I don't think so" (as cited in Peoples, 2022, para. 9). Others urged Democrats to lean into abortion. Following a victory for pro-choice advocates on a 2022 Kansas ballot measure, Emily's List spokesperson Christina Reynolds argued "What we saw last night is this can drive turnout in a way that hasn't happened before" (as cited in Linskey & Shepard, 2022, para. 11). In addition to the decision to emphasize abortion as a campaign issue (or not), others noted that a strategic *frame* was equally important. The *New York Times* reported that President Biden "was uncomfortable even using the word abortion," preferring "broader phrases, like 'reproductive health'

DOI: 10.4324/9781003440833-6

**70** Media Messages in the 2022 Midterm Election

and 'the right to choose'" (Shear, 2022, para. 2). On the Republican side, NBC News reported that senate candidate Blake Masters "scrubbed" his campaign website to "soften" the language on abortion (Smith & Caputo, 2022).

This chapter asks how abortion communication permeated the 2022 midterms, and what these dynamics tell us about the nature of policy representation. This approach utilizes a unique data source: a corpus of every abortion statement on candidates' campaign websites between 2008 and 2022. The findings support four interconnected arguments about abortion messaging. First, abortion is increasingly discussed by Democrats in competitive districts, while Republicans consistently use abortion as a "base" strategy in safe districts. Second, Democratic messaging on abortion has been gradually increasing since 2008—*Dobbs* accelerated a trend that was already underway. Third, the parties frame abortion in different ways. Even across the short span of eight elections, the number of "consensus" candidates has observably shrunk as abortion messaging became increasingly partisan. Fourth, the way candidates (especially Democrats) frame abortion reflects underlying strategic calculations rooted in district extremity, gender, and incumbency.

### Issues, Framing, and the *Dobbs* Decision

A healthy democracy requires that constituents have the ability to hold their representatives accountable for the positions they take. Based on the theory of promissory responsiveness (Mansbridge, 2003), constituents are able to assess the performance of elected officials by listening to candidates' commitments on the campaign trail. Voters then use this information to inform their decisions at the ballot box. As a result, campaign communications serve a vital role in safeguarding our democratic institutions.

Nevertheless, many social scientists argue that voters pay little attention to politics, so much so that robust communication on issues of the day holds little weight in a competitive election (Guntermann & Lenz, 2022). That said, emerging evidence suggests that abortion might be different (Dancey & Goren, 2010; Goren & Chapp, 2017). Abortion is deeply entrenched in social and cultural norms around sexuality, gender, and family values (Luker, 1984). As such, abortion is an issue that evokes strong emotional responses (Koleva et al., 2012; Luker, 1984). Given this, voters may respond differently to rhetoric focused on this specific issue, making abortion communication electorally consequential (Goren & Chapp, 2017).

Policy communication can theoretically affect voters in different ways. At one level, issues can be *primed* as a basis of candidate evaluation, such that voters are thinking about these issues when casting a vote (Druckman, 2004; Zaller, 1992). Through priming, candidates exact a degree of control over what issues are on the top of voter's minds when they enter the ballot box. For example, an incumbent candidate in a good economy might want to prime economic considerations as a basis of candidate evaluation, while a challenger in the same environment would want to prime an alternative basis of evaluation (Vavreck, 2009). By the same logic, candidates "prime" issues like abortion when the public mood makes it a winning issue for a particular party or candidate. Priming does not necessarily change voter's preferences per se. Rather, priming raises the salience of issues as the basis of evaluation. Candidates are strategic about which issues they prime, taking public opinion, current events, and candidate personality into consideration (Druckman et al., 2004).

While priming brings a specific issue to the forefront of a voter's mind, candidates employ differing frames to direct the conversation around said issue. On any given issue, candidates can choose to emphasize certain considerations and deemphasize others. Candidates select frames based on the specific considerations they hope to raise in the minds of voters. To take one classic example, if a controversial group wishes to stage a rally in a public square, proponents will likely frame this as a free speech issue, while opponents might frame the rally in terms of public safety (Nelson & Oxley 1999). Frames can shift voters' belief importance, impacting how they prioritize their issue preferences when they head to the polls (Nelson & Oxley, 1999).

Like priming, candidates strategically employ framing (Klar et al., 2013). Even candidates advocating for the same policy position can utilize disparate frames to appeal to specific voters. For example, a politician discussing education might do so with an equality frame, making the argument that the government should fund education so that every child has the opportunity to succeed. Conversely, they could use an economic frame, contending that education should be funded so the country can have a competitive workforce on the global stage. Not only do frames have a substantial impact on public opinion (Sniderman & Theriault, 2004), they also showcase candidates' perceptions of the issue landscape.

The strategic logic of priming and framing in campaigns rests on two main theoretical foundations. First, candidates are single-minded seekers of reelection (Mayhew, 1976). They need to first get elected before they can accomplish any policy objectives. Accordingly, candidates communicate strategically in order to maximize their vote total. The second foundation posits that candidates pursue this reelection goal by managing their risk environment (Druckman et al., 2009). Candidates have different levels of risk depending on any number of circumstances including incumbency, popularity in the district, money in their campaign war chest, and broader national forces like the economy and presidential popularity. Each of these circumstances plays into the risk environment, influencing which issues candidates choose to prime, and how candidates subsequently frame these issues. Imagine a long-shot Democratic challenger campaigning in a Republican district against a Republican incumbent. In this scenario, the Democrat needs to chip away at the incumbent's electoral base to build a constituency, so they might

**72** Media Messages in the 2022 Midterm Election

take higher-risk positions on a variety of issues. The Republican, in contrast, will likely play it safe to avoid an unforced error. In fact, many incumbents facing "cakewalk" electoral environments do not bother to hazard clear issue-stances in the first place (Chapp et al., 2019).

Researchers have identified a number of abortion frames available to candidates. Saurette and Gordon (2013) identified four traditional pro-life frames used on the political right, including a legislative change frame, a frame that is critical of women, a frame grounded in religion, and a "fetal-centric" set of arguments. Ainsworth and Hall (2010) concurred that religious arguments are common, and also pointed to an emphasis on the family which prioritizes traditional values and morals. Lowe and Page (2019) added to this literature, arguing that pro-life groups often use an equality and right to life frame, which allows them to combat the women's rights-based argument found in pro-choice rhetoric. Lowe and Page also provided evidence of women-centered rhetoric on the anti-abortion side. Although the abortion debate is frequently boiled down to fetal rights versus women's rights, anti-abortion groups try to subvert this narrative by contending that abortion harms women, often using the slogan "Women Deserve Better Than Abortion." This argument focuses on motherhood and frames abortion as unnatural and dangerous.

For Democrats, the name "pro-choice" itself helps describe the central frame. Based on analysis of pro-choice frames in U.S. Congressional races from 1976 to 2000, Jaenicke (2002) highlighted bodily autonomy and rights-based discourse as the most popular frames. Ainsworth and Hall (2010) argued that the discourse surrounding a woman's right to choose is often accompanied by a focus on the importance of safe and legal abortions from a public health perspective. This public health frame dovetails with Jaenicke's finding that pro-choice advocates often argue for government assistance alongside legalization.

How does this brief review inform expectations about the 2022 midterms? Research suggests that Republicans had a number of frames available, including legislative action, fetal rights, religion, and family/motherhood. Democrats have women's rights, bodily autonomy, healthcare, and safety available as potential frames. However, while the literature is a helpful guide, several caveats are in order. First, not all of the studies reviewed above examine congressional campaign rhetoric. It is likely that the rhetoric from movement activists differs considerably from the calculated ways candidates prime and frame issues to win elections. Second, 2022 was different. All the aforementioned research was conducted before the *Dobbs* ruling, and it is possible that the universe of available frames shifted faster than the scholarship. For these reasons, the content analytic procedure adopted in this paper is largely exploratory, even though previous studies inform expectations. In order to deduce expectations, this paper makes use of the concepts of "prevailing" and "alternative" frames (Wedeking, 2010). Prevailing frames are the most commonly deployed frames in elite discourse,

Post-*Roe* Politics  **73**

while alternative frames introduce a different dimension or "thought structure" into policy debate (Wedeking, 2010). As this chapter turns to expectations about which frames will be utilized and why, the prevailing/alternative dichotomy is a helpful distinction to form expectations.

The next question is what factors might influence a candidate's abortion risk calculus, and how will candidates use priming and framing to manage these risks? When will Republicans emphasize "right to life" versus "religious" language? When will Democrats use prevailing versus an alternative frame? In the case of abortion, three factors will likely influence how candidates understand the risk environment: issue ownership, incumbency status, and gender.

Issue ownership describes policy areas in which one party is considered more competent and trustworthy by the majority of the population (Petrocik, 1996). For example, Republicans are typically seen as better able to handle crime while Democrats "own" social security. Candidates take advantage of this dynamic by messaging on their party's "owned issues," particularly when these issues are also prominent in the news cycle (Ansolabehere & Iyengar, 1994). Tying issue ownership back to the idea of risk, it makes little sense to prime an issue that is not owned by one's party, unless, perhaps, the candidate is in such a "safe" district that they are more worried about a primary challenge than the general election. When forced to talk about an issue the other party "owns," candidates will highlight features of the issue in which they are seen as more competent (Petrocik, 1996).

Will issue ownership matter in abortion messaging? On one hand, Egan (2013) noted that the concept of issue ownership is most relevant in the case of "consensus" issues where voters agree on policy ends. Issue ownership dynamics are less likely to be at play in the case of a divisive issue like abortion. At the same time, abortion politics are shifting. A recent *Pew Research Center* study (2022) finds that 62% of Americans think abortion should be legal in all or most cases, and 57% disagree with the Supreme Court ruling which overturned *Roe*. Likewise, the 2022 American National Election Study (ANES) pilot study asked voters to "Please tell us which political party—the Democrats or the Republicans—would do a better job handling [the issue of abortion], or is there no difference," and found that 45.6% of respondents said Democrats do a better job, compared to 28.8% of respondents preferring Republicans. Incredibly, of the twelve policy areas the survey asked about, abortion was the most Democratically owned issue based on unweighted percentages from the 2022 ANES pilot study. This suggests that Democrats will be more likely to prime abortion, relative to their Republican counterparts. Republicans are likely to campaign on this issue in heavily Republican "safe" districts where the issue might help deter a future primary challenge. Safe seat Republicans and incumbents will likely utilize "prevailing" partisan frames to signal partisan bona fides to voters.

**74** Media Messages in the 2022 Midterm Election

Researchers have established that gender is an often-used heuristic for how voters evaluate candidates (Sanbonmatsu, 2002). For example, Schneider (2014a) found that female candidates are rated significantly higher than male candidates on abortion issues regardless of messaging strategy or party. Insofar as abortion functions as an "owned issue" for women, it is likely that female candidates will capitalize on this ownership and discuss abortion more often than male candidates. In fact, using candidate website data, Schneider (2014b) found that female candidates are more likely to run on stereotype-congruent platforms than their male counterparts. Further, women will likely utilize frames associated with other issues they maintain ownership benefits over and discuss abortion in terms of healthcare and women's rights (Alexander & Andersen, 1993). Evidence suggests that these effects may vary based on a candidate's party. Gender and party can interact, such that female Republicans and female Democrats are each seen as having unique emergent traits (Schneider & Bos, 2016).

A candidate's gender can also influence frame selection because of the U.S. primary structure. Lawless and Pearson (2008) found that primaries may be a key source of the disparity of representation between men and women as female candidates are perceived by competitors as more vulnerable. This results in women in both parties contending with more competitive primaries as they are more likely to attract primary challengers. Ideologically extreme voters are able to exert disproportionate influence on candidate selection which forces candidates in competitive primaries to adopt ideologically extreme positions to appeal to voters (Brady et al., 2011). Given female candidates' propensity to attract competition in primaries, women are expected to utilize less equivocating and prevailing frames. Alexander and Andersen (1993) also suggest that regardless of party or expressed ideology, women are perceived as more liberal than their male counterparts. In a competitive primary setting this is particularly problematic for Republican women and offers additional incentive for them to rely on more extreme and/or alternative frames.

Incumbency is another factor which the literature suggests will be highly predictive of frame choice. The incumbency advantage incentivizes incumbent candidates to refrain from risk-taking and focus on their legislative accomplishments. Challengers on the other hand must raise issue-based appeals in order to try to compete with the familiarity advantage of the incumbent (Druckman et al., 2020). Based on this dynamic, incumbents will most likely stake out prevailing partisan frames to avoid risky discourses. Challengers are incentivized to engage in risk-taking behavior and employ potentially costly alternative frames. In the case of abortion, challengers might use novel or untested alternative frames to persuade voters.

In summary, campaigns try to prime issues that are a favorable basis of evaluation, and frame these issues in favorable terms. What "favorable" looks like depends on factors like party-based issue ownership, gender, and incumbency. Each of these factors theoretically influences the risk calculus involved with taking a stance on a hot-button issue, though what this looks like in practice is an open question. Put more concretely, evolving Democratic issue ownership on abortion will likely incentivize Democrats to talk about the issue more in 2022 than in 2008, though given that incumbents don't need to take risks, it is unclear if incumbent Democrats truly have any incentive to elevate abortion in the national discourse. Accordingly, this study asks how candidates altered priming and framing strategies on a rapidly evolving issue. Were long-shot candidates more likely to prime a "risky" issue like abortion following the Dobbs ruling? Did "safe" incumbents respond by avoiding the issue completely? Moreover, did the parties develop novel approaches to framing given uncertainty surrounding the issue?

## Methodology: Understanding Abortion Messaging

The literature suggests an underlying logic to whether candidates will "run on abortion," or avoid the issue completely. This said, there is relatively little consensus on the universe of possible abortion frames. Moreover, the *Dobbs* decision created unprecedented circumstances, leading to uncertainty in how candidates might campaign in a changed environment. For this reason, this chapter uses an exploratory content analytic approach called "topic modeling" to identify underlying clusters of words that tend to appear together (Grimmer et al., 2022). The approach is as follows:

To begin, it is necessary to identify a corpus of text to analyze. While televised campaign advertising is one strong contender, television is limited for a number of reasons. First, the heavy use of visuals does not lend itself to automated content analysis of language per se. Second, because television advertising is expensive, there is relatively little television content available in uncompetitive districts—limiting the ability to explore district competitiveness as an independent variable. Given these limitations, this chapter turns to text from campaign websites. While websites are not frequently visited by the general public, they do serve as good indicators of the overall thrust of a campaign's messaging strategy (Druckman et al., 2009). Moreover, web content is inexpensive to produce and is a mainstay of virtually every congressional campaign. This provides for the ability to compare competitive and uncompetitive races on roughly even ground.

This chapter draws on the "Congressional Campaign Collection," an archive of website text maintained at St. Olaf College. From 2014 to the present, researchers identified every major-party candidate on a general election ballot and scraped the text from every "issues page" (e.g., "abortion policy," "reproductive rights," or "pro-life"), home page, and bio page. From 2008 to 2012, campaign pages were accessed through the Library of Congress's (n.d.) "United States

Elections Web Archive" and the Oberlin College and Northwestern University (n.d.) "Congressional Candidate Website Project," both of which archive congressional campaign websites. Trained student researchers used uniform procedures to collect and catalog text. Stopwords ("a," "the") were eliminated in order to whittle the text files down to the content words that differentiate abortion frames. To sample abortion text, the authors used a "keyword in context" procedure through the R package quanteda (Benoit et al., 2018). The following words were used to identify abortion passages: "pro-choice," "prochoice," "pro choice," "pro-life," "prolife," "pro life," "abortion," "unborn," "fetus," "roe," "reproductive," "heartbeat," and "embryo." These keywords were selected to yield a sample of passages on the political "right" and political "left."

Once abortion passages were selected, the next step was to characterize how each candidate framed abortion. To do so, the authors selected a bandwidth of the fifteen words prior to and fifteen words after each keyword. The resulting sample of abortion passages (sometimes multiple passages per candidate) were then aggregated at the candidate level. Next, structural topic models (STM) were applied to the subset of abortion passages to identify words that tended to cluster together on a particular candidate's webpage. The authors explored several different approaches to topic modeling, ultimately choosing a four-topic model for each party that fit the data well and led to sensible interpretation. These topic scores were the basis for all subsequent analysis.

## Stability and Change in Abortion Campaigning, 2008–2022

As a first cut at the data, Figure 4.1 displays the percentage of candidates in a given year who mentioned abortion on the issue pages of their website.

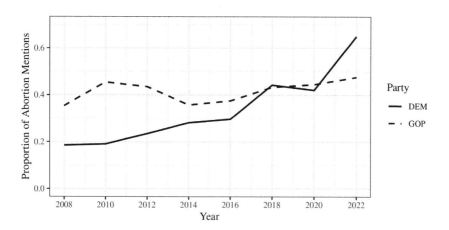

**FIGURE 4.1** Congressional Candidate Abortion Statements, 2008–2022.

The dashed line in Figure 4.1 illustrates that from 2008 to 2022, Republicans campaigned in a strikingly consistent manner. In any given year, roughly 42% of Republican candidates staked out a position on abortion. Given this stability, it is worth asking if abortion tends to be—consistent with expectations—a "base" strategy in safe Republican districts or a strategy used to appeal to undecided voters in competitive districts. Using Cook Political Report Partisan Voting Index scores (a common approach to operationalizing district lean relative to national presidential voting) as rough indicators of district lean reveals that 61% of Republicans in the reddest districts ran on abortion, while only 32% of Republicans in the bluest districts did so. This pattern is relatively consistent for every election in the dataset. For Republicans, abortion issue is primarily a base strategy, though not exclusively so.

In contrast to Republicans, Democrats' strategy has shifted considerably in the past two decades. First, Democrats have grown increasingly comfortable talking about abortion. In 2008, only 19% of Democratic websites mentioned abortion. In 2022, 65% did so. While the increase in abortion messaging between the 2020 and 2022 campaigns suggests a *Dobbs* effect, *Dobbs* is not the whole story. As the data show, abortion has steadily become a more important part of Democratic campaigns. Until recently, Democrats have used abortion fairly evenly across different types of districts. In fact, in 2008 and 2010, Democratic strategy mirrored the "base" approach of Republicans in some ways. For example, in 2008 25% of "safe seat" Democrats in deep blue districts ran on abortion, while only 13% of Democrats in competitive districts mentioned the issue (using Cook PVI scores between -4 and 4 to operationalize competitive districts). However, over time Democratic strategy shifted, such that Democrats in competitive districts are now clearly the most likely to stake out a position on abortion. In 2022, a staggering 86% of Democrats running in competitive congressional races brought up abortion. In addition, previewing an argument developed later in this chapter, female Democrats, but not Republicans, are also significantly more likely to bring up abortion. Across all years in the sample, 44% of female Democrats issued an abortion statement, while only 29% of male Democrats did so ($\chi^2$ = 54.1, p <.001). Interestingly this gender difference was not observed among the Republican candidates, where 35.4% of Republican men discussed abortion compared to 35.7% of Republican women ($\chi^2$ =.024, $p$ >.05). Drawing on the notion that abortion is a woman-owned issue, part of the steady increase in abortion messaging on the Democratic side likely reflects a greater number of women running for office (178 Democratic women in 2022, versus only 96 in 2008) (Center for American Women and Politics, 2022).

To summarize, in 2008 abortion was primarily a "base" strategy for both parties (particularly Republicans). From 2008 to 2022, Republican candidates were especially consistent in the types of districts where they have used the abortion strategy. On the other hand, Democratic strategy has changed.

**78** Media Messages in the 2022 Midterm Election

Democrats ran on abortion more often, particularly as more Democratic women have sought office. Democrats also appear to have shifted strategy, running on abortion in "swing" rather than "safe" districts. This pattern is consistent with the expectation that abortion may by becoming an "owned" Democratic issue.

While Figure 4.1 addresses where and when abortion was "primed" as a political issue, it is also likely that candidates deploy specific abortion "frames" for electoral advantage. Although the literature informs some expectations about what frames might be deployed, 2022 was a novel campaign environment. Accordingly, this chapter uses STM to identify latent topics (or "frames") in each of the candidates' abortion statements. This exploratory approach identifies groups of words that regularly appeared together, rather than impose preconceptions about what frames would be present.

Table 4.1 displays Republican and Democratic frames separately. Four latent frames characterized the rhetoric for each party. After qualitatively inspecting campaigns scoring high on particular topics, labels were assigned to characterize the underlying frame. STM produces a "theta" score for each campaign. Theta estimates the proportion of words assigned to each of the four topics for each candidate. In practice, no candidates use word tokens exclusively from a single latent topic. For example, a Democrat might primarily frame abortion as a "women's rights" issue while also using some of the words from the healthcare frame. The "average theta" column displays the mean proportion of words that were classified under each topic (illustrating Democrats primarily used "women's rights" words and Republicans primarily used "unborn" words). Theta tells us how different types of words appeared across the entire corpus, but not the "bottom line" framing decisions specific candidates ultimately made. For this reason, Table 4.1 also displays the "Dominant topic," which is the frequency with which a particular topic had the highest theta for a given candidate. In other words, rather than think about a campaign as deploying multiple frames proportionally, the "Dominant topic" column illustrates how often a particular topic was the defining feature of a particular campaign.

It is important to note that some candidates use multiple frames roughly equally. For example, incumbent Scott Perry's 2022 campaign website (PA-10) stated, "All life, born and unborn, is sacred and must be defended. I supported efforts in Congress to protect the rights of the unborn, block taxpayer funding for abortion, and defund Planned Parenthood while shifting its funding to local health clinics." The STM identified this as primarily an "unborn rights" frame, but it also had aspects of the "legislation" frame (identifies efforts in Congress) and the "morality" frame (uses the word "sacred"). Specifically, the topic models estimated theta scores of .39 for "unborn rights," which we call the "Dominant topic," a score of .36 for "legislation," and .2 for morality and religion.

The prevailing frame for Republicans was "unborn rights" (characterizing 36% of the documents). This frame can be thought of as a counter-frame to

Post-*Roe* Politics **79**

**TABLE 4.1** Top Frames by Party

| Party | Frame | Most Frequent & Exclusive Words | Average Theta | Dominant Frame |
|---|---|---|---|---|
| Republican | Legislation & Funding | abort, fund, act feder, taxpay, protect, vote prohibit, require, cosponsor, pain, co-sponsor | 0.223 | 23.0 |
| Republican | Abortion Circumstances | abort, issu, state, women, mother, can, wade, count, decis, roe, suprem, case, rape | 0.189 | 18.0 |
| Republican | Religion & Morality | life, believ, concept, human, protect, begin, must, begin, sanctity, natur, god, tradit, marriag | 0.269 | 23.0 |
| Republican | Unborn Rights | will, right, pro-lif, support, protect, congress, nation, blain, list, work, continu, susan, second | 0.319 | 36.0 |
| Democrat | Exceptions & Morality | about, need, issu, believ, life, pregnanc, republican, pro-lif, phil, partial, rare, incest, rape | 0.222 | 22.2 |
| Democrat | Women's Rights | women, right, support, plan, women, make, will, pay, violence, parenthood, earn, opportune, proud, endors | 0.281 | 29.1 |
| Democrat | Judicial | right, wade, reproduct, state, law, decis, court, suprem, overturn, privacy, preced, codifi | 0.225 | 21.4 |
| Democrat | Healthcare | acess, health, care, women, service, include, protect, coverag, insur, cost | 0.272 | 27.3 |

Democratic "women's rights" messaging, claiming to be champions for rights of the unborn (Lowe & Page, 2019). John Rutherford (FL-4, 2016) provides one typical example: "John is a strong defender of the lives of the unborn and will fight passionately in Washington to protect life." Likewise, Iowa's 2022 3rd district GOP challenger Zach Nunn used this frame to situate his abortion position as advocacy for the rights of the vulnerable generally: "I will always stand with Iowa's most vulnerable – that means protecting our seniors, our disabled, and our unborn. I am a recognized pro-life leader, committed to fighting for the unborn."

Nearly a quarter of Republicans framed abortion in terms of religion or morality, using phrases like "God," "creator," and "sacred." Like the previous frame, this frame includes a focus on the life of the developing fetus. However, this frame drops the language of rights, instead using the language of religion and personal morality. Some candidates used explicitly Christian language to justify their position. For example, Renee Ellmers (NC-2, 2010) stated, "I believe in the sanctity of human life and that life begins at conception. As a mom, Christian and nurse, my beliefs have deepened through experience." Other candidates, like Pete Olson (TX-22, 2010) use non-sectarian language that nevertheless invokes a higher power: "I believe that life begins at conception and every life has a soul." In addition, many candidates also listed their abortion position ("pro-life") alongside other concepts ("religious liberty in schools"), semantically linking these issues without explicitly using religious justifications for policies.

Republicans also regularly framed abortion in terms of "legislation and funding." These statements protest "taxpayer funded abortion" and regularly mention specific legislative proposals, such as "defunding Planned Parenthood." For example, Alabama's 6th District Republican Gary Palmer advocated for "the Defund Planned Parenthood Act, which would create a moratorium on any funding for Planned Parenthood, as well as H.R. 3504, the Born-Alive Abortion Survivors Protection Act, which provides greater protection for infants that survive the abortion procedure." This frame centers on proposed legislation and the use of tax dollars, rather than the morality of abortion policy per se.

The least common frame in our sample—defining roughly 18% of Republicans' abortion rhetoric—was the "circumstances" frame. In some ways this frame can be thought of as a "compromise" stance, advocating for pro-life policies while also carving out exceptions. Scott Tipton's (CO-3, 2018) website was typical: "I am pro-life and I believe abortion should be limited to cases that involve rape, incest, or threat to the life of the mother." In addition to enumerating *personal circumstances* under which abortion should (or should not) be legal, candidates using this frame also regularly used court decisions to argue that *state circumstances* should determine abortion policy. Jeremy Shaffer's (PA-17, 2022) position was typical:

> With the Supreme Court overturning R*oe v. Wade* the question of abortion now returns back to the individual states (where it was for approx. 200 years). I have long advocated for a pro-life policy that allows for exceptions for life of the mother, rape and incest which will again now be determined by our state government.

By mentioning that abortion legality is a question for states, Shaffer is essentially creating some ambiguity in his own position, even while identifying as pro-life. Claire Gustafson, New Jersey's 1st district Republican in 2020, also scored high on this topic, and interestingly, is quite self-conscious about the framing of the abortion debate: "We have allowed the Democrats to frame the debate on abortion…They falsely claim abortion is a choice when the truth is the majority of the time the 'choice' is made before conception – a simple trip to the 'family planning aisle' at the drug store could prevent an unwanted pregnancy. For me, abortion is never an option, but I also understand there are exceptions to every rule."

The circumstances frame has a strategic purpose, creating gray areas between stark abortion absolutes. For this reason, while Republicans did not *typically* prime abortion in heavily Democratic districts, when they chose to do so they frequently used the "circumstances matter" argument. This suggests that Republicans in these long-shot races strategically attempt to move the conversation away from the pro-life/pro-choice dichotomy. The circumstances frame was used roughly 40% of the time in districts with a PVI score larger than D+4. In contrast, in competitive districts this frame was deployed only 13% of the time. In R+4 or greater districts, circumstances framing was used less than 10% of the time. The correlation between a district's PVI score and the "exceptions and alternatives" frame was $-.366$ (p <.001).

Not surprisingly, Democrats deployed very different language when discussing abortion. The prevailing frame was "equal rights," using phrases like "reproductive rights" and "reproductive freedom" to defend abortion. Debbie Mucarsel-Powell (FL-26, 2020) provided one illustrative example: "As a mother, sister, and daughter, I will fight for women's rights, especially for women of color who face additional barriers to full equality." The "rights" frame was also frequently linked to abortion advocacy organizations, as was the case with Stephanie Murphy's (FL-7, 2020) statement: "Stephanie strongly supports women's reproductive rights and has consistently stood up to efforts to defund Planned Parenthood."

The "equal rights" frame stands in contrast to the "exceptions and morality" frame, which made up 22% of abortion statements. This frame articulates circumstances under which abortion should be allowed (rather than an absolute right) and distinguishes the role of government in abortion from the candidate's personal morality. Consider Barry Welsh, the Democrat running against Mike Pence in Indiana's 6th in 2008. Welsh argued that "Congressman Pence and I both agree that abortion is not the personal choice of either of us; we disagree on making criminals of those that are faced with this difficult decision." This dovetails with the Republican "circumstances" frame both rhetorically and strategically. Indeed, Democrats were most likely to deploy this language in heavily Republican districts—the correlation between a district's PVI score and the exceptions frame was .369 (p < .001). Some Democrats scoring high on this topic advocated for choice while also advocating for abortion reduction, not unlike the "safe, legal, and rare" mantra used by Bill Clinton in his 1992 campaign (for an interesting account of this phrase, see North, 2019). For example, Democrat Bob Lorinser (MI-1) stated, "I am an advocate of life and a proponent of choice, privacy, and individual liberty. I will support proven measures to reduce abortion." Interestingly, the model assigned (the few and far between) pro-life Democrats to this topic, suggesting rhetorical similarity between pro-life positioning and the language of exceptions. Karen Hyer (UT-3, 2010) was typical: "I believe in the sanctity of life at all times and circumstances, from the earliest stages to the last days. I oppose abortion, except to preserve the life of the mother, or in cases of rape or incest."

Democrats used "abortion as healthcare" framing roughly 27% of the time. For example, in Colorado's 1st congressional district in 2016, incumbent Diana Degette argued that "Diana is fighting to protect access to birth control coverage under the Affordable Care Act and ensuring that women have comprehensive reproductive health care they need." While the spirit of these pages was similar to the equal rights frame, the emphasis of these pages was on women's health generally, including contraception options and mammograms.

Finally, the judicial frame referred to the constitutional status of abortion, arguing that the fate of abortion would be determined by the composition of the Supreme Court. For example, following *Dobbs,* Jon Haire (TX-36, 2022) wrote, "Women's rights have suffered serious blows—most drastically at the hands of the Republican-appointed Justices on the U.S. Supreme Court who, on June 24, 2022, reversed the landmark *Roe v. Wade* decision that had stood for nearly 50 years." Similarly, Brad Ettinger (MN-1, 2022) used Dobbs as a rationale to codify the protections afforded by *Roe* in Congress

> The Supreme Court created a chaotic situation for people all across our district and the nation when they overturned *Roe vs. Wade*… As a member of Congress, I will lead the fight to pass legislation codifying *Roe v. Wade* into national law.

How have messaging strategies changed over time? Figures 4.2 and 4.3 address this question, plotting the average theta scores over time. As Figure 4.2 illustrates, Republican strategy has been relatively static. "Unborn rights" language (represented by the solid black line) is the most common abortion frame, and it shows little evidence of change over time. There is a steady decrease in "exceptions" words over time (the dashed gray line), suggesting a modest decrease in Republicans staking out moderate positions on abortion. The most remarkable thing about Figure 4.2 is that, despite *Dobbs* marking a conservative policy victory fifty years in the making, most Republican

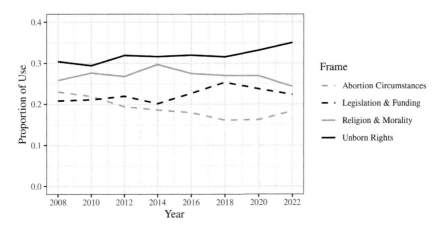

**FIGURE 4.2** Republican Frames 2008–2022.

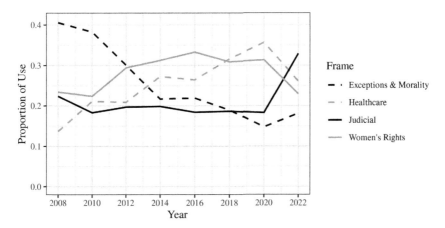

**FIGURE 4.3** Democratic Frames 2008–2022.

candidates in 2022 adopted a rhetorical posture similar to prior years. In fact, only twenty-four Republican candidates even mentioned *Roe* by name on their 2022 websites (a small increase from earlier years).

In contrast, Democratic strategy has changed substantially since 2008. First, the "exceptions" frame, once the most common in the party, has fallen into disuse. As the dashed black line in Figure 4.3 shows, the use of this frame plummeted after 2010. The reason for this dramatic change may be due in part to political serendipity. 2010 was a wave election for Republicans, sweeping out swing district Democratic incumbents like Kathy Dahlkemper, Jim Oberstar, and Steve Driehaus who were conservative on abortion. Other conservative

**84** Media Messages in the 2022 Midterm Election

Democrats (like Bart Stupak) declined to seek reelection. This, coupled with a 2010 redistricting cycle largely controlled by GOP-majority legislatures, left relatively few abortion moderates in the House, and, with fewer moderate districts, relatively little incentive to frame abortion as a circumstantial right.

Of course, wave elections and redistricting are not the only reason this frame has fallen into disuse. Party coalitions are also changing. As late as 2004, the national Democratic party platform included the language, "we strongly support family planning and adoption incentives. Abortion should be safe, legal, and rare," holding up abortion as a right, while also implying that "circumstances matter" (Woolley & Peters, 2020). By 2020 the national Democratic party had dropped equivocating language, arguing "comprehensive health services, including access to reproductive care and abortion services, are vital to the empowerment of women and girls" (Woolley & Peters, 2020). It is out of the scope of this paper to determine if an absence of candidates like Oberstar led to a changing Democratic abortion posture, or if a changing party line discouraged conservative and moderate Democrats from running. However, while the direction of these causal arrows is not known, it is clear that Democrats' posture on abortion has moved considerably in the space of eight elections. Abortion is increasingly characterized as an absolute right, regardless of circumstances.

Two other features of Figure 4.3 are noteworthy. First, abortion was routinely framed as routine healthcare. In practice, these issue statements often appeared as part of a candidate's overall healthcare vision (i.e., single payer healthcare, affordable prescription drugs, and reproductive choice) rather than a women's issue per se. Second, the proportion of Democrats referring to the judiciary jumped substantially in 2022—a clear reaction to the *Dobbs* ruling.

Taken together, Figures 4.1–4.3 provide evidence consistent with the notion that abortion is becoming an "owned issue." However, the extant literature also suggests that two candidate-level factors—incumbency and gender—could impact the candidate's rhetorical calculus. To adjudicate between these competing factors, candidates' theta scores are regressed on a dummy variable for incumbency (1 = incumbent), a dummy variable for candidate gender (1 = female), and a dummy variable for 2022, since the evidence presented earlier points to year-specific effects (1 = 2022). Because examining three variables across eight models can be cumbersome to look at, Figure 4.4 summarizes the results as a coefficient plot. Positive values (dots on the right side of the figure) indicate a positive relationship between the variable and the frame, while negative values (dots on the left side of the figure) represent negative relationships. When the error band crosses zero, the relationship is not statistically significant.

Several things about Figure 4.4 stand out. First, Democrats were more responsive to the changed 2022 environment than Republicans. While 2022 Republicans were more likely to use "unborn rights" framing and less likely to use "morality" framing, these differences were substantively small. By contrast,

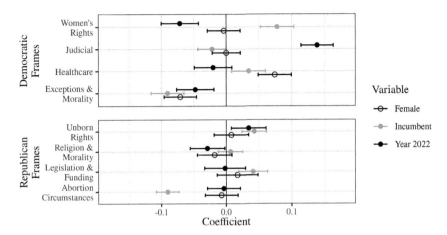

FIGURE 4.4  Predicting Candidates' Abortion Framing.

Democrats significantly increased the proportion of time spent talking about the Supreme Court at the expense of the other frames. Rather than framing abortion about healthcare or rights, abortion in 2022 was about the levers of power. This, coupled with the increase in abortion priming from Figure 4.1, points to a Democratic full court press on abortion: talk about abortion a lot, and frame the issue through the lens of a reckless Supreme Court.

The data support the expectation of gender differences, but only for Democrats. Democratic women were more likely to adopt the alternative "healthcare" frame, deviating from the prevailing "women's rights" frame. Democratic women were less likely to use the "moderate" strategy of framing abortion in terms of exceptions or personal morality. While not a focus of this study, women were not significantly more or less likely to reference advocacy groups. As Lawless and Pearson (2008) noted, women tend to attract more primary challengers. It is plausible that female Democrats were staking out fewer "compromising" positions to defend against a challenge from the left. It is puzzling that this same dynamic was not present for Republican women, even though they face the same primary challenge problem. It is possible that, for Republican women, abortion is simply not an issue used to fend off challenges. Schneider and Bos (2016) argued that female Republicans have unique opportunities to present themselves as "family values" candidates, so it is possible that this is a missed opportunity to deploy an alternative frame.

Incumbents of both parties also behaved largely as predicted. Following Druckman, Kefir, and Parkin (2009), the expectation is that incumbents are risk-averse (having already built winning coalitions in their districts) and are likely to adopt the "prevailing" frames used by their party. Consistent with this expectation, incumbents of both parties adopted the prevailing frame—"unborn rights" for Republicans and "women's rights" for Democrats. Incumbents of both parties also avoided the risky "expectations" or "circumstances" frame. Strategically, avoiding compromising language on abortion should help incumbents deter potential primary challengers (Parsneau & Chapp, 2017). Republican incumbents were also more likely to frame abortion in terms of concrete legislation, which makes sense given that incumbents were more likely to have sponsored actual bills. Finally, Democratic incumbents were more likely to deploy the healthcare frame. This finding—incumbents using an alternative frame—was not predicted. Speculatively, this signals a possible sea change in prevailing Democratic abortion rhetoric.

## Conclusions

This research supports several conclusions about the 2022 campaign environment. The *Dobbs* decision did nothing to quiet the abortion debate in the U.S. Particularly for Democrats, abortion is increasingly a centerpiece of congressional campaigns. Moreover, while Republicans typically use abortion as a base strategy, for Democrats abortion is a strategy used in competitive races. This rhetorical pattern is broadly consistent with the notion that abortion is becoming a Democratic-owned issue. To be clear, public opinion scholars do not think of abortion as a "consensus issue." In fact, abortion is typically thought of as the quintessential non-consensus policy, such that taking a stance will always have some sort of political cost (Egan, 2013). Despite these costs, Democratic House candidates went "all in" on this strategy in 2022, a sign of what campaigning may come to look like in a polarized era. Should this pattern continue, some revision of the conventional wisdom around abortion politics may be in order. Notably, this trend was underway before Dobbs, even though the Dobbs decision likely amplified this change.

In addition to an increased willingness to take on hot-button issues in swing districts, both parties are increasingly engaged in non-consensus message framing. Candidates of both parties are less likely to acknowledge "exceptions" to abortion or distinguish between their own personal morality and the law. This has important implications for social cleavages in the electorate at large. Goren and Chapp (2017) suggest that polarized abortion positions can drive patterns of partisan switching and religious realignment. The polarized and widespread abortion campaigning documented in this chapter, coupled with the dynamics documented by Goren and Chapp (2017), suggests that the 2022 elections have likely deepened social and political fissures. These changes in abortion framing are strategic. The evidence supports the theoretical framework that candidate rhetoric is guided by risk evaluations (Druckman et al., 2009). Particularly for

Democrats, 2022 campaigning represented a departure from previous messaging efforts, with a focused message on the role of the courts and abortion access.

It is important to discuss two significant limitations to this chapter. First, websites are just one source of political communication, and are unlikely to be regularly visited by most members of the general public. Rather, websites are most often visited by partisan activists, voters intending to donate, and journalists covering the campaign. This said, research suggests that websites are good indicators of the overall rhetorical thrust of a campaign (Druckman et al., 2009). For this reason, while it is unlikely that the text in our dataset had a direct impact on many voters, it remains a good proxy for broader campaign dynamics.

Secondly, STM use a large corpus of text to extract a small number of topics, thus sacrificing some nuance for greater interpretability. Take, for example, the use of the phrase "reproductive freedom." This phrase gained popularity among Democratic candidates in a post-Dobbs campaign environment—it was used by forty-seven Democrats in 2022. Comparatively, in 2008 the phrase was used only eight times. Why wasn't this novel framing detected by the topic models? The answer is that across the entire corpus, the phrase was still uncommon. STM is designed to identify the frames that are most common across an entire dataset. Missing these nuanced changes is a significant methodological limitation. Interestingly, Democratic candidates who used the phrase "reproductive freedom" also tended to score high on the emerging "judicial" topic that spiked in 2022, suggesting that women's reproductive freedom is increasingly rhetorically linked to a legal/institutional framework. Exploring this linkage is an important direction for future research.

Prior to the election, pundits and strategists disagreed substantially on how campaigns should address abortion in a post-*Roe* environment. While the data do not permit speculation on the efficacy of different strategies, the evidence does highlight how campaign decisions played out in real time. Although abortion attitudes are deeply held and some of the most stable fixtures in American public opinion (Goren & Chapp, 2017), the Dobbs decision altered the information environment around abortion, and in turn altered the risk calculus encountered by candidates. Campaigns will continue to experiment with message strategies that resonate with voters for the foreseeable future.

## References

Ainsworth, S. H., & Hall T. E. (2011). *Abortion politics in Congress: Strategic incrementalism and policy change.* Cambridge University Press.

Alexander, D., & Andersen, K. (1993). Gender as a factor in the attribution of leadership traits. *Political Research Quarterly, 46*(3), 527–545. https://doi.org/10.1177/1065912 99304600305

## 88 Media Messages in the 2022 Midterm Election

American National Election Study. (2022, December 14). *ANES 2022 pilot study.* https://electionstudies.org/data-center/2022-pilot-study/

Ansolabehere, S., & Iyengar, S. (1994). Riding the wave and claiming ownership over issues: The joint effects of advertising and news coverage in campaigns. *The Public Opinion Quarterly, 58*(3), 335–357. https://doi.org/10.1086/269431

Benoit, K., Watanabe, K., Wang, H., Nulty, P., Obeng, A., Müller, S., & Matsuo, A. (2018). "quanteda: An R package for the quantitative analysis of textual data." *Journal of Open Source Software, 3*(30), Article 774. https://doi.org/10.21105/joss.00774

Brady, D., Hahrie, H., & Pope, J. (2011). Primary elections and candidate ideology: Out of step with the primary electorate? *Legislative Studies Quarterly, 32*(1), 79–105. https://doi.org/10.3162/036298007X201994

Center for American Women and Politics. (2022). *Congress.* Rutgers Eagleton Institute of Politics. https://womenrun.rutgers.edu/2022-report/congress/

Chapp, C., Roback, P., Johnson-Tesch, K., Rossing, A., & Werner, J. (2019). Going vague: Ambiguity and avoidance in online political messaging. *Social Science Computer Review, 37*(5), 591–610. https://doi.org/10.1177/0894439318791168

Chong, D., & Druckman, J. N. (2007). Framing public opinion in competitive democracies. *The American Political Science Review, 101*(4), 637–655. https://doi.org/10.1017/S0003055407070554

Dancey, L., & Goren, P. (2010). Party identification, issue attitudes, and the dynamics of political debate. *American Journal of Political Science, 54*(3), 686–699. https://doi.org/10.1111/j.1540-5907.2010.00454.x

Druckman, J. N. (2004). Political preference formation: Competition, deliberation, and the (ir)relevance of framing effects. *The American Political Science Review, 98*(4), 671–686. https://doi.org/10.1017/S0003055404041413

Druckman, J. N., Jacobs, L. R., & Ostermeier, E. (2004). Candidate strategies to prime issues and image. *Journal of Politics, 66*(4), 1180–1202. https://doi.org/10.1111/j.0022-3816.2004.00295.x

Druckman, J. N., Kefir, M. J., & Parkin, M. (2009). Campaign communications in U.S. congressional elections. *American Political Science Review, 103*(2), 343–366. https://doi.org/10.1017/S0003055409990037

Druckman, J. N., Kefir M. J, & Parkin, M. (2020). Campaign rhetoric and the incumbency advantage. *American Politics Research, 48*(1), 22–43. https://doi.org/10.1177/1532673X18822314

Egan, P. (2013). *Partisan priorities: How issue ownership drives and distorts American politics.* Cambridge University Press.

Gamson, M., & Modigliani, A. (1989). Media discourse and public opinion on nuclear power: A constructivist approach. *American Journal of Sociology, 95*(1), 1–37. https://doi.org/10.1086/229213

Goren, P., & Chapp, C. (2017). Moral power: How public opinion on culture war issues shapes partisan predispositions and religious orientations. *American Political Science Review, 111*(1), 110–128. https://doi.org/10.1017/S0003055416000435

Grimmer, J., Roberts, M. E., & Stewart, B. M. (2022). *Text as data: A new framework for machine learning and the social sciences.* Princeton University Press.

Guntermann, E., & Lenz, G. (2022). Still not important enough? COVID-19 policy views and vote choice. *Perspectives on Politics, 20*(2), 547–561. https://doi.org/10.1017/S1537592721001997

Jaenicke, D., W. (2002). Abortion and partisanship in the US Congress, 1976–2000: Increasing partisan cohesion and differentiation. *Journal of American Studies, 36*(1), 1–22. https://doi.org/10.1017/S0021875802006758

KAConsulting, The Tarrance Group, & Republican National Committee. (2022, September 13). *2022 research – abortion.* https://thehill.com/wp-content/uploads/sites/2/2022/09/RNC-Data-Issue-Memo.pdf

Klar, S., Robison, J., & Druckman, J. N. (2013). Political dynamics of framing. In T. N. Ridout (Ed.), *New directions in media and politics* (pp. 191–210). Routledge.

Koleva, S. P., Graham, J., Iyer, R., Ditto, P. H., & Haidt, J. (2012). Tracing the threads: How five moral concerns (especially purity) help explain culture war attitudes. *Journal of Research in Personality, 46*(2), 184–194. https://doi.org/10.1016/j.jrp.2012.01.006

Lawless, J., & Pearson K. (2008). The primary reason for women's underrepresentation? Reevaluating the conventional wisdom. *The Journal of Politics, 70*(1), 67–82. https://doi.org/10.1017/S002238160708005X

Library of Congress. (n.d.). *United States elections web archive.* www.loc.gov/collections/ united-states-elections-web-archive/about-this-collection/

Linskey, A., & Shepard, K. (2022, August 3). Democrats emboldened after Kansas abortion vote, as they eye fall campaign. *The Washington Post.* www.washingtonpost.com/ politics/2022/08/03/democrats-abortion-midterms-kansas/

Lowe, P., & Page, S., J. (2019). Rights-based claims made by UK anti-abortion activists. *Health and Human Rights, 21*(2), 133–144. www.jstor.org/stable/26915383

Luker, K. (1984). *Abortion and the politics of motherhood.* University of California Press.

Mansbridge, J. (2003). Rethinking representation. *The American Political Science Review, 97*(4), 515–528. https://doi.org/10.1017/S0003055403000856

Mayhew, D. R. (1976). *Congress: The electoral connection.* Yale University Press.

Messerly, M., & Ollstein, A. M. (2022, October 18). Anti-abortion groups: It's time for Republicans to stop avoiding the issue. *Politico.* www.politico.com/news/2022/10/18/anti-abortion-groups-gop-midterms-00062182

Nelson, T., & Oxley, Z. (1999). Issue framing effects on belief importance and opinion. *Journal of Politics, 61*(4), 1040–1067. https://doi.org/10.2307/2647553

North, A. (2019, October 18). How the abortion debate moved away from "safe, legal, and rare." *Vox.* www.vox.com/2019/10/18/20917406/abortion-safe-legal-and-rare-tulsi-gabbard

Oberlin College & Northwestern University. (n.d.). Congressional candidate website project. *Archive-It.* https://archive-it.org/organizations/316?fc=meta_Collector%3AOberlin+College+%26+Northwestern+University&totalResultCount=6&sort=f_collectionName.desc

Parsneau, K., & Chapp, C. (2017). Partisan extremity in the 2014 midterm elections: How primaries and incumbency influence polarized position-Taking on campaign websites. In T. S. Sisco, J. C. Lucas, & C. J. Galdieri (Eds.), *Political communication and strategy: Consequences of the 2014 midterm elections* (pp. 175–186). University of Akron Press.

Peoples, S. (2022, October 9). Nevada Senate race tests potency of abortion focus for Dems. *AP News.* https://apnews.com/article/abortion-2022-midterm-elections-inflation- crime-nevada-7f2356f8d2be07e61389d70c6001e696

Petrocik, J. (1996). Issue ownership in presidential elections, with a 1980 case study. *American Journal of Political Science, 40*(3), 825–50. https://doi.org/10.2307/2111797

*Pew Research Center*. (2022, July 6). Majority of public disapproves of Supreme Court's decision to overturn Roe v. Wade. www.pewresearch.org/politics/2022/07/06/majority-of-public-disapproves-of-supreme-courts-decision-to-overturn-roe-v-wade/

Sanbonmatsu, K. (2002). Gender stereotypes and vote choice. *American Journal of Political Science, 46*(1), 20–34. https://doi.org/10.2307/3088412

Saurette, P., & Gordon, K. (2013). Arguing abortion: The new anti-abortion discourse in Canada. *Canadian Journal of Political Science, 46*(1), 157–185. https://doi.org/10.1017/S0008423913000176

Schneider, M. (2014a). The effects of gender-bending on candidate evaluations. *Journal of Women, Politics & Policy, 35*(1), 55–77. https://doi.org/10.1080/1554477X.2014.863697

Schneider, M. (2014b). Gender-based strategies on candidate websites. *Journal of Political Marketing, 13*(4), 264–290. https://doi.org/10.1080/15377857.2014.958373

Schneider, M. C., & Bos, A. L. (2016) The interplay of candidate party and gender in evaluations of political candidates. *Journal of Women, Politics & Policy, 37*(3), 274–94. https://doi.org/10.1080/1554477X.2016.1188598

Shear, M. D. (2022, August 7). Biden is an uneasy champion on abortion. Can he lead the fight in post-Roe America? *The New York Times*. www.nytimes.com/2022/08/07/us/politics/biden-abortion-catholic-history.html

Smith, A., & Caputo, M. (2022, August 25). *In Arizona, Blake Masters backtracks on abortion and scrubs his campaign website. NBC News*. www.nbcnews.com/politics/2022-election/arizona-blake-masters-backtracks-abortion-scrubs-campaign-website-rcna44808

Sniderman, P. M., & Theriault, S. M. (2004). The structure of political argument and the logic of issue framing. In W. E. Saris, & P. M. Sniderman (Eds.), *Studies in public opinion: Attitudes, nonattitudes, measurement error, and change* (pp. 133–165). Princeton University Press.

Vavreck, L. (2009). *The message matters: The economy and presidential campaigns*. Princeton University Press.

Wedeking, J. (2010). Supreme Court litigants and strategic framing. *American Journal of Political Science, 54*(3), 617–631. https://doi.org/10.1111/j.1540-5907.2010.00450.x

Woolley, J. T., & Peters, F. (2020) *American Presidency Project*. [Web.] Retrieved from www.presidency.ucsb.edu

Zaller, J. R. (1992). *The nature and origins of mass opinion*. Cambridge University Press.

# 5

# WINNING STORIES AMID PARTISANSHIP

## Narratives in Political Advertisements and Overperforming Candidates in the 2022 U.S. Midterm Election

*B. Theo Mazumdar*

The 2022 U.S. midterm election was notable for confounding expectations. Many observers had predicted a Republican "red wave." Conventional wisdom held that President Biden's stubbornly low approval ratings, a well-documented historical precedent of the president's party losing seats in midterm elections (e.g., Zeidenstein, 1972), and an economic outlook sullied by persistent inflation would deliver a strong Republican plurality in the House of Representatives and the retaking of the majority in the Senate. This red wave did not materialize. Republicans won only a small majority in the House of Representatives and the Democrats held control of the Senate, ultimately gaining a seat and bolstering their majority.

Yet, the 2022 midterm election is also worthy of attention for the candidates who surpassed expectations. For example, in competitive House districts in states like New York, Michigan, Washington, and Florida, candidates of both major parties notched impressive wins. Some of these victors outperformed an existing district partisan lean in their favor; others won despite a partisan lean that advantaged their opponents. What accounts for such strong performances in competitive districts? One approach that can contribute to explicating these winning campaigns conceptualizes their political advertisements as narratives. Political advertisements are powerful weapons in contemporary electoral campaigns (Shen et al., 2023; Vafeiadis et al., 2018). Political advertisements have the capacity to motivate and persuade voters by appealing to emotion (Brader, 2005). Political ads also do the work of informing voters about candidate issue positions (Patterson & McClure, 1976; Vafeiadis et al., 2018; Zhao & Bleske, 1995), allow candidates to build their desired images (Johnston & Kaid, 2002)

DOI: 10.4324/9781003440833-7

**92** Media Messages in the 2022 Midterm Election

and may function as potent attacks that place foes on the defensive (Vesnic-Alujevic & Van Bauwel, 2014).

Narrative is a core but often overlooked component of political advertisements. Culturally shared narratives are central to identify formation and meaning-making at both the individual and collective levels (Shanahan et al., 2014). Narratives deployed strategically by political actors are believed to have several important capabilities, including the crucial capacity to persuade audiences (Groth, 2019). Unsurprisingly, much political information is disseminated in narrative form (Hinyard & Kreuter, 2007; McLaughlin et al., 2019; Polletta, 2015; Poletta & Callahan, 2017). Indeed, public adoption of a campaign's constructed narratives has been construed as the primary goal of a campaign for elective office (Kreiss, 2012). From this perspective, compelling narratives in formats such as advertising are the very key to winning political campaign messaging (Kreiss, 2012).

A body of research has explored the underlying mechanisms by which narratives in political advertisements influence viewers. Narratives may, for example, be cognitively processed in a unique manner stemming from the presence of emotion (Shen et al., 2023). Narratives may also result in audience transportation into the story world and subsequent persuasive effects (Green, 2004). Narratives may furthermore engender audience empathy, visualization, and reduced counterarguing (McLaughlin et al., 2019; Shen et al., 2023).

However, very little attention has been paid to identifying and analyzing the plotted stories that are disseminated in political advertisements. This chapter addresses this gap, and in so doing seeks to make two contributions. First, the analysis helps to elucidate the 2022 U.S. midterm elections and their results. Second, this study is among the first to foreground, in relation to political advertisements, the qualitative analysis of narrative approach that befits a narrative ontology (cf., Groth, 2019). More specifically, the video advertisements of 17 victorious, overperforming candidates for the House of Representatives in the 2022 midterm elections are analyzed. Overperforming candidates, following the data analysis site FiveThirtyEight.com (Best et al., 2022), were winning Republican and Democratic candidates who outperformed the extant partisan lean in their competitive districts. The video ads posted to the candidates' YouTube channels (but also aired on TV) in the calendar year 2022 until Election Day are included in the study. Qualitative narrative analysis of the strategically constructed narratives allows for the discernment of the key or main stories disseminated by the victors. These are comprised of sub-narratives, each of which is also identified, along with their goals, plots and main characters. The study furthermore permits identification of the prominent emotions embedded in the video political advertisement narratives.

The chapter proceeds with a literature review of political advertisements, of narratives of the political, and of narratives in political advertisements specifically. The study methodology is then described, after which the results and analyses of narratives are presented. The chapter concludes with a discussion of the utility of narrative approaches to political advertisements as a lens through which to view both the 2022 midterm election and campaign messaging strategy more broadly.

## Literature Review

### Political Advertisements

Political advertisements serve a range of functions on behalf of contemporary candidates for elective office. Political ads allow unknown or lesser-known candidates to gain name recognition and connect themselves to target audiences (Vesnic-Alujevic & Van Bauwel, 2014). Political advertising may also enable candidates to attract new voters, raise money, and serve as an effective vehicle by which to attack opposing candidates (Vesnic-Alujevic & Van Bauwel, 2014). The provision of information is also a function of political advertisements. Such information-rich ads allow candidates to define their images or explain issues and their positions relative to those issues (Johnston & Kaid, 2022). Political advertisements may be central to congressional races in particular. Congressional races feature smaller constituencies, less available information about the candidates, and lower voter turnout, in comparison to presidential elections (Brazeal & Benoit, 2001).

Early scholarship maintained that both the media, generally, and political advertising, in particular, have minimal effects on voter behavior (Brader, 2005; Granato & Wong, 2004, Lazarsfeld et al., 1944). However, in recent decades an emergent scholarly consensus holds that political campaigns and political communication formats like advertising do influence individual voting behavior and election outcomes (Granato & Wong, 2004). Meta-analytic research of political advertising scholarship finds that this influence occurs primarily by shaping voters' preferences, likelihood of voting, and vote choice (Benoit et al., 2007).

A robust body of literature has investigated the manner in which certain messaging strategies in political advertisements elicit effects (Shen et al., 2023). Many of these studies focus on the consequences of negative political advertisements and their influence on voter turnout (Brader, 2005; Lau et al., 2007). Other messaging strategies like the presence of character-based ads versus issue-based ads (Dardis et al., 2008) and the dissemination and reception of like-minded (opinion-congruent) political advertising instead of cross-cutting (opinion-incongruent) political advertising (Matthes & Marquart, 2015) have also received attention. Limited scholarship has additionally investigated the use of emotion—particularly enthusiasm appeals and fear appeals—by which to motivate and persuade voters through political advertisements (e.g., Brader, 2005; Van Steenburg, 2015).

With regard to video political advertisements in particular, the preeminence of image ads is a central concern (Johnston & Kaid, 2002; Vesnic-Alujevic & Van Bauwel, 2014). Thirty-second commercials have become commonplace, and research has shown them to be as effective as longer advertisements (Denton et al., 2024). This truncated format may not leave room for issue positioning; therefore, image construction advertisements, which stress the candidate's character and personal qualities and are articulated though a clear representational identity, may be gaining prominence (Johnston & Kaid, 2002; Vesnic-Alujevic & Van Bauwel, 2014). Political advertisements have been found to have three basic functions, though scholars sometimes use varying terminology: acclaim, attack, and defend (Benoit, 1999; Vesnic-Alujevic & Van Bauwel, 2014). Acclaim advertisements bolster the candidate's own qualities. Attack ads diminish the opponent's qualities. Finally, defense ads are reactions to an opponent's attacks.

Political advertisements proliferate in contemporary U.S. political campaigning. Franz et al. (2023) report the advertising spending on traditional media (broadcast TV, cable TV, satellite TV, and radio) in the 2022 midterm election cycle. The 2022 midterm elections set a record for ad volume in any election cycle with 4.8 million total broadcast television ad airings across gubernatorial, Senate, and House of Representatives races. With regard to House races, 1.41 million television ads aired on broadcast stations, compared to 1.37 million airings in the 2020 election cycle and 1.32 million airings in the 2018 midterm cycle. The 1.58 million advertisement airings in Senate races, while falling short of a record for any election cycle, did establish a record for a midterm election and was a marked increase from the 1.33 million Senate ad airings in 2018, the previous midterm election cycle. Three quarters ($3.2 billion) of the $4.3 billion spent on ads for traditional media were spent on broadcast television, while one-fifth ($866 million) was spent on cable television. The influence of outside groups—organizations not officially affiliated with the campaigns—grew. Such groups were responsible for about 35% of all ads in House races and 40% of those in Senate races, both record highs.

Fowler et al. (2023) document the candidate-sponsored digital advertising spending in the 2022 midterm election cycle, with a focus on the available metrics provided by Meta (Facebook and Instagram) and Google (YouTube and search-related ads). Nearly $150 million was spent on Senate and House of Representatives election cycle digital advertising. Sixty percent of this digital ad spending was in Senate races. Fowler et al. (2023) identify three broad patterns in the data. First, a few candidates accounted for the vast majority of the digital ad spending, while most candidates spent little, and in many cases, nothing. Second, Senate candidates spent more on YouTube and search-related ads, while

House of Representatives candidates emphasized Instagram and Facebook. Finally, Google's share of the advertising spending increased compared to 2020, possibly cutting into Meta's share of the market (Fowler et al., 2023).

Together, these data indicate that campaigns and their aligned outside groups are not abandoning traditional broadcast television advertising for online social media, despite claims to the contrary that note the steady decline in live television broadcast viewership over the last decade (Franz et al., 2023).

### Narratives, Narratives of the Political, and Narratives in Political Advertisements

Political information is often disseminated in narrative form (Hinyard & Kreuter, 2007; McLaughlin et al., 2019; Polletta, 2015; Poletta & Callahan, 2017). Scholars have thus devoted considerable attention to the role of narratives in politics. A narrative is fundamentally a story, an instance of discourse. Polkinghorne (1995) described the components of stories: characters, a plot, and a delimited temporal period whose time sequence need not be linear (e.g., beginning, middle and end). The plot—a "type of conceptual scheme by which a contextual meaning of individual events can be displayed"—draws together events and actions into an organized whole (p. 7). Plots delineate a segment in time in which events are conjoined as contributors to a particular outcome. Stories, then, involve human attempts to progress to a clarification, solution, or unraveling of some incomplete solution (Polkinghorne, 1995). Stories often invoke numerous events, actors, and places; narratives can thus be viewed as comprised of various sub-narratives which contribute to a larger narrative (Manners & Murray, 2016; Tekin & Meissner, 2022).

The concept of narrative has received multi-disciplinary focus from scholars since the 1980s (Fisher, 1987; Patterson & Monroe, 1998; Spence, 1984; White, 1981). Groth (2019) explained that this "narrative turn" in the humanities and social sciences was a rejection of positivist approaches holding that the social world can be objectively observed and analyzed. Instead, scholars began to explore the manner in which perceptions of the world are mediated subjectively through stories; the modalities by which narratives are transmitted; the effects of such narratives; and the relationships between differentiated narratives. Fisher (1987) argued that humans are primarily storytelling beings and that all meaningful human communication is most usefully interpreted as narratives. Culturally shared narratives reflect who we are: they are fundamental expressions of human experiences, of values, and of individual and group identities (Shanahan et al., 2014). Narratives also shape who we are, since culturally shared compelling narratives influence our preferences and beliefs (Shanahan et al., 2014). Narratives are fundamentally vivid and emotionally involving, which can make them memorable and enhance the likelihood that audiences will accept

**96** Media Messages in the 2022 Midterm Election

the messages inherent to the narrative (Appel & Richter, 2007; Green & Brock, 2005). Stories thus do important work at both the individual and collective levels with regard to influence, meaning-making and identity-formation. Put simply, it is often through narrative that humans make sense of, and find meaning in, the world around them.

### Narratives of the Political

Narratives of the political—often referred to as "political narratives"—can be defined as "stories about sociopolitical issues, which exist within an imagined community where the actions of political actors and/or the outcomes of political events have important causal effects" (McLaughlin & Velez, 2019, p. 22). They contain a range of archetypes like dramatic binaries of heroes and villains, which generate public interest in the drama, since conflict and suspense often capture the public's interest rather than substantive discussions of political policies and issues (Anker, 2005; Coe et al., 2004; Iyengar et al., 2004; McLaughlin & Velez, 2019). Narratives of the political are disseminated by many different sources. These include politicians, journalists, and given participatory culture, digital media users. They are delivered through various offline (e.g., TV) and Internet-based media (e.g., Twitter, now X and YouTube), set in various contexts (e.g., national, state, or local elections) and concentrate on a range of topics (McLaughlin & Velez, 2019).

According to Groth (2019), narratives of the political have several important capacities. They can shape worldviews and play an important role in the construction of social realties, of political ideologies, and of political systems. Narratives of the political may furthermore address risk and future possibilities and may help people understand political processes. This latter explanatory capacity is central to parsing the influence of political narratives. Such narratives can help distill political value systems and complex political processes into easily comprehensible stories. These stories, for example, create divisions between righteous political actors and corrupt opponents who are responsible for evil and wrong in society. This explanatory dimension in turn creates orientation and order: those audience members who are part and parcel of this evil and wrong, contrasted by those who have the wherewithal to see through the rank corruption and conspiracy. Through this order, narratives of the political may validate or reinforce worldviews and conceptions of the political system. As Groth (2019) observes, the story of an establishment swamp that needs to or can only be drained by political outsiders, for example, has been a powerful means by which to explain the populist worldview of "us" (a righteous and genuine public) versus "them" (members of a corrupt out-group). Narratives of the political may additionally spur audiences to imagine how an election will affect them personally (Jamieson, 1996) and even prompt individuals to see themselves as important actors within the story (McLaughlin et al., 2017).

Certain narratives of the political not only have ordering and explanatory powers, but also the performative capacity to motivate and organize collective action (Groth, 2019; Mayer, 2014). These stories have the resilience to endure in the increasingly digitally-mediated public sphere; they may motivate receptive audiences to share content, add details to it, and to organize in attempt to gain advantage from further dissemination of the narrative (Groth, 2019). This was the case with regard to the many far-right groups whose online discourses invoked the narrative of a stolen U.S. election in 2020—groups who ultimately converged on and violently breached the U.S. Capitol in the domestic terror attack of January 6, 2021.

### Narratives as Political Strategy

Narratives of the political may be used as strategy, deployed intuitively or intentionally in formats like political advertisements to advance relatively specific goals (Groth, 2019). According to Tekin and Meissner (2022), strategic narratives can be understood as constructs of reality resulting from various sub-narratives and two primary elements, plot and goal. The plot is determined by space, or where the political actor constructing the narrative is situated geographically and institutionally; by time, or when the story unfolds; and by relationality, or how the political actor stands relative to the audience. The goal delineates the objective toward which the constructed narrative is aimed. Thus, political actors often position themselves narratively as protagonists uniquely equipped to defeat an imminent threat (McLaughlin & Velez, 2019). In the case of a candidate for elective office, there is a related goal of vanquishing an unqualified opponent for the betterment of the relevant society. Strategic narratives of the political may be found in shared communicative spaces like those facilitated by socially oriented digital media (Groth, 2019). They may also appear in discourses ranging from domestic politics to foreign affairs and international relations (Groth, 2019; Roselle et al., 2014). Strategic narratives of the political do not always need to be enumerated in full. References to culturally shared and socially available stories may evoke political framings and signal policy positions, obviating the need to tell the whole story (Groth, 2019).

Narratives deployed strategically by political actors are believed to have the ability to persuade audiences, to mediate messages and political stances, and to sell policy positions (Groth, 2019). They may also help to achieve public support broadly and to position potent "metanarratives" such as conservatism, liberalism or socialism (Lyotard, 1984). As Groth (2019) describes, these capacities are reflected culturally in the phrase "controlling the narrative." Conventional wisdom holds that stories told at the right time, in the right way, stressing the appropriate aspects and geared toward the appropriate audiences are effective politically and can be used to frame political positions as preferable. With regard to emotion-based appeals like fear and enthusiasm, politicians use cues like words, images or sounds to craft emotional appeals and help "unleash" the desired emotional response in audiences (Brader, 2005, p. 390).) Strategic narrative messaging may also help control the news cycle and harm opponents by proffering a contrasting worldview or forcing these rivals to mount a defense against accusations (Groth, 2019).

### Narratives in Political Advertisements

A limited body of research has investigated narratives in political advertisements, specifically. Many of these are quantitative studies focused on the mechanisms undergirding their persuasive effects. These include the concepts of narrative transportation, which occurs when the mental capacities and systems of a narrative audience or reader become focused on the events taking place in the political narrative (Green & Brock, 2000; McLaughlin & Valez, 2019); visualization, or the process of "cognitively stimulating future political scenarios and imagining the potential effects of these scenarios" (McLaughlin et al., 2019, p. 761); empathy—sharing another person's thoughts and feelings (Campbell & Babrow, 2004)—which may drive audience involvement with characters in a narrative (Shen et al., 2023); and reduced counterarguing, since story-involved readers or audiences may be less motivated to counterargue and thus more susceptible to influence (Bilandzic & Busselle, 2013; Shen et al., 2023).

Few studies have concentrated on the narratives themselves that are disseminated in political advertising. For example, Vafeiadis et al. (2018) content analyzed the narrative characteristics contained in TV and online advertisements of gubernatorial and senatorial candidates in the U.S. 2014 midterm elections. These authors identified three narrative types in the advertisements. Voter stories were fully formed narratives, with coherent issue-based storylines featuring protagonists, plots, and resolutions. Testimonials were abbreviated ads that are similar to anecdotes and contain the presentation of characters and evidence, without delving into coherent plots that might be featured in longer narratives. Finally, autobiographical ads were the candidates' personal accounts of their life stories and include such information as upbringing, education, and professional experience. Statistically significant relationships were observed between winning candidates and the presence of autobiographical ads, including those that featured family members in the ads, and between losing candidates and the presence of negative attack ads and anonymous ad announcers.

Surprisingly, very few studies have employed narrative inquiry to investigate qualitatively the particular stories (e.g., their unique characters and plots) that are deployed in political advertisements. For instance, Bartlett and Rayner (2014) employed the framework of public narratives to analyze the campaign materials disseminated by the various branches of the Australian Labor Party and the Liberal Party of Australia in federal and state electoral campaigning from 2004 to 2013. This framework conceptualizes public stories as a device that allows groups, agencies, and institutions to provide an external account of themselves and provide a basis for shared understanding. The Australian campaign narratives were thus examined for plot (involving the main characters and key focal points); for drama (involving what is at stake); for explanation (involving how the events are organized and how causality is attributed); and for selective appropriation (involving the frames or symbols that are utilized). Bartlett and Rayner (2014) found that just six narratives achieved a dominant presence in the campaign materials across nine years: "new hope," "time's up," "job isn't done," "experience vs. inexperience," "we've listened and learned," and "fear" (pp. 54–59). Bartlett and Rayner (2014) concluded that each story seemed to have a fitting place for use at different points in the election cycle. They also observed that none of the stories appeared to be associated with election wins for the party in question (though this matter warrants statistical correlation, not present in the study). These authors furthermore raised the interesting questions of whether the political actors and parties were consciously replicating previously used narratives, or whether they were unconsciously being influenced by past campaigns—and why.

Based on this previous research, this chapter has the goal of identifying and analyzing the narratives contained in the political advertisements of winning candidates in House of Representatives races in the 2022 U.S. midterm elections. Of particular interest are those candidates who overperformed by achieving notable victories in partisan yet competitive districts. In light of this goal and the preceding literature review, the following research questions are identified:

RQ1: What were the common strategically constructed main narratives and sub-narratives, and their narrative components (goals, plots, and characters) in the video advertisements of overperforming 2022 U.S. midterm House of Representatives candidates (those who achieved notable victories in partisan yet competitive districts)?

RQ2: What were the primary emotions embedded in the narrative video advertisements of overperforming 2022 U.S. midterm House of Representatives candidates?

## Method

The political advertisements selected for analysis were those of 17 overperforming, victorious Republican and Democratic candidates in competitive U.S. House of Representatives districts, as shown by the data site FiveThirtyEight.com (Best et al., 2022). Midterm election overperformance was the difference between each competitive House district's partisan lean (average margin difference between how a district votes and how the country votes overall) and the winning candidate's victory margin, as of November 18, 2022 (Best et al., 2022).

Candidate video advertisements were included if they were uploaded to YouTube anytime between January 1, 2022, and Election Day (November 8, 2022). These ads were either posted to the official YouTube channel of each candidate or to the candidate's campaign YouTube channel. Two candidate ads posted to Vimeo were also included. Only the ads that contained the proximate clause, "I'm candidate X, and I approve this message," were included. The presence of this clause signaled that the advertisement was not just posted to the candidate's YouTube channel, but also aired on television. Since 2002, election law has required candidates for federal office to include in television and radio ads a statement by the candidate that identifies the candidate and informs audiences that the candidate approves the communication (Jung & Critcher, 2018). Thus, the advertisement narratives included in the study were those that had been most widely viewed, appearing both on television and on YouTube.

The political advertisement scripts were first transcribed using YouTube's "show transcript" feature, then verified manually. The two Vimeo ads were transcribed manually. The ad transcripts were then imported to MAXQDA (https://www.maxqda.com), a qualitative research software. All coding was completed in MAXQDA. The unit of analysis was each individual video political advertisement script. In total, 65 ads were analyzed.

Four sets of analyses were performed, based in part on FiveThirtyEight.com's calculation of partisan lean and electoral performance, described above. The first analysis involved 22 videos posted to YouTube and two videos posted to Vimeo, by six winning Republican candidates who overperformed in Republican-leaning districts. The second analysis featured 11 videos posted to YouTube by four winning Republican candidates who overperformed in Democratic-leaning districts. The third analysis considered 25 videos posted to YouTube by five winning Democratic candidates who overperformed in Democratic-leaning districts. The fourth and final analysis involved five videos posted to YouTube by two winning Democratic candidates who overperformed in Republican-leaning districts. See Table 5.1 for the overperforming candidates, their district partisan leans and their victory margins. The other overperforming candidates listed by FiveThirtyEight.com (Best et al., 2022) did not upload to YouTube ads that were also featured on TV in the time period considered.

**TABLE 5.1** Overperforming Winning Candidates in the 2022 U.S. Midterm Election, by District Partisan Lean and Victory Margin

| Candidate | District Partisan Lean | Victory Margin |
|---|---|---|
| **Republican Candidates in Republican-Leaning Districts** | | |
| Carlos Gimenez (FL-28) | R+13 | +42% |
| Nicole Malliotakis (NY-11) | R+10.5 | +23.5% |
| Andrew Garbarino (NY-2) | R+6 | +22% |
| Laurel Lee (FL-15) | R+7.5 | +17.5% |
| Cory Mills (FL-7) | R+14 | +17.5% |
| Marc Molinaro (NY-19) | R+1 | +2.5% |
| **Republican Candidates in Democratic-Leaning Districts** | | |
| George Devolder-Santos (NY-3) | D+4.5 | +8.5% |
| Anthony D'Esposito (NY-4) | D+11 | +4% |
| Brandon Williams (NY-22) | D+2.5 | +1% |
| Mike Lawler (NY-17) | D+7.5 | +1% |
| **Democratic Candidates in Democratic-Leaning Districts** | | |
| Haley Stevens (MI-11) | D+15 | +23% |
| Chrissy Houlahan (PA-06) | D+9 | +17% |
| Marilyn Strickland (WA-10) | D+12 | +14% |
| Hillary Scholten (MI-3) | D+3 | +13% |
| Kim Schrier (WA-8) | D+2 | +7% |
| **Democratic Candidates in Republican-Leaning Districts** | | |
| Marie Gluesenkamp Pérez (WA-3) | R+9 | +2% |
| Yadira Caraveo (CO-8) | R+3 | +1% |

The qualitative analysis of narrative methodology was employed. This approach gathers stories as data (the individual ads) and employs analytic procedures to produce categories and taxonomies from the common narrative elements (Polkinghorne, 1995). This process is similar to qualitative thematic analysis and therefore consistent with inductive approaches to theory-building (Naeem et al., 2023). Thematic analysis entails identifying and reporting patterns in a data set, which are subsequently interpreted for their inherent meaning (Braun & Clarke, 2006; Naeem et al., 2023). In narrative analysis, the focus is to interpret the "themes" or elements for their narrative contribution. Tekin and Meissner's (2022) operationalization of the concept of constructed narrative was employed. Five steps were followed, adapted from Naeem et al. (2023), in order to limit bias, enhance rigor and achieve thoroughness: 1) transcription

**102** Media Messages in the 2022 Midterm Election

and familiarization with data; 2) inductive and open coding, resulting in the initial codes and the primary characters featured in the stories; 3) narrative "theme" development through axial coding, resulting in the sub-narratives, goals (operationalized here as the strategic intention behind the sub-narratives) and plots; 4) narrative conceptualization through interpretation; and 5) development of the conceptual model in the form of the main narratives.

## Results and Discussion

With regard to the advertisements of the six winning Republican candidates who overperformed in Republican-leaning districts, two key narratives were identified: *America is under existential threat* and *fighting for you* (see Table 5.2). The former establishes the stakes if the opponent and other Democrats win: the destruction of the country you know and love. It paints a dystopian portrait of

TABLE 5.2 Analysis of Narratives: Winning 2022 Republican Candidates Who Overperformed in Republican-Leaning Districts

| Key Narrative | Sub-narrative | Goal | Plot | Characters |
|---|---|---|---|---|
| **America is under existential threat** | *The America you knew is no longer recognizable* | Sets the stakes, emphasizes that, and how, Democratic policies are ruining America | The Democrats are destroying the America you knew through their policies on the economy, crime and immigration. | Biden, opponent, candidate, cops, criminals, Nancy Pelosi, families |
| | *The American Dream is threatened* | Establish Democrats as the destroyers of the American Dream | Our kids' ability to obtain the American Dream is being destroyed by Democrats through censorship, debt and an oppressive economy. | Candidate, opponent, Democrats, kids, grandkids |
| | *The Democrats are subverting America* | Disqualify Democrats based on morality and ethics | Democrats are willfully and maliciously subverting American freedoms, to your detriment | Opponent, President Biden, cops, middle class families |

Winning Stories Amid Partisanship **103**

**TABLE 5.2** (Continued)

| Key Narrative | Sub-narrative | Goal | Plot | Characters |
|---|---|---|---|---|
| | *The Democrats are coming for you* | Scare audiences into believing Democrats pose a threat to them personally | Democrats want to control you and punish you if you don't cooperate. | IRS agents, opponent, Biden, middle class families |
| **Fighting for you** | *The right personal background for the job* | Assure voters that the candidate has the right life experiences and values to represent them | Candidate has persevered and overcome obstacles to become a person and politician that you can relate to or respect | Candidate, "us" |
| | *Fighting the liberal agenda* | Reassure voters that candidate will fight for their policy priorities | The candidate will go to Washington and work tirelessly to fight the liberal agenda and advance the policy positions that voters want | Candidate, opponent, Biden, residents of the district, Washington |
| | *Getting things done* | Remind audiences that the candidate has already delivered results for them and will continue to do so | The candidate has bold ideas and the results to show for them, including working with the other party if need be | Candidate, President Biden |
| | *Keeping you safe* | Position the candidate as a guardian for constituents | Through my policies I'll keep you and your family physically safe, and safeguard American democracy | Candidate, Gov. DeSantis, police |

American life under Democratic policies and control. This key narrative was comprised of four sub-narratives. The first, *the America you knew is no longer recognizable*, attempts to put on record the manner in which Democrats are ruining America. The plot revolves around the destruction caused by the Democrats in the form of a ravaged economy, rampant crime and unchecked immigration. For example, an advertisement from Marc Molinaro (NY-19) (2022) called "TV Ad: Representing US" featured citizens screaming in reaction to "sky high gas prices," "rising crime," and "runaway inflation." It then informed viewers that "Joe Biden and Nancy Pelosi are to blame" (prompting another citizen scream), and that "one party rule in Albany and Washington is destroying New York" (prompting yet another citizen scream).

The second sub-narrative, *the American Dream is threatened*, is somewhat similar to the first, but employs the commonly invoked metanarrative of the American Dream. This sub-narrative is more abstract and designed to fill viewers with the emotions of worry and anxiety. Kids and grandkids are thus important characters in this narrative. The plot coalesces around the destruction of American identity caused by Democrats, the opponent. This story of destruction emphasizes values more than policies. For instance, an ad from Carlos Gimenez (FL-28) (2022) called "American Dream" featured a rigged game of chess as a metaphor for the disappearing American Dream. Gimenez argued: "It's unfair to our children and grandchildren. They deserve better: we must protect the American Dream."

A third sub-narrative under the *America is under existential threat* key narrative is *the Democrats are subverting America*. This sub-narrative seeks to disqualify Democrats, the opponent, based on unethical and immoral conduct. The plot depicts Democrats as willfully and maliciously subverting American freedoms and values. There is little ambiguity in the advertisements' accusations of deliberate subversion rather than wrong-headed policies. For example, in an advertisement titled "Inflation," Andrew Garbarino (NY-2) (2022) referred to "Biden's Build Back Better *scheme*," while Nicole Malliotakis (NY-11) (2022) stated, "Biden and Max Rose? They prefer turning to countries that hate America. That's unconscionable". Gimenez (2022), in a spot called "Freedom," asserted that "threats to freedom start at the top with President Biden: he emboldens evil regimes, outsources jobs to communist China, restricts parents' rights, and has paved the way for censorship right here at home." The emotion associated with this sub-narrative is outrage.

Finally, the fourth sub-narrative is *the Democrats are coming for you*. This sub-narrative centers on the emotion of fear and a plot that depicts Democrats as power-hungry manipulators who want to control voters and punish them for resistance. Protagonists like middle class families are juxtaposed with antagonists like Internal Revenue Service (IRS) agents. In an ad called "They're Coming," Malliotakis (2022) warned viewers about a "new reality … a financial war waged on middle class families. The first assault: a massive tax increase, then billions spent to build an army of IRS agents unleashed on families like yours. Thanks to

Max Rose and Biden, you might be hearing a knock at your door very soon." Cory Mills' (FL-7) (2022) advertisement, "Cory Mills Ad: 'Control'," demonstrates both this and the previous sub-narrative. Mills asserted that "in America, our enemy is different, but their objective is the same: total government control." These four sub-narratives comprising the *America is under existential threat* key narrative establish the Democratic opposition as the archetypal villain against whom the Republican hero is positioned. This familiar binary likely draws into the drama viewers and possesses explanatory capacity, allowing audiences to identify which party is wrong and ultimately align themselves against the bad actors. The potent emotions of fear and anger are pervasive in these sub-narratives, likely enhancing their capacity to persuade. The American Dream metanarrative furthermore serves as a kind of public story (Bartlett & Rayner, 2014), signaling a shared understanding that is easily comprehensible and does not require the presentation of a fully developed plot.

The second key narrative associated with the winning Republican candidates who overperformed in Republican-leaning districts is *fighting for you*. This key narrative establishes relationality, or how the actor stands relative to the audience, as the candidate is positioned as the action-oriented advocate whom voters expect and need. This key narrative also demonstrates the manner in which stories reflect shared cultural identity. The hardworking warrior–advocate protagonist is a persona to which audiences can aspire and with whom they can identify. The first of four sub-narratives, *the right personal background for the job*, serves to assure or reassure voters that the candidate has the appropriate values and life experiences to represent them. The plot features action involving perseverance and the surmounting of obstacles to become a person and politician that voters can relate to and respect. This is likely persuasive as an identity and ethos-based appeal, establishing both that the audience can identify with the candidate—*I am one of you*—and that the candidate has the right kind of inner qualities to do the job. The character of "us" also takes an important position in this sub-narrative. For example, a Molinaro (2022) ad titled "The Choice" featured a narrator relating how "Mark Molinaro gets it. Growing up on food stamps, he's lived it. As county executive he's made the tough choices: cutting taxes, balancing budgets, working every day to keep us safe." The ad thus invites the audience into a collective understanding of an in-group (*us*), and by extension, establishes a shared understanding of the out-group (*them*).

A second sub-narrative is *fighting the liberal agenda*. This sub-narrative reassures voters that the candidate will fight the liberal agenda in the combative manner they desire. The plot involves the candidates' tireless work to beat back the unflinching agenda thrust on America by liberals. Important characters are the protagonists, residents of the district, and the antagonist, Washington, D.C. This Washington, D.C., antagonist also functions as the story setting or space, achieving cultural congruence with the notion of a corrupt swamp (outside of which the candidate is positioned) and with the pugilistic tone of the Trump era of U.S. politics. Garberino (2022), in an ad called "Winter," described how he is "fighting to rein in inflation and for more domestic oil and gas production so Long Islanders can stay warm this winter." In this excerpt, the Washington, D.C., setting (where the fight takes place) is implied rather than directly stated and contrasted with the Long Island nexus of the candidate's activity and efforts. The prominent emotion is determination.

The third sub-narrative under the *fighting for you* key narrative is *getting things done*. This reminds audiences that the candidate has delivered for voters, and by extension will continue to do so. The candidate–protagonist, as capable pragmatist, is the most important character in the story. This is demonstrated by Garberino's (2022) ad titled "Real Results." A narrator informed viewers that "Andrew Garberino is getting real stuff done: ensuring 9/11 survivors and first responders get the health care promised; repairing local roads like the LIE; protecting the bay." The focus in this sub-narrative is on the results of the fight rather than the fight itself, for example the securing of healthcare and the upkeep of infrastructure and vital resources.

Finally, the *keeping you safe* sub-narrative positions the candidate as a guardian for constituents. This sub-narrative is more emotion-based than *getting things done*. The candidate and police are important characters in this story. The plot weaves together the physical safety of voters' families and the safeguarding of American democracy, alluding to the well-established Republican law-and-order narrative without needing to complete the story. An advertisement called "Split Second Ad" portrayed the split-second decisions that police officers have to make, and candidate Laurel Lee (FL-15) (n.d.) voiced her commitment "to safeguard our elections. In congress, I'll defend the rule of law and those who serve it." The emotions involved are resoluteness and sense of responsibility. Together, these four sub-narratives under the *fighting for you* key narrative establish that Republicans are the hero, the other half of the villain–hero archetypal dramatic binary.

With regard to the four winning Republican candidates who overperformed in Democratic-leaning districts, one key narrative was identified: *stark contrast with opponent* (see Table 5.3). This key narrative contrasts a feckless, misguided, and damaging adversary with a strong, well-equipped candidate who can fix the downward American trajectory engendered by the Democrats (and by extension, the opponent). It clarifies by placing into stark relief who the "good guys" are. Four sub-narratives comprise this key narrative. The first, *defending the American Dream that is under attack*, presents the candidate as uniquely able to rescue the American Dream that the opponents/Democrats are destroying. The core of this narrative focuses on the Republican candidate's ability to salvage American values. It is more empowering than anxiety-riddled, with corresponding emotions invoking resolute determination. For example, the narrator in a George Devolder-Santos (NY-3) (2022) ad called "Living the

Winning Stories Amid Partisanship **107**

**TABLE 5.3** Analysis of Narratives: Winning 2022 Republican Candidates Who Overperformed in Democratic-Leaning Districts

| Key Narrative | Sub-narrative | Goal | Plot | Actors |
|---|---|---|---|---|
| **Stark contrast with opponent** | *Defending the American Dream that is under attack* | Position candidate as uniquely able to save the American Dream that the opponents/ Democrats are destroying | My opponent, President Biden and the Democrats are destroying the American Dream for our future, but I have the ability to return the American Dream to our state and nation. | Candidate, candidate's spouse, The American Dream, Biden, opponent, Democrats |
| | *Have the personal background required to fix the mess created by opponents* | Establish for voters that the candidate has the right kind of experience to rectify the damage done by the opponents | My background gives me the insight and experience to fight on your behalf: to save the nation from the mess that my opponent, Biden, and the Democrats have created. | Candidate, opponent, Biden |
| | *Enacting policies to repair the damage opponents have done* | Inform voters that the candidate has the policy positions and solutions to counter the damage done by the opponents | I have worked hard, or plan to work hard, on specific issues to fix the damage that has been done or would be done by opponent's disastrous policies | Candidate, opponent |
| | *Keeping you safe when my opponent/ Democrats won't* | Attack the opponent by instilling fear in voters but give them a clear remedy: elect the candidate | Opponent's, Democrats', and Biden's policies on crime, drugs and illegal immigration are making you unsafe: I can fix this and safeguard you from these dangers. | Candidate, opponent, Biden, police, dangerous criminals |

Dream" related how "George Santos is fighting back: Standing up to Biden to save his family's dream and lead New York forward. Our defender of the American Dream: George Santos for congress." This sub-narrative draws on the same metanarrative as *the American Dream is threatened* sub-narrative described above. However, the focus is turned on its head: the plot features the heroic protection of the American Dream rather than the destruction of it (committed by Democrats). It thus creates orientation and order by establishing who, in contrast to the opponent, can protect the culturally shared idea of America.

The second and third sub-narratives within this key narrative are: *have the personal background required to fix the mess created by opponents* and *enacting policies to repair the damage opponents have done.* These parallel stories situate the candidates as prominent protagonists who have the very life experiences, career background, and policy experience that are necessary to remedy the damage done by Democrats (and that would be done by the opponent). For example, in an ad titled "Defending the Middle Class," Brandon Williams (NY-22) (2022) explained, "Six submarine patrols in 500 Days at Sea. I'm Brandon Williams, former nuclear submarine officer. My next mission: defending Central New York from Joe Biden and Francis Canole's far left agenda." These sub-narratives are similar to *the right personal background for the job* sub-narrative described above, but they are not best interpreted as solely acclaim ads. Rather, they deploy acclaim, or the bolstering of the candidate's own qualities, deliberately as a mechanism by which to advance the story's plot and drama, and in so doing launch an attack against the opponent.

The final sub-narrative, *keeping you safe when my opponent/Democrats won't*, also follows this acclaim–attack story structure, but invokes more pathos than the previous two sub-narratives. The goal is to attack the opponent by instilling fear in voters but also, crucially, to supply a clearly stated remedy: elect the candidate and empower the candidate to make the necessary changes to achieve fear avoidance, an important consideration in the use of fear to persuade audiences (e.g., Perloff, 2023). For example, Anthony D'Esposito (NY-4) (2022) asserted that:

> Biden and Laura Gillen will continue allowing millions to illegally pour into our country, and the drug cartels to flood our neighborhoods with deadly fentanyl from China. I spent over a decade in the NYPD working to get drugs off of our streets. I'll make sure we finally get serious about border security and shut down the flow of deadly fentanyl from Mexico into Nassau County.

The candidate is positioned as the hero, with the villain portrayed as the opponent who is enabling foreign invaders to attack, physically and symbolically, the United States. Thus, setting is also important, with the juxtaposition of home (the security of "our streets") and foreign (the threatening or even deviant, for

Winning Stories Amid Partisanship **109**

example China or Mexico). This sub-narrative also holds the potential to invite audiences to imagine how the election will affect them personally, argued to be an important capacity of narratives of the political (Jamieson, 1996).

Turning to the Democrats who overperformed in Democratic-leaning districts, two key narratives were discerned (see Table 5.4). The first key narrative, *you can trust me*, serves to assuage concerns about voting for a Democrat when

**TABLE 5.4** Analysis of Narratives: Winning 2022 Democratic Candidates Who Overperformed in Democratic-Leaning Districts

| *Key Narrative* | *Sub-narrative* | *Goal* | *Plot* | *Actors* |
|---|---|---|---|---|
| **You can trust me** | *Share your values* | Affirm shared values that differentiate the candidate from Republicans and serve as a defense against Republican attacks. | You, along with me, can overcome threats to the moral fabric of this nation through shared values of outrage, courage, loyalty and determination. | Candidate, Supreme Court, women, family members, military veterans |
| | *Service embedded in local values and local priorities* | Establish trust on the basis of familiar, local priorities and value systems. | A candidate nurtured by local values and priorities can draw on those qualities to overcome disfunction in Washington and achieve results | Local district, local workers, candidate, President Obama, Congress |
| | *Personal background as beacon* | Establish aspects of biography that will lead to perceptions of credibility by voters. | I have never shied away from hard work, diverse life experiences, and taking on career challenges, these experiences will serve a guiding light in Congress | Candidate, Dad, Mom, patients |

(*Continued*)

# 110 Media Messages in the 2022 Midterm Election

**TABLE 5.4** (Continued)

| Key Narrative | Sub-narrative | Goal | Plot | Actors |
|---|---|---|---|---|
| | *Results delivered* | Give voters an alternative to Republicans' solutions for the problems of the Biden administration. | There are serious problems facing the country now, I have tackled them, and will continue to tackle them in the future, no matter what it takes and who I have to challenge. | Candidate, "us", the Biden Administration, Congress |
| | *Endorsed by credible third parties* | Reassure voters that a Democrat is worthy of your vote, despite full Democratic control of federal government | We (farmers, law enforcement, Republicans and Democrats) have seen many candidates come and go, we are confidently lending our support to the candidate, who has displayed bipartisan outreach, established values and a desire for solutions over party loyalty. | Candidate, Republican politician endorsers, farmers, Republican mayor, Democratic mayor, retired or late-career law enforcement professional, police |
| | *Will work across the aisle and hold President Biden accountable* | Demonstrate to voters that candidate won't simply rubberstamp the positions of Democratic leaders | Political gridlock in Washington is failing voters, I am willing to work with, or call out, a member of either party if that is necessary to get things done. | Democrats, Republicans, "anyone," Washington, D.C., Biden, Trump |

## TABLE 5.4 (Continued)

| Key Narrative | Sub-narrative | Goal | Plot | Actors |
|---|---|---|---|---|
| | *Taking on Big Business* | Prime an alternate explanation for current challenges, rather than the perceived failings of the Biden administration (the opponent's attack line) | I am fearlessly taking on corporations because they are taking advantage of citizens and harming the economy. | Oil and drug companies, corporations, families, small businesses |
| **Far right-wing danger lurks** | *Fringe opponent is not fit for office* | Disqualify opponent while presenting candidate as a worthy contrast | Virtuous citizen protagonists under threat from a far-right, extreme opponent and ideology, but can be overcome by voting for and supporting me. | Candidate, veterans, women, local leaders, opponent, Marjorie Taylor Greene |
| | *American institutions have changed alarmingly* | Keep anger stoked at the way America has changed | Most Americans thought these changes would never happen, but institutions are changing rapidly to their detriment; I will fight to reverse these changes. | Citizens, candidate, Supreme Court, D.C. politicians |

Democrats were in charge of both the executive and legislative branches of government. By re-establishing a common identity and reminding audiences of a shared value set, this key narrative demonstrates both the identity-related and explanatory capacities of narratives of the political. Seven sub-narratives were identified. *Share your values* affirmed a value set—a common messaging strategy—but also served as a means by which to go on the offensive and as

**112** Media Messages in the 2022 Midterm Election

a defense against Republican attacks. For example, in an ad called "Uphold," Hillary Scholten (MI-3) (2022) recounted:

> Working cases at the nation's top law enforcement agency, I swore an oath to uphold the rule of law. So when someone broke the law, that meant they went to jail or were deported. Because it was always about keeping people safe. That's a matter of right and wrong, not Right or Left.

Prominent characters were the candidate, the Supreme Court, women, family members, and military veterans. Notable emotions were resoluteness and conviction.

The second sub-narrative, *service embedded in local values and local priorities*, sought to mollify voters' doubts by establishing trust built upon local values. The plot coalesced around the candidate, nurtured by local values and priorities, able to draw on those qualities to overcome disfunction in Washington and achieve results. Notable protagonists were the candidate, local districts and local workers. For example, Scholten (2022) narrated an ad called "Built to Last—Hillary Scholten", in which she asserted, "When it's made in West Michigan, it's built to last. I think it's time Congress got back to valuing that kind of hard work and the quality that comes with it." Similarly, the Kim Schrier (WA-8) (2022) campaign uploaded an ad called "Walk," in which Schrier claimed: "to understand someone better, walk a mile in their shoes. Or, ride along in their patrol car. That's what I do, with local police officers here in Washington, to hear their concerns firsthand. Then fight for them in Congress." These stories also employ the hero–villain archetypal binary, but in a manner that positions one setting (the local) as the hero working against a kind of villain in another setting (Washington, D.C., or Congress), likely a shrewd narrative contrast to deploy when a candidate is of the party in power. Time is furthermore a prominent narrative element, as these stories of the acquisition of local values and priorities unfolded over many years. Moreover, these stories had the potential to be persuasive due to the use of a powerful emotion in persuasion: pride.

The third and fourth sub-narratives—*personal background as beacon* and *results delivered*—buttressed the candidates' histories and offered further reassurance to voters. These sub-narratives function as acclaim ads, and the latter had an important additional goal of giving voters a viable alternative to Republicans' solutions for the problems of the Biden administration. For instance, in an ad called "One Chip at a Time" by the Chrissy Houlahan (PA-06) (2022) campaign, a narrator asked:

> How do we beat inflation? It begins down here. Chrissy Houlahan's the expert in Congress, who wrote the book on supply chain management at MIT. She worked with both parties to pass the Chips Act, getting minerals

into made-in-America computer chips faster, so we can build more products here instead of China. Her plan is the best inflation fighting blueprint to come out of Congress.

These stories thus served an important clarifying function. They make clear that there is an alternative protagonist, the candidate–expert who is part of the audience political in-group, and who can anchor a different story of ameliorating a problem like inflation, rather than Republicans.

The fifth sub-narrative, *endorsed by credible third parties*, added a crucial aspect of credibility as it is focused on the endorsements of politicians and public figures who may not be expected to align ideologically with a contemporary Democratic politician. In this story, character is paramount. Central characters included Republican politician endorsers, farmers, Republican and Democratic mayors, along with current and retired law enforcement personnel. The plot concentrates on the journey of these credible third-party endorsers to lend their support to the deserving candidate. For instance, the Schrier (WA-8) (2022) campaign uploaded an ad titled, "Police," in which a late-career (or retired) law enforcement officer stated: "I've been in law enforcement for over 36 years and I've seen a lot of politicians talk about police. But Kim Schrier is different. She listens to us, and she delivers." Emotions imbued in this sub-narrative relate to respect and admiration. Time, in addition to character, is salient in this sub-narrative. The credibility boost bestowed by the trusted characters unfurled over time, rather than during limited, recent interactions.

The sixth and seventh sub-narratives made additional contributions to the *you can trust me* key narrative. The *will work across the aisle and hold President Biden accountable* sub-narrative assured voters that candidates would work in a bipartisan manner and even go against their party if necessary to achieve results. In this sub-narrative, an important character is "anyone," which serves as an antagonist with respect to the plot. Therefore, anyone who interfered with the ability of the candidate to deliver for constituents would be defeated by the protagonist–candidate, even if that person or group was of the same party or even the president. With regard to space, the candidate is situated institutionally in the symbolic nation, rather than in a political party. Time is also important, as this story is forward-looking and future-oriented, rather than focused on the past or present. The *taking on big business* sub-narrative contained a plot in which a determined fighter (the candidate as protagonist) stood up to an antagonist (big business) that was taking advantage of ordinary Americans. This story utilizes a tried-and-true progressive archetypal binary: the righteous people's warrior–hero who stands up to the corrupt corporate villain. The emotions of combativeness and righteousness are embedded in this sub-narrative. This story also served an additional goal: to prime an alternate explanation for current challenges, rather than the perceived failings of the Biden administration; in other words, to insulate the candidate from the opponent's attack line. Thus, the Schrier (WA-8) (2022) campaign ad, "Because," insulated the candidate from attacks on the high inflation rate rooted in a Democratic presidency: "I'm taking on the oil and drug companies because they're ripping us off." These stories therefore function as a kind of narrative defense. The seven sub-narratives under the *you can trust me* key narrative furthermore reassure audiences that it is still permissible to view the candidate and the Democratic party as the hero, which serves a clarifying role for constituents.

The second key narrative with regard to Democrats who overperformed in Democratic-leaning districts was *far right-wing danger lurks.* This key narrative sought to remind audiences of the villain by positioning Republicans as an extremist threat. It served to remind voters that if they have concerns about the nation now, under Democratic control, a much worse alternative exists should the Republicans and the opponent emerge victorious. Time is thus a central component in this key narrative, with a focus on the present and future rather than on the past. The *fringe opponent is not fit for office* sub-narrative sought to disqualify the opponent while clarifying the candidate as a contrast worthy of support. This sub-narrative emphasized virtuous citizen protagonists under threat from a far-right, extreme opponent and ideology. Protagonist characters were veterans, women, local leaders, and the candidate. Antagonists were the opponent and Marjorie Taylor Greene, the narrative archetype of a far-right extremist. For example, the Scholten (2022) ad "No Other Candidate—Hillary Scholten" depicted two retired, local Republican leaders. One of them observes: "The other guy, John Gibbs, endorsed a plan to terminate Social Security and Medicare! That's about the worst idea I've ever heard! We earned those benefits, Mr. Gibbs! This one's easy: I'm voting for Hillary Scholten!" In another example, the Schrier (2022) campaign stated that the opponent "supports a national ban on abortion, overturning protections here in Washington and putting women's lives at risk. Larkin even said he "aligns with Marjorie Taylor Greene" and said, "this isn't the time for moderation." That's Matt Larkin, the definition of dangerous." The emotion of fear is prominent in this sub-narrative.

The second and final sub-narrative within the *far right-wing danger lurks* key narrative was *American institutions have changed alarmingly.* The setting of the institutional change became an important narrative component. This sub-narrative had a goal of keeping voters' anger stoked at the manner in which American institutions have changed rapidly for the worse. This was likely effective, as the emotions of anger (and relatedly, belittlement) are potentially potent emotions in persuasion (Heinrichs, 2020). The plot centered both on citizens who never thought these changes would occur and on the candidates who would fight to stop such transformations. Antagonists were the Supreme

Court and D.C. politicians. For example, the Schrier (2022) campaign ad, "Extreme," stated:

> Some thought it would never happen: the Supreme Court taking away a woman's right to choose, a right to privacy that existed for almost fifty years .... Now some D.C. politicians want to ban all abortions with no exceptions for rape, incest, or the life of the mother. As a doctor and mother, I am outraged. As your congresswoman, I won't stand for it.

In this example, the Supreme Court is presented as an institution that in previous times was thought to be resistant, and even impervious, to alarming change. This propels the narrative of unwanted transformation, allowing the candidate–protagonist to emerge as the savior who can ensure the survival of what had been thought to be safe.

Finally, with regard to the Democrats who overperformed in Republican-leaning districts, only five videos were available to be analyzed. These featured one key narrative, *populist identity makes it acceptable to vote for me* (see Table 5.5). This key narrative was constructed to establish a voting permission structure among audiences who may be hostile to the candidates' party ideology.

**TABLE 5.5** Analysis of Narratives: Winning 2022 Democratic Candidates Who Overperformed in Republican-Leaning Districts

| Key Narrative | Sub-narrative | Goal | Plot | Actors |
|---|---|---|---|---|
| **Populist identity makes it acceptable to vote for me** | *I'm one of you* | Position candidate as much more like the voter than opponent is | I have led a life that you can recognize, therefore, I can be your representative and fight for you. | Candidate, shop owner, mother |
| | *Opponent is aligned with special interests* | Contrast candidate's populist identity with that of the opponent | My opponent is not looking out for you because they are not like you; I am, and I will fight alongside you. | Special interests, corporate PACs, candidate, working Washingtonians, extremist Republicans, opponent, special interest donors, struggling Colorado families |

The sub-narrative, *I'm one of you,* established that despite potential ideological differences, the candidate has more in common with the voters than not in common. The plot depicted the candidate as having led a life that voters can recognize, with similar struggles and obstacles; therefore, the candidate could be your representative and fight for you. Invoking a sense of shared identity was critical. For instance, Marie Gluesenkamp Pérez (WA-3) (2022), in an ad titled, "Marie Gluesenkamp Pérez (WA-03) – Not Your Typical Candidate for Congress," explained, "I'm not your typical candidate for Congress." A narrator then takes over: "Marie Gluesenkamp Pérez. Auto repair shop owner, mother and Democrat for Congress." Gluesenkamp Pérez concluded the ad by stating, "I will fight for working Washingtonians just like *me*"—an illuminating choice of pronoun in contrast to the customary use of "you" (emphasis added). Character, in relation to the audience, thus also emerged as a central narrative component. The other side of the populist narrative coin is to depict the opponent as not like "you." Therefore, the second sub-narrative is *opponent is aligned with special interests.* This plot featured the antagonist opponent working in cahoots with special interests that do not prioritize the interests of ordinary voters. For instance, Yadira Caraveo (CO-8) (2022) stated, in an ad titled, "Dr. Yadira Caraveo for Congress: WORSE": "But Barbara Kirkmeyer voted no instead, choosing to protect her special interest donors instead of helping struggling Colorado families. Extremist Barbara Kirkmeyer isn't just a typical politician. She's worse." This was an attack ad that also did the work of reassuring voters that they could view the candidate as sharing an identity, even if there were policy and ideological differences. The emotions associated with this final sub-narrative are skepticism, anger and resentment.

## Discussion

Scholars recognize the centrality of narrative in politics and increasingly in the video advertisements of candidates for elective office. Yet, this chapter represents one of the few studies to analyze the plotted stories themselves: the narratives at the heart of the political advertisements deployed by the campaigns. On the one hand, these analyses support previous research that found, for example, that the majority of ads serve a function that acclaims, attacks, or defends (Benoit, 1999; Vesnic-Alujevic & Van Bauwel, 2014). In addition, these analyses support the theorizing that narratives of the political engage audiences in the drama and clarify by invoking culturally congruent archetypes (Anker, 2005; Coe et al., 2004) and metanarratives (Lyotard, 1984) like the American Dream. For example, both the overperforming Republicans and Democrats employed key narratives that align with the commonly invoked binary of the hero (the candidate or candidate's party) and the villain (opposition). These analyses also demonstrated the utility of Tekin and Meissner's (2022) approach, wherein the plot is determined by space (where the political actor constructing the narrative is situated geographically and institutionally), by time, and by relationality (how the political actor stands relative to the audience). The concept of public narratives (Bartlett & Rayner, 2014), which envisions stories as devices that allow groups, agencies, and institutions to provide an external account of themselves, was furthermore applied in this study.

On the other hand, the analysis of narrative methodology employed, following Tekin and Meissner's (2022) concept of constructed narrative, permits insight and a degree of nuance that may have been unattainable using more commonly applied narrative lenses. This approach views strategic narratives as constructs of reality (the key narratives) stemming from various sub-narratives and the elements of character, plot, and goal. The overperforming Republicans in districts whose lean was Republican positioned their hero story as one of action, of struggle, and of conflict with the villain opposition: *fighting for you*. They situated the villain opposition as representing a threat to the very nation itself and to Americans' way of life: *America is under existential threat*. This included, for instance, the threat-based sub-narrative, *the Democrats are coming for you*. The overperforming Democrats in districts whose lean was Democratic, by contrast, positioned their hero story as one of trust, rooted in values, credibility gained, and results achieved: *you can trust me*. The menacing opposition was much less prominent than in the corresponding Republicans' key narrative (*fighting for you*). Democrats situated the villain opposition as representing and enacting alarming normative, policy, and institutional change—*far right-wing danger lurks*—which likely engendered fear but did not stress the end of America as we know it.

The overperforming Republicans in districts whose lean was Democratic displayed a main narrative of *stark contrast with opponent*, perhaps expected from the party out of power. The overperforming Democrats in districts whose lean was Republican, in contrast, sought to create a permission structure for voters: *populist identity makes it acceptable to vote for me*.

The identification of sub-narratives that comprised the key narratives yielded fruitful insights. For example, overperforming Republicans in Republican-leaning districts told stories about the Democrats' destruction of the American Dream (*the American Dream is threatened*, part of the key narrative, *America is under existential threat*). This was contrasted notably by overperforming Republicans in Democratic-leaning districts, who alluded to the same destruction of the American Dream. These Republicans, however, adopted an important narrative change: they deployed plots in which they were centered as fighter protagonists who had the ability to stem the damage and safeguard the future (*defending the American Dream that is under attack*, part of the key narrative, *stark contrast with opponent*). This sub-narrative therefore positioned these Republicans as having the agency and wherewithal to stem the decline or collapse of the American Dream. Indeed, as the key narrative, *stark contrast with opponent* indicated, all the relevant sub-narratives elevated the candidates as protagonists who were capable of taking action to halt the damage wrought by the Democrats.

This study also discerned several prominent emotions embedded in the campaign narratives of the overperforming candidates. Such identification of emotion also carries scholarly promise, given the degree to which the persuasiveness of narratives is widely attributed to emotion (Brader, 2005; Van Steenburg, 2015). One example relates to the key narrative *you can trust me*, and to the *share your values* sub-narrative (Democratic candidates who overperformed in Democratic-leaning districts). These narratives situated trust in a plot centered on the candidate protagonists equipping themselves with local values for the fights in store in Washington. The central emotion identified is pride in the local culture and in its value system—an emotion, intertwined with shared identity, which may have carried considerable persuasive potential. The identification of other prominent emotions like fear and anger, along with potential presence of qualities like credibility, also proved fruitful, especially when contextualized by insights from persuasion theory.

This approach and these findings are also promising with respect to unpacking the 2022 U.S. midterm election results. The analyses of narratives in this study contribute to understanding why the predicted "red wave" did not come to fruition in 2022. For example, the midterm elections were a time of norm trampling and perceived extremism; select Democrats' use of narratives concentrating on the risk of extreme opponents and unrecognizable institutions likely achieved their goal of disqualifying from some voters' consideration Republican candidates. Some 2022 Democrats thus appeared to effectively tell a story of a horrifying worse alternative: the fringe, extreme opponent. Against a considerable headwind, 2022 Democrats may have survived in competitive districts by telling stories about trustworthiness rooted in local values and buttressing credibility perceptions through emotion-filled narratives of how a candidate's personal background, values system, track record, and endorsements from respected out-group members engendered an advocate-warrior who was worthy of support, despite being of the same party as an unpopular president.

Moreover, this study of winning narratives allows for inferences to be made with regard to political strategy more broadly. For example, a midterm candidate not of the president's party, but running in a district with an opposing party lean, might be well advised to deploy "contrast" narratives. The insight gained is not in the contrast itself, but rather in the story plots about destruction, decline, and chaos necessarily juxtaposed against the plots of empowered actors with the unique ability to fix, improve, and fight for the nation or district. A midterm candidate who is of the party in control of government, by contrast, may still attain victory even in a district that has the opposite party lean. This may be accomplished through a populist narrative—a story plot in which the candidate joins the voters in navigating life and sharing struggles ("us")—rather than making a non-narrative claim to solve constituents' problems from afar ("you").

There are a few important qualifications and limitations to this study that warrant mention. First, in addition to the narratives, an array of factors—from other prominent forms of messaging like speeches, to candidate quality, to unique local dynamics, and to the presence of a Donald Trump endorsement—likely played consequential roles in determining which candidates emerged victorious. No causal claim with regard to the narratives and the election victories is, or should be, made. Second, one of the analyses conducted (Democratic candidates who overperformed in Republican-leaning districts) included just five video advertisements, a small sample. Third, only the verbal components of the advertisements were analyzed. This is consistent with some extant analyses of political advertisements; however, it is acknowledged that visual aspects of campaign advertisements play an attention-worthy role in the construction and interpretation of the narratives.

Future studies should continue to investigate the campaign advertisement key narratives, and their subordinate sub-narratives, associated with winning candidates. In addition, scholars should consider the advertisement narratives of other groups of politicians: losing candidates, for instance, in addition to third-party candidates or newcomers. Additional comparative approaches may also hold utility. For example, the literature would benefit from the study of incumbent advertisement narratives compared to those of challengers, of shifts in candidate advertisement narratives across elections, and of the advertisement narratives of one nation's candidates for elective office in relation to another's. Qualitative analysis of narrative as methodology deserves a starring role in the scholarly consideration of political campaign advertisements.

## References

Anker, E. (2005). Villains, victims and heroes: Melodrama, media, and September 11. *Journal of Communication*, *55*(1), 22–37. https://doi.org/10.1111/j.1460-2466.2005. tb02656.x

Appel, M., & Richter, T. (2007). Persuasive effects of fictional narratives increase over time. *Media Psychology*, *10*(1), 113–134. https://doi.org/10.1080/1521326070 1301194

Bartlett, D., & Rayner, J. (2014). "This campaign is all about..." Dissecting Australian campaign narratives. *Communication, Politics & Culture*, *47*(1), 51–68.

Benoit, W. (1999). *Seeing spots. A functional analysis of presidential TV ads 1952–1996*. Praeger.

Benoit, W., Leshner, G., & Chattopadhyay, S. (2007). A meta-analysis of political advertising. *Human Communication*, *10*(4), 507–522. https://epublications.marque tte.edu/comm_fac/9

Best, R., Lodhi, H., & Skelley, G. (2022, November 21). *A red wave in Florida. A blue riptide in Michigan*. FiveThirtyEight. https://projects.fivethirtyeight.com/republic ans-house-election-margin/

Bilandzic, H., & Busselle, R. (2013). Narrative persuasion. In J. P. Dillard & L. Shen (Eds.), *The persuasion handbook: Developments in theory and practice* (2nd ed., pp. 200–219). Sage.

Brader, T. (2005). Striking a responsive chord: How political ads motivate and persuade voters by appealing to emotions. *American Journal of Political Science*, *49*(2), 388– 405. https://doi.org/10.1111/j.0092-5853.2005.00130.x

Braun V., & Clarke V. (2006). Using thematic analysis in psychology. *Qualitative Research in Psychology*, 3(2), 77–101. https://doi.org/10.1191/1478088706qp063oa

Brazeal, L. M., & Benoit, W. L. (2001). A functional analysis of congressional television spots, 1986-2000. *Communication Quarterly*, *49*(4), 436–454. https://doi.org/ 10.1080/01463370109385640

Campbell, R. G., & Babrow, A. S. (2004). The role of empathy in responses to persuasive risk communication: Overcoming resistance to HIV prevention messages. *Health Communication*, *16*(2), 159–182. https://doi.org/10.1207/S15327027HC1602_2

Caraveo, Y. (2022, November 3). *Dr. Yadira Caraveo for congress: WORSE* [Video]. YouTube. www.youtube.com/watch?v=YJ3CS7w5QsQ

Coe, K., Domke, D., Graham, E. S., John, S. L., & Pickard, V. W. (2004). No shades of gray: The binary discourse of George W. Bush and an echoing press. *Journal of Communication*, *54*(2), 234–252. https://doi.org/10.1111/j.1460-2466.2004.tb02626.x

Dardis, F. E., Shen, F., & Edwards, H. H. (2008). Effects of negative political advertising on individuals' cynicism and self-efficacy: The impact of ad type and message exposures. *Mass Communication & Society*, *11*(1), 24–42. https://doi.org/10.1080/ 15205430701582512

Denton, R. E., Voth, B., Trent, J. S., & Friedenberg, R. V. (2024). *Political campaign communication: Principles and practices* (10th ed.). Rowman & Littlefield.

D'Esposito, A. (2022, October 21). *D'Esposito for congress – keep Nassau safe* [Video]. YouTube. www.youtube.com/watch?v=2pfpyvHDbdw

Devolder-Santos, G. (2022, September 8). *Living the dream* [Video]. YouTube. www. youtube.com/watch?v=-K-BMZAG2eY

Fisher, W. R. (1987). *Human communication as narration: Toward a philosophy of reason, value, and action*. University of South Carolina Press.

Fowler, E. F., Franz, M. M., Neumann, M., Ridout, T. N., & Yao, J. (2023). Digital advertising in the 2022 midterms. *The Forum*, *21*(1), 53–73. https://doi.org/10.1515/ for-2023-2006

Franz, M. M., Ridout, T. N., & Fowler, E. F. (2023). Television advertising in the 2022 midterms. *The Forum*, *21*(1), 27–51. https://doi.org/10.1515/for-2023-2005

Garbarino, A. (2022, August 11). *Inflation* [Video]. YouTube. www.youtube.com/ watch?v=HL5ab4GyDc

Garbarino, A. (2022, September 28). *Winter* [Video]. YouTube. www.youtube.com/ watch?v=qgltQ2usvjo

Garbarino, A. (2022, October 19). *Real results* [Video]. YouTube. www.youtube.com/watch?v=v9HR_vGBcOY

Gimenez, C. (2022, October 16). *American dream* [Video]. YouTube. www.youtube.com/watch?v=Wb4l0IohKU0

Gimenez, C. (2022, November 4). *Freedom* [Video]. YouTube. www.youtube.com/watch?v=eaJGAzcH9K8

Gluesenkamp Pérez, M. (2022, July 20). *Marie Gluesenkamp Perez (WA-03) – Not your typical candidate for congress* [Video]. YouTube. www.youtube.com/watch?v=WDCnL4Ng4Yg

Granato, J., & Wong, M. C. S. (2004). Political campaign advertising dynamics. *Political Research Quarterly*, *57*(3), 349–361. https://doi.org/10.2307/3219846

Green, M. C. (2004). Transportation into narrative worlds: The role of prior knowledge and perceived realism. *Discourse Processes*, *38*(2), 247–266. https://doi.org/10.1207/s15326950dp3802_5

Green, M. C., & Brock, T. C. (2000). The role of transportation in the persuasiveness of public narratives. *Journal of Personality and Social Psychology*, *79*, 701–721. https://doi.org/10.1037/0022-3514.79.5.701

Green, M. C., & Brock, T. C. (2005). Persuasiveness of narratives. In T. C. Brock & M C. Green (Eds.), *Persuasion: Psychological insights and perspectives* (2nd ed., pp. 117–142). Sage Publications, Inc.

Groth, S. (2019). Political narratives / narrations of the political: An Introduction. *Narrative Culture*, *6*(1), 1–18. https://doi.org/10.13110/narrcult.6.1.0001

Heinrichs, J. (2020). *Thank you for arguing: What Aristotle, Lincoln, and Homer Simpson can teach us about the art of persuasion* (4th ed.). Broadway Books.

Hinyard, L. J., & Kreuter, M. W. (2007). Using narrative communication as a tool for health behavior change: A conceptual, theoretical, and empirical overview. *Health Education & Behavior*, *34*(5), 777–792. https://doi.org/10.1177/1090198106291963

Houlahan, C. (2022, October 24). *One chip at a time* [Video]. YouTube. www.youtube.com/watch?v=fk313wY2XKQ

Iyengar, S., Norpoth, H., & Hahn, K. S. (2004). Consumer demand for election news: The horserace sells. *The Journal of Politics*, *66*(1), 157–175. https://doi.org/10.1046/j.1468-2508.2004.00146.x

Jamieson, K. H. (1996). *Packaging the presidency: A history and criticism of presidential campaign advertising*. Oxford University Press.

Johnston, A. & Kaid, L. L. (2002). Image ads and issue ads in U.S. presidential advertising: Using videostyle to explore stylistic differences in televised political ads from 1952 to 2000. *Journal of Communication*, *52*(2), 281–300. https://doi.org/10.1093/joc/52.2.281

Jung, M. H., & Critcher, C. R. (2018). How encouraging niceness can incentivize nastiness: An unintended consequence of advertising reform. *Journal of Marketing Research*, *55*(1), 147–161. https://doi.org/10.1509/jmr.14.0654

Kreiss, D. (2012). Acting in the public sphere: The 2008 Obama campaign's strategic use of new media to shape narratives of the presidential race. In J. Earl & D. A. Rohlinger (Eds.), *Media, movements, and political change* (pp. 195–223). Emerald Group Publishing Limited. https://doi.org/10.1108/S0163-786X(2012)0000033011

Lau, R. R., Sigelman, L., & Rovner, I. B. (2007). The effects of negative political campaigns: A meta-analytic reassessment. *The Journal of Politics, 69*(4), 1176–1209. https://doi.org/10.1111/j.1468-2508.2007.00618.x

Lazarsfeld, P. F., Berelson, B., & Gaudet, H. (1944). *The people's choice: How the voter makes up his mind in a presidential campaign.* Duell, Sloan and Pearce.

Lee, L. (n.d.). *Split second ad* [Video]. Vimeo. https://vimeo.com/votelaurel

Lyotard, J.-F. (1984). *The postmodern condition: A report on knowledge.* University of Minnesota Press.

Malliotakis, N. (2022, October 17). *Biden or me* [Video]. YouTube. www.youtube.com/watch?v=UMC3GEmrTFo

Malliotakis, N. (2022, October 31). *They're coming* [Video]. YouTube. www.youtube.com/watch?v=U2U6wGMAYSQ

Manners, I., & Murray, P. (2016). The end of a noble narrative? European integration narratives after the Nobel Peace Prize. *Journal of Common Market Studies, 54*(1), 185–202. https://doi.org/10.1111/jcms.12324

Matthes, J., & Marquart, F. (2015). A new look at campaign advertising and political engagement: Exploring the effects of opinion-congruent and -incongruent political advertisements. *Communication Research, 42*(1), 134–155. https://doi.org/10.1177/0093650213514600

Mayer, F. W. (2014). *Narrative politics: Stories and collective action.* Oxford University Press. https://doi.org/10.1093/acprof:oso/9780199324460.001.0001

McLaughlin, B., Thompson, B. A., & Krause, A. (2017). Political fiction: Political e-mails during the 2014 U.S. midterm election. *Social Science Computer Review, 36*(3), 277–295. https://doi.org/10.1177/0894439317718536

McLaughlin, B., & Velez, J. A. (2019). Imagined politics: How different media platforms transport citizens into political narratives. *Social Science Computer Review, 37*(1), 22–37. https://doi.org/10.1177/0894439317746327

McLaughlin, B., Velez, J. A., Gotlieb, M. R., Thompson, B. A., & Krause-McCord, A. (2019). React to the future: Political visualization, emotional reactions and political behavior. *International Journal of Advertising, 38*(5), 760–775. https://doi.org/10.1080/02650487.2018.1556193

Mills, C. (2022, July 11). *Cory Mills ad: 'Control'* [Video]. YouTube. www.youtube.com/watch?v=jlAV0C63VXA

Molinaro, M. (2022, July 27). *TV ad: Representing US* [Video]. YouTube. www.youtube.com/watch?v=zPB8KAvohVk

Molinaro, M. (2022, October 24). *The choice* [Video]. YouTube. www.youtube.com/watch?v=KCwh5iUs0p4

Naeem, M., Ozuem, W., Howell, K., & Ranfagni, S. (2023). A step-by-step process of thematic analysis to develop a conceptual model in qualitative research. *International Journal of Qualitative Methods, 22.* https://doi.org/10.1177/16094069231205789

Patterson, M., & Monroe, K. (1998). Narrative in political science. *Annual Review of Political Science, 1*, 315–331. https://doi.org/10.1146/annurev.polisci.1.1.315

Patterson, T. E., & McClure, R. D. (1976). *The unseeing eye: The myth of television power in national politics.* Putnam.

Perloff, R. M. (2023). *The dynamics of persuasion: communication and attitudes in the twenty-first century* (8th ed.). Routledge.

Polkinghorne, D. E. (1995). Narrative configuration in qualitative analysis. *International Journal of Qualitative Studies in Education, 8*(1), 5–23. https://doi.org/10.1080/0951839950080103

Polletta, F. (2015). Characters in political storytelling. *Storytelling, Self, Society, 11*(1), 34–55. https://doi.org/10.13110/storselfsoci.11.1.0034

Polletta, F., & Callahan, J. (2017). Deep stories, nostalgia narratives, and fake news: Storytelling in the Trump era. *American Journal of Cultural Sociology, 5*(3), 392–408. https://doi.org/10.1057/s41290-017-0037-7

Roselle, L., Miskimmon, A., & O'Loughlin, B. (2014). Strategic narrative: A new means to understand soft power. *Media, War & Conflict, 7*(1), 70–84. https://doi.org/10.1177/1750635213516696

Scholten, H. (2022, September 14). *Uphold* [Video]. YouTube. www.youtube.com/watch?v=76chtNcc734

Scholten, H. (2022, October 20). *No other candidate —Hillary Scholten* [Video]. YouTube. www.youtube.com/watch?v=qhI7yU6vCtU

Scholten, H. (2022, October 24). *Built to last—Hillary Scholten* [Video]. YouTube. www.youtube.com/watch?v=aBHgYPF58iA

Schrier, K. (2022, August 3). *Extreme* [Video]. YouTube. www.youtube.com/watch?v=BhYbvj-O9zQ

Schrier, K. (2022, September 21). *Police* [Video]. YouTube. www.youtube.com/watch?v=p-58iPDgQ_U

Schrier, K. (2022, October 4). *Walk* [Video]. YouTube. www.youtube.com/watch?v=IeIlXkDVLSk

Schrier, K. (2022, October 12). *Definition* [Video]. YouTube. www.youtube.com/watch?v=W4k7vvCv27I

Schrier, K. (2022, November 4). *Because* [Video]. YouTube. www.youtube.com/watch?v=U30cL0TGb8Q

Shanahan, E. A., Adams, S. M., E., Jones, M. D., & McBeth, M. K. (2014). The blame game: Narrative persuasiveness of the intentional causal mechanism. In M. D. Jones, E. A. Shanahan, & M. K. McBeth (Eds.), *The science of stories* (pp. 69–88). Palgrave Macmillan. https://doi.org/10.1057/9781137485861

Shen, F., Yang, G., Conlin, J., & Diddi, P. (2023). Effects of issue- and character-based narrative political ads on ad evaluations. *Journal of Media Psychology: Theories, Methods, and Applications, 35*(6), 325–334. https://doi.org/10.1027/1864-1105/a000374

Spence, D. P. (1984). *Narrative truth and historical truth: meaning and interpretation in psychoanalysis.* W.W. Norton.

Tekin, F., & Meissner, V. (2022). Political differentiation as the end of political unity? A narrative analysis. *The International Spectator, 57*(1), 72–89. https://doi.org/10.1080/03932729.2022.2018823

Vafeiadis, M., Li, R., & Shen, F. (2018). Narratives in political advertising: An analysis of the political advertisements in the 2014 midterm elections. *Journal of Broadcasting & Electronic Media, 62*(2), 354–370. https://doi.org/10.1080/08838151.2018.1451858

Van Steenburg, E. (2015). Areas of research in political advertising: A review and research agenda. *International Journal of Advertising, 34*(2), 195–231. https://doi.org/10.1080/02650487.2014.996194

Vesnic-Alujevic, L., & Van Bauwel, S. (2014). YouTube: A political advertising tool? A case study of the use of YouTube in the campaign for the European Parliament elections 2009. *Journal of Political Marketing, 13*(3), 195–212. https://doi.org/10.1080/15377857.2014.929886

White, H. (1981). The value of narrativity. In W. J. T. Mitchell (Ed.), *On narrative* (pp. 1–23). University of Chicago Press.

Williams, B. (2022, September 29). *Defending the middle class* [Video]. YouTube. www.youtube.com/watch?v=GN4P2InrzXI

Zeidenstein, H. (1972). Measuring Congressional seat losses in mid-term elections. *The Journal of Politics, 34*(1), 272–276. https://doi.org/10.2307/2129440

Zhao, X., & Bleske, G. L. (1995). Measurement effects in comparing voter learning from television news and campaign advertisements. *Journalism & Mass Communication Quarterly, 72*(1), 72–83. https://doi.org/10.1177/107769909507200106

# 6
# HOW CONGRESS MANAGED SOCIAL MEDIA AGENDA FRACTURE AND INVERSION DURING THE 2022 ELECTION

*Jason B. Reineke, Kenneth R. Blake, and Jun Zhang*

Political elites often speculate as to what issues will be most effective in driving voters to the polls. Politicians seek to take advantage of events and topics related to those issues to advance toward their goals. In the 2022 United States midterm elections, polling consistently pointed to the economy, and particularly the topic of inflation, as the main issue at the forefront of voters' minds and at the top of the media agenda. The economy and inflation, along with immigration, crime, and low approval ratings for President Joseph Biden were popularly believed to be advantageous issues for Republicans, who were expected to take control of the House of Representatives by a wide margin, and perhaps the United States Senate, in part because of the prominence of these issues prior to the election. The importance that voters attributed to issues perceived to be advantageous to Democrats, like abortion following the United States Supreme Court's decision in *Dobbs v. Jackson Women's Health Organization,* 597 U.S. 215 (2022), protecting democracy in the aftermath of the January 6, 2021, attack on the U.S. Capitol by a crowd that tried to stop certification of the 2020 presidential election, and gun control declined as the election neared (Cohn, 2022). Ultimately, Republicans did take the House, but only by a narrow majority, while Democrats retained control of the Senate.

The present research investigates how discussion of prominent issues increased and decreased over the approximately two-year term of the 117th U.S. Congress, including the 2022 midterm elections. Academic access to the Twitter application programming interface (API) provided text and metadata for all tweets by sitting members of the U.S. Congress as well as by several news media outlets frequently retweeted or quoted by the respective parties during that time period. Simultaneously, Brandwatch data counted mentions

DOI: 10.4324/9781003440833-8

**126** Media Messages in the 2022 Midterm Election

of the same issues in social media posts by the general U.S. public. This research examines changes in the relative frequencies with which these groups mentioned the issues considered, with special attention to partisan differences in those changes. Overall, these data depict partisan attempts to build and manage fractured agendas and may provide insights about the effects and function of these processes in the contemporary political media context. The data and analyses present here also represent a distinct moment in time. As discussed in more detail below, the Twitter API used in this research became unavailable after the billionaire owner of Tesla and SpaceX Elon Musk bought Twitter later in 2022 and after rebranded the platform as X (Stokel-Walker, 2024; Capoot, 2023). However, similar data can still be obtained through Brandwatch and other social media listening platforms.

### Agenda Fracture and Inversion

Classic agenda-setting theory (e.g., McCombs & Shaw, 1972; McCombs & Valenzuela, 2021) stipulates that media organizations don't tell the public what to think but do tell the public what issues to think about, especially in terms of the relative importance of issues to one another in the agenda. As the theory has evolved in the decades since its founding, agenda setting has grown to include the proposition that media outlets similarly emphasize issue and object attributes more or less relative to one another (McCombs et al., 1997). Furthermore, media may emphasize the connections between issues, objects, and their attributes relatively more or less as well (McCombs et al., 2014). The media's agenda-setting effect on audience cognitions is one of accessibility or salience, or the ability to recall from the top of the mind what the most important issues being discussed are at a given time (Feezell, 2018; Price & Tewksbury, 1997; Scheufele & Tewksbury, 2007).

Media agendas do not exist in a vacuum, nor are they solely determined by the decisions of media content producers and distributors. Interested entities attempt to shape media messages to pursue their goals. Political actors approach communication and media strategically in their efforts to win elections, influence elite and public perceptions, and implement policies (Serazio, 2014). These efforts include attempts to manage (McNair, 2008) or build (Arceneaux et al., 2022) political agendas. Doing so involves understanding, emphasizing, and directing attention toward issues that are perceived to be beneficial to candidates, campaigns, and the policy implementation. It also means avoiding, perhaps even ignoring, topics that are perceived to be disadvantageous to political goals. Issues that are politically advantageous to a politician, campaign, or party are said to be *owned*. Previous research has shown that issue ownership differs between parties, is driven by elites, and creates different partisan agendas (Petrocik, 1996). Although party issue ownership is generally stable, it is not absolute, and non-owner parties can attempt to take over issue ownership, sometimes successfully (Conway et al., 2015; Petrocik, 1996; Petrocik et al., 2003).

When such shifts occur, they can stem from changes that partisan communicators perceive in the utility of maintaining or owning issues, and they can manifest as variations, over time, in the volume of discussion from partisan communicators about the issue. In turn, the variation can contribute to the *fragmentation* of partisan political agendas, or the phenomena of different political elites, political media, and audiences focusing on different issues at different times for different reasons rather than forming a relatively consonant media agenda (Serazio, 2014). The public agenda endures despite fragmentation (Bulkow et al., 2012; Feezell, 2018). With this in mind, the present research reconceptualizes fragmentation somewhat as *fracturing*—while partisan political agendas are still generally part of the same whole, they may break and depart, even widely, from each other as partisan communicators perceive different political advantages or disadvantages associated with discussing specific issues. It seems likely that there will usually be some response or discussion of a potentially disadvantageous issue remaining among the party that perceives it as such. However, the amount of communication dedicated to the issue by that party is expected to be less, perhaps far less, than that for the party that perceives advantage and seeks to maintain or take issue ownership.

Examples of such hypothesized phenomena abound, including in the context of the 2022 midterm elections. As mentioned above, the *Dobbs* decision fundamentally changed the political communication dynamics involving issues of abortion, reproductive freedom, and women's health care. We propose that what was previously perceived as an issue strategically favorable to Republicans, and was therefore discussed relatively more by them prior to *Dobbs*, became perceived as more favorable to Democrats and discussed relatively more by them, especially framed as a matter of reproductive freedom, after *Dobbs*. Abortion remains an important agenda item overall, but how much it is discussed by Democratic and Republican partisans is expected to observably change.

Similarly, changes in economic realities and perceptions, in conjunction with the partisan affiliation of the president, would be expected to lead to shifts in who is talking more about the economy. The economy can reasonably be expected to maintain a fairly high position on the agenda overall. However, a booming economy favorable to the president is likely to be discussed relatively more by the president's party. Economic downturns are likely to be seized upon by the president's opponents as proof that things would be better were they in power, making them more likely to mention the economy relatively more under such conditions.

Thus, if a party begins to perceive an owned issue as disadvantageous, party communicators will de-emphasize the issue, and maybe even avoid mentioning it altogether. The issue would fall on that party's issue agenda as a

## 128 Media Messages in the 2022 Midterm Election

result. Meanwhile, if a competing party perceives the issue as having become advantageous to the party's goals, the party will switch from de-emphasizing or avoiding the issue to emphasizing it, thereby pushing the issue higher on the party's issue agenda in an attempt to take issue ownership. This process may progress to an *inversion*, meaning a point on the timeline at which the issue's volume of discussion by the party taking ownership substantially and persistently exceeds the issue's volume of discussion by the party giving up ownership.

For example, if the partisan trend lines in discussion of abortion not only shift, but cross each other for abortion or reproductive freedom, such that Democrats not only discuss the issue more than they did before *Dobbs*, but also thereafter discuss it even more than Republicans, whose discussion of the issue is expected to be in decline, an inversion will have taken place. Similarly, if Republicans, sensing a perception of economic stagnation, not only talk about the economy more than they did previously, but surpass declining Democratic discussion of the economy, an inversion will have taken place there as well.

### Social Media, News Media, and Political Communication

Social media have agenda-setting functions (Lewandowsky et al., 2020). For example, Feezell (2018) found that participants exposed to hard news stories selected from *The New York Times* and *The Washington Post* on Facebook tended to indicate greater salience of the issues discussed in those stories than did participants who were not exposed. However, this effect was more powerful for those with low political interest.

News outlets and political leaders adopted Twitter as a means to communicate with the public (Barberá & Zeitzoff, 2017), and political communication research has focused particular attention on the platform (Vergeer, 2015). For instance, Gilardi et al. (2022) found that the traditional media agenda was related to the social media agenda of politicians on Twitter in Switzerland. They identified two advantages of using Twitter in agenda-setting research. First, researchers can collect data regarding the political agendas of both politicians and the public on the platform, and these data follow the same format and symbolic references, making them easy to analyze and compare. Second, the timestamp of Twitter data allows researchers to acutely capture the temporal patterns of interactions between agendas.

These principles have been applied previously to other national-level political communication research questions in the U.S. and abroad. Arceneaux et al. (2022) found that tweets, among other campaign communication, had inter-campaign effects across the 2018 gubernatorial and U.S. Senate races in Florida, respectively. In other words, partisan issue agendas in campaign communication, including Twitter, were related to each other in these races. Ausserhofer and Maireder (2013) found that Austrian political Twitter was primarily managed by political elites and that the amount of political topic discussion in this context was driven by the topic's proximity to media or technology issues. Topics with short-lived news cycles in legacy media tended to be higher on the Austrian political Twitter agenda as well.

Conway and colleagues have studied Twitter's role in agenda setting and agenda building across the 2012 (Conway et al., 2015), 2016 (Conway-Silva et al., 2018) and 2020 (Conway et al., 2022) U.S. presidential primary elections, especially in terms of the time order of agenda building. The findings across these studies are mixed. During the 2012 presidential primary election season, primary candidates and the parties effectively managed social media to influence and build the news media agenda across most issues, including the economy, employment, energy, foreign policy, health care, and taxes. One exception was the issue of the budget. News media consistently led, but a reciprocal relationship was evident, too, in which political elites responded and in turn influenced the news media agenda. The 2012 results did not indicate issue ownership differences in the amount of tweets by candidates or parties (Conway et al., 2015).

In contrast, during the 2016 presidential primary season the news media agenda consistently led the political agenda of candidates on Twitter, although, for some issues, reciprocal relationships were once again evidenced (affirmative action, banking, gun control, immigration, and social welfare for Democratic candidates; and banking, employment, foreign policy, health care, and social welfare for Republican candidates). For many issues, candidates and news media were all discussing the same issues at the same time (Conway-Silva et al., 2018). This last observation may be interpreted to indicate that perhaps even time series lags on the order of days, as used in Conway-Silva et al.'s (2018) work, may not adequately capture the speed with which stories develop on Twitter.

In the most recent of this series of studies, the researchers wrote that "intermedia agenda-setting power was more even-handed during the 2020 nomination season compared to 2012 and 2016" (Conway et al., 2022, p. 247). The results revealed consistently reciprocal relationships between the agendas of candidates and news media outlets across issues. However, the influence of news outlet agendas on candidates' Twitter agendas was somewhat weaker than that observed in the previous two studies.

Shifting attention to Congress, Barberá et al. (2019) analyzed all tweets sent by members of the House and Senate during the 113th U.S. Congress from January 2013 to December 2014. They compared topic counts in those tweets to topic counts among four samples of Twitter users: the general public, the attentive public who follow a major news media outlet, Republican supporters, and Democratic supporters. They also compared both the Congressional and public Twitter agendas with the Twitter agendas of the 36 largest media outlets in the U.S. as reviewed by the Pew Research Center. Barberá et al.'s (2019) results indicate that members of Congress were well able to lead party supporters and

**130** Media Messages in the 2022 Midterm Election

the attentive public on attention to issues, but they did not similarly lead the general public's issue attention. Instead, the reverse occurred: the issue agenda of members of Congress tended to follow the issue agenda of the public, with the Twitter agenda of Republican supporters showing the most influence on the agendas of both Democratic and Republican members of Congress, although members of Congress from both parties were strongly responsive to their own respective supporters. The media agenda was responsive to the attentive public, and relatively less so to members of Congress. The media agenda had the greatest impact on the agendas of members of Congress and party supporters.

### The Present Research

The present research adds to the literature in several important ways. First, it contributes additional analysis of the numerous and varied Twitter discussions by and surrounding members of Congress in the context of the 117th U.S. Congress in 2021 and 2022 leading up to and through the 2022 midterm elections. The findings provide valuable insight into the content of Congress's agenda on the platform, and how it compares to the agenda of news media and the social media agenda of the public in the aftermath of the January 6, 2021, attack on the Capitol and during the first two years of Joseph Biden's presidency.

This study has a few important similarities and differences when compared to its immediate predecessors that provide additional perspective. Unlike Conway et al.'s (2015, 2018, 2022) focus on presidential primary candidates, but like Barberá et al. (2019), this study focuses on sitting members of the U.S. Congress, with incumbent candidates, most (but not all) of whom were up for re-election in the 2022 midterms. Furthermore, the present research uses Brandwatch, a social media listening platform that monitors online conversations across various sources, to capture the broader public social media agenda rather than the Twitter samples used by Barberá et al. (2019) and the exclusive focus on presidential candidates and news media outlets of Conway et al. (2015, 2018, 2022).

Unlike Conway et al.'s (2015, 2018, 2022) focus on traditional newspapers of record as media outlets, or the large list from the Pew Research Center used by Barberá et al. (2019), the present research identified the most influential media outlets using Twitter itself. This study is also less concerned than Conway et al. (2015, 2018, 2022) or Barberá et al. (2019) with granular time-order analysis, which seems to both consistently reveal reciprocity (rather than more convincingly answering the question of who leads whom) and fail to fully capture the speed at which the platform functions. Instead, the present research focuses on relative, comparative trends over the entire timeline of the data. Finally, particular attention is paid here to potential shifts in issue ownership and the possibility of agenda inversion that may result.

## Methods

Academic-level access to the Twitter 2.0 API, the academictwitteR package (Barrie & Ho, 2021) for R (R Core Team, 2022), and a custom R script were used to collect all available tweets, retweets and quoted tweets posted by members of the 117th U.S. Congress to their main Twitter accounts between January 3, 2021, the day the 117th Congress convened, and January 3, 2023, the day it ended. Defunct as of early 2023, academic-level access to the Twitter 2.0 API, or application programming interface, allowed academic researchers to collect large volumes of Twitter content and metadata at no cost. Meanwhile, academictwitteR was an add-on package for the R programming language that allowed R code users who had obtained academic access credentials to easily access and use the API. Following Musk's purchase of the platform, free academic API access ended. The change rendered the academictwitteR package inoperable. Shortly after, the package's developers discontinued the package's development and support.

Twitter account handles were identified from a GitHub repository (Tauberer, 2023), supplemented by information from the U.S. House of Representatives Press Gallery (U.S. House of Representatives, n.d.) and searches of the Twitter platform. Tweets were captured in two phases, one in October of 2022 that captured all available member tweets to date, and a second in January 2023 that captured subsequent tweets through January 3, 2023.

Analysis of the October data identified the seven media outlets retweeted and quoted most frequently by Republican members, and the seven media outlets retweeted and quoted most frequently by Democratic members. For Republican members, the list consisted of, in descending order of popularity, *Fox News*, *Newsmax*, the *Washington Examiner*, *Daily Caller*, the *New York Post*, *Townhall. com*, and *The Wall Street Journal*. Top choices for Democratic members were *The New York Times*, *The Washington Post*, *The Associated Press*, *CNN*, *NBC News*, *ABC News*, and *National Public Radio* (NPR). All tweets from these sources were collected for the period between January 3, 2021, and January 3, 2023.

The tidytext package for R (Silge & Robinson, 2016) yielded word frequency counts for the text of Congressional tweets, both in total and broken down by party. Another of the many free add-on packages for R, tidytext provides R coders with a set of easy-to-use text mining functions useful for deriving analyzable data from unstructured text files. Guided by the word frequency counts, the analysis focused on tweets about any of three issues, immigration, abortion, and the economy/inflation, or about either of two individuals, former U.S. President Donald Trump and current U.S. President Joseph Biden. Case insensitive electronic searches for keywords related to these issues and individuals then categorized each tweet as either mentioning or not mentioning each topic. To identify and count tweets about immigration, the terms "border,"

**132** Media Messages in the 2022 Midterm Election

"bidenbordercrisis," "immigra," "illegal aliens," and "alien" were used. Including the term "immigra" and using R's grepl function to search for the terms meant that a tweet could be coded as mentioning immigration if it included any word starting with "immigra," such as "immigrant," "immigrants," and, of course, "immigration." Meanwhile, tweets about abortion were identified by searching for the terms "abort," "reproductive rights," "unborn," "right to life," "right to choose," and "roe v." Terms for tweets about the economy were "inflation," "rising prices," "economic," and "economy." Tweets about Trump were found using the terms "trump," "donald trump," and "maga." Keywords for tweets about Biden were "biden," "joe biden," and "uncle joe." The grepl code was set to ignore capitalization. Accordingly, a search for "joe biden" detected "joe biden," "Joe Biden," and any other mix of capital and lowercase letters used to form Biden's name. These counts were aggregated by week and type of source, with each week beginning on a Monday and concluding the following Sunday.

Next, Brandwatch queries were used to produce weekly tallies, by topic, of social media posts by the general U.S. public that mentioned the keywords described above. Brandwatch is a web-based subscription platform that enables users to access historical and live data from a variety of social media and online news sources, such as Twitter, Reddit, and YouTube. Brandwatch was recognized as a social media listening platform leader in the 2020 Forrester Wave (Liu & Dawson, 2020) and has been used for collecting Twitter data in many previous studies (e.g., Borah et al., 2022). Brandwatch extrapolates volume based on the sampled mentions. Stacked-area charts, bivariate correlations, and paired and independent-samples t-tests were used to identify and evaluate patterns in the data. R's *corrplot* package (Wei & Simko, 2021) was used to compute correlations and represent them visually. T-tests were computed in base R.

## Results

The R script captured 2,134,539 tweets in all, 1,011,987 from 523 members of Congress and 1,122,552 from the 14 media outlets retweeted most frequently by Democratic and Republican members. Table 6.1 shows descriptive statistics for each type of source in the dataset. Given that there were only two independent members of Congress who used Twitter, the analysis focused on contrasts between Democratic and Republican members and their preferred media outlets.

The Brandwatch query of social media traffic from the general public projected 1,095,302,917 posts in all, with subtotals by topic ranging from 90,197,451 posts mentioning one of the "abortion" search terms to 423,904,768 posts mentioning one of the "Trump" search terms. Unfortunately, Brandwatch projections for the first three weeks of the 117th Congress's term were unavailable. Graphics show tweet totals from Congressional and media sources during those first three weeks, even though the general public totals are missing. The first three weeks

## How Congress Managed Social Media Agenda Fracture and Inversion **133**

**TABLE 6.1** Congressional and Preferred Media Outlet Twitter Data Descriptives

| Source | Total tweets | Mean tweets/ source | Standard deviation | Median | Min. | Max. |
|---|---|---|---|---|---|---|
| Democratic members | 581,830 | 2,187 | 1,358 | 1,943 | 231 | 10,411 |
| Democratic-preferred media | 511,647 | 73,092 | 32,460 | 70,593 | 30,670 | 137,349 |
| Independent members | 2,338 | 1,169 | 320 | 1,169 | 943 | 1,395 |
| Republican members | 427,819 | 1,678 | 1,396 | 1,344 | 15 | 11,913 |
| Republican-preferred media | 610,905 | 76,363 | 52,074 | 69,778 | 6,520 | 158,897 |

were, however, excluded from the data when calculating correlations. Given the disproportionately high volume of public social media posts relative to the number of Congressional and media tweets, counts of public social media posts were re-expressed in units of 5,000.

The most-tweeted individual term among Republican members of Congress was "Biden" ($n = 58,281$). The runner-up was "border," typically in the context of immigration. The next-most-common terms were "energy" ($n = 25,069$) and "inflation" ($n = 22,140$). Both of the latter terms usually referenced economic hardships. Among Democratic members, "health" came in as the top term ($n = 46,679$) and referred to everything from "mental health" to "reproductive health" to "health care spending." The next-most-tweeted terms were "families" ($n = 43,736$), "people" ($n = 42,979$), "American" ($n = 38,870$), "care" ($n = 37,680$), "support" ($n = 37,248$), and so on. The term "abortion" received 9,396 mentions among Democrats and 3,662 among Republicans, although the word's plural form, "abortions," was mentioned more often by Republicans ($n = 1,686$) than Democrats ($n = 671$). Democrats also held a near monopoly on the term "reproductive" ($n = 5,212$), which Republicans tweeted only 44 times. Republicans favored the term "unborn," mentioning it 1,799 times compared to only eight mentions by Democrats.

### Topic Volume by Week and Source

Figure 6.1 uses a stacked-area chart to compare aggregate volume from all sources for each of the topics examined across each of the 105 weeks of the 117th Congress. Recall that volume from the general public was recast in units of 5,000 but is indistinguishable, both in this chart and in the descriptive statistics given below, from the single-item volume counts for Congressional and media sources.

Biden's volume, shown in the topmost region of the chart, was the most consistently large throughout the period, averaging 2,392 per week with a standard deviation of 660. Trump's volume, shown in the second region from the top, averaged 1,454 per week with a standard deviation of 773 and features a relatively high volume at the start of the period—during the aftermath of the 2020 election and the January 6, 2021, attack on the U.S. Capitol—and again toward the end of the period. The latter period coincides with televised hearings regarding the January 6 attack, the FBI's retrieval of classified documents from Trump's Mar-a-Lago, Florida, home, and Trump's return to politicking during the run-up to the 2022 midterm elections. The economy and immigration showed lower but steady topic volume across the period, averaging 1,130 ($SD$ = 456) and 827 ($SD$ = 362) weekly mentions, respectively. Abortion received relatively few mentions for the first two thirds of the period, but mentions spiked during the final third of the period, at first with the leak of the U.S. Supreme Court's *Dobbs v. Jackson Women's Health Organization*, 597 U.S. 215 (2022), ruling and again with the release of the final ruling that overturned *Roe v. Wade*, 410 U.S. 113 (1973). Weekly abortion mentions averaged only 460 across the period but showed a standard deviation of 648 mentions, reflecting the measure's end-of-period volatility.

The inset in the upper-right corner of Figure 6.1 shows little correlation among the weekly topic volume counts across the period. Small, but significant, positive correlations emerged for the Biden/immigration, abortion/economy, and Trump/economy pairings, and one small-but-significant negative correlation appeared for the Trump/immigration pair. But all other pairs show nonsignificant correlations, and the inset omits their coefficients.

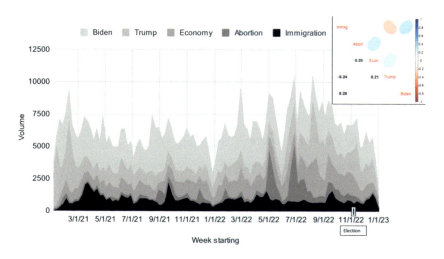

**FIGURE 6.1**   Total Topic Volume by Week.

## Immigration

Figure 6.2 depicts the weekly volume of references to immigration by each of the sources examined. Several peaks punctuate the figure, and most correspond to external events related to the immigration issue. The first peak, for example, aligns with Spring 2021 news coverage about the typical surge in Southern U.S. border crossings that occurs when migrants from Central and South America take advantage of relatively cooler weather that is more favorable for traveling on foot to the U.S. The Spring 2022 rise in volume may be connected to the same phenomenon. The second major peak from the left in the figure corresponds to media coverage of a September 19, 2021, ruling by the U.S. Senate's parliamentarian that barred Senate Democrats from using a budget reconciliation procedure to pass an immigration reform bill with a simple majority vote instead of amassing the two-thirds majority needed to break a likely Republican filibuster of the bill. The next-to-last peak probably marks an uptick in volume stemming from Florida Governor Ron DeSantis's decision to fly a planeload of immigrants to Martha's Vineyard, Massachusetts, on September 14, 2022, and the final peak may pertain to the U.S. Supreme Court's December 19, 2022, decision to halt the expiration of Title 42, a Trump-era policy restricting immigration to the U.S. because of COVID-19.

Republican members of Congress tweeted about immigration an average of 361 times per week ($SD$ = 196.11), while their Democratic colleagues tweeted about the topic an average of only 87 times a week ($SD$ = 58.42). A paired-samples t-test found the difference significant $t(104)$ = 15.70, $p < 0.05$). Similarly, Republican-preferred media out-tweeted Democratic-preferred media regarding

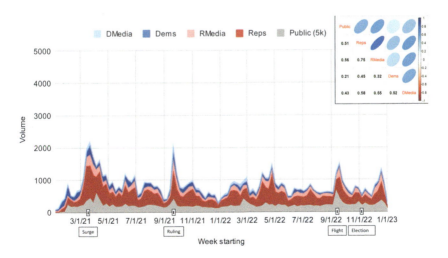

FIGURE 6.2  Immigration Topic Volume, by Week and Source.

136  Media Messages in the 2022 Midterm Election

immigration by a weekly average of 131 ($SD$ = 69.69) to 53 ($SD$ = 25.87), a difference that was also statistically significant $t$(104) = 13.47, $p$ < 0.05). Furthermore, the peaks in immigration-related tweets—driven, evidently, by Republican and Republican-preferred media tweeting—typically corresponded to peaks in immigration-related social media posts by the general public, represented by the bottom layer in the figure. The inset's correlation data show a strongly positive relationship between the tweet volumes of Congressional Republicans and their preferred media outlets as well as the general public. Meanwhile, immigration-related tweet volumes among Congressional Democrats and their preferred media correlate positively, and both correlate positively—although less so—with public social media volume.

### Abortion

Figure 6.3 looks fundamentally different in a number of ways. Early in the Congressional term, Republicans seemed to tweet about abortion relatively more often than their Democratic counterparts did. But social media volume about abortion remained low across all sources relative to, for example, volume about the immigration topic explored above. However, volume spiked—most noticeably among public social media users—around September 1, 2021, at about the time a Texas law took effect banning abortion after a detectable "fetal heartbeat." Somewhat more abortion-related tweet volume became evident among Congressional Democrats between then and the May 2, 2022, leak of the Supreme Court's *Dobbs v. Jackson Women's Health Organization,* 597 U.S. 215

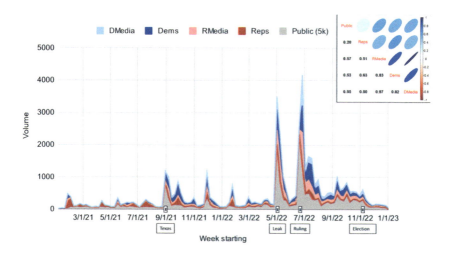

**FIGURE 6.3**   Abortion Topic Volume, by Week and Source.

(2022), ruling draft. Democratic tweet volume about abortion increased even more after the court released its final ruling on June 24, 2022, and remained relatively high through the midterm election in November. During the same period, Congressional Republicans grew relatively quiet about abortion. T-tests provide evidence supporting these patterns. A paired-samples t-test, for example, found that the average weekly abortion tweet volume among Democrats ($M = 100.13$, $SD = 152.49$) significantly exceeded $t(104) = 3.86$, $p < 0.05$) the average weekly abortion tweet volume among Congressional Republicans ($M = 54.63$, $SD = 70.78$). Furthermore, Democrats in Congress posted, on average, about one fewer abortion-related tweets per week than their Republican colleagues ($M = -0.74$, $SD = 74.40$) before the leak of the *Dobbs v. Jackson Women's Health Organization*, 597 U.S. 215 (2022), draft ruling. After, however, Congressional Democrats posted, on average, about 134 more abortion-related tweets per week than Congressional Republicans did ($M = 134.14$, $SD = 142.33$), a statistically significant increase, $t(45) = 5.32$, $p < 0.05$.

Unlike Republican members of Congress, Republican-preferred media outlets ramped up the volume of their abortion-related tweets in the wake of the *Dobbs v. Jackson Women's Health Organization* (2022) draft ruling's leak. Prior to the leak, they out-tweeted Democratic-preferred media outlets on abortion by about five tweets a week on average ($M = 5.00$, $SD = 15.26$). After, they out-tweeted Democratic-preferred media outlets on abortion by just over 22 tweets per week on average ($M = 22.42$, $SD = 47.17$), $t(39) = 5.32$, $p < 0.05$). Similarly, the week-to-week comparison across the Congressional term showed Republican-preferred media outlets tweeting about abortion an average of 72 times per week ($SD = 125.08$) compared to an average of 61 times per week ($SD = 111.81$) among Democratic-preferred media outlets, $t(104) = 3.61$, $p < 0.05$). As the correlation inset shows, volume among Republican-preferred media outlets in fact correlated strongly both with volume among Democratic-preferred media outlets and with volume among Democratic members of Congress, and all three correlated moderately well with volume in the general public. Congressional Republicans correlated significantly, but weakly, with the general public on weekly abortion volume.

## Economy

Figure 6.4 shows yet another distinct pattern, depicting a steady rise in the volume of public social media posts about the economy corresponding, perhaps not coincidentally, to rising inflation and consumer prices over the period. Republicans and Democrats in Congress matched each other nearly tweet for tweet here, with Republicans tweeting an average of 319 times a week ($SD = 159.88$), and Democrats tweeting an average of 320 times a week ($SD = 178.88$), a nonsignificant difference ($t(104) = 0.03$, $p = 0.98$). Republican-preferred media

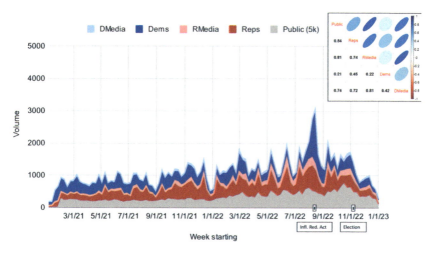

FIGURE 6.4   Economy Topic Volume, by Week and Source.

outlets did outpace Democratic-preferred media outlets on the topic, tweeting about the economy an average of 111 times a week ($SD = 65.03$) compared to 70 times a week ($SD = 30.51$) among Democratic-preferred outlets. Weekly volume among all groups correlated positively, although correlations for Democratic members of Congress lag conspicuously in the figure's inset, especially with Republican-preferred media outlets and the general public. But none of the Congressional or media groups seemed to produce notable spikes in public volume. Instead, the public volume gradually built steadily until after the midterm election. Even the mid-August flurry of tweets by Congressional Democrats about the August 16, 2022, passage of the Inflation Reduction Act seemed to have little impact on the public's tweet volume. This peak, the figure's most prominent feature, may account for a sizable chunk of the relatively low correlations evident between Congressional Democrats' volume and the volume of the other groups in the study, including the general public.

## *Trump*

Public tweet volume dominates Figure 6.5. The public averaged 807 ($SD = 488.67$) 5,000-tweet units about Trump per week, or, in raw terms, right around 4 million tweets a week. The volume dwarfed the weekly average volume among Republican-preferred media outlets ($M = 267.58$, $SD = 139.03$), Congressional Democrats ($M = 124.29$, $SD = 208.66$), Democratic-preferred media outlets ($M = 196.30$, $SD = 191.36$), and especially Congressional Republicans ($M = 58.45$, $SD = 42.43$). Democratic members of Congress, along with their

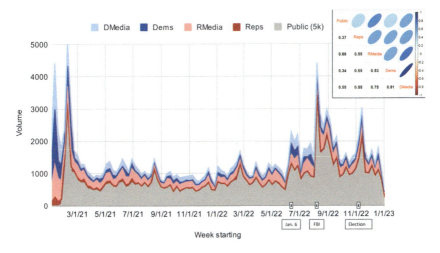

FIGURE 6.5 "Trump" Topic Volume, by Week and Source.

preferred media outlets, seemed especially interested in tweeting about Trump during and after the televised House hearings in the summer of 2022 about the January 6, 2021, attack on the U.S. Capitol. The interest persisted, if to a lesser degree, after the FBI retrieved classified documents from Trump's home in Mar-a-Lago, Florida. But as the 2022 midterms neared, Congressional Democrats seemed to join their Republican colleagues in trying to say as little as possible about the former president. Despite this pattern, Congressional Democrats' higher frequency of tweeting about Trump compared to their Republican colleagues proved statistically significant ($t(104) = 3.74$, $p < .05$). Republican-preferred media outlets, however, reversed the pattern, tweeting about Trump significantly more times per week, on average, than Democratic-preferred media outlets did ($t(104) = 7.02$, $p < .05$). Trump-related volume from Democratic-preferred media outlets correlated strongly with volume from Congressional Democrats and appreciably with Republican-preferred media outlets. Remaining correlations were lower, but still positive and significant.

### Biden

Congressional Republicans reluctant to tweet about their own party's recent president nonetheless tweeted with seeming abandon about their rival party's current president, as shown in Figure 6.6. They averaged 779 tweets a week about Biden ($SD = 285.47$) compared to 192 a week ($SD = 173.10$) among Congressional Democrats, a difference that was statistically significant ($t(104) = 18.93$, $p < .05$). Similarly, Republican-preferred media outlets tweeted

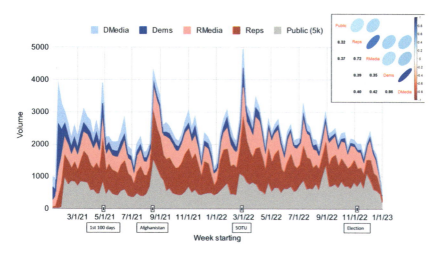

FIGURE 6.6  "Biden" Topic Volume, by Week and Source.

much more often about Biden ($M$ = 565.75, $SD$ = 148.49) than did Democratic-preferred media outlets ($M$ = 254.64, $SD$ = 147.87), $t(104)$ = 19.02, $p$ <.05. The weekly volume of tweets about Biden among Congressional Democrats may not look all that different from the volume of their weekly tweets about Trump in Figure 6.5, but it is significantly greater ($t(104)$ = 3.07, $p$ <.05).

Peak volumes in the figure correspond to Biden's first 100 days in office, the August 2021 withdrawal of U.S. troops from the airport in Kabul, Afghanistan, and Biden's 2022 State of the Union Address. Corresponding spikes in public social media posts about Biden are evident, but weekly post averages from the public remain largely flat across the period. Public post volume correlated weakly with Congressional Republican volume and Republican-preferred media volume and insignificantly with Congressional Democratic volume and Democratic-preferred media volume. The strongest correlations appeared between the two Congressional factions and their preferred media outlets.

## Discussion

This research considers the 117th Congress and 2022 midterms election in terms of agenda setting, agenda building, social and news media and the attributes these factors manifested together in that context. While news, political, and public agendas trended together as described by agenda-setting theory in the social media space, the data presented also show that those agendas are fractured relative to one another on a partisan and source basis.

Members of Congress appear to collectively attempt to build agendas by managing, maintaining, and relatively emphasizing and de-emphasizing issues and topics. Although the volume of mentions of the issues and topics generally increases and decreases together across partisan and news Twitter agendas and the public social media agenda, there are also noticeable differences and diversions between different agendas. The partisan differences in volume may indicate issue ownership. Some issues and topics clearly have greater attention among Congressional Democrats or Republicans, and among their respective favored media outlets.

Two issues were of particular note with regard to issue ownership and agenda building. First, abortion's place in the agendas seems to illustrate an example of possible issue ownership and fractured agenda *inversion.* Prior to the *Dobbs v. Jackson Women's Health Organization,* 597 U.S. 215 (2022), ruling, abortion appears to have been a Republican-owned issue. After, it appears to have become a Democratically-owned issue. Interestingly, Republican-favored media may have contributed to the magnitude of this shift by continuing to discuss abortion at a relatively high volume after the ruling, continuing to draw attention to an issue that Congressional Democrats seemed to perceive as advantageous and were eager to engage with while Congressional Republicans appeared to avoid discussion of the issue after the ruling.

Second, Congressional Democrats appeared to make a concerted effort to take ownership of economic issues with the passage of the Inflation Reduction Act, but this attempt failed, and Congressional Republicans maintained ownership of the issue. The Inflation Reduction Act was a wide-ranging bill that addressed issues as diverse as deficit reduction, prescription drug prices, domestic energy production, and environmental issues. However, despite its name, the law's impact on so-called kitchen table economic issues associated with inflation, such as the rising prices of groceries and other consumer goods, may have been at best delayed and perhaps even non-existent. The increased volume of Democratic tweets about the economy that followed the passage of this major legislation still did not correlate strongly with media or public tweets, and shortly thereafter Democratic tweets about the economy returned to near their previous level. Republican and Republican-preferred media tweets correlated more strongly with public social media discussion of the economy than Democratic and Democrat-preferred media tweets, respectively. Public perceptions of the economy, at least those expressed on social media, do not appear to have been strongly influenced by the passage of the Inflation Reduction Act or Democrats' attempts to promote attention to the law and build the economic agenda and issue ownership around it. The overall structure of the fractured economic agenda was largely unchanged by, and after the 2022 midterms.

However, Democratic efforts on the economy may not have been entirely ineffective. Though the public may not have been persuaded, Democrats appear to have at least challenged an issue that should have been a reliable strategic benefit to Republicans. On both abortion and the economy, contrary to the popular

**142** Media Messages in the 2022 Midterm Election

narrative that Republicans were at a distinct issue agenda advantage in the 2022 midterms, Republicans were actually, at least for a time as the election neared, on issue defense in the social media space. Though Republicans successfully maintained ownership of the economy by election day, they had lost abortion. This might help to explain some part of why Republicans underperformed electoral expectations in the 2022 midterms, despite other campaign wins and structural advantages that did give Republicans a majority in the House.

If communication patterns regarding abortion and the economy suggest fracturing as an attempt to take issue ownership, the patterns involving Trump and Biden may indicate fracturing as in terms of issue disownership. As Figures 6.5 and 6.6 indicate, Democrats and Republicans alike showed curiously little interest in calling attention to their respective party heads. Among both, calling attention instead to the head of the other party seemed like the preferred strategy. Particularly as Trump's legal troubles mounted in the wake of the January 6 hearings and the FBI raid of his Mar-a-Lago home, Republican members of Congress may have perceived Trump as both risky to oppose and risky to support. If so, then saying as little about him as possible would have seemed like a relatively safe alternative. Loudly attacking Biden, by contrast, perhaps provided a way to maintain visibility while hazarding little. After all, Biden's approval ratings were hovering in the low 40s, even as the midterm election approached.

Democratic members of Congress, meanwhile, no doubt were just as aware as their Republican counterparts of Biden's lethargic approval ratings. They may have seen little benefit in boosting his profile, especially as they appeared to gain political traction from passage of the Inflation Reduction Act and overturning of Roe v. Wade. Attacking Trump, the way Republicans were attacking Biden, may have seemed advantageous in the weeks immediately after the January 6 hearings and the FBI raid on Trump's home. But with the midterm election quickly approaching, giving Trump's supporters a reason to rally around him probably quickly began to seem unwise. The relatively greater willingness of partisan media to talk about both Biden and Trump, but especially Trump, may have been due to the substantial level of public discussion about Trump. News media profit by offering content audiences want, not by ignoring what audiences are talking about.

Future research should attempt to determine why and how attempts to maintain and take ownership and build agendas succeed or fail. There may be guidance to help answer these questions in Birkland's (1998) work on focusing events in agenda setting. No matter how much one tweets about an issue, things that happen externally to even the most strategically sound political communication have an impact on perceptions and voting behavior. Democrats passed a bill that, at least in name, addressed the economic inflation troubling the nation. But public discussion tracked more closely with that of Republicans and their preferred media outlets, perhaps because the realities of inflation most important to the public may not have seemed to favorably change with the passage of the bill. Similarly, despite widespread Republican abandonment of abortion discussion, public and media alarm at the realities resulting from the overturn of *Roe v. Wade,* 410 U.S. 113 (1973),was consistent with the increased volume of Democratic tweets about the issue.

The present research did not directly consider how issue framing may contribute to agenda fracturing and inversion. For example, did reframing of abortion from an issue focused on ideas mainly pertaining to the beginning of human *life* to those mainly pertaining to health and reproductive *freedom* contribute to fracturing, inversion, and issue ownership? Future research should examine the interconnections between agenda setting and framing in this manner.

Another aspect of the agenda-setting and agenda-building model that the data presented here could not address is the cognitive processes of people in terms of interaction, incorporation, reaction, and behavior relative to the social media communication examined. From a cognitive perspective, did 2022 midterm voters think about the issues used to build the agendas described in this paper in terms of accessibility? If this was the case, they would remember what was being talked about. Or did they apply some issues, but not others, when they stepped into the voting booth? If this was the case, they would vote based on the personal and expected effects on themselves and others. Is there a threshold or some other aspect of issue attention in an agenda that may make an issue more likely to be applicable? Perhaps more interestingly, did differences in accessibility versus applicability of issues, and the specific issues that were more or less applicable, differ on a partisan or voter-turnout basis? Future research should examine the complex relationships between fractured agendas, agenda building, cognitions, and voting behavior.

As the data for this research were collected, major changes were also happening with Twitter. In late October of 2022, billionaire Elon Musk completed an acquisition of the company and took it private (Conger & Hirsch, 2022). In the weeks and months that followed, Musk implemented massive changes to Twitter's staff and policies. These events raise at least two important questions about the future of research like that described here. First, will Musk's ownership and leadership have an impact on how elites and everyday users interact with each other and use (or decline to use) the platform? Might there be partisan effects, such that Republicans and their preferred media outlets use the platform more, while Democrats and their preferred media do so less? Will technical and functional changes increase or decrease the platform's influence overall?

Second, will research like this even be possible going in the future? In March of 2023, it was reported the Musk was considering a price point of nearly $500,000 per year for even the most limited of access to Twitter's API (Stokel-Walker, 2023); access that has previously been free upon approval for academic use. A similar data collection to that reported here would therefore cost something like $1 million under that proposed scheme. Indeed, our team's API access was terminated by July of 2023. By February of 2024, it was reported that Musk had put in place a paid API access plan starting at $42,000 per month (Stokel-Walker, 2024). This creates a noteworthy obstacle to gaining further knowledge about political communication in the social media space. As of this writing, our team only has access to data like that collected for this study via Brandwatch.

Agendas that were once more whole are now more separated. It is easy to see why this state is typically referred to as fragmentation—broken into narrow shards, with pieces of issues, publics, media, and nations wielded as tools to advance interests. Though split and turned in this manner, news, political, and public agendas, social media and traditional media agendas, are separated, but still connected. So perhaps *fractured* is a better way to think about these divisions. And fragments are shattered pieces, presumably broken forever. But, though they may break again and in different ways, fractures can also heal.

## References

Arceneaux, P., Albishri, O., & Kiousis, S. (2022, February). How candidates influence each other in electoral politics: Intercandidate agenda-building in Florida's 2018 midterm election. *Journal of Political Marketing*. https://doi.org/10.1080/15377 857.2022.2040690

Ausserhofer, J., & Maireder, A. (2013). National politics on Twitter. *Information, Communication & Society*, *16*(3), 291–314. https://doi.org/10.1080/13691 18X.2012.756050

Barberá, P., Casas, A., Nagler, J., Egan, P. J., Bonneau, R., Jost, J. T., & Tucker, J. A. (2019). Who leads? Who follows? Measuring issue attention and agenda setting by legislators and the mass public using social media data. *American Political Science Review*, *113*(4), 883–901. https://doi.org/10.1017/S0003055419000352

Barberá, P., & Zeitzoff, T. (2017). The new public address system: Why do world leaders adopt social media? *International Studies Quarterly*, *62*(1), 121–130. https://doi.org/10.1093/isq/sqx047

Barrie, C., & Ho, J. C. (2021). academictwitter: An R package to access the Twitter academic research product track v2 API endpoint. *Journal of Open Source Software*, *6*(62), Article 3272. https://doi.org/10.21105/joss.03272

Birkland, T. A. (1998). Focusing events, mobilization, and agenda setting. *Journal of Public Policy*, *18*(1), 53–74. https://doi.org/10.1017/S0143814X98000038

Borah, P., Keib, K., Trude, B., Binford, M., Irom, B., & Himelboim, I. (2022). "You are a disgrace and traitor to our country": Incivility against "the squad" on Twitter. *Internet Research*, *32*(5), 1646–1661. https://doi.org/10.1108/INTR-06-2021-0363

Bulkow, K., Urban, J., & Schweiger, W. (2012). The duality of agenda-setting: The role of information processing. *International Journal of Public Opinion Research*, *25*(1), 43–63. https://doi.org/10.1093/ijpor/eds003

Capoot, A. (2023, July 24). *Elon Musk rebrands Twitter to 'X,' replaces iconic bird logo.* CNBC. www.cnbc.com/2023/07/24/elon-musk-rebrands-twitter-to-x-replaces-iconic-bird-logo.html

Cohn, N. (2022, October 24). A Republican advantage: As headlines shift in the weeks before the midterms, so to voters' top concerns. *The New York Times.* www.nytimes.com/2022/10/24/briefing/republican-polling-midterms.html

Conger, K., Hirsh, L. (2022, October 27). Elon Musk completes $44 billion deal to own Twitter. *The New York Times.* www.nytimes.com/2022/10/27/technology/elon-musk-twitter-deal-complete.html

Conway, B. A., Kenski, K., & Wang, D. (2015). The rise of Twitter in the political campaign: Searching for intermedia agenda-setting effects in the presidential primary. *Journal of Computer-Mediated Communication, 20*(4), 363–380. https://doi.org/10.1111/jcc4.12124

Conway, B. A., Tsetsi, E., Kenski, K., & Shmargad, Y. (2022). Tipping the Twitter vs. news media scale? Conducting a third assessment of intermedia agenda-setting effects during the presidential nomination season. *Journal of Political Marketing, 21*(3-4), 247–258. https://doi.org/10.1080/15377857.2022.2099582

Conway-Silva, B. A., Filer, C. R., Kenski, K., & Tsetsi, E. (2018). Reassessing Twitter's agenda-building power: An analysis of intermedia agenda-setting effects during the 2016 presidential primary season. *Social Science Computer Review, 36*(4), 469–483. https://doi.org/10.1177/0894439317715430

Dobbs v. Jackson Women's Health Organization, 597 U.S. 215 (2022). www.supremecourt.gov/opinions/21pdf/19-1392_6j37.pdf

Feezell, J. T. (2018). Agenda setting through social media: The importance of incidental news exposure and social filtering in the digital era. *Political Research Quarterly, 71*(2), 482–494. https://doi.org/10.1177/1065912917744895

Gilardi, F., Gessler, T., Kubli, M., & Müller, S. (2022). Social media and political agenda setting. *Political Communication, 39*(1), 39–60. https://doi.org/10.1080/10584609.2021.1910390

Lewandowsky, S., Jetter, M., & Ecker, U. K. H. (2020). Using the president's tweets to understand political diversion in the age of social media. *Nature Communications, 11*(1), 5764. https://doi.org/10.1038/s41467-020-19644-6

Liu, J., & Dawson, S. (2020). *The Forrester wave™: Social listening platforms, q4 2020.* Forrester. www.forrester.com/report/the-forrester-wave-social-listening-platforms-q4-2020/RES157487

McCombs, M., Llamas, J. P., Lopez-Escobar, E., & Rey, F. (1997). Candidate images in Spanish elections: Second-level agenda-setting effects. *Journalism & Mass Communication Quarterly, 74*(4), 703–717. https://doi.org/10.1177/107769909707400404

McCombs, M., & Valenzuela, S. (2021). *Setting the agenda: Mass media and public opinion* (3rd ed.). John Wiley & Sons.

McCombs, M. E., & Shaw, D. L. (1972). The agenda-setting function of mass media. *Public Opinion Quarterly, 36*(2), 176–187. https://doi.org/10.1086/267990

McCombs, M. E., Shaw, D. L., & Weaver, D. H. (2014). New directions in agenda-setting theory and research. *Mass Communication and Society, 17*(6), 781–802. https://doi.org/10.1080/15205436.2014.964871

McNair, B. (2008). The internet and the changing global media environment. In A. Chadwick & P. N. Howard (Eds.), *Routledge handbook of internet politics* (pp. 217–229). Routledge. https://doi.org/10.4324/9780203962541

Petrocik, J. R. (1996). Issue ownership in presidential elections, with a 1980 case study. *American Journal of Political Science, 40*(3), 825–850. https://doi.org/10.2307/2111797

Petrocik, J. R., Benoit, W. L., & Hansen, G. J. (2003). Issue ownership and presidential campaigning, 1952-2000. *Political Science Quarterly, 118*(4), 599–626. www.jstor.org/stable/30035698

Price, V., & Tewksbury, D. (1997). News values and public opinion: A theoretical account of media priming and framing. In G. A. Barett & F. J. Boster (Eds.), *Progress in communication sciences: Advances in persuasion* (Vol. 13, pp. 173–212). Ablex.

R Core Team. (2022). *R: A Language and Environment for Statistical Computing* (Version 4.2.2). [Computer software] R Foundation for Statistical Computing. www.R-project.org/

Roe v. Wade, 410 U.S. 113 (1973). www.oyez.org/cases/1971/70-18

Scheufele, D. A., & Tewksbury, D. (2007). Framing, agenda setting, and priming: The evolution of three media effects models. *Journal of Communication, 57*(1), 9–20. https://doi.org/10.1111/j.0021-9916.2007.00326.x

Serazio, M. (2014). The new media designs of political consultants: Campaign production in a fragmented era. *Journal of Communication, 64*(4), 743–763. https://doi.org/10.1111/jcom.12078

Silge, J., & Robinson, D. (2016). tidytext: Text mining and analysis using tidy data principles in R. *Journal of Open Source Software, 1*(3), 37. https://doi.org/10.21105/joss.00037

Stokel-Walker, C. (2023, March 10). *Twitter's $42,000-per-month API prices out nearly everyone*. Wired. www.wired.com/story/twitter-data-api-prices-out-nearly-everyone/

Stokel-Walker, C. (2024, February 27). Under Elon Musk, X is denying API access to academics who study misinformation. *Fast Company*. www.fastcompany.com/91040397/under-elon-musk-x-is-denying-api-access-to-academics-who-study-misinformation

Tauberer, J. (2023). *legislators-current.csv* [GitHub dataset]. Retrieved July 20, 2022, from https://github.com/unitedstates/congress-legislators

U.S. House of Representatives. (2022). *Members' official twitter handles*. U.S. House of Representatives Press Gallery. Retrieved July 20, 2022, from https://pressgallery.house.gov/member-data/members-official-twitter-handles

Vergeer, M. (2015). Twitter and political campaigning. *Sociology Compass, 9*(9), 745–760. https://doi.org/10.1111/soc4.12294

Wei, T., & Simko, V. (2021). *R package 'scorrplot': Visualization of a correlation matrix (Version 0.92)* [Computer software]. https://github.com/taiyun/corrplot

# SECTION III

# News Narratives

2022 Media Coverage and Public Perception

# 7
# THE IMPACT OF DIGITAL PARTISAN NEWS ALGORITHMS IN THE 2022 MIDTERM ELECTION

*Hyun Jung Yun and Jae Hee Park*

The 2022 midterm elections unfolded and served as an important path-breaking point in American election history. Unlike the expected red wave under the less popular Democratic Party president, the midterm election tendencies of out-party gains and in-party losses, known as "surge and decline theory" and "referendum theory" (Campbell, 2022), were nullified in the 2022 midterm elections. Scholarly speculations attempting to make sense of another unique political outcome of the 2022 midterm elections in the rapidly changing political world include theories of a strong Trump effect vs. weak Biden effect, voters' modest expectations for a divided government, increased in-person vote casting, and divided confidence in the voting system, among others (Pew Research Center, 2022). These different scholarly perspectives all emphasize the significance of political information in their theoretical approaches and consider how this information is provided, consumed, and validated in the rapidly changing media and communication environment (Duda & Turek, 2024; Mitchell et al., 2020).

The current research investigates the expanded roles of digital political information that shaped a significant part of the 2022 midterm campaign and election outcomes (Trzcińska, 2024). This study specifically focuses on digital partisan news delivered via digital new algorithms. Digital news algorithms have been explored in various parameters across different disciplines of political science, marketing, psychology, and others. Among the scholars' and practitioners' arguments of various causes, effects, benefits, and concerns of online news algorithms, the core thesis shared is that online news algorithms work as generators and channels (Feezell et al., 2021). News organizations and commercial advertisers utilize digital news algorithms to cultivate viewers' interests and generate more attention and revenues (Latzer et al., 2016). Partisan news organizations and political professionals, such as party leaders

DOI: 10.4324/9781003440833-10

## 150 Media Messages in the 2022 Midterm Election

and campaign managers, use digital news algorithms to create echo chambers for their political purposes and generate more personalized and polarized news interests for their target viewers and voters. This chapter examines the patterns of digital news funneled through digital partisan news algorithms surrounding the intensifying political polarization during the 2022 midterm elections.

## Theoretical Underpinnings

### The 2022 Midterm Election: Deviations, Divisions, and Controversies

The 2022 midterm election marked a significant turning point in American election history. Amid ongoing partisan-sorting and polarization, the 2022 election deviated from typical election by effectively serving as two separate party elections. This divergence provided evidence that challenged conventional midterm election theories, such as the "surge and decline theory" and "referendum theory." According to the surge and decline theory, during presidential election years, congressional candidates of the president's party are more likely to win, getting benefits from the energy in the presidential campaigns, while the president's party candidates are more likely to lose in the off-year midterm elections when presidents' executive actions divide the congressional floor (Campbell, 1960). In the 2022 midterm elections under the Democratic president, Joe Biden, the Republican Party gained control of the House of Representatives, however, by a much smaller margin than expected, and failed to obtain control of the Senate. The Democratic Party lost control of the House of Representatives by a small, nine seat margin while gaining three Senate seats, earning the party's Senate majority (Politico, 2023). Compared to the average loss of 28 House seats and four Senate seats in the president's party in the midterm elections from 1934 to 2018 (Woolley, 2022), the Democratic Party's margin of loss was much smaller in the House elections, and the gains in the Senate flipped the general midterm election expectation in 2022. It implies that the surge and decline theory was a fading perspective in the 2022 midterm elections.

Moreover, the referendum theory that predicts congressional election outcomes based on the president's popularity during midterm elections turned out to be a weak indicator in the 2022 midterm elections. The referendum theory assumes presidential popularity has a positive relationship with in-party shares of the Senate and House votes and a negative relationship with out-party shares of the Senate and House votes (Campbell, 2010). In American election history since 1936, there have been six presidents whose approval ratings were in the low 40s% before President Biden, and the average loss of House seats was 36 and the average Senate seat loss was four (Woolley, 2022). However, despite President Biden's relatively low approval rating of 43–44% during his first-term midterm election, this did not significantly decrease the Democratic House vote share and even increased the Democratic Senate vote share in the 2022 midterm election (Woolley, 2022). The unexpected election results provided evidence that midterm elections are turning away from conventional wisdom and traditional expectation.

As the traditional theories of "surge and decline" and "referendum" lose their theoretical credibility in explaining overall election patterns, campaign professionals and scholars are looking elsewhere for insights into the changing midterm elections, carefully analyzing election results for new understanding. Some argue that Trump's persistent rhetoric about a stolen election was more impactful than Biden's moderate political rhetoric, and that Trump's involvement in the midterm elections negatively affected outcomes for Republican candidates. Former president Donald Trump was actively involved in the highly-contested Republican Senate campaigns in Arizona, Georgia, Nevada, New Hampshire, Pennsylvania, and Wisconsin, and the Republican Senate candidates in five out of the six toss-up election states were defeated (Patterson, 2023). Others discuss that the sharply polarized abortion issue (Amenta, 2022) regenerated Democratic Party voters' interest and motivation in the election. That resulted in narrowing down the enthusiasm gap between Democrats and Republicans, a shift that is unusual in midterm elections when supporters of the president's party are typically less motivated to participate (Hill, 2014; Politico, 2023). Other scholars attribute the causes to broader factors with the current political system, such as voters' modest expectations for a divided government, varying levels of confidence in the voting system, and other related issues (Pew Research Center, 2022).

While different, these conclusions all share the common aspect of including political information polarization in their arguments. Political polarization has increased in American elections over the last four decades (Fiorina & Abrams, 2008), and has reached a point where theoretical wisdom and political expectations in campaigns and elections flip. Previous research has been flooded with conflicting and inconclusive one-dimensional perspectives on the causes, processes, and consequences of political polarization in American politics (Fiorina & Abrams, 2008; Prior, 2013). This chapter expands the theoretical common ground with an inclusive and interactive approach, inviting overarching partisan-sorting, emerging digital media, and demand-supply information algorithms in order to provide a better understanding of this path-breaking midterm election. The study assembles theoretical and practical pieces together to understand why the 2022 midterm elections played out as seemingly two separate partisan elections rather than a whole election, observing how the supply and demand of partisan campaign information in the digital media era was cultivated, distributed, and consumed in the 2022 midterm elections.

### Digital Partisan News Algorithm

There have been various scholarly approaches to understanding the roles of digital news algorithms in American politics (Entman & Usher, 2018; Feezell et al., 2021; Thorson et al., 2021). An algorithm, as a black box, processes a series of information and cultivates outcomes variously and unknowingly, depending on an interactive exchange and deep learning between an algorithm and a user (Pasquale, 2015). Therefore, the effects of digital news algorithms are less trackable, and the scholarly findings are sporadic. Feezell and her colleagues (2021) suggested that algorithm-driven news can increase news users' political participation, but partisan polarization depends on the modes of news delivery. Thorson and his colleagues (2021) provided evidence that social media users sorted by algorithms are more likely to be exposed to the types of political news that match the algorithm type, however, the extent of this news varies and is not easily generalizable. Entman and Usher (2018) argued that digital platform algorithms disconnect the traditional news elites and the public and create "newer ideological media" which digitalize different information paths for the political left, center, and right (p. 304).

The processes and outcomes of digital news algorithms are a complex web of online and offline professional news makers, digital news aggregators and distributors, and digital news consumers (Wallace, 2018). News producers and makers who are affiliated with news organizations have both internal pressures to meet the organizational economic and political interests and external pressures to meet societal and political demands from audiences within the society and political system (Dunaway & Graber, 2022). Politically conservative news organizations, such as Fox News Channel, and their news producers are inclined to create news with an ideologically conservative philosophy to serve their target audiences' preferences. By the same token, politically liberal news organizations, like MSNBC, and their news makers tend to produce more liberal news with liberal political values to satisfy target audiences' political demands (Dunaway & Graber, 2022). Digital news aggregators and distributors collect news content from various news organizations, sort news stories, and send the news out via different pipelines for different digital audiences. Digital news aggregators utilize different formulas and designs of digital news algorithms for the purposes of news feeder apps. For example, Google News, as a digital news aggregator, curates stories relevant to users based on previous news consumption but may prevent conflicting ideas and news from being in news consumers' feeds (Lazer, 2015). However, news aggregators mainly collect and sort stories based on news demands and popularity but care less about the truthfulness or falsehoods of information, leaving the choices and acceptances to news consumers (Coddington, 2019). Digital news consumers, as both news seekers and receivers, are often more selective in their news diets and seek out more personalized news for their news appetites. In other words, political news consumers are more likely to select and accept ideologically congruent digital news stories and websites (Tsfati & Nir, 2017).

The dynamics of digital news algorithms, driven by the interactive and cyclical information processes among news makers, news feeders, and news consumers, amplify their intended political purposes, functions, preferences, and outcomes. This effect is particularly evident in partisan news algorithms, where the inputs and outputs are more apparent (Hasell, 2021). News producers from partisan media organizations make more consistent partisan news content that meet both the political standards and expectations of their news organizations and news consumers (Shultziner & Stukalin, 2021). Digital news aggregator apps create better-defined algorithm paths for specific digital partisan news consumers. The functional mappings and designs, through parameterizing processes, aim to collect and disseminate more engaging political information to improve online interactions (Canavilhas & Satuf, 2016; Webster, 2014). Partisan digital news consumers also expect personalized partisan news to be delivered to them through their choices of news aggregator apps (Cardenal et al., 2019). Digital partisan news algorithms and the consistent news diets of partisan digital news consumers co-generate the paths and aftermaths of digital partisan news. This algorithm interaction accelerates the interactive production, distribution, and consumption of such news (Canavilhas & Satuf, 2016).

Beyond the purposive operational information processes of digital news algorithms, digital partisan news stories utilize news content strategies to meet the interests of news makers, spreaders, and receivers. As legacy partisan news outlets have been using selective partisan news framing and appeals for political purposes (Han & Federico, 2018), digital partisan news stories filtered through digital news algorithms repeat politically-intended partisan framing and strategies (Mayerhöffer & Heft, 2022). Various news framings evaluated across different subject matters in scholarly research prove that specific framing strategies have been adopted for news stories to achieve political and socio-economic purposes (De Vreese, 2005). Among the different types of news framing, the episodic vs. thematic framing approach has been widely and reliably used in news-making practices and research (De Vreese, 2005). Studies have found that political partisan news stories invite episodic news framing frequently because it is easier to be produced by partisan news makers, to be delivered through the paths of partisan news algorithms, and to be understood by partisan news consumers (Gooch, 2018). Moreover, episodic news framing is a more human-interested approach and a more emotionally provocative strategy that better meets partisan political purposes than broader thematic framing (Gross, 2008).

Related to the partisan news framing strategy, more reactive and triggering news appeals have also been used for political partisan news purposes. Categorizing news appeal strategies as logical, emotional, or source credibility

**154** Media Messages in the 2022 Midterm Election

appeals has been widely adopted in academic research and political dialogues (Flanagin & Metzger, 2017). Among logical, emotional, and source credibility appeals, political partisan news stories are more likely to utilize emotional and source-oriented appeals since the strategies are often more effective for partisan news organizations' political purposes of promoting specific political issues and figures, because digital partisan news algorithms' purpose is to attract target audiences for human-interested stories and to engage partisan digital news consumers (Hasell & Weeks, 2016; Landreville & Niles, 2019).

### Digital Political Polarization

Whether news algorithms supplement or replace traditional journalistic professionalism, both news producers and consumers recognize that these algorithms play a dominant role in determining which news content is highlighted and how it is distributed in today's media landscape (Carlson, 2018). Digital partisan news algorithms repeatedly push ideologically aligned news content into the partisan pipelines the algorithms design and operate (Canavilhas & Satuf, 2016). As a result of digital partisan news algorithms, digital news consumers cannot escape the partisan digital domain, continuously receiving sorted political news content relevant to their partisan preferences and repeating partisan news selections and consumptions (Canavilhas & Satuf, 2016). The ongoing cycle of digital partisan news feeds driven by partisan algorithms, combined with the consistent partisan news consumption habits of digital consumers, only deepens political divides and polarization between liberal Democrats and conservative Republicans (Tyler et al., 2022).

Partisan digital news algorithms do more than just deliver biased news; they also foster partisan public opinions that stem from partisan news feeding, further increasing political polarization. Partisan public opinions across different ideological online environments are being hardened by repeated partisan news consumption (Tyler et al., 2022; Yun, 2020). Digital comments on online news have become an important channel for shaping the public's perceptions, attitudes, and behaviors, which in turn fuel political debates, divides, and polarizations (Han et al., 2023; Yun, 2020). Online political agreements among like-minded partisan voters are more likely to increase in-party biases, while online political disagreements are more likely to increase out-party prejudices, intensifying the divide between Democrats and Republicans (Han et al., 2023; Suhay et al., 2018).

### Research Question & Hypotheses

The core theoretical argument in this study is that digital news algorithms contribute to political polarization in American elections via the interactive and cyclical information processes fed by digital partisan news algorithms and consumed by digital partisan news consumers to meet the political purposes of news makers, news distributors, and news consumers in campaigns and elections. Based on this review of the literature, this chapter proposes the following research question and hypotheses:

RQ1 How do digital news algorithms influence the types of news framing and appeals used in digital partisan news articles to engage digital partisan news consumers?

H1 Digital partisan news algorithms funnel ideologically aligned digital news to polarized digital algorithm channels.

H2 Digital partisan news algorithms cultivate ideologically aligned digital public opinions for polarized digital algorithm spheres.

## Methodology: Content Analysis

### Samples and Coders

During the 2022 midterm elections, from October 24 to November 18, the researchers and five student coders examined different ideological news algorithms (liberal vs. neutral vs. conservative) across the most widely downloaded and highly rated online news aggregator apps (Google News, Flipboard, Opera News, News Break, Smart News) (Hochman, 2022). Among the most downloaded news aggregators, the apps that had a rating higher than 4 out of 5 and had no fees and no geographic or scope limitations were selected.

### Coding Procedures and Content Analysis Measures

The five student coders had three separate 30-minute coder training sessions, reviewing coding procedures, content analysis measures, and codebook items. In order to identify digital algorithms' information processes for different ideological algorithm paths across the news aggregator apps, each student coder spent 20 minutes on a pre-assigned ideological algorithm track (liberal, neutral, or conservative), clicking and reading digital news articles in the same political ideology on his/her own pace, in one online news app daily rotating as follows: Google News on Mondays, Flipboard on Tuesdays, Opera News on Wednesdays, News Break on Thursdays, and Smart News on Fridays. The coders analyzed the last news article fed at the end of each of the 20-minute liberal, neutral, or conservative news consumption periods. The coding procedure was adopted for the reliability of the study to replicate the real-world news consumers' digital news diets. According to Milliot (2021), American

**156** Media Messages in the 2022 Midterm Election

online news consumers stay on online news apps on average between 12 and 20 minutes at a time. Therefore, the 20-minute-long period was adopted as the time span. The unit of the content analysis is the last news article viewed at the end of each 20-minute news consumption session and the entirety of the digital page the article is on, including comments and other links to the article, visible on the article page.

The textual content analysis form consists of the following measures: news article framing (episodic vs. thematic), news article appeal (logical, emotional, or source credibility), news article ideological thermometer (liberal [1] – conservative [100]), ideological algorithm alignment (very unaligned [1] – very aligned [7]), number of partisan statements (pro-Democrat, pro-Republican, anti-Democrat, and anti-Republican), comments' tone (negative [1] – positive [7]), comments' ideological thermometer (liberal [1] – conservative [100]), comments' agreement to news articles (disagree [1] – agree [7]), and hostile comments (low [1] – high [7]). At the end of the three coder training sessions, the coders completed one content analysis form each for the same sample news article. The five coders achieved a Cronbach's Alpha intercoder reliability value of .83.

The five coders pooled a total of 100 digital news articles from the different ideological news algorithm tracks, fed by the news algorithms' information processes after being led by each coder's consistent partisan news consumption, 20 each from the five news aggregator apps of Google News, Flipboard, Opera News, News Break, and Smart News. During the four surrounding weeks of the 2022 midterm elections, the coders collected and analyzed 36 digital news articles and their associated digital pages funneled in by liberal news algorithms, 28 digital news articles and the digital pages by neutral news algorithms, and 36 digital news articles and the digital pages by conservative news algorithms.

## Results

### Digital Partisan News Framing & Appeal

The one overarching research question in the study was if there are any consistent patterns of news framing and appeals that the digital partisan news algorithms repeat to feed digital partisan news consumers. This study found that digital partisan news algorithms indeed have an algorithm habit of sorting digital news articles with a pattern of news framing. A chi-squared test showed that conservative (85.71%) and liberal (82.86%) news algorithms were more likely to feed episodic news than neutral (57.14%) news algorithms ($\chi^2 = 8.283$, $p \leq .016$). However, there was no statistically significant difference in thematic framing across partisan news articles fed by different partisan news algorithms (see Table 7.1). As discussed in other studies (Gross, 2008), episodic news framing is an effective strategy for partisan news makers to utilize for their news

TABLE 7.1 Partisan News Framing in Digital Partisan News Algorithms

| Digital Partisan News Algorithm | Framing | |
|---|---|---|
| | Episodic | Thematic |
| Liberal | 82.86% | 63.89% |
| Neutral | 57.14% | 60.71% |
| Conservative | 85.71% | 72.22% |
| | $\chi^2 = 8.283, p \leq .016$ | $\chi^2 = 1.041, p \leq .594$ |

TABLE 7.2 Partisan News Appeals in Digital Partisan News Algorithms

| Digital Partisan News Algorithm | Appeal | | |
|---|---|---|---|
| | Logical | Emotional | Source Credibility |
| Liberal | 30.56% | 27.78% | 41.67% |
| Neutral | 67.86% | 14.29% | 17.86% |
| Conservative | 22.22% | 30.56% | 47.22% |
| | $\chi^2 = 15.295, p \leq .004$ | | |

interests and their partisan audiences' preferences. The result reconfirms that the framing strategies used by digital partisan news algorithms were similar to traditional electronic partisan news channels (Han & Federico, 2018).

Furthermore, this study confirmed that partisan news algorithms were more likely to feed news articles with emotional and source credibility appeals, while neutral news algorithms tended to provide more news with logical appeals ($\chi^2 = 15.295, p \leq .004$). Conservative and liberal digital news algorithms served more news articles with emotional appeals (30.56% and 27.78% respectively) and source appeals (47.22% and 41.67% respectively) than neutral news algorithms (14.29% with emotional appeal and 17.86% with source credibility appeal). Notably, neutral news algorithms fed most of the news stories with a logical appeal (67.86%), while digital partisan algorithms provided much fewer logical news articles (22.22% in conservative news algorithms and 30.56% in liberal news algorithms) (see Table 7.2). As expected, partisan news tended to be driven by more emotional appetites and subjective source credibility appeals, such as citing high-profile politicians from the two major parties (Hasell & Weeks, 2016; Landreville & Niles, 2019).

### Digital Partisan News Algorithm Paths and Political Polarization

Digital partisan news algorithms processed the partisan news consumers' news selection preferences and provided ideologically congruent digital news to the partisan news consumers. According to ANOVA tests, digital partisan news

**158** Media Messages in the 2022 Midterm Election

algorithms funneled ideologically aligned news articles, feeding more partisan-leaning news stories with pro-Democrat, pro-Republican, anti-Democrat, or anti-Republican statements to the corresponding partisan news consumers. The digital news articles fed by the conservative news algorithms were ideologically more extremely conservative ($M = 75.39$, $SE = 2.82$), the digital news articles that flowed through the pipeline of the liberal news algorithms were ideologically more liberal ($M = 35.03$, $SE = 2.61$), and the digital news articles aggregated by the neutral news algorithms were ideologically moderate ($M = 49.25$, $SE = 1.62$) ($F = 70.851$, $p \leq .001$) when compared across different ideological news algorithms (see Table 7.3). These findings confirmed H1 speculating that digital partisan news algorithms contributed to delivering more ideologically aligned partisan news to polarized digital algorithm channels in the 2022 midterm elections.

The degrees of ideological alignments among the digital news articles in liberal partisan algorithms ($M = 5.89$, $SE = 0.27$) and in conservative news algorithms ($M = 5.67$, $SE = 0.29$) were stronger compared to the mixed-toned articles in neutral news algorithms ($M = 4.75$, $SE = 0.43$) ($F = 3.253$, $p \leq .043$). Furthermore, the digital news articles fed by conservative news algorithms consisted of more pro-Republican statements ($M = 3.69$, $SE = 0.35$, $F = 67.487$, $p \leq .001$) and anti-Democrat statements ($M = 2.42$, $SE = 0.53$, $F = 16.401$, $p \leq .001$) than digital news articles funneled by the liberal ($M = 0.31$, $SE = 0.13$ for pro-Republican statements and $M = 0.14$, $SE = 0.10$ for anti-Democrat statements) and neutral ($M = 0.32$, $SE = 0.13$ for pro-Republican statements and $M = 0.07$, $SE = 0.07$ for anti-Democrat statements) news algorithms. However, the digital news articles fed by liberal news algorithms contained more pro-Democrat statements ($M = 2.03$, $SE = 0.43$, $F = 8.370$, $p \leq .001$) and anti-Republican statements ($M = 2.83$, $SE = 0.67$, $F = 12.865$, $p \leq .001$) compared to digital news articles delivered by conservative ($M = 0.33$, $SE = 0.14$ for pro-Democrat statements and $M = 0.31$, $SE = 0.18$ for anti-Republican statements) and neutral ($M = 0.79$, $SE = 0.27$ for pro-Democrat statements and $M = 0.11$, $SE = 0.06$ for anti-Republican statements) news algorithms (see Table 7.3).

### *Digital Partisan News Algorithm Spheres and Political Polarization Cultivator*

Digital partisan news algorithms cultivated ideologically aligned digital public opinions on the digital pages where the partisan news articles were fed, confirming H2 about the effect of digital partisan news algorithms on digital public opinion polarization. The online new consumers' comments on the digital news articles delivered by conservative news algorithms were more conservative ($M = 76.16$, $SE = 3.52$) and the online comments on the digital news articles provided by liberal news algorithms were more liberal ($M = 41.15$, $SE = 3.27$),

**TABLE 7.3** Partisan News Properties in Digital Partisan News Algorithms

| Digital Partisan News Algorithm | Ideological Thermometer | Ideological Alignment | Pro-Democrat Statements | Pro-Republican Statements | Anti-Democrat Statements | Anti-Republican Statements |
|---|---|---|---|---|---|---|
| | *Mean (S.E.)* | *Mean (S.E.)* | *Mean (S.E.)* | *Mean (S.E.)* | *Mean (S.E.)* | *Mean (S.E.)* |
| Liberal | 35.03 (2.61) | 5.89 (0.27) | 2.03 (0.43) | 0.31 (0.13) | 0.14 (0.10) | 2.83 (0.67) |
| Neutral | 49.25 (1.62) | 4.75 (0.43) | 0.79 (0.27) | 0.32 (0.13) | 0.07 (0.07) | 0.11 (0.06) |
| Conservative | 75.39 (2.82) | 5.67 (0.29) | 0.33 (0.14) | 3.69 (0.35) | 2.42 (0.53) | 0.31 (0.18) |
| | $F = 70.851, p \leq .001$ 1 (Liberal) – 100 (Conservative) | $F = 3.253, p \leq .043$ 1 (Very Unaligned) – 7 (Very Aligned) | $F = 8.370, p \leq .001$ | $F = 67.487, p \leq .001$ | $F = 16.401, p \leq .001$ | $F = 12.865, p \leq .001$ |

**160** Media Messages in the 2022 Midterm Election

**TABLE 7.4** Partisan News Comments in Digital Partisan News Algorithms

| Digital Partisan News Algorithm | Ideological Thermometer | Agreement | Tone | Hostile View |
|---|---|---|---|---|
| | Mean (S.E.) | Mean (S.E.) | Mean (S.E.) | Mean (S.E.) |
| Liberal | 41.15 (3.27) | 4.46 (0.20) | 3.71 (0.24) | 4.19 (0.25) |
| Neutral | 51.65 (6.72) | 4.38 (0.34) | 3.11 (0.32) | 4.13 (0.51) |
| Conservation | 76.16 (3.52) | 4.88 (0.28) | 2.58 (0.25) | 5.09 (0.30) |
| | $F = 21.496$, $p \leq .001$ | $F = .996$, $p \leq .375$ | $F = 5.258$, $p \leq .007$ | $F = 3.011$, $p \leq .055$ |
| | 1 (Liberal) – 100 (Conservative) | 1 (Disagree) – 7 (Agree) | 1 (Negative) – 7 (Positive) | 1 (Low) – 7 (High) |

while the digital comments on the neutral news articles aggregated by neutral news algorithms stayed more moderate ($M = 51.65$, $SE = 6.72$) ($F = 21.496$, $p \leq .001$) (see Table 7.4). However, the comments left on digital news articles did not necessarily more agree with, or were more hostile to, the news articles across liberal, neutral, and conservative news algorithms. As expected by previous research, the digital public opinion sphere invited cross-cutting views (Yun, 2020), resulting in both agreeing and disagreeing perspectives in digital public spheres. However, in the context of the 2022 midterm elections, digital comments on conservative news articles were more negative ($M = 2.58$, $SE = 0.25$), while digital comments on liberal news articles were relatively more positive ($M = 3.71$, $SE = 0.24$) ($F = 5.258$, $p \leq .007$) (see Table 7.4). The Republican out-party candidates in midterm elections were more likely to attack and blame the incumbent party candidates, and the out-party's negativity toward the incumbent party appeared to contribute a higher degree of negativity in the conservative dialogues in conservative news algorithm spheres (Espinoza, 2023).

## Discussion

This study provides evidence of digital political polarization that outweighs the theoretical patterns of American midterm elections, such as in-party disadvantages, out-party advantages, and presidential referendum gauges. This chapter found that digital news algorithms process partisan digital news consumers' preferences and funnel ideologically aligned partisan news to partisan news consumers, while using digital news with episodic framing, emotional appeal, and partisan source credibility. The digital partisan news stories fed by digital partisan news algorithms fertilize digital partisan public opinion. Digital partisan news sites serve as partisan dialogue spheres for polarized digital political discourse. In the 2022 midterm elections, those dynamics of digital partisan

The Impact of Digital Partisan News Algorithms **161**

news algorithms solidified political polarization via filtered campaign messages that paved two separate party elections, overshadowing the conventional whole election patterns, such as out-party advantages and the president's referendum, in the election outcomes.

However, one of the notes to be discussed in the 2022 midterm election from the study results was that conservative news algorithms and their conservative digital news articles were ideologically more strongly conservative, by about 10 degrees farther toward the conservative side of the ideological spectrum on a scale of 100, than the liberal digital news algorithms and their partisan news articles on the liberal side of the ideological spectrum. Moreover, the political discourse was more negative in conservative political domains than in liberal political domains. In other words, although the digital comments in partisan news were not necessarily hostile to, or in agreement with, the partisan news articles, the public views were more negative in conservative digital news sites than the public comments expressed in the liberal digital news sites. The patterns of the discrepancy between the liberal digital domain and the conservative digital domain and the ideological consistency, strength, and negativity within partisan digital spheres have been observed in the field of digital political communication. The netizens of conservative online spheres tended to be more exceedingly and cohesively conservative compared to the liberal netizens who were less extreme in their liberal ideology (Han et al., 2023; Yun, 2020). Digital algorithms re-enhance the partisan pattern via the interactive and cyclical information processes of political polarization (Canavilhas & Satuf, 2016). Moreover, higher negativity in the out-party news and the out-party political discourse has been filled with more attacks and blame for the incumbent party in American election history (Campbell, 1960). The Republican out-party under the Democratic Party presidency appeared concurrently with the perception of a seemingly red wave that was expected to overshadow the 2022 midterm campaign and elections, which turned out as a more perceived campaign atmosphere rather than the actual election outcome (Woolley, 2022). The perceived expectations of voters are cemented by their exposures to preferred information and consumption of curated information that are overly amplified by digital partisan news algorithms in the new media era (Lai, 2022).

This chapter examined the manner in which digital news algorithms generate politically aligned algorithm routes for digital partisan news consumers in the 2022 midterm elections. Despite the evident findings that digital partisan news algorithms contributed to digital polarization in the elections, this study could provide more sophisticated clarification in patterns, depths, and degrees of polarization during the election season with larger and more stratified samples of digital news consumers. The study traced down 100 different algorithm paths across liberal, conservative, and neutral digital domains by pre-trained partisan news consumers, limiting the various scopes of real-world applications. For more

**162** Media Messages in the 2022 Midterm Election

practical applications of digital news algorithms for campaign professionals, future research should revisit the study for various digital news consumers across different age groups and geopolitical locations and with different levels of education and income in addition to partisanship, who use digital political news media with various digital habits in different depths and time spans.

Moreover, a longitudinal approach, comparing the dynamics of digital partisan news algorithms in different political contexts of election years from non-election years would further clarify the effects of digital algorithms in American campaigns and elections and increase the reliability and validity of the study. Most importantly, for a better comprehensive understanding and effective utilization of digital news algorithms, future research must investigate the degrees of political polarization derived from digital partisan news algorithms in American political discourse in order to weigh the impact on American democracy. With the findings of digital partisan algorithms that were powerful enough to reverse conventional wisdom in the 2022 midterm elections, this current research leaves more responsibility for future studies in cultivating healthier ways to apply digital algorithms to polarized American politics and to fertilize fair and balanced political dialogues on American political soil.

## References

Amenta, E. (2022). Why US conservative movements are winning: It's not Trump – It's the institutions. *Mobilization, 27*(1), 27–45. https://doi.org/10.17813/1086-671X-27-1-27

Campbell, A. (1960). Surge and decline: A study of electoral change. *Public Opinion Quarterly, 24*(3), 397–418. www.jstor.org/stable/2746724

Campbell, J. E. (2010). The seats in trouble forecast of the 2010 elections in the U.S. House. *PS: Political Science and Politics, 43*(4), 627–630. https://doi.org/10.1017/S1049096510001095

Campbell, J. E. (2022, July 5). *The 2022 house midterm by the numbers*. RealClear Politics. www.realclearpolitics.com/articles/2022/07/05/the_2022_house_midterm_by_the_numbers_147840.html

Canavilhas, J., & Satuf, I. (2016). Who brings the news? Exploring the aggregators apps for mobile Devices. In J. M. Aguado, C. Feijoo, & I. J. Martinez (Eds.), *Emerging perspectives on the mobile content evolution* (pp. 220–238). IGI Global.

Cardenal, A. S., Aguilar-Paredes, C., Galais, C., & Pérez-Montoro, M. (2019). Digital technologies and selective exposure: How choice and filter bubbles shape news media exposure. *The International Journal of Press/Politics, 24*(4), 465–486. https://doi.org/10.1177/1940161219862988

Carlson, M. (2018). Automating judgment? Algorithmic judgment, news knowledge, and journalistic professionalism. *New Media & Society, 20*(5), 1755–1772. https://doi.org/10.1177/1461444817706684

Coddington, M. (2019). *Aggregating the news: Secondhand knowledge and the erosion of journalistic authority*. Columbia University Press. https://doi.org/10.7312/codd18730

De Vreese, C. H. (2005). News framing: Theory and typology. *Information Design Journal + Document Design, 13*(1), 51–62. www.jbe-platform.com/content/journals/10.1075/idjdd.13.1.06vre

Duda, R., & Turek, M. (2024). *The crossroads elections: European perspectives on the 2022 U.S. midterm elections.* (Eds.). Routledge. https://doi.org/10.4324/978100 3440895

Dunaway, J. L., & Graber, D. A. (2022). *Mass media and American politics* (11th ed.). CQ Press.

Entman, R. M., & Usher, N. (2018). Framing in a fractured democracy: Impacts of digital technology on ideology, power and cascading network activation. *Journal of Communication, 68*(2), 298–308. https://doi.org/10.1093/joc/jqx019

Espinoza, M. (2023). An overview of the Republican party after the 2022 midterm elections. In P. Finn, T. Furse, C. Harrington, & M. Espinoza (Eds.), *Exploring the 2022 US midterms brief* (pp. 41–45). American Politics Group of the Political Studies Association. https://scholarworks.utrgv.edu/cgi/viewcontent.cgi?article=1062&cont ext=pol_fac

Feezell, J. T., Wagner, J. K., & Conroy, M. (2021). Exploring the effects of algorithm-driven news sources on political behavior and polarization. *Computers in Human Behavior, 116*, Article 106626. https://doi.org/10.1016/j.chb.2020.106626

Fiorina, M. P., & Abrams, S. J. (2008). Political polarization in the American public. *Annual Review of Political Science, 11*, 563–588. https://doi.org/10.1146/annurev.poli sci.11.053106.153836

Flanagin, A., & Metzger, M. J. (2017). Digital media and perceptions of source credibility in political communication. In K. Kenski & K. H. Jamieson (Eds.), *The Oxford handbook of political communication* (pp. 417–436). Oxford University Press. https:// doi.org/10.1093/oxfordhb/9780199793471.013.65

Gooch, A. (2018). Ripping yarn: experiments on storytelling by partisan elites. *Political Communication, 35*(2), 220–238. https://doi.org/10.1080/10584609.2017. 1336502

Gross, K. (2008). Framing persuasive appeals: Episodic and thematic framing, emotional response, and policy opinion. *Political Psychology, 29*(2), 169–192. www.jstor.org/ stable/20447111

Han, J., & Federico, C. M. (2018). The polarizing effect of news framing: Comparing the mediating roles of motivated reasoning, self-stereotyping, and intergroup animus. *Journal of Communication, 68*(4), 685–711. https://doi.org/10.1093/joc/jqy025

Han, J., Lee, Y., Lee, J., & Cha, M. (2023). News comment sections and online echo chambers: The ideological alignment between partisan news stories and their user comments. *Journalism, 24*(8), 1836–1856. https://doi.org/10.1177/1464884921 1069241

Hasell, A. (2021). Shared emotion: The social amplification of partisan news on Twitter. *Digital Journalism, 9*(8), 1085–1102. https://doi.org/10.1080/21670 811.2020.1831937

Hasell, A., & Weeks, B. E. (2016). Partisan provocation: The role of partisan news use and emotional responses in political information sharing in social media. *Human Communication Research, 42*(4), 641–661. https://doi.org/10.1111/hcre.12092

Hill, S. J. (2014). A behavioral measure of the enthusiasm gap in American elections. *Electoral Studies, 36*, 28–38. https://doi.org/10.1016/j.electstud.2014.06.012

Hochman, A. (2022, August 30). *Top apps ranking: Top news and magazines apps ranking –Most popular news & magazine apps in united states.* Similarweb. www. similarweb.com/apps/top/google/app-index/us/news-magazines/top-free/

Lai, S. (2022). Data misuse and disinformation: Technology and the 2022 elections. Commentary: Brookings. www.brookings.edu/articles/data-misuse-and-disinformation-technology-and-the-2022-elections/

Landreville, K. D., & Niles, C. (2019). "And that's a fact!": The roles of political ideology, PSRs, and perceived source credibility in estimating factual content in partisan news. *Journal of Broadcasting & Electronic Media, 63*(2), 177–194. https://doi.org/10.1080/08838151.2019.1622339

Latzer, M., Hollnbuchner, K., Just, N., & Saurwein, F. (2016). The economics of algorithmic selection on the Internet. In J. Bauer & M. Latzer (Eds.), *Handbook on the economics of the internet* (pp. 395–425). Edward Elgar Publishing.

Lazer, D. (2015). The rise of the social algorithm: Does content curation by Facebook introduce ideological bias? *Science, 348*(6239), 1090–1091. www.science.org/doi/10.1126/science.aab1422

Mayerhöffer, E., & Heft, A. (2022). Between journalistic and movement logic: Disentangling referencing practices of right-wing alternative online news media. *Digital Journalism, 10*(8), 1409–1430. https://doi.org/10.1080/21670811.2021.1974915

Milliot, J. (2021, July 29). *Reading time rose 21% in second half of 2020.* Publishers Weekly. www.publishersweekly.com/pw/by-topic/industry-news/publisher-news/article/87009-reading-time-rose-21-in-second-half-of-2020.html

Mitchell, A., Jurkowitz, M., Oliphant, J. B., & Shearer, E. (2020, December 15). *Most republicans approve of Trump's post-election messaging, but about a third say it has been wrong.* Pew Research Center. www.pewresearch.org/wp-content/uploads/sites/20/2020/12/PJ_2020.12.15_Trump_Post-Election-Message_FINAL.pdf

Pasquale, F. (2015). *The black box society: The secret algorithms that control money and information.* Harvard University Press. www.jstor.org/stable/j.ctt13x0hch

Patterson, T. E. (2023, February 23). *2022 midterms, looking back and beyond.* McGraw Hill Talk Webinar: Harvard University. https://scholar.harvard.edu/thomaspatterson/teaching

Pew Research Center. (2022, December 1). *Public has modest expectations for Washington's return to divided government.* www.pewresearch.org/politics/2022/12/01/public-has-modest-expectations-for-washingtons-return-to-divided-government/

Politico. (2023, February 23). *2022 elections.* www.politico.com/2022-election/results/

Prior, M. (2013). Media and political polarization. *Annual Review of Political Science, 16*, 101–127. https://doi.org/10.1146/annurev-polisci-100711-135242

Shultziner, D., & Stukalin, Y. (2021). Distorting the news? The mechanisms of partisan media bias and its effects on news production. *Political Behavior, 43*(1), 201–222. https://doi.org/10.1007/s11109-019-09551-y

Suhay, E., Bello-Pardo, E., & Maurer, B. (2018). The polarizing effects of online partisan criticism: Evidence from two experiments. *The International Journal of Press/Politics, 23*(1), 95–115. https://doi.org/10.1177/1940161217740697

Thorson, K., Cotter, K., Medeiros, M., & Pak, C. (2021). Algorithmic inference, political interest, and exposure to news and politics on Facebook. *Information, Communication & Society, 24*(2), 183–200. https://doi.org/10.1080/1369118X.2019.1642934

Trzcińska, J. (2024). Media coverage of the 2022 campaign. In R. Duda & M. Turek (Eds.), *The crossroads elections: European perspectives on the 2022 U.S. midterm elections.* (pp. 192–203). Routledge. https://doi.org/10.4324/9781003440895

Tsfati, Y., & Nir, L. (2017). Frames and reasoning: Two pathways from selective exposure to affective polarization. *International Journal of Communication, 11*, 301–322. https://ijoc.org/index.php/ijoc/article/view/5793/1898

Tyler, M., Grimmer, J., & Iyengar, S. (2022). Partisan enclaves and information bazaars: Mapping selective exposure to online news. *The Journal of Politics, 84*(2), 1057–1073. www.journals.uchicago.edu/doi/abs/10.1086/716950?journalCode=jop

Wallace, J. (2018). Modelling contemporary gatekeeping: The rise of individuals, algorithms and platforms in digital news dissemination. *Digital Journalism, 6*(3), 274–293. https://doi.org/10.1080/21670811.2017.1343648

Webster, J. G. (2014*). The marketplace of attention: How audiences take shape in a digital age.* The MIT Press. https://doi.org/10.7551/mitpress/9892.001.0001

Woolley, J. T. (2022. August 30*). The 2022 midterm elections: What the historical data suggest.* The American Presidency Project. www.presidency.ucsb.edu/analyses/the-2022-midterm-elections-what-the-historical-data-suggest

Yun, H. J. (2020). Divided and crosscutting blogosphere political dialogues: Revisiting the Spiral of Silence and the Bandwagon Effect. *Quarterly Review of Business Disciplines, 7*(3), 245–265. https://faculty.utrgv.edu/louis.falk/qrbd/QRBDnov20.pdf#page=65

# 8

## REPLY "STOP"

### Dominant Media Frames of SMS-Based Political Communication as a Consumer Problem

*Ryan Cheek and Samuel Allen*

Fifteen billion political text messages were sent to U.S. mobile phones in the 2022 midterm election in the United States (Ford, 2023). Political texts are preferred by campaigns for many of the same reasons such texts are often reviled by consumers: texts are difficult to ignore, mimic personalized communication, and are insufficiently regulated (Thurlow & Poff, 2013). Through an ideological rhetorical analysis of a coded news coverage corpus, the research reported in this chapter examines media framings of mass political texting in the 2022 midterm elections.

The role that media framing plays in constructing political texting as a problem is an understudied phenomenon. Most political communication research has investigated the effectiveness of text messaging in voter turnout (Bhatti et al., 2017; Dale & Strauss, 2009; Malhotra et al., 2011). Another line of research has explored how the use of informational mobile media is positively associated with political participation (Campbell & Kwak, 2010; Martin, 2015; Neumayer & Stald, 2014). Where other studies have focused on the effects of Short Message Service (SMS) texts as campaign communication (Bergh et al., 2021; Bhatti et al., 2017; Shaul-Cohen & Lev-On, 2020; Shaw et al., 2022). We extend this research by offering an ideological rhetorical analysis of the ways mass media frames the phenomenon of political texting and argue such an analysis can inform policymaking, public understanding, and future scholarship about the increasingly technological practice of political communication.

Mass media outlets tended to frame the uses of political campaign text messaging in 2022 with an apocalyptic tenor. Headlines foregrounded the annoyance of campaign messages invading personal phones (Price, 2022) and

DOI: 10.4324/9781003440833-11

framed barrages of messages as without recourse (Balmert, 2022). When media outlets offered solutions, they emphasized individual responsibilities to resist the influx of text messages (Steigerwald, 2022) and obfuscated the importance of a robust regulatory approach to ameliorating the harms of political texting. In the next two sections the research methodology and methods of data collection are described, then the study findings are thematically reported and discussed, and finally the chapter ends with some brief conclusions about the phenomenon of SMS-based political communication practices going into the 2024 election and beyond.

## Ideological Rhetorical Analysis of Political Texting News Coverage

Grounded in ideology theory (Hall, 1986; van Dijk, 2005) and rhetorical criticism (Makus, 1990; Wander, 1983), the methodology applied in the present study focuses on highlighting the perspectives on political texting as captured by national and local news coverage of the phenomenon. Ideologies are "the mental frameworks [...] which different classes and social groups deploy in order to make sense of, define, figure out and render intelligible the way society works" (Hall, 1986, p. 29). Colloquially, most people recognize ideologies when framed as worldviews or paradigms that shape how groups of people understand and interact with their reality.

Ideologies are expressed in popular culture and through mass media as narratives that define the terms, scope, blame, harm, and solutions to problematic phenomena. This media framing involves "selecting" a particular aspect of the situation and making those aspects more "salient" in their selections (Entman, 1993, p. 52). Attending closely to the expression of perspectives and the conceptual relationships represented within a text, rhetorical critics may apply their craft to help expose what masquerades "largely unconsciously as common sense" (Makus, 1990, p. 502). Through normalizing processes, ideologies configure how economic, social, and political problems are understood by a group, which then subsequently constrains what solutions become available for imagination and realization.

News coverage can, sometimes overtly and sometimes covertly, act as a normalizing process to gain audience adherence to a particular ideology (van Dijk, 2009). Since journalists cannot advocate for a viewpoint within a story without breaking the pretense to objectivity, they instead must frame stories around the perspectives of various stakeholders in a controversy. Read critically and systematically, the perspectives expressed in media coverage are a window into the "general attitudes and specific personal models, which form the basis of discourse production" (van Dijk, 2005, p. 33). Narrative elements such as protagonists, antagonists, bystanders, witnesses, and plots are all derived from

**168** Media Messages in the 2022 Midterm Election

whose perspective is represented in the story and how that perspective is framed in the context of a problematic phenomenon.

As a result of the occupational bias toward objectivity (Reese, 1990), stories published by news organizations attempt to reflect the perspectives of issue stakeholders, but like a broken mirror, the segmented perspectives conglomerate into refractions of reality as understood by different interest groups. The news story, then, becomes a terrain where interpretations of a problem or issue (e.g., who is at fault, what the harm is, who benefits) compete for narrative dominance. In the next section, the methods used to collect and code the corpus of news coverage for analysis are explained in detail.

## Collecting and Coding News Coverage of Political Text Messaging

In this study, we analyzed a corpus of news coverage from 2022 to address the following research questions:

RQ1: How was political texting framed in news coverage during the 2022 U.S. midterm elections?

RQ2: What ideologies were expressed in news coverage related to political texting during this period.

RQ3: Who benefited and who was harmed by mass media framings of political texting. Through a careful analysis of news stories, we identified emergent patterns of communication that connected each represented character segment to a perspective on the benefits, hams, blame, and solutions to the issue.

Figure 8.1 illustrates the four-phase process undertaken to systematically answer the research questions by analyzing both text and visual content from a small corpus of media articles on SMS political marketing during the 2022

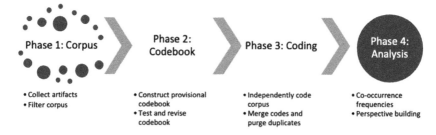

FIGURE 8.1 Four Phases of the Research Process.

U.S. midterm elections. In phase one, researchers built a corpus of news coverage to study. To do that, a clean browser was setup for research to collect the first 50 unique news articles on Google News containing one or more of the following search terms: SMS political marketing, SMS political texting, political text messages, and campaign text messages. Google News was chosen because it has no paywall and collects a mix of national and local media outlets across print and broadcast media. Research has shown that Google News is a better choice to capture a broad swath of coverage while alternatives like LexisNexis miss a lot of news coverage because of wire service exclusions (Weaver & Bimber, 2008). Since many news stories are syndicated, an important step in our artifact collection was eliminating duplicate news content. Articles were captured as PDF documents to preserve formatting and visual elements. After initial screening, 11 articles were excluded from the sample because they did not meet the inclusion criteria that articles must be: about the use of SMS marketing by political campaigns during the midterm election cycle in the United States; dated between June 1st, 2021, and December 31st, 2022; and unique from other articles in the sample. The sampling period extends almost two months after the 2022 elections to capture process stories about political text messaging that can run several weeks after election day, especially from local outlets.

The qualitative data analysis software package Atlas.ti was used to develop a codebook, code data, and produce co-occurrence tables and models for analysis. In phase two, after a review of relevant literature and an initial scan of the artifacts, the researchers developed a provisional coding scheme and tested it on nine randomly drawn articles representing 23% of the usable corpus. Krippendorff's c-a binary, a measure of inter-coder agreement about the presence or absence of a code within an annotation (Krippendorff, 2011), was used to guide a norming discussion about coding scheme adjustments. Through a process of "negotiated agreement" (Campbell et al., 2013), researchers ended the provisional coding process by confirming 32 codes spread among the following six frames (or code groups): perspective, metaphor, benefit, harm, fault, and solution. Pictures in the corpus were tagged with a picture code to separate their co-occurrences with various frames from textual annotations. Table 8.1 is a truncated codebook with the definitions used for the 24 codes that are most important for understanding the analysis in the discussion sections.

In phase three, researchers, independently and without conferral, coded the corpus ($n - 39$) using the refined codebook. At a minimum, codes were applied at the sentence level to ensure sufficient context to make sense of each annotation. Once coding was completed, eight codes were removed from results because they were not found in the sample with enough frequency by one or both coders to make inferences about. After removing those eight codes, the remaining coded sample achieved a global reliability rating of .667 using Krippendorff's c-a binary as configured in Atlas.ti, which indicates an

# 170 Media Messages in the 2022 Midterm Election

**TABLE 8.1** Truncated Codebook Containing All Codes Found Relevant to the Study

| Groups | Codes | Definition | Example |
|---|---|---|---|
| Perspective | Academics | Sentence expresses the perspective of an academic | "The studies found that people who opted in to texts reminding them to vote actually were more likely to vote after getting the reminder, said Melissa Michelson, a professor of political science at Menlo College in Atherton, California." (Kaul, 2022) |
| | Campaigns | Sentence expresses the perspective of a campaign | "Scott Goodstein, who led Barack Obama's pioneering texting program during the 2008 cycle and was the lead digital adviser to Bernie Sander's 2016 campaign, said the Democratic committees' defense of unsolicited messages is short-sighted." (Cohen, 2022) |
| | Lawmakers | Sentence expresses the perspective of a lawmaker | "Lawmakers expressed anger about misleading information in Monday's unsolicited text message and the confusion it created among voters." (McCormick, 2022) |
| | Anti-spam industry | Sentence expresses the perspective of the anti-spam industry | "Almost 50 million political robotexts were sent to Arizona phones in September and October alone, according to the latest estimates by RoboKiller, a company that markets a spam-blocking app." (Brown, 2022) |
| | Marketing industry | Sentence expresses the perspective of SMS marketing vendors | "Movement Labs said it reached out to each voter that received a message from the firm echoing the sentiments of the two secretaries of state." (Schonfeld, 2022) |

Reply "STOP"  **171**

**TABLE 8.1**  (Continued)

| Groups | Codes | Definition | Example |
|---|---|---|---|
| | Receivers | Sentence expresses the perspective of a person or persons who receive texts from political campaigns | " 'I feel like my phone is constantly blowing up with texts," said Harris, an Anchorage health care worker specializing in women's health." (Early, 2022) |
| | Regulators | Sentence expresses the perspective of a government entity with oversight responsibility and rulemaking authority but not lawmaking authority | " 'The Supreme Court decision has created a loophole that I think lots of actors, good and bad, are using and exploiting,' Jessica Rosenworcel, the chairwoman of the F.C.C., said in an interview." (Singer, 2022) |
| Benefits | Benefits campaigns | Sentence expresses the sentiment that in the status quo, political campaigns are beneficiaries of SMS political marketing technology | "Political campaign text messages are a cheap and easy way to get voters' attention." (Michael, 2022) |
| | Benefits democracy | Sentence expresses the sentiment that in the status quo, democracy and democratic institutions are beneficiaries of SMS political marketing technology | "These text messages are permitted because political speech is sacrosanct under the First Amendment and the government is loath to limit it, Geronimo said." (Balmert, 2022) |
| | Benefits individuals | Sentence expresses the sentiment that in the status quo, individual receivers are beneficiaries of SMS political marketing technology | "Shobe said he and his family are among those receiving a lot of political text messages. And while he takes steps to keep them from pouring in, he said he likes that candidates can use texting as a tool because he ultimately likes their voices to be heard as they make their cases for voters to support them." (Loging, 2022) |

(*Continued*)

## 172 Media Messages in the 2022 Midterm Election

**TABLE 8.1** (Continued)

| Groups | Codes | Definition | Example |
|--------|-------|------------|---------|
| Faults | Fault of campaigns | Sentence expresses the sentiment that political campaigns are at fault for the problems with SMS political marketing technology | "In other words, texting is a handy method for political actors to quietly propagate the same kind of divisiveness and disinformation that already abounds on social media—only away from the public scrutiny of academic researchers, fact-checking groups and journalists." (Singer, 2022) |
| | Fault of lawmakers | Sentence expresses the sentiment that lawmakers and current laws are at fault for the problems with SMS political marketing technology | "Utah's Division of Consumer Protection said while the texts and calls might be annoying, they are legal, citing Utah's Telephone and Facsimile Solicitation Act." (Harrison, 2022) |
| | Fault of regulators | Sentence expresses the sentiment that regulators and insufficient government regulation are at fault for the problems with SMS political marketing technology | "The FCC has flipped-flopped on the issue, though more federal intervention may be coming" (Cohen, 2022) |
| Harms | Harms campaigns | Sentence expresses the sentiment that SMS political marketing technology harms political campaigns | " 'Of course, I didn't send them,' Higgins said. 'It's ridiculous. I mean, who would send texts like that?' Higgins stopped short of saying the texts cost him the election. 'But I had about 10 to 20 people, while I was out at the polls (on Election Day), telling me they got it or knew someone who did.' " (Holleman, 2022) |

**TABLE 8.1** (Continued)

| Groups | Codes | Definition | Example |
|---|---|---|---|
| | Harms democracy | Sentence expresses the sentiment that SMS political marketing technology harms democracy and democratic institutions | "Today's massive volume of unregulated political mobile spam is turning into a tactic of voter suppression." (Goodstein, 2022) |
| | Harms individuals | Sentence expresses the sentiment that SMS political marketing technology harms individual receivers | "Unlike email, many people still view texting as a sacrosanct channel for communicating with friends, family or co-workers. That is why some Americans regard unsolicited political texts as privacy invasions." (Singer, 2022) |
| Metaphors | Militaristic | Sentence expresses a military related metaphor in relation to SMS political marketing technology | "Have you been getting bombarded with unwanted political text messages on your personal cell phone?" (Goodstein, 2022) |
| | Natural disaster | Sentence expresses a natural disaster related metaphor in relation to SMS political marketing technology | "Coloradans should prepare for a tsunami of anonymous political text messages as 2022 campaign season kicks into gear" (Fish, 2022) |
| Solutions | Solution is campaigns | Sentence expresses the sentiment that the solution to the problems with SMS political marketing technology is for political campaigns to better regulate themselves | "In this polarized climate, hundreds of Americans told us they agree on one thing: Campaigns must stop spamming voters' phones with unwanted political texts." (Singer, 2022) |

(*Continued*)

## 174 Media Messages in the 2022 Midterm Election

**TABLE 8.1** (Continued)

| Groups | Codes | Definition | Example |
|---|---|---|---|
| | Solution is regulation | Sentence expresses the sentiment that the solution to the problems with SMS political marketing technology is better government regulation | "It's time for the Federal Communications Commission's (FCC) new leadership to step in and put an end to the billions of unwanted political text message spam." (Goodstein, 2022) |
| | Solution is individuals | Sentence expresses the sentiment that the solution to the problems with SMS political marketing technology is individual receivers taking action themselves | "Although there is no way to completely block campaign texts, there are some things you can do to minimize them:• Don't give out your phone number. • Reply with the word 'STOP.'" (Michael, 2022) |
| | Solution is lawmaking | Sentence expresses the sentiment that the solution to the problems with SMS political marketing technology is for lawmakers to take action | "Some states have laws meant to prevent state- and local-level political campaigns from autodialing robotexts that can ping thousands of cell phones at a time." (French, 2022) |
| | Solution is telecom companies | Sentence expresses the sentiment that the solution to the problems with SMS political marketing technology is for telecommunication companies to adopt better regulations (10DLC) | "Mobile providers, including Verizon and AT&T, along with dozens of services that facilitate texting campaigns, recently signed on to an effort to standardize industry practices." (Singer, 2022) |
| | There is no solution | Sentence expresses the sentiment that there is no adequate solution to problems with SMS political marketing technology | "Both McParland and Lottsfeldt say getting texts from campaigns likely isn't going away anytime soon." (Early, 2022) |

acceptable level of agreement to trust the coding scheme that was developed and applied (O'Connor & Joffe, 2020). After measuring for basic agreement, researchers merged project files and purged duplicate codings with software assistance. In merging codes, researchers opted to keep longer segments over shorter ones to capture as much detail and co-occurrence between codes as possible. A total of 606 annotations remained for analysis after the merge was complete.

Phase four consisted of producing co-occurrence tables and visualizations to analyze the coded corpus of news coverage from a variety of angles. A co-occurrence is an instance where two codes were identified in the same segment of text. In total, 1,465 code co-occurrences and 297 unique co-occurrence relationships were observed in the merged corpus. Analysis started with identifying the most significant co-occurrence relationships in the corpus, defined in this study as the top 10% of co-occurrence relationships when ranked by the total frequency of code co-occurrences observed in the merged corpus. Table 8.2 lists the 29 significant co-occurrence relationships by frequency of code co-occurrences observed, which in total accounted for 457 code co-occurrences

**TABLE 8.2** Significant Co-Occurrence (c/o) Relationships

| First code | Second code | Frequency of co-occurrence |
| --- | --- | --- |
| Harms Individuals | Perspective of Receivers | 53 |
| Harms Individuals | Fault of Campaigns | 34 |
| Pictures | Perspective of Receivers | 26 |
| Fault of Campaigns | Perspective of Receivers | 24 |
| Benefits Campaigns | Perspective of Campaigns | 23 |
| Benefits Campaigns | Perspective of Academics | 20 |
| Harms Individuals | There is No Solution | 17 |
| Harms Individuals | Metaphor: Natural Disaster | 16 |
| Harms Individuals | Benefits Campaigns | 16 |
| Benefits Campaigns | Fault of Campaigns | 15 |
| Harms Individuals | Metaphor: Militaristic | 14 |
| Harms Individuals | Perspective of Marketing Industry | 14 |
| Harms Individuals | Perspective of Regulators | 14 |
| Fault of Campaigns | Harms Democracy | 13 |
| Harms Individuals | Fault of Lawmakers | 13 |
| Harms Individuals | Solution is Individual | 13 |
| Benefits Democracy | Perspective of Campaigns | 12 |
| Solution is Lawmaking | Perspective of Lawmakers | 11 |
| Fault of Regulators | Solution is Government Regulation | 11 |
| Fault of Lawmakers | Solution is Lawmaking | 11 |
| Fault of Lawmakers | Perspective of Regulators | 11 |
| Solution is Regulation | Perspective of Regulators | 10 |

*(Continued)*

**TABLE 8.2** (Continued)

| First code | Second code | Frequency of co-occurrence |
| --- | --- | --- |
| There is No Solution | Perspective of Receivers | 10 |
| Harms Individuals | Fault of Regulators | 10 |
| Harms Individuals | Perspective of Academics | 10 |
| Harms Campaigns | Perspective of Campaigns | 9 |
| Benefits Campaigns | Fault of Lawmakers | 9 |
| Fault of Campaigns | Perspective of Campaigns | 9 |
| Harms Individuals | Perspective of Anti-spam Industry | 9 |

*Note.* The top 10% of co-occurrence relationships observed as ranked by total code co-occurrence frequency recorded.

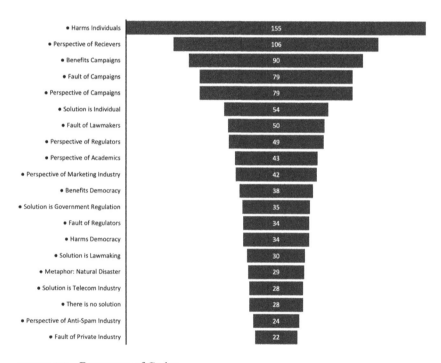

FIGURE 8.2   Frequency of Codes.

or about 31% of the total code co-occurrences observed in news coverage of political texting during the 2022 U.S. midterm elections.

Another measure used to inform where to focus analysis was the frequency of each code applied. The 20 most frequent codes are represented in Figure 8.2.

Frequency is a way to think about the relative amount of news coverage dedicated to the various phenomena captured by the coding scheme. Quantifications of the coded corpus helped spotlight areas ripe for ideological rhetorical criticism, but numbers alone cannot provide a full picture of how the mass media framed political texting as a phenomenon. The remainder of this chapter explicates and reinforces the findings by adding "thick descriptions" (O'Connor & Joffe, 2020, p. 4) of the perspectives captured through the methodology applied.

In the next section, we offer a narrative of the rise of mass political texting from its humble beginnings as a technological novelty used by under-resourced organizers to its ubiquitous presence in every modern campaign run in the 2022 midterm elections.

## From Novel to Nuisance: Rise of Text Messaging in U.S. Political Communication

As text messaging emerged as a novel and important tool in U.S. political campaigning, scholars observed a critical influx in campaign text messaging across the world (Stelter, 2008). Early research on text messaging focused particular attention to the uses of text messaging as a critical technological channel shaping communication culture, particularly among young people (Blanchfield, 2006; Epstein, 2015; Kasesniemi, 2003). Given the early uses of text messaging for organizing youth protest movements and mobilizing international connections, it is perhaps not surprising that the presidential campaign of Barack Obama was a watershed moment for using text messaging as a political campaign tool in a national U.S. election as his campaign attempted to harness both young voters' energy and international connection.

In 2008, the Obama campaign announced his vice-presidential running mate to millions via text (Nielsen, 2008). The Obama campaign VP text was both a pragmatic effort to attract supporters by developing voter and donor lists and a gesture of participatory democracy that drew on the novelty, interactivity, and appearance of sociability of text messaging (Thurlow & Poff, 2013). The effectiveness of the Obama campaign's use of text messaging, along with other technologies such as e-mail and online video, helped popularize the use of those tools in political campaigns. However, the Obama campaign's use of text messaging also opened important discussions about the challenges new technologies pose for campaign communication etiquette and consideration of "mobile advocacy dos and don'ts" (Verclas, 2008, p. 63). While some raised concerns that political text messaging campaigns strategies may leave the older voters behind (Ling, 2008), the growth of political text messaging over the subsequent decade and a half suggests the broad acceptance of the strategic usefulness of campaign text messaging and targeting an ever-wider audience (Green & Gerber, 2019).

**178** Media Messages in the 2022 Midterm Election

By 2012, the uses of text messaging went well beyond a tool for grabbing attention. Shortly before the election, the Federal Election Commission approved the use of text-to-donate fundraising and both the Obama and Romney campaigns quickly adopted the tactic. Subsequent campaigns continued to adapt to new technologies and regulatory environments. In the 2016 presidential campaign of Bernie Sanders, for example, the campaign circumvented regulations on mass texting that require explicit opt-in consent by the receiver by turning to a new texting technology platform, Hustle, which enabled individuals to text other individuals, a communication that did not clearly require opt-in consent from the receiver (Glover et al., 2020). By 2016, the use of text messaging for campaign fundraising and voter mobilization was no longer a novel tool for select campaigns. Instead, it quickly became a set element for both Republican and Democratic campaigns. Katy Steinmetz, writing for *Time* magazine during the 2018 midterm election, took notice of the rise in political text messaging and warned that it was "only the beginning" (Steinmetz, 2018). She was right.

The 2020 presidential election, shaped as it was by pandemic contexts that limited face-to-face campaigning, became so defined by the ubiquitous use of text messaging that some started to refer to the race as the "texting election" (Zarroli, 2020, para. 7). Professional communicators working on political campaigns during the 2020 presidential primary election found themselves without traditional message operations such as door-knocking campaigns, in-person town halls, and candidate meet and greets. To solve this problem, these communicators rapidly reassigned resources dedicated to traditional political communication outreach to emergent political communication technologies such as Short Message Service-based peer-to-peer text messages (Glover et al., 2020). In the wake of the texting campaign of 2020, the novelty of Obama's 2008 text messaging campaign faded into the past. The rapid rise in political campaign text messaging left many in 2022 feeling that "political texts" were simply "the worst" (Wallsten, 2022). News media coverage amplified this narrative in 2022–often framing the "barrage," or "flood," of text messages as "annoying, but legal."

To directly answer RQ1, which asked how news coverage framed political texting, we found news coverage of political texting shifted from describing the practice as a novelty when the technology first emerged over a decade ago to now primarily framing political texting as an unregulated nuisance that the public must endure. This shift is exemplified in the arguments made by one of the most cited figures across multiple articles, Scott Goodstein. Goodstein, the former Obama text messaging campaign manager, has become a vocal advocate for enhanced federal regulations of text messaging. Given his credibility as a foundational figure in the emergence of political text messaging, Goodstein is one of the few voices expressed in the sample of news coverage that suggested unregulated texting harms individuals, democratic engagement, and campaigns who will generate public backlash to the litany of messages on their phones. Goodstein (2022) blames the Federal Communications Commission and lawmakers for failing to close loopholes. However, rather than relying on the telecom industry to self-regulate text messaging, Goodstein suggests the only viable path forward is for the FCC to address clear loopholes that make P2P spam texting the new normal.

While Goodstein suggests government regulation is a necessary solution, the most prominent frames across the corpus of media articles centered the perspectives of text message receivers and the annoyance of spam text messaging for those individuals. Framing the issue around individual user experiences, the next most common codes took on the perspectives of the campaigns who were acknowledged both to be at fault for their text messaging practices, but also the primary beneficiaries of those same practices. While less frequent, the fault was often directed to lawmakers and regulatory agencies who were framed as unwilling and unable to take the necessary actions to constrain political campaigns text message practices. The least prominent framing of fault, although still present, was directed at the private telecom industries. Given the distribution of fault, it was not uncommon for the media to suggest government regulations and lawmaking as potential solutions, but then acknowledging that no such action was likely to take place. While this led some media to come to frame the issue as having no solution, the most common solutions were for individuals to attempt to solve the problem themselves.

This framing is explored more in the next section where RQ2, which asked what ideologies were expressed in news coverage of political texting during this period of time, is addressed through a close reading of how news coverage framing of the harms, benefits, and solutions to mass political texting.

## "Annoying, but Legal": Regulatory Failures of Political Text Messaging

There are two basic methods of mass political texting that campaigns in the 2022 midterm elections used to reach potential voters, volunteers, and donors: a robotexting method often referred to as app-to-peer (A2P) texting, which can send a message to thousands of phone numbers with one push of a button; and peer-to-peer texting, where a button push is required to send each message to each individual. Federal regulations of mobile communications include the 1991 Telephone Consumer Protection Act (TCPA) which requires opt-in consent for robocalls and auto-dialers contacting individuals, and the 2003 CAN-SPAM Act, which regulate commercial autodialing programs. Whereas current federal laws and regulations impose several compliance

**180** Media Messages in the 2022 Midterm Election

burdens on A2P texting campaigns (such as requiring receivers to opt-in), statutory and regulatory language does not consider the P2P texting boom in political marketing from 2016 onward.

In 2022 midterm media coverage, much of the reporting found fault with the regulatory environment, citing legal loopholes that enabled campaigns to increasingly annoy voters by text messaging. One common narrative frame was that regulations of mobile communications have not kept pace with the rapid emergence of political text messaging campaigns:

> You can opt out of scam text messages pitching the latest fitness fad. You can block that annoying relative's emoji-laden message. But you can't escape the latest Ohio Senate polling numbers delivered to your cellphone. That's because the National Do Not Call Registry does not apply to political text messages. (Balmert, 2022, para. 1)

Framed as a legal loophole, the gray area of definition that questions if P2P texting campaigns constituted autodialer, was critical to the widespread adoption by political campaigns in 2018 and 2020. This regulatory environment since has been shaped by political efforts of the P2P Alliance to exempt campaigns from autodialing regulations, a perspective that in 2018 and 2020 was upheld by the Federal Communications Commission, Federal Election Commission, and the Supreme Court. The P2P texting loophole ties the hands of regulators, who in the sample of news coverage often pointed to the need for lawmakers to act. However, lawmakers are politicians, many of whom have come to depend on P2P texting services in their electoral campaigns. As shown in Figure 8.2, results from the present study show that news coverage blamed primarily two entities: campaigns and lawmakers.

All elected lawmakers, even the ones publicly advocating for cracking down on political texting, have a fundamental conflict of interest that makes statutory resolution of this problem unlikely. Although campaigns and lawmakers are conceptually different entities, which is why they were coded differently in this study, in many cases they are two sides of the same coin. Since lawmakers must run modern campaigns to maintain or advance their political position, they have a perverse incentive not to act. Although that insight was rarely admitted in the news coverage studied, two significant co-occurrence findings (refer to Table 8.2) were the links between the "benefits campaigns" code and both the "fault of campaigns" and "fault of lawmakers" codes, suggesting that news coverage in the sample rhetorically connected campaigns and lawmakers as a source of fault while also recognizing that as a unified entity these same people benefited by not acting to ameliorate the harms of political texting.

Metaphorical language (Lakoff & Johnson, 2008) was employed often when news coverage described the harm caused by mass political texting.

Two significant co-occurrence relationships (refer to Table 8.2) were found between "harms individuals" and both of the "metaphor: natural disaster" and "metaphor: militaristic" codes. Terms associated with water-based natural disasters (e.g., torrent, flood, tsunami, etc.) were widely used by individuals, regulators, lawmakers, and academics to describe the looming danger of mass political texting. Framing problems as naturogenic elides attributions of fault for the abuses of mass political texting. "Political discourse is replete with variously demeaning metaphors that derogate the enemy" (van Dijk, 2005, p. 30), which helps explain why media outlets relied on battle-oriented terminology when representing the perspective of political campaigns in the sampled news coverage (e.g., onslaught, hitting, bombardment, etc.). The construction of political texting as a weapon to be used in battle fits the competitive ethos of campaigns, but it is a framing that may also be helping campaigns rationalize their increasing reliance on P2P texting programs to supply their operations with cash and volunteers.

Directly answering RQ2, which asked what ideologies were expressed in news coverage related to political texting during this period, the primary ideological expression found in the news coverage was a neoliberal individualism that delegitimized government solutions to political texting while empowering the private entities who are benefiting from the status quo. "Harm to individuals" was the most frequent code (refer to Figure 8.2) in the sample of news coverage that the researchers analyzed. In fact, almost every perspective captured by the coding scheme had a significant co-occurrence relationship with the "harms individual" code. The exception was the "perspective of campaigns" which instead had significant co-occurrence relationships with "harms campaigns" and "benefits democracy" codes, suggesting deflection of responsibility and the rationalization of political texting as necessary for the greater good. This framing connects to neoliberal individualism in two ways. First, by individualizing the problem as a consumer-centric one, rather than say the free market and democratic system writ large. Second, the harm individual framing invites regulatory scrutiny, but the media laments that it is unlikely any policy action will be taken, instead framing individual action as the only available solution.

Some of the potential harm to individuals identified in the sample was serious, such as texting becoming a major source of polarization and disinformation, or the risk of being scammed by identity-thieves posing as campaign volunteers (Kraftt & Donovan, 2020). Summarizing a collection of comments about P2P texting gathered by a prominent news organization, one journalist (Singer, 2022) wrote that many people "found the electioneering texts annoying, polarizing, occasionally dubious and definitely intrusive" (para 4.). However, most of the harm to individuals identified centered on less serious issues such as being helplessly spammed and annoyed by political campaigns, as one headline put it, "Political texts are annoying, but legal" (Price, 2022). A visual example of this framing is observed in Figure 8.3, which is a screen clip of a news broadcast taken from a

FIGURE 8.3  Example of "Annoying, but Legal" Media Coverage.

video transcript captured in the sample. Given the commonplace media framing of individual annoyance as the reported harm of political campaign texting spam, more serious discussions of the risks of current political texting practices to exacerbate polarization and disinformation were less frequently discussed.

Beyond the federal P2P statutory and regulatory loopholes, the legality of political texting was occasionally framed as a constitutional matter beyond even lawmakers' ability to solve, as one election attorney paraphrased in the sample put it "unsolicited messages, as annoying as they may be, are a form of political speech protected by the First Amendment" (French, 2022, para. 6). Coverage also cited state statutes as another obstacle to solving problematic political texting campaigns. For example, as another article put it "Utah's Division of Consumer Protection said while the texts and calls might be annoying, they are legal, citing Utah's Telephone and Facsimile Solicitation Act" (Harrison, 2022, para. 12). Public belief in the inevitability of annoying political texting, as demonstrated in Table 8.2, is underscored by the significant co-occurrence relationship between the "harms individuals" and "there is no solution" codes. Far from nihilistically rejecting solutions, this framing sets up the rhetorical conditions to mitigate accountability for politicians and marketing firms to curb the problematic P2P operations they have come to rely on for modern political campaigns. Framing the problem as inevitable and beyond government intervention merges with a framing that displaces the responsibility of mitigating harm onto those that are harmed. In the next section, RQ3, which asks who benefited and who was harmed by mass media framings of political texting, is addressed by tracing the link between neoliberal ideology and the market-based commodification of political text spam.

## Reply 'STOP': Commodification via Individualizing Market Solutions to Political Spam

Cultural theorist Stuart Hall argued that individualism is one of "the ruling ideological principles of the bourgeois lexicon" and "key political themes which, in our time, have made a powerful and compelling return to the ideological stage" (Hall, 1986, p. 35) of neoliberalism. Neoliberal individualism is an ideology that places the rational choice-making individual at the heart of a political economy driven by the free market and celebrates a negative conception of individual liberty that frees the individual from constraint to maximize their own wellbeing (Freeden, 1996). A consequence of this ideologically motivated individualist rhetoric is that those most capable of solving large societal problems are excused from any obligation to act while those most harmed by systemic failures are blamed for not being accountable enough for solving their own victimization. Inevitability claims provide rhetorical cover for officials to avoid placing meaningful guardrails on the use of political texting as a mass persuasion tool. Such claims also tend to obscure the responsibility of campaigns and their vendors to curtail their own abuse of SMS-powered mass marketing technology. Meanwhile those being spammed are admonished for giving out their number in the first place and advised to reply "STOP" (Michael, 2022) to unwanted text messages or told if they just return their ballot then campaigns would leave them alone (Brown, 2022). The failure of regulatory agencies and lawmakers to reign in political marketers and campaigns has been set up as a justification for people to just deal with it.

A connected finding is the significant co-occurrence relationship found between the "harms individuals" and "solution is individual" codes. That finding along with the very high frequency of "solution is individual" as an applied code suggests a news coverage framing adhering to a neoliberal ideology of individualism that turns systemic failures into personal problems for folks to work out by themselves. Adding texture for readers to understand this individualizing rhetorical maneuver, in one coded annotation, the author first concedes the harm to individuals that mass political texting campaigns may be "annoying, and some could even be scams" before suggesting that it is up to the individuals to "keep from falling for them" (Cassulo, 2022, paras. 2–3). Another exemplar of this move similarly acknowledged the inevitability of receiving campaign texts before listing the actions individuals should take if they are annoyed:

> Although there is no way to completely block campaign texts, there are some things you can do to minimize them: Don't give out your phone number. Reply with the word "STOP." Campaigns should honor opt-out requests. Check out the settings in your phone- select the "filter unknown senders" or enable spam protection. (Michael, 2022, para. 9)

**184** Media Messages in the 2022 Midterm Election

Given that the preponderance of the news coverage characterized political text messaging as a significant harm to individuals and offered little optimism for a regulatory or legal solution to the rapid expansion of campaign texting, a commonplace discourse around market-based solutions became a prominent feature in many stories. Perhaps not surprisingly, two of the most common solution frames were promoted through the perspectives of an emergent anti-spam technology sector and the telecom industry seeking to commercialize the complaints of consumers facing a barrage of campaign text messages. Although political texting is in one sense bad for telecom businesses, the industry quickly adapted to monetize their regulatory role by charging campaigns to be part of a registry.

An emergent anti-spam technological sector, headlined most frequently by Robokiller, was commonly cited across news media as a critical figure in navigating public annoyance with the swell of campaign text messages. Robokiller was generally cited in news articles for two reasons: first, they were cited as an authoritative source on the magnitude of campaign text messaging circulating during the 2022 midterm elections (French, 2022). Second, their anti-spam software was promoted as one of the only solutions available to consumers experiencing "Hell on Your Cell," as one outlet headlined their article (Brown, 2022). Media stories which amplified the sense of a harmful explosion of political text messages facing consumers in the 2022 midterm elections, often coupled with a fatalist discourse that suggested there was no solution available to the public, became a rhetorical rationale for private consumers to purchase anti-spam protections as the only realistic available option for receivers to mitigate the annoying rise of political texts. Ultimately, the anti-spam industry benefits from the sense that there is a significant threat to consumers and no imminent regulatory solution because they can then sell anti-spam protection as a consumer solution.

Answering RQ3, which asked who benefits and who is harmed by the predominant media frames of political text messaging, we suggest mass media framings are elevating private interests, who are reaping the benefits of a neoliberal individualistic framing. It was not only the emergent anti-spam industry, but the media also took note of the telecom industry's efforts to take on the role as the most relevant actor to resolve the harmful spread of political text messaging. Although telecom businesses and cell phone makers are harmed by political texting spam, they have turned a problem into an opportunity. Reacting to consumers asking them to solve the problem, telecom companies monetized the solutions and now sell them back to consumers. One of the most prominent storylines in media coverage of the 2022 midterm elections centered on the implementation of new telecom rules restricting the use of political text messaging (Cohen, 2022). Known colloquially as "10DLC Rules," for the regulations on 10-digit long codes, mobile carriers put into effect a policy delayed from 2020 which require campaigns to register with a private Campaign Registry before embarking on mass text campaigns or face high messaging rates, slower delivery rates, and sometimes blocking campaigns from sending text messages altogether (CTIA, 2022).

Drawing extensively on the perspective of telecom companies, these stories amplified the notion that political text messaging was harmful to individuals, who were framed not as citizens, but as consumers. Speakers from the telecom industry spread blame for the harmful text explosion across unscrupulous campaigns targeting vulnerable consumers and an absent regulatory and lawmaker solution on the horizon. In the wake of the failed regulatory environment, as FCC, FEC, and state attorneys general have failed to enforce existing regulatory statutes, the telecom industry framed their actions as the only potential solution to the barrage of political text messaging harming their consumers. Telecomm takes on the position of gatekeeper and monetizes the approval process along the way all in the name of protecting consumer privacy while extracting more from the text messaging process. Although they were largely ignored, 10DLC was criticized by lawmakers and campaigns as a potential threat to democratic engagement because it will stamp out progressive grassroots organizations and cement media gatekeeping (Changa, 2022). Mass media framings of SMS-based political communication technology are contributing to the neoliberal commodification of the problem rather than fostering solutions founded in good governance. In the last section of this chapter, the implications of the research findings presented are discussed in the context of future uses and advancements in SMS-based political communication technology.

## On the Future of SMS-based Political Communication Technology

At approximately 50 political texts sent out to every phone in the U.S., SMS-based political texting programs reached new heights in the 2022 midterm elections (Ford, 2023). A once rare and novel political communication technology, SMS-based marketing has become a staple of any well-organized campaign and it is not difficult to understand why that is the case. Texting is an incredibly cheap and effective means of communicating with potential voters. However, after the 2022 midterm elections, experts and campaigns are beginning to worry about oversaturation. The present study supports such a concern as every perspective captured in the sampled news coverage recognized the potential harm mass political texting may inflict.

A disempowering and delegitimizing narrative frame positing texting as an annoying, but completely legal political communication technology that cannot be reined in by the government, and will not be reined in by political campaigns who presume to benefit most from text usage, is present in the sampled news coverage. Through this framing, audiences are led to believe that the best chance at a solution is to act individually by not giving out phone numbers, by reporting texts as spam, by replying STOP to political texters, or by paying for an anti-spam

## 186 Media Messages in the 2022 Midterm Election

application like Robokiller to block messages before the intended receiver has any chance to be annoyed (Brown, 2022). To the extent a systemic level solution is consistently offered in the news coverage, it is the largely ineffective new 10DLC rules major telecom companies recently adopted to, according to them, protect their customers. However, the 10DLC rules are mostly a bureaucratic and financial barrier that well-resourced political campaigns can easily overcome while subjecting less-resourced grassroots organizers to the potential editorial power of the telecom industry.

Individualizing responsibility lets government officials, politicians, and campaign operatives off the hook for curbing the harm that mass political texting poses to individuals and society. With this frame, news coverage about political texting is enabling the privatized takeover of the entire problem-solution dynamic. SMS-based political communication is poised to continue growing into the 2024 presidential election and beyond. More than just grow, it is likely the phenomenon will also evolve to incorporate advancements in artificial intelligence and natural language processing techniques to make mass political texting more efficient at targeting and more effective at persuading potential voters. The use and abuse of SMS-based political communication technology will not be abated without government intervention. In the meantime, the American electorate is unlikely to get relief from political texting spam anytime soon.

### References

Balmert, J. (2022, January 31). Tired of receiving political text messages? Here's why you're getting so many. *The Cincinnati Enquirer.* www.cincinnati.com/story/news/politics/electi ons/2022/01/31/tired-political-text-messages-do-not-call-list-wont-help/6613616001/

Bergh, J., Christensen, D. A., & Matland, R. E. (2021). When is a reminder enough? Text message voter mobilization in a European context. *Political Behavior*, *43*(3), 1091–1111. https://doi.org/10.1007/s11109-019-09578-1

Bhatti, Y., Dahlgaard, J. O., Hansen, J. H., & Hansen, K. M. (2017). Moving the campaign from the front door to the front pocket: Field experimental evidence on the effect of phrasing and timing of text messages on voter turnout. *Journal of Elections, Public Opinion and Parties*, *27*(3), 291–310. https://doi.org/10.1080/17457 289.2016.1270288

Blanchfield, T. (2006). The texting phenomenon: Countries across the world use text messaging to help with campaigns. *Campaigns & Elections*, *27*(6), 42. www. thefreelibrary.com/The texting phenomenon: countries across the world use text messaging...-a0148657679

Brown, J. (2022, November 4). Hell on your cell: Arizonans got 50 million campaign robotexts this fall. *Tucson Sentinel.* www.tucsonsentinel.com/local/report/110422_ robocall_campaigning/hell-your-cell-arizonans-got-50-million-campaign-robote xts-this-fall/

Campbell, J. L., Quincy, C., Osserman, J., & Pedersen, O. K. (2013). Coding in-depth semistructured interviews: Problems of unitization and intercoder reliability and agreement. *Sociological Methods & Research, 42*(3), 294–320. https://doi.org/10.1177/0049124113500475

Campbell, S. W., & Kwak, N. (2010). Mobile communication and civic life: Linking patterns of use to civic and political engagement. *Journal of Communication, 60*(3), 536–555. https://doi.org/10.1111/j.1460-2466.2010.01496.x

Cassulo, E. (2022, November 4). Tech byte: Don't fall for political texting scams. *WDEF.* www.wdef.com/tech-byte-dont-fall-for-political-texting-scams/

Changa, A. (2022, August 9). Advocates sound alarm about new texting policy that could have negative impacts on Black voter outreach. *News One.* https://newsone.com/4387691/10dlc-sound-alarm-new-texting-policy-voter-outreach/

Cohen, R. (2022, July 19). Campaigns may have lost their most effective–and annoying–outreach tool. *Vox.* www.vox.com/2022/7/19/23268260/midterms-texting-10dlc-campaigns-optin-mobile

CTIA. (2022). Keeping consumers spam free during election season. *CTIA Blog.* www.ctia.org/news/keeping-consumers-spam-free-during-election-season

Dale, A., & Strauss, A. (2009). Mobilizing the mobiles: Text messaging and turnout. In P. G. Gulati, P. C. Williams, V. Gueorguieva, & C. Panagopoulos, & A. Slotnick (Eds.), *Politicking online: The transformation of election campaign communications* (pp. 152–162). Rutgers University Press.

Early, W. (2022, November 1). 'My phone is constantly blowing up': Alaska voters contend with increase in campaign text messages. *Alaska Public Media.* https://alaskapublic.org/2022/11/01/my-phone-is-constantly-blowing-up-alaska-voters-contend-with-increase-in-campaign-text-messages/

Entman, R. M. (1993). *Framing: Toward clarification of a fractured paradigm. Journal of Communication, 43*(4), 51–58.

Epstein, I. (Ed.). (2015). *The whole world is texting: Youth protest in the information age.* Sense Publishers. https://doi.org/10.1007/978-94-6300-055-0

Fish, S. (2022, May 2). Coloradans should prepare for a tsunami of anonymous political text messages as 2022 campaign season kicks into gear. *The Colorado Sun.* https://coloradosun.com/2022/05/02/anonymous-political-text-messages-colorado/

Ford, A. (2023, January 26). Billions of political text messages were sent last year–and there is little to stop more from coming. *NBC News.* www.nbcnews.com/data-graphics/15-billion-political-text-messages-sent-2022-rcna64017

Freeden, M. (1996). *Ideologies and political theory: A conceptual approach.* Oxford University Press.

French, R. (2022, November 16). Hate the flood of political texts? Here's what Michigan can and can't do. *Bridge Michigan.* www.bridgemi.com/michigan-government/hate-flood-political-texts-heres-what-michigan-can-and-cant-do

Glover, K., Gursky, J., Joseff, K., & Woolley, S. C. (2020). Peer-to-peer texting and the 2020 U.S. election: Hidden messages and intimate politics. *Center for Media Engagement.* https://mediaengagement.org/research/peer-to-peer-texting-and-the-2020-election.

Goodstein, S. (2022). How the FCC can protect consumers from unwanted political text message spam. *The Hill.* https://thehill.com/opinion/campaign/3497156-how-the-fcc-can-protect-consumers-from-unwanted-political-text-message-spam/

Green, D. P., & Gerber, A. S. (2019). *Get out the vote: How to increase voter turnout.* Brookings Institution Press.

Hall, S. (1986). The problem of ideology-Marxism without guarantees. *Journal of Communication Inquiry, 10*(2), 28–44. https://doi.org/10.1177/01968599860 1000203

Harrison, A. (2022, October 17). Residents in Utah consider voter privacy in light of upcoming election. *KJZZ.* https://kjzz.com/news/local/voter-privacy-upcoming-elect ion-november-utah-ballot-phone-number-email-driver-license-social-security-num ber-text-messages-primary-midterm-republican-democrat

Holleman, J. (2022). West St. Louis County political contest had share of 'shenanigans.' *St. Louis Post-Dispatch.* www.stltoday.com/news/local/columns/joe-holleman/west-st-louis-county-political-contest-had-share-of-shenanigans/article_3c8a2fc3-ede4-598f-a00f-5c905fdeff37.html

Kasesniemi, E.-L. (2003). *Mobile messages: Young people and a new communication culture.* Tampere University Press.

Kaul, G. (2021, October 5). What's behind the flood of political texts blowing up voters' phones this year. *MinnPost.* www.minnpost.com/politics-policy/2021/10/whats-beh ind-the-flood-of-political-texts-blowing-up-voters-phones-this-year/

Krafft, P. M., & Donovan, J. (2020). Disinformation by design: The use of evidence collages and platform filtering in a media manipulation campaign. *Political Communication, 37*(2), 194–214. https://doi.org/10.1080/10584609.2019.1686094

Krippendorff, K. (2011). Computing Krippendorff's alpha-reliability. *University of Pennsylvania Library.* https://repository.upenn.edu/asc_papers/43

Lakoff, G., & Johnson, M. (2008). *Metaphors we live by.* University of Chicago Press.

Ling, R. (2008). Should we be concerned that the elderly don't text? *The Information Society, 24*(5), 334–341. https://doi.org/10.1080/01972240802356125

Loging, S. (2022, October 26). Flood of campaign text messages leading up to election day, *KWCH.* www.kwch.com/2022/10/26/flood-campaign-text-messages-leading-up-election-day/

Makus, A. (1990). Stuart Hall's theory of ideology: A frame for rhetorical criticism. *Western Journal of Speech Communication, 54*(4), 495–514. https://doi.org/10.1080/ 10570319009374357

Malhotra, N., Michelson, M. R., Rogers, T., & Valenzuela, A. A. (2011). Text messages as mobilization tools: The conditional effect of habitual voting and election salience. *American Politics Research, 39*(4), 664–681. https://doi.org/10.1177/1532673X1 1398438

Martin, J. A. (2015). Mobile news use and participation in elections: A bridge for the democratic divide? *Mobile Media & Communication, 3*(2), 230–249. https://doi.org/ 10.1177/2050157914550664

McCormick, L. (2022, August 3). 12 Kansas lawmakers plan to close text messaging 'loophole' for ballot initiatives. *KHSB.* www.kshb.com/news/local-news/investigati ons/12-kansas-lawmakers-plan-to-close-text-messaging-loophole-for-ballot-init iatives

Michael, O. (2022, November 7). Campaigns turn to text messages hoping to sway voters in Tennessee. *NewsChannel 5.* www.newschannel5.com/news/campaigns-turn-to-text-messages-hoping-to-sway-voters-in-tennessee

Neumayer, C., & Stald, G. (2014). The mobile phone in street protest: Texting, tweeting, tracking, and tracing. *Mobile Media & Communication, 2*(2), 117–133. https://doi. org/10.1177/2050157913513255

Nielsen. (2008, August). Obama's V.P. text message reaches 2.9 million. *The Nielsen Company.* www.nielsen.com/insights/2008/obamas-text-message-reaches-29-mill ion-and-makes-history/

O'Connor, C., & Joffe, H. (2020). Intercoder reliability in qualitative research: Debates and practical guidelines. *International Journal of Qualitative Methods, 19.* https://doi. org/10.1177/1609406919899220

Price, S. (2022, October 25). Political texts are annoying, but legal. *KFMB-TV.* www. cbs8.com/article/news/politics/elections/political-texts-are-annoying-and-legal/509-b2433b9d-c3de-4f66-a128-018fa393879e

Reese, S. D. (1990). The news paradigm and the ideology of objectivity: A socialist at the Wall Street Journal. *Critical Studies in Media Communication, 7*(4), 390–409. https:// doi.org/10.1080/15295039009360187

Rodgers, K. (2022, August 18). Constantly getting political texts? Here's what you should know. *WJXT.* www.news4jax.com/news/politics/2022/08/18/constantly-getting-politi cal-texts-heres-what-you-should-know/

Schonfeld, Z. (2022, November 1). Company says text messages with false voting information sent in error. *The Hill.* https://thehill.com/homenews/campaign/3714055-company-says-text-messages-with-false-voting-information-sent-in-error/

Shaul-Cohen, S., & Lev-On, A. (2020). Smartphones, text messages, and political participation. *Mobile Media & Communication, 8*(1), 62–82. https://doi.org/10.1177/ 2050157918822143

Shaw, D. R., Dun, L., & Heise, S. (2022). Mobilizing peripheral partisan voters: A field experimental analysis from three California congressional election campaigns. *American Politics Research, 50*(5), 587–602. https://doi.org/10.1177/1532673X221094295

Singer, N. (2022, November 5). Fed up with political text messages? Read on. *The New York Times.* www.nytimes.com/2022/11/05/technology/political-text-messages-pelosi-trump.html

Steigerwald, A. (2022, November 1). Tired of receiving texts from campaigns? Here's how you can stop them. *WBNS.* www.10tv.com/article/news/politics/elections/politi cal-text-messages/530-dfa1b1ba-5740-49a8-a95f-2f621280c3bf

Steinmetz, K. (2018, October 24). Why politicians are texting you so much–and it's only the beginning. *Time.* https://time.com/5432309/politician-campaigns-midterm-elect ion-text-messages/

Stelter, B. (2008, August 17). Enticing text messengers in a get-out-the-vote push. *The New York Times.* www.nytimes.com/2008/08/18/us/politics/18message.html

Thurlow, C., & Poff, M. (2013). Text messaging. In S. C. Herring, D. Stein, & T. Virtanen (Eds.), *Pragmatics of computer-mediated communication* (pp. 163–189). De Gruyter Mouton. https://doi.org/10.1515/9783110214468

van Dijk, T. A. (2005). Discourse analysis as ideology analysis. In C. Schäffne & A.L. Wenden (Eds.), *Language & peace* (pp. 41–58). Routledge.

van Dijk, T. A. (2009). News, discourse, and ideology. In K. Whal-Jorgensen & T. Hanitzsch (Eds.), *The handbook of journalism studies* (pp. 211–224). Routledge.

Verclas K. (2008). Mobile advocacy dos and don'ts. In J. D. Lasica & C. M. Firestone (Eds.), *Civic engagement on the move: How mobile media can serve the public good* (pp. 63–68). The Aspen Institute.

Wallsten, S. (2022). Political texts are the worst. *Technology Policy Institute.* https://tech policyinstitute.org/publications/content-moderation/political-texts-are-the-worst/

Wander, P. (1983). The ideological turn in modern criticism. *Communication Studies, 34*(1), 1–18. https://doi.org/10.1080/10510978309368110

Weaver, D. A., & Bimber, B. (2008). Finding news stories: a comparison of searches using LexisNexis and Google News. *Journalism & Mass Communication Quarterly, 85*(3), 515–530. https://doi.org/10.1177/107769900808500303

Zarroli, J. (2020, October 7). Getting lots of political messages on your phone? Welcome to 'the texting election. *NPR.* www.npr.org/2020/10/07/920776670/getting-lots-of-political-messages-on-your-phone-welcome-to-the-texting-election

# 9

# OF RED WAVES, ELECTION DENIERS, CANDIDATE QUALITY AND OTHER ISSUES

## Political Cartoons during the 2022 Midterm Elections

*Jody C Baumgartner and Hanna Kassab*

Editorial cartoons hold a special place in the hearts and minds of many historians and political aficionados. Often hearkening back to Thomas Nast's cartoons targeting Boss Tweed and his Tammany Ring, they point to the insightful, pointed, and often contrary political messages of this genre and the power they have to affect social and political change. Whether they do affect change is an open question, but most would agree that editorial cartoons are a valuable and entertaining form of political messaging.

This essay reviews editorial cartoons produced during the 2022 election campaign season. The analysis draws on a sample of 227 cartoons from four separate online sources, reviewing the main themes, subjects, and topics found in the sample. Because midterm elections typically lack a main, singular unifying theme or narrative, several mini, or smaller themes are identified by employing the theory of topical congruence, which suggests that the topics and subjects of political humor will mirror news of the day. In addition to cartoons about both political parties and several nationally prominent politicians, there were a number of cartoons about the red wave, election deniers, the lack of candidate quality, and the issues of abortion and inflation.

The research adds to a diverse, but relatively small body of literature that examines editorial or political cartoons. Findings shed light on the nature of the messages of editorial cartoons, particularly in context of a midterm election campaign and as they relate to news coverage.

DOI: 10.4324/9781003440833-12

## Review of Political Cartoon Research

There is not an overwhelming amount of research on political cartoons. A number of comprehensive, book-length treatments of the subject exist, which include historical overviews of the genre, how cartoonists work, and examinations of the main themes represented (e.g., Hess & Northrop, 2011; Lordon, 2006). Works examining cartoons about high-profile happenings, issues, or events are well represented. One such example is Solomon's (1984) analysis of how the Great Depression was depicted in cartoons in *The New Yorker*. Another examined cartoons published during the second World War, focusing on the hostile racial stereotypes used to depict Axis powers (Somers, 1996). Other examples include research focused on 9–11 and its aftermath (Diamond, 2002; Hoffman & Howard, 2007), the global financial crisis of 2008 (Bounegru & Forceville, 2011), and the Coronavirus pandemic (Baumgartner & Kassab, 2022).

Consistent with research focused on editorial cartoons produced during and about high-profile events, there has been a fairly consistent stream of research focused on U.S. presidential elections over the past few decades. For example, drawing on cartoons culled from a variety of sources, Hill (1984) explored the themes, primarily negative, found in cartoons about candidate Jimmy Carter during the presidential campaign of 1976. Similarly, DeSousa and Medhurst (1982) explicated themes from cartoons about eight candidates during both the nomination and general election phases of the campaign during the 1980 presidential campaign.

Cartoons about the 1988 presidential campaign were the focus of two scholarly works. One examined the exaggerated ways in which 12 candidates were depicted in cartoons throughout the nomination and general election campaign seasons (Buell & Maus, 1988). Cartoons published during the presidential campaign of 1988 were also the subject of a book-length treatment by Edwards (1997). In her analysis, she also explicated the images, metaphors, and narratives found in political cartoons throughout the campaign.

Cartoons focused on George W. Bush, Bill Clinton, and Ross Perot during the presidential campaign of 1992 were the subject of Koetzle and Brunell's (1996) content analysis. In another content analysis, Sewell (1998) examined cartoons about the 1996 Republican nomination candidates and the incumbent Bill Clinton. In her examination of cartoons about the 2000 presidential campaign, Edwards (2001) explored "metaphoric portrayals" of the issue of character for Al Gore and competence for George W. Bush. The character traits and situation themes found in depictions of the 2004 major party presidential and vice-presidential candidates, as well as those of Green Party candidate Ralph Nader, were the subject of Conners' (2005) analysis.

Cartoons published during the presidential election season of 2008 were the subject of several articles and book chapters. Two were focused on the historic reality that the Democratic nomination was a contest between a woman (Hillary Clinton) and an African-American (Barack Obama), both firsts. Conners (2010) focused on gender-related themes found in cartoons depicting Clinton and race-related themes in those about Obama. Gender, and by extension, Clinton, was the subject of Edwards' 2007 examination of cartoons from various sources. In a similar analysis, Conners (2009) compared depictions of Clinton in cartoons from various sources to how she was being characterized on late night talk shows.

In addition to these analyses which centered on representations of race and gender, two other studies focused on the 2008 campaign. Using cartoons (from Cagle syndication service and *The New Yorker*) depicting presidential and vice-presidential candidates, including those seeking their party nomination, Edwards (2009) focused on political symbols in these cartoons. In their study, Zurbriggen and Sherman (2010) similarly focused on representations of Obama, Clinton, and John McCain in cartoons culled from GoComix. Finally, Conners (2014) collected over 500 cartoons from Cagle syndication service featuring Obama and 2012 challenger Mitt Romney in her study.

Typically, the initial focus of editorial cartoon analysis, whether implicit or explicit, is on what subjects are being depicted. A secondary focus is often how subjects are being represented. This can amount to a general evaluation of whether the subject in question (e.g., a political candidate) is portrayed in a positive or negative light, or, whether a particular personality trait, physical characteristic, policy position, and so on, of the subject in question is highlighted. This often leads to researchers exploring various themes, narratives, or messages in these cartoons.

This said, we note while much work in this area is interpretive in nature, it is descriptive and largely atheoretical. The present analysis breaks somewhat with this tradition. Here we introduce the theory of topical congruence in an attempt to provide a certain theoretical rigor to the study of editorial cartoons. The theory of topical congruence suggests that the subjects, narratives, themes, and messages of editorial cartoons will mirror those found in the day's news coverage. In other words, editorial cartoons largely follow the news in terms of what or who they are portraying, and the themes or narratives being represented.

The theory is grounded in and consistent with the previously cited research, as well as observations, about political cartoons. One need only examine editorial cartoons on a daily basis to conclude that their content, broadly understood, follows the day's news events. For example, the Cagle syndication service (Cagle.com) categorizes its cartoons by date, artist, and importantly, by topic. These topics invariably are aligned with the general direction of major news coverage. Therefore the theory of topical congruence can be thought of as an offshoot of intermedia agenda setting (Atwater et al., 1987; Harder et al., 2017), where dominant news narratives drive those of editorial cartoons.

In addition, the theory is also consistent with some research on political humor. One study in particular empirically demonstrated that there was a significant and positive correlation between the targets and subjects of jokes told on late night television and what was found in the headlines of daily newspapers (Baumgartner et al., 2019). While there is a conceptual difference between the political satire of editorial cartoons and simple political jokes told on late night talk shows, both are examples of political humor. Therefore, one could expect to see similar patterns with respect to subjects and themes portrayed in each.

Finally, the theory of topical congruence is consistent, at least implicitly, with a good deal of research on editorial cartoons. It is easy to see, for example, how the theory guides the types of cartoons produced during wartime (Somers, 1996), national crises (Diamond, 2002; Hoffman & Howard, 2007), and economic recessions or depressions (Bounegru & Forceville, 2011; Solomon, 1984). One recent article focused on cartoons drawn during the Coronavirus pandemic provided some empirical support for the theory (Baumgartner & Kassab, 2022).

Topical congruence is especially useful in an analysis of editorial cartoons during midterm election campaigns, inasmuch as the subjects one might expect to see portrayed are less obvious than those in presidential races. Presidential elections typically have a single, or at best, two main media narratives. In 2000, for example, it was the frat boy (George W. Bush) versus the stiff guy (Al Gore). In 2008, to simplify only slightly, it was political rock star Barack Obama. In 2016, it was the brash, combative, narcissistic outsider (Donald Trump) versus the woman who would do anything to win (Hillary Clinton).

However, midterm elections are different from presidential elections in many ways. First, there is less media attention paid to midterm elections than to presidential elections. Citizens are more engaged and more likely to vote during presidential elections. In addition, presidential elections are typically focused on national domestic and foreign policy issues, while during midterm election season the focus is on state and local issues or those relating to majority control of Congress.

It is this latter factor that is responsible for the fact that midterms typically lacking a single unifying theme or narrative. Beyond generic stories about, for example, how many seats a president's party is expected to lose, there are few unifying themes present. Exceptions like the Republican Party's 1994 "Contract with America" are just that—exceptions. The present analysis is focused on explicating the major mini-narratives in editorial cartoons during the 2022 campaign, drawing on the assumptions present in this theory.

## Data: The Cartoons

This analysis draws on editorial cartoons culled from four separate online sources. The first, *US News*, hosts a wide range of editorial cartoons from a number of cartoonists, including Drew Sheneman, Tom Stiglich, and Nick Anderson (www.usnews.com/cartoons). The second, *Townhall*, is a conservative news and political commentary website that features cartoons from Gary Varvel, Margolis & Cox, and A. F. Branco (https://townhall.com/political-cartoons). The third, *GoComics*, hosts the work of cartoonists like Lalo Alcaaz, Clay Bennett, and Michael Ramirez (www.gocomics.com/comics/political). The final source, from which the plurality of the cartoons were culled, was Cagle.com. The Cagle syndication service serves more than 1,000 clients, representing more than 60 cartoonists, who include four Pulitzer Prize winners: Adam Zyglis (*Buffalo News*), Mike Keefe (*Denver Post*), Steve Sack (*Minneapolis Star Tribune*), and Kevin Siers (*Charlotte Observer*).

Both authors went to each of these sites daily, starting the day after Labor Day (September 6, 2022) through the Monday after Election Day (November 14, 2022), and downloaded any cartoon that seemed related to the midterm congressional elections. Excluded from this analysis were all cartoons which were not directly related to the election. In addition, cartoons that appeared on more than one than day (in other words, duplicates) were not included. A total of 267 election-related cartoons were collected over a period of 70 days.

There is a good deal of variation in editorial cartoon research with respect to the method employed to categorize or code cartoons, ranging from formal coding to simple, impressionistic interpretation. Categorizing cartoons for this analysis was a fairly straightforward process, primarily because it is not that challenging to identify the objects or subjects depicted in editorial cartoons.

First, a preliminary set of broad and general topics, themes or subjects (plural) represented in the cartoons, was inductively constructed. Selection of these initial categories was guided generally by topical congruence theory, an impressionistic sense of what news organizations were talking about during the campaign season, as well as an initial read of the cartoons while collecting them. Categories included both objects depicted in the cartoons, like candidate (generic, at this stage), party (either), Joe Biden, Donald Trump, or subjects and themes, including "red wave," "election deniers," and "citizen fatigue." Both authors then examined and categorized the first 100 cartoons. Following this, topics and subjects were re-evaluated based on the results of this preliminary round. A second, more fine-tuned classification was then constructed, followed by another categorization of the first 100 cartoons. A reconciliation of this round produced the final version of the classification scheme.

Included were categories for citizens, each political party, President Biden, Donald Trump, and several nationally known candidates, including Herschel Walker, John Fetterman, Mehmet Oz, and Kari Lake. Other categories included themes or subjects like the so-called Republican "red wave," election deniers (which included the issue of ballot security and a "democracy at risk" theme), poor candidate quality, citizen fatigue with the campaign, admonitions to vote, as well as the issues of abortion and inflation.

The theory of topical congruence suggests that cartoon topics or subjects will mirror those found in the news. To confirm that these topics and subjects were found in news stories throughout the campaign, the online Television Explorer, part of the GDELT Project's Television Comparer, was consulted. This tool employs data from the Internet Archive's Television News Archive to examine television news coverage from over 150 stations since 2009 (GDELT Project, 2017). Searches were conducted of the three main cable network channels (CNN, Fox News, MSNBC). The first searches were for non-political news terms (e.g., "Elon Musk," "Queen Elizabeth," "Russia," "Ukraine"). These searches served as baselines of sorts (data not included).

Comparison searches of most of the identified cartoon categories were then conducted. Some few of the cartoon category terms were excluded (e.g., "vote") from this round of searches, inasmuch as they were too general. These searches showed that the cartoon categories selected for this analysis were the subject of an amount of aggregate news coverage that was greater than the baseline searches (See Table 9.1). This confirmed the idea that the themes, objects and subjects selected for inclusion in the analysis were indeed the subject of considerable news coverage throughout the campaign season, thus validating their inclusion in the classification scheme employed in the analysis.

**TABLE 9.1** GDELT Project Television Comparer Values for News Stories, by Category

| Category | GDELT Value |
| --- | --- |
| *Themes* | |
| Candidate Quality | 2.20 |
| Election Deniers | 6.18 |
| Red Wave | 9.47 |
| *Political Parties* | |
| Democratic Party | 47.02 |
| Republican Party | 81.00 |
| *Presidents & Ex-Presidents* | |
| Joe Biden | 39.35 |
| Donald Trump | 77.66 |
| *Well-Known Candidates* | |
| John Fetterman | 115.33 |
| Mehmet Oz | 81.48 |
| Herschel Walker | 136.48 |
| *Issues* | |
| Abortion | 12.68 |
| Inflation | 9.78 |

Each category was constructed as a dummy variable, coded as either "1" or a "0" depending on whether the object or subject was depicted in the cartoon. Cartoons were then categorized according to a non-exclusive strategy, meaning that if more than one object or subject was depicted, each was coded as "1" for that cartoon. This strategy allowed for less ambiguity in categorizing cartoons, inasmuch as there was no need to weigh different objects against each other in an attempt to determine a singular subject, theme, and so on. Further, it allowed for an analysis of how various subjects and themes intersected.

Excluded from the sample were 21 cartoons that were geared toward readers in specific states and not likely to be of interest to those in other states. In addition, 19 cartoons were excluded because they did not fit our classification scheme or it was felt they could be interpreted differently by different analysts. This left a final $N$ of 227 cartoons from 63 different artists.

To get a sense of how closely the number of daily editorial cartoons tracked with news coverage about the midterm elections, the generic term "midterm election" was used in a Television Explorer search of news coverage. Data were then downloaded, and daily scores were totaled by week. These scores were then multiplied by 10 to make them comparable to the total number of cartoons devoted to the midterm elections. Figure 9.1, below, shows that as

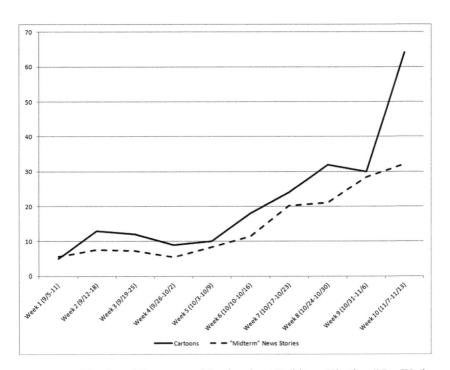

FIGURE 9.1    Number of Cartoons and Stories about "Midterm Elections" Per Week.

**198** Media Messages in the 2022 Midterm Election

the campaign season progressed, the number of stories and cartoons about the election increased.

In an attempt to more formally confirm the preliminary finding that cartoon topics and subjects mirrored news coverage, bivariate correlations were run between weekly news data values and the number of cartoons coded for each category. The mean value of the 12 Pearson R values was .662 (SD = .256), and of the 12 relationships which were measured, seven were significant (data not shown). Although this test hardly constitutes definitive proof of the validity of the theory of topical congruence, at minimum it is suggestive.

## Analysis

Table 9.2 details the number and percentage of cartoons coded for each category, as well as the number coded for only one category. Relatively few (14, or 6.2%) cartoons in the sample were identified as fitting only one category. Of these, nine were references to one of the two political parties (4 to Republicans, 5 to Democrats). The remaining were focused the red wave (1), Herschel Walker (1), admonitions to vote (1), and election deniers, broadly defined (2). A total of 197 cartoons in the sample (86.8%) referenced two, three, or four separate objects, subjects, or themes. Six cartoons were coded for five or six references.

**TABLE 9.2** Number and Percentage of Cartoons in Each Category

| Category | Number (Exclusive) | Percentage |
|---|---|---|
| *Themes* | | |
| Candidate Quality | 99 (0) | 43.6% |
| Election Deniers | 33 (2) | 14.5 |
| Red Wave | 36 (1) | 15.9 |
| Vote! | 29 (1) | 12.8 |
| *Political Parties* | | |
| Democratic Party | 36 (5) | 17.2 |
| Republican Party | 51 (4) | 22.5 |
| *Presidents and Ex-Presidents* | | |
| Joe Biden | 18 (0) | 7.9 |
| Donald Trump | 26 (0) | 11.5 |
| *Well-Known Candidates* | | |
| John Fetterman | 17 (0) | 7.5 |
| Kari Lake | 5 (0) | 2.2 |
| Mehmet Oz | 6 (0) | 2.6 |
| Herschel Walker | 23 (1) | 10.1 |
| *Issues* | | |
| Abortion | 31 (0) | 13.7 |
| Inflation | 24 (0) | 10.6 |

Quite arguably, the single greatest theme that was present in news coverage and commentary throughout the 2022 midterm elections was the prediction of a "red wave," or a larger than expected Republican victory. This theme was present in a total of 36 cartoons (15.9%) in the sample. Some of these cartoons reflected the confidence many felt about Republican chances. Bill Day's "There's Always 2024" (October 27, 2022) was one such. In it, a donkey is pictured on the shore, about to be engulfed by an enormous red wave. The donkey's thought balloon reads, "Well, there's always 2024." Others were more skeptical, like R.J. Matson's "Red Wave Drought Before Mid-Term Elections" (September 13, 2022). In it, an elephant is shown atop a surfboard labeled "2022," mired in a red puddle in the middle of a desert.

Interestingly, most (22) red wave cartoons were published after Election Day. Virtually all of these revolved around the idea that the Republican win was smaller than expected. Perhaps predictably, a majority (17) also included references to the Republican Party; ten referenced Trump, and six, both the Republican Party and Trump. Approximately one-quarter (8) contained a reference to the Democratic Party. Another nine red wave cartoons saw the artist bemoan a perceived lack of candidate quality in the elections, another common theme throughout cartoons in the sample.

Ninety cartoons, or 39.7% of the sample, contained references to either the Democratic or the Republican Party. This is hardly surprising, inasmuch as nationally, the coverage of midterm elections focuses for the most part on the two main parties and their battle for control of each house of Congress. The majority of cartoons that referenced one of the two parties (51, or 56.7%) targeted the Republican Party. This percentage is consistent with news coverage of the parties. A Television Explorer search for coverage about both parties shows that stories about the Republican Party constituted approximately 63 percent of the total.

Most of the cartoons that referenced the Republican Party were negative. Pat Bagley's "GOP In Disarray" (September 21, 2022) was a good example. In it, three elephants are shown looking at declining "GOP Polls." One remarks to the others, "We've got to stop running on what we really think." As noted, a good number also focused on the red wave theme, and Trump was featured in nine of these cartoons.

Of the two policy issues recorded, inflation and abortion, the issue of abortion was dominant in cartoons which referenced Republicans. There were 20 cartoons focused on one of these two issues. Fifteen were about abortion. One example was Robert Ariail's "Roe vs. Grave: GOP Midterms," from September 6, 2022. Here, one sees an elephant strolling past a tombstone which reads "Roe v. Wade." Ironically, the elephant is whistling, implying it is free from worry. Another theme that was present in a fair number (7, or 13.7%) of cartoons about the Republican Party was election denial, or attempts to steal the election.

Finally, 21 cartoons that depicted the Republican Party also lamented the lack of quality candidates.

An additional 39 cartoons in the sample included representations of the Democratic Party. Of these, only five were focused solely on the party itself. Steve Kelley's cartoon from September 14, 2022, titled "The Sole of The Nation," featured a man kicking a donkey with the sole of his shoe. As a result, the donkey drops several leaflets headlined "inflation," "DOJ Abuses," and other issues with which the Democrats were perceived to be having trouble. The red wave theme was present in eight Democratic cartoons; again, unsurprising given that many analysts were predicting a big Republican win.

President Biden was included in almost one-quarter (9) of these cartoons, also to be expected given that sitting presidents are informal party leaders and have a vested interest in gaining or maintaining congressional majorities. In many of these cartoons, Biden was depicted as an albatross around the neck of the party. For example, in his cartoon of November 8, 2022, Gary Varvel drew a Democratic donkey falling through the sky, skydiving with a broken parachute and an anchor labeled "Biden" around its neck.

Another 11 of the cartoons referencing the Democratic Party contained references to inflation. The messages in these were similar to those found in the cartoons that included Biden, namely, that inflation was hurting the party. A final theme found in this set of cartoons was the issue of candidate quality. A total of 14 cartoons contained negative messages about candidate quality, a slightly lower percentage than those associated with the Republican Party.

In addition to Biden's role as leader of the Democratic Party, it is reasonable to assume that there would have been a number of editorial cartoons depicting him during the fall 2022 campaign season, inasmuch as presidents are the subject of continuous news coverage. Biden was featured in 18 (7.9%) of the cartoons in the sample. Of these, half overlapped with cartoons depicting the Democratic Party. A.F. Branco's October 26, 2022, cartoon titled "If Republicans Win…" is a good example. In it, a figure is depicted bound with a rope that reads "green agenda," a hood that reads "woke agenda," and has a cast that reads "crime." Biden, eating an ice cream cone, tells the figure, "If Republicans win it'll get a lot worse." All but two Biden cartoons intersected with cartoons focused on poor candidate quality, and 77.8% (14) were negative in tone. Most of these were produced by cartoonists known for their anti-leftist orientation: A. F. Branco, Tom Stiglich and Gary Varvel.

Interestingly, as the informal leader of the Republican Party, Trump was featured in 26 cartoons, more than Biden. This is somewhat consistent with a comparative Television Explorer search of news about each throughout the campaign season, which showed Trump featured in double the amount of news coverage than Biden. Trump, of course, has rarely been out of the news spotlight since leaving office in 2021. Moreover, he was quite active in publicly

# Red Waves, Election Deniers, Candidate Quality and Other Issues 201

promoting various congressional candidates throughout 2022. Nine cartoons depicting Trump associated the former president with the Republican Party, while 10 focused on the red wave theme.

The idea that Trump was a major player in the elections and may well continue to be a presence in national politics was depicted in Bill Bramhall's cartoon of November 9, 2022, titled "Behind Us." The cartoon is a rear view of a man and woman sitting on their couch watching television, which reads "2022 Elections." The woman says, "I'm glad that's behind us," an ironic comment given that Trump is shown looming directly behind them. Trump was portrayed in overwhelmingly negative terms in a full 80.8 percent (21) of these cartoons, which also featured the theme of poor candidate quality. In another six he was associated with election deniers, another clearly negative reference.

Continuing with the focus on political actors, the next general category of subjects is a small set of candidates who seemed to receive a fair amount of national news coverage, either because of the perceived importance or closeness of their race, their fame or infamy, or some combination of these factors. These include, in order of the attention they seemed to receive, Herschel Walker, Republican, running for the U.S. Senate in Georgia; both candidates for the U.S. Senate in Pennsylvania, Democrat John Fetterman and Republican Mehmet Oz; and Kari Lake, Republican candidate for governor in Arizona. A Television Explorer search of news coverage of all four of these candidates throughout the campaign season revealed that there were actually more stories about each than about Biden, Trump, or either political party.

Herschel Walker was the candidate most depicted in the sample, seen in a full 10.1 percent (23) of the cartoons. This was likely the result of his anti-abortion stance combined with the scandals generated when ex-girlfriends went public claiming he had paid for them to have abortions. Fourteen of the Walker cartoons were abortion-related. For instance, the October 20, 2022, cartoon by Pat Byrnes titled "To Save The Life" is a good example. It shows Walker talking to a woman protester who is holding a sign saying, "My Body, My Choice." Walker says to the woman, "I'm opposed in all cases, except to save the political life of the father." In addition, all but two Walker cartoons were also coded for targeting poor candidate quality. In other words, depictions of Walker were negative, focused either on his hypocrisy or his perceived lack of intelligence. Finally, in terms of other subjects, eight of the cartoons depicting the Georgia candidate also contained references to the Republican Party.

The Pennsylvania U.S. Senate race between Fetterman and Oz drew a considerable amount of national attention. This was partly due to Oz's celebrity status as well as attention paid to Fetterman's cognitive health following his spring 2022 stroke and October debate performance. A total of 30 cartoons targeted these two candidates. Fetterman alone was featured in 17; Oz was the sole target in six; an additional seven saw both candidates depicted. For

**202** Media Messages in the 2022 Midterm Election

example, in his October 11, 2022, cartoon titled, "Fetterman Versus Oz," Clay Jones showed Fetterman as a large brute, wearing a hooded sweatshirt, saying, "me, hoodie… shorts," while Oz is a flying fowl, saying, "quack quack, I'm a quack quack." The cartoon neatly captured the caricature of each that emerged throughout the election. There were no patterns evident with respect to other themes present beyond poor candidate quality, one that was present in all 30 of these cartoons.

The final candidate featured was Kari Lake, who appeared in five cartoons. Consistent with mainstream news coverage, all of these largely painted her in a negative light. All five, for example, were also coded for poor candidate quality, while election denier was a theme in two. One of these by artist by Ed Wexler, from October 19, 2022, titled "Will Only Accept If I Win Poof I Win," drew a direct parallel to Trump. In it, the first panel depicted Lake claiming she would "only accept the elections results if" she won. A middle panel is taken up by the word "poof!" In the final panel, Lake is redrawn with a Trumpish hairstyle, claiming she won.

In all, there were 99 cartoons (43.6%) in the sample which touched on the subject of poor candidate quality. These cartoons, by their very nature, contained negative messages. The dissatisfaction felt by many over poor candidate quality was well captured in David Fitzsimmons November 1, 2022, cartoon titled "Candidate Choices." In it, one sees a voter marking a ballot in a voting booth. The side of the panel shows the ballot itself, with the voter selecting "sane human being" over "lunatic," "normal person" over "complete wingnut," and "intelligent candidate" over "rabid troll."

As might be expected, the theme of candidate quality intersected with a number of other themes. Many contained references to both Trump or the Republican Party, with 21.2% targeting one or the other. Others took aim at Biden (16.2%) or the Democratic Party (14.1%). Other themes were present as well. For example, 19.2% of the candidate quality cartoons focused on abortion, although most of these (73.4%) targeted Walker. Election deniers or denial was the subject of 11.1% of the poor candidate quality cartoons, and citizen fatigue with the campaign another 12.1%.

A final subcategory of cartoons followed themes related to substantive issues of abortion or inflation, each appearing in roughly comparable percentages of the sample. Cartoons featuring the issue of abortion constituted 13.7% of the sample. Of these, the Republican Party was targeted in almost half (15, or 48.4%); Walker was in 14. The issue of inflation appeared in 24 cartoons, and of these, the Democratic Party shared the focus in 11 (45.8%). As an illustration, the cartoon titled "Midterm Issues," published September 29, 2022, by Dick Wright, depicted a scene of a gas station, in front of which are two signs. One sign reads, "Inflation, Gas," with an up arrow, while the other sign says, "Democrats Midterm Odds," with a down arrow.

Finally, there were a fair number of cartoons produced about the electoral process as it played out in the 2022 midterm elections. One category centered around the prospects of election result denial, ballot security, or the fundamental notion that democracy may be in peril as the result of either or both. In total, there were 33 of these cartoons in the sample. One cartoon, titled "The Fix is In" (Pat Bagley, October 11, 2022) depicted a far-right rally. On stage was a sign that read, "God & Guns," with the candidate on stage—holding a Bible—proclaiming "We're gonna fix these elections for good!" In terms of intersection patterns, 11 of these cartoons also targeted poor candidate quality. Seven contained a reference to the Republican Party, and another six to Trump.

Another fairly common theme was that of citizen fatigue with the campaign season. A full 16.7% (38) of the cartoons advanced this idea. A cartoon by Daryl Cagle from November 9, 2022, was typical. Titled, "After the Election, Get Off My Lawn," it showed a couple in front of their suburban home, the man using a hose to drive away an elephant and donkey from their lawn. No patterns were evident in this subset of cartoons, save for the fact that 12 of them also addressed the topic of poor candidate quality.

The last subcategory of cartoons was those which encouraged people to vote. A total of 29 cartoons were coded for this category. Many shared a focus with a partisan preference for the vote, such as Steve Kelley's "The Sole of the Nation" (from September 16, 2022), which encouraged people to vote against Democrats on the basis of the "border crisis," "DOJ abuse," "inflation," and the "crime epidemic." Another, by Jimmy Margulies, was produced on November 3, 2022. In this cartoon, titled "Gas Prices vs. Democracy," Margulies suggests that casting a vote based on high gas prices ignores the "threat that Republicans posed" for democratic government. Some few simply reminded readers how important it was to vote, like Adam Zyglis' "How to Fight Fascism (in 2022)" (November 9, 2022), which depicted the iconic scene of Iwo Jima Marines, this time raising "a pen, instead" of a flag, to mark a ballot.

## Discussion

Midterm elections typically lack a single unifying theme. As a result, several smaller storylines emerge in news coverage throughout the fall campaign season. In 2022, several of these themes were fairly predictable. It was natural to assume, for example, there would be stories about each political party, the president, and in this case the former president, in their respective roles as unofficial party leader. In addition, it could also be anticipated that there would be a focus on at least a few individual politicians who, for whatever reason, had attracted the attention of the national press. Who those might be, however, would be more difficult to predict, as would the identification of other themes.

**204** Media Messages in the 2022 Midterm Election

The present analysis took this reality as its starting point. Several themes were initially identified, based on an overall read of campaign news coverage and cartoons as the campaign unfolded. The theory of topical congruence suggests that the subjects or topics of editorial cartoons should mirror news coverage. A reasonable amount of support for this theory was found, comparing descriptive analyses of the subjects covered in the cartoons and news coverage data from the same period. This came first by way of a formal quantitative test which relied on bivariate correlations between cartoon and news story categories. This test was limited in that it relied on reducing broad categories to quantitative values, and only seven of the 12 categories were significantly correlated. However in retrospect, the selected cartoon themes seemed, on the face if things, to fit with news coverage of the elections.

In terms of subjects or themes, several stood out. As might have been expected, there were a number of cartoons focused on the so-called red wave, or the idea that many were expecting a decisive Republican win. A number of cartoons focused on this theme. However it should be noted that the red wave theme served cartoonists well after the election as well, as the Republican margin of victory (in terms of seats in Congress) fell short of expectations. These cartoons showed smaller "waves," consistent with the narrow Republican win in the House and not having captured the Senate.

Also expected were a number of cartoons about each political party. This is because midterms are typically framed in terms of which party will have a majority in each house of Congress after the elections. In 2022, there were slightly more cartoons focused on the Republican as opposed to the Democratic Party. This was also to be expected, inasmuch as much of the commentary and news coverage in the run-up to the elections was focused on an expected Republican victory. Most of the cartoons focused on the Republican Party were also, it should be noted, negative. From this it might be natural to surmise that there was, or is, a pro-Democratic bias among editorial cartoonists. This idea would be consistent with a recent finding that cartoons produced during the Coronavirus pandemic reflected a clear left-wing bias (Baumgartner & Kassab, 2022). However, the Democratic Party was also the target of cartoonists' pens in the fall of 2022. The party was negatively depicted as being weighed down by Biden's low approval ratings, as well as by issues like rising inflation, gas prices, and crime rates.

There were also significantly more cartoons produced targeting Trump as opposed to Biden (26 as opposed to 18). This too might reasonably be construed as evidence that cartoonists are biased in favor of Biden or opposed to Trump. However, it should be remembered that Trump was extremely active during the campaign and was also under investigation for potentially mishandling classified documents. Other individuals targeted by cartoonists included, in order of the number of cartoons in the sample depicting them, Herschel Walker, John

Fetterman, Mehmet Oz, and Kari Lake. Here it is easier to set aside questions of partisan bias and simply acknowledge that these individuals were the subject of considerable news coverage and commentary. Based on the theory of topical congruence, it was therefore natural to see them lampooned by cartoonists.

Moreover, it should be noted that in addition to their celebrity politician status, these individuals collectively presented numerous comedic handles. Research on late night television comedy shows that some politicians (notably, presidents) are simply easier to lampoon, based on their backgrounds, previous experience, public statements, looks, and more. Others seem to have fewer of these comic handles. Barack Obama was one such example (Lichter et al., 2015). Like Trump and Biden, Walker, Fetterman, Oz, and Lake seemed to present comics, including editorial cartoonists, with an abundance of material with which comics might target them.

Beyond the focus on political actors (parties, party leaders, candidates), editorial cartoonists focused on several substance or process-related issues. The main substantive issues in this regard included abortion and inflation. The focus on abortion was the result of two factors. First, many Democrats attempted to nationalize the elections with a focus on the *Dobbs* decision overturning *Roe.* v. *Wade*. The other factor was the scandal surrounding Herschel Walker's stated opposition to abortion and allegations made by past girlfriends that he at least implicitly approved of them. There were slightly more cartoons focused on this issue than on inflation. However, by no means did cartoonists ignore that issue, nor did they attempt to paint it in a positive light. This said, references to inflation were made as part of a game schema approach, or how the issue affected Democratic chances for victory.

It is not clear how many Republican candidates could fairly be described as election deniers, or whether election deniers and election security did (or does) pose an existential threat to democracy. This said, there were any number of news stories focused on this issue, and this attention was reflected in editorial cartoons. Given that there were relatively few instances during the post-election period of challenges to official election results, it could be that the degree of focus in editorial cartoons was disproportionate to reality.

The most common process-oriented theme present in the sample was the perceived lack of candidate quality. There were a total of 99 cartoons that made some reference to this. Most overlapped with other subjects or topics, but the idea that there was a dearth of qualified individuals running for office was common. Similar to the idea that election deniers were both common and a threat to U.S. democratic governance, it could be that this perception did not match reality. However, together with the election deniers theme and the overall negative tone of the overwhelming majority of other cartoons, one could be excused for coming away with a pessimistic view of American democracy as the result of viewing these cartoons.

The one clearly positive note that was struck overall was the process-related idea present in many cartoons that voting is important. This is an ever-present theme in commentary, and at least implicitly in much news coverage itself, in any election. But it is particularly important in midterm elections. It is well understood that midterm elections attract less news coverage, attention, and in the end, less participation than do presidential elections. This is in part due to the fact that they lack the central focus of the selection of a president. In addition, midterm elections are in large part local affairs, which tends to make midterm election coverage more diffuse than news during a presidential election. But the idea that editorial cartoonists found a focus in the advocacy and promotion of voter turnout is, from a normative perspective, important.

Most research on editorial cartoons share a common focus. While specific methodological approaches may differ, the objective of such analyses is an approach that attempts to identify and explicate targets, subjects, messages, themes, and so on, of the various cartoons. The research in this chapter shares that focus. The chapter attempted to identify what political cartoonists were focused on throughout the fall midterm election campaign. The various foci included the informal heads of the respective political parties (Biden and Trump), high-profile candidates, as well as several issues and themes.

In this respect this chapter differs somewhat from most research on editorial cartoons. The vast majority of scholarship in this area (and it is relatively sparse) looks at higher-profile and more singularly focused events, such as presidential elections, war, economic crises, and other crises like the Coronavirus pandemic. During a presidential election, for example, the main focus is on two candidates. The fact that midterm elections in the U.S. typically lack this type of focus made this analysis somewhat more challenging. There were, in short, more subjects, targets, and themes to identify and account for.

The subjects, topics and themes found in the sample of editorial cartoons in the sample were also reflective of news and commentary throughout the 2022 midterm campaign. One study, for example, showed that in addition to the expected horse race coverage that dominated much news coverage of the 2022 midterm elections, there were a number of stories that focused on the low approval or both Trump and Biden, rising inflation and gas prices and high crime rates (Trzcińska, 2024).

Of course this analysis was not without its limitations. For example, the sample size was somewhat small, but this was at least in part a function of the relative lack of cartoons produced. More, unlike a good deal of other research on editorial cartoons, it was often to pinpoint the main target or subject of the cartoons in question. This difficulty was a product of the fact that midterm elections are, as noted, more diffuse in their foci. This lack of focus also affected news coverage tracking data. Both of these limitations point to the idea that the formal test of topical convergence, statistically correlating cartoon and news coverage data, was not terribly strict. This said, previous research (e.g., Lichter et al., 2015) suggests that the jokes told by late night talk show hosts follow news coverage, and there is good reason to expect that editorial cartoons follow a similar trajectory, inasmuch as they are a form of satire.

What determines what cartoonists draw? This review, guided by the theory of topical congruence, as well as a broad overview of research on editorial cartoons, suggest that cartoonists follow developments in the news in their selection of topics, subjects, themes, and so on. While this may seem almost self-evident, this analysis offers some confirmation of the theory, inasmuch as midterm elections do not typically offer easy and obvious subjects and themes for cartoonists to pick up on, at least compared with presidential elections. It is also consistent with research that shows that the jokes told on late night talk shows follow the news (Baumgartner, Lichter & Morris, 2019). In fact the theory of topical congruence can be thought of as a humor-specific variant of intermedia agenda setting.

One implication of this analysis, as well as some previous research (e.g., Baumgartner & Kassab, 2022) is that the work of editorial cartoonists may not necessarily be the cutting edge of social or political commentary or satire. The perception among many satire and editorial cartoon aficionados is that these individuals offer insights that few others could. However it might be the case that their voices are just like the many others in the cacophony of ordinary political commentary. This suggestion is not intended to devalue their work, but perhaps to add perspective with regard to what they do and how they do it.

## References

Atwater, T., Fico, F., & Pizante, G. (1987). Reporting on the state legislature: A case study of inter-media agenda-setting. *Newspaper Research Journal, 8*(2), 53–61. https://doi.org/10.1177/073953298700800206

Baumgartner, J. C., & Kassab, H. (2022). Critic or cheerleader? Editorial cartoons during the 2020 Coronavirus pandemic. *Newspaper Research Journal, 43*(4), 448–466. https://doi.org/10.1177/07395329221112389

Baumgartner, J. C., Lichter, S. R., & Morris, J. S. (2019). Research note: Negative news and late-night comedy about presidential candidates. *Humor, 32*, 605–617. https://doi.org/10.1515/humor-2018-0067

Bounegru, L., & Forceville, C. (2011). Metaphors in editorial cartoons representing the global financial crisis. *Visual Communication, 10*(2), 209–229. https://doi.org/10.1177/1470357211398446

Buell, E. H., & Maus, M. (1988). Is the pen mightier than the word? Editorial cartoons and 1988 presidential nominating politics. *PS: Political Science & Politics, 21*(4), 847–858. https://doi.org/10.2307/420024

Conners, J. L. (2005). Visual representations of the 2004 presidential campaign: Political cartoons and popular culture references. *American Behavioral Scientist, 49*(3), 479–487. https://doi.org/10.1177/0002764205280920

Conners, J. L. (2009). She's not laughing: Political humor and Hillary Clinton's campaign for president. In T. F. Sheckles (Ed.), *Cracked but not shattered* (pp. 189–202). Lexington Books.

Conners, J. L. (2010). Barack versus Hillary: Race, gender, and political cartoon imagery of the 2008 presidential primaries. *American Behavioral Scientist, 54*(3), 298–312. https://doi.org/10.1177/0002764210381703

Conners, J. L. (2014). Binders of bayonets for Big Bird: Analysis of political cartoon images of the 2012 presidential debates. *American Behavioral Scientist, 58*(9), 1144–1156. https://doi.org/10.1177/0002764213506203

DeSousa, M. A., & Medhurst, M. J. (1982). Political cartoons and American culture: Significant symbols of campaign 1980. *Studies in Visual Communication, 8*(1), 84–98. https://doi.org/10.1111/j.2326-8492.1982.tb00061.x

Diamond, M. (2002). No laughing matter: Post-September 11 political cartoons in Arab/Muslim newspapers. *Political Communication, 19*(2), 251–272. https://doi.org/10.1080/10584600252907470

Edwards, J. L. (1997). *Political cartoons in the 1988 presidential campaign: Image, metaphor, and narrative*. Garland Publishing.

Edwards, J. L. (2001). Running in the shadows in campaign 2000: Candidate metaphors in editorial cartoons. *American Behavioral Scientist, 44*(12), 2140–2151. https://doi.org/10.1177/00027640121958249

Edwards, J. L. (2007). Drawing politics in pink and blue. *PS: Political Science & Politics, 40(2)*, 249249–253. https://doi.org/10.1017/S1049096507070382

Edwards, J. L. (2009). Presidential campaign cartoons and political authenticity. In R. E. Denton (Ed.), *The 2008 presidential campaign: The communication perspective* (pp. 191–208). Rowman & Littlefield.

GDELT project. (2017, October 9). GDELT 2.0 television API debuts! https://blog.gdeltproject.org/gdelt-2-0-television-api-debuts/

Harder, R. A, Sevenans, J., & Van Aelst, P. (2017). Intermedia agenda setting in the social media age: How traditional players dominate the news agenda in election times. *The International Journal of Press/Politics, 22*(3), 275–293. http://doi.org/10.1177/1940161217704969.

Hess., S., & Northrop, S. (2011). *American political cartoons: From 1754–2010*. Routledge.

Hill, A. (1984). The Carter campaign in retrospect: Decoding the cartoons. In J. M. Medhurst &T. W. Benson (Eds.), *Rhetorical dimensions in media: A critical casebook* (pp. 182–203). Kendall/Hunt.

Hoffman, D. R., & Howard, A. D. (2007). Representations of 9-11 in editorial cartoons. *PS: Political Science and Politics, 40*(2), 271–274. https://doi.org/10.1017/S1049096507070424

Koetzle, W., & Brunell, T. L. (1996). Lip-reading, draft-dodging, and Perotnoia: Presidential campaigns in editorial cartoons. *Harvard International Journal of Press/politics, 1*(4), 94–115. https://doi.org/10.1177/1081180X96001004008

Lichter, R. S., Baumgartner, J. C, & Morris, J. S. (2015). *Politics is a joke!: How TV comedians are remaking political life*. Westview Press.

Lordon, E. J. (2006). *Politics, ink: How America's cartoonists skewer politicians, from King George III to George Dubya*. Roman and Littlefield.

Nilsen, A. P., & Nilsen, D. L. F. (2008). Political cartoons: Zeitgeists and the creation and recycling of satirical symbols. In J. C Baumgartner & J. S. Morris (Eds.), *Laughing matters: Humor and American politics in the media age* (pp. 67–80). Routledge.

Sewell, E. H., Jr. (1998). Torture-by-tedium, or editorial cartoons during the 1996 presidential campaign. In R. E. Denton (Ed.), *The 2008 presidential campaign: The communication perspective* (pp. 191–208). Rowman & Littlefield.

Solomon, E. (1984). Eustace Tilley sees the thirties through a glass monocle, lightly: "New Yorker" cartoonists and the Depression years. *Studies in American Humor, 3*(2/3), 201–219. www.jstor.org/stable/42573187

Somers, P. P., Jr. (1996). Right in the Führer's face. *American Journalism, 13*(3), 333–353. https://doi.org/10.1080/08821127.1996.10731837

Trzcińska, J. (2024). Media coverage of the 2022 campaign. In R. Duda & M. Turek (Eds.), *The crossroads elections: European perspectives on the 2022 U.S. midterm elections* (pp. 192–203). Routledge.

Zurbriggen, E. L., & Sherman, A. M. (2010). Race and gender in the 2008 U.S. presidential election: A content analysis of editorial cartoons. *Analyses of Social Issues and Public Policy, 10*(1), 223–247. https://doi.org/10.1111/j.1530-2415.2010.01211.x

**SECTION IV**

# Midterm Communication in the States

## Case Studies from Arizona, Nevada, Florida, Texas, and Kansas

# 10

# THE LIMITS OF BEING "100% PRO-LIFE"

## Rhetorical Trajectory and Abortion in the American Southwest

*Calvin R. Coker and Desmond J. McCarthy*

The 6–3 decision by the United States Supreme Court to overturn *Roe v. Wade* and *Planned Parenthood v. Casey* in *Dobbs v. Jackson Women's Health Organization* was and continues to be profoundly unpopular among a plurality of the American public. In July of 2022, 57% of Americans expressed disapproval of the majority's ruling—including 82% of Democrats—alongside a deluge of think pieces and condemnations from legal, media, and political elites prepared due to a leak of the majority draft two months prior (*Pew Research Center*, 2022; Winderman & Hallsby, 2022). That public opinion deficit extended well beyond the Court to the detriment of the Republican Party, in part due to the controversial three appointments made during the Trump administration. The centrality of abortion, and antagonism toward the Court, even mitigated the expected ascension of the Republican Party to national majorities in the House and Senate in the 2022 midterms, with the existence of a "Roe Wave" facilitating the retention of a Democratic majority in the Senate (Ball, 2022).

This chapter argues the aftermath of *Dobbs* constituted a moment where the rhetorical trajectory of the abortion debate was altered through political discourse, and that alteration breaks from the broader rhetorical stalemate endemic to national discussions of abortion in the United States. Though some pundits situated reproductive rights as simply one more intensely polarized issue for the U.S./American public, this chapter submits the strategies employed by Senator Mark Kelly (D-AZ) and Senator Catherine Cortez Masto (D-NV) against relatively standard Republican opponents suggest changes to the broader landscape of abortion rhetoric. Those changes respond to the material conditions engendered by *Dobbs*, wherein at least 13 states significantly contracted access to abortion following the ruling (Chu et al., 2023), but also an altered public

DOI: 10.4324/9781003440833-14

understanding of the political arm of the anti-abortion movement. Kelly and Cortez Masto's respective strategies—accusations of paternalism and treating democratic frameworks as safeguards of rights—had demonstrably limited rhetorical purchase pre-*Dobbs*. Following the overturn of *Roe* and *Casey,* however, these strategies fit within and alter the broader rhetorical trajectory of abortion discourses in the United States such that advocates for reproductive choice can, through campaign discourses, access new forms of rhetorical invention.

Though there are varied implications for this rhetorical invention in the 2022 midterms, we would isolate two. First, this analysis confirms that scholars should not treat inventional strategies in down ballot races as less important because of their reduced reach or geographically tailored messaging. Rather, both campaigns suggest that local races, with all their idiosyncrasies, can be crucibles for the innovation of rhetorical strategies based on national contexts which invite shifting understanding of seemingly calcified political issues. As abortion access in the United States was dramatically imperiled because of *Dobbs*, the 2022 midterms were one of the first widely visible political opportunities for pushback against anti-abortion legislation and jurisprudence. Though the rhetorical landscape pre-*Dobbs* was calcified around <choice> and <life>, the strategies employed in these Senate campaigns offer rhetorical resources which forcefully respond to the material gains of the anti-abortion movement to break that calcification. Second, the comparative success of these strategies demonstrates the possibility of a shifting interpretation of the modern Republican and Democratic parties in the United States. Where previously accusations of paternalism or appeals to majoritarian frameworks regarding safeguarding abortion access could have been comparatively easily dismissed as hyperbole (Coker, 2020), the altered contours engendered by *Dobbs* and the campaign strategies suggest the Republican Party may face increased skepticism among a plurality of citizens and unaligned media and political elites.

The chapter proceeds as follows. First, a section outlines the theoretical underpinnings of the project, with focus on how *Dobbs* offered a moment wherein rhetors could successfully alter the rhetorical trajectory of the U.S. abortion debate. The chapter then details the context of the Arizona and Nevada Senate races before situating the respective strategies alongside and against the broader rhetorical landscape of abortion access. The chapter concludes by expanding on the above implications.

## Abortion, Rhetorical Trajectories, and Politics in the American Southwest

This analysis is informed by the litany of scholars who have studied the U.S. abortion debate to great effect (e.g., Coker, 2017a, 2020; Condit, 1990;

Dubriwny & Siegfried, 2021; Rowland, 2017) and theorizing on how the contours of a given debate can calcify or shift over time. This section, first, details the theoretical underpinnings of rhetorical trajectories to demonstrate how the aftermath of *Dobbs* constituted a moment of possible alteration. It then summarizes the existing landscape of abortion rhetoric in the United States to substantiate the notion that, prior to *Dobbs,* rhetorical invention was limited due to a stale discursive landscape characterized by "overweighing" terms not conducive to effective policy or argumentative clash (Condit, 1990). It concludes by discussing how the two Senate races in American Southwest are appropriate vehicles to locate the seeds of change to the rhetorical trajectory of the abortion debate.

Griffin's (1984) foundational work on how some discourse can demonstrate a definable "dialectical progression" developed a theoretical vocabulary of "rhetorical trajectories" (p. 111). That vocabulary has been fruitfully employed in the study of political speeches and campaigns to clarify the interrelationship of past and present discourses alongside understanding of how rhetors are constrained or empowered in context. Griffin suggests that critics can develop an understanding of how "particular state[s] of readiness [are] achieved" (p. 127) in looking to (un)changing bodies of discourse over time while being attuned to exigencies that can alter trajectories or set them on "collision courses" between rhetors, movements, or institutions (Dionisopoulos et al., 1992, p. 93). Building from Griffin's scholarship, Dionisopoulos and colleagues (1992) note that fruitful analysis identifies how a body of discourse features a "progression or curve of development that a speaker establishes as he or she attempts to turn a vision into a reality" (p. 94). To that end, Rowland and Jones (2001) suggest that two key markers of a defined rhetorical trajectory concern how a system of symbols acquires a "long term influence" while becoming "part of the dominant political vocabulary" (p. 57). As such, the paragraphs below substantiate the extant rhetorical trajectories of the abortion debate in the United States and isolate how *Dobbs* and the subsequent midterm campaign facilitate altered trajectories.

Prior to the overturn of *Roe* and *Casey,* the abortion debate in the United States was characterized by longstanding rhetorical gridlock (e.g., Coker, 2017a, 2020, 2023a; Condit, 1990; Lake, 1984; Ziegler, 2020). This intransigence was overdetermined, as there were rhetorical, political, and cultural barriers to significant policy gains for either anti-abortion forces or those committed to reproductive access. Rhetorically, the dominance of two organizing terms—<choice> and <life>—presented multifold problems to the enactment of liberalized abortion access (Coker, 2017a; Lake, 1984). Dubriwny and Siegfried (2021) crystalize the problem with <choice> as an inability to capture the multiplicity of experiences for pregnant people to the detriment of broader organizing or policy intelligibility. Similarly, anti-abortion activists have

**216** Media Messages in the 2022 Midterm Election

gradually expanded <life> to an extension of humanity toward children in utero, even if the most extreme policy examples of fetal personhood were ultimately rejected (Coker, 2017a; Rowland, 2017).

That rhetorical gridlock did not necessarily translate, however, into *policy* gridlock. Many locales in the United States experienced an almost uninterrupted implementation of restrictions on abortion clinics from the mid-2000s until the 2016 Supreme Court decision in *Whole Women's Health v. Hellerstedt,* which foreclosed on Texas's brazen moves to regulate providers out of existence. Despite that policy trajectory, *Dobbs* constituted a shock to the political system even though the overturn of *Roe* and *Casey,* to the six conservative justices in the Majority's opinion's point, did not on explicitly alter access to abortion in the United States. *Dobbs* solidified the existence of a patchwork of abortion access wherein the ability to get safe, affordable, expedient reproductive care was heavily dependent on the partisan valence of the state where one lived. As such, *Dobbs* was a kairotic moment in the broader trajectory of abortion rhetoric because the persistence of *Roe*, with all its corresponding flaws and weaknesses (Gibson, 2008), had shaped the propensity of activists to move beyond <choice> as an organizing term. The overturn, and midterm election a scant five months later, constitute an opportunity for altering the broader rhetorical trajectory of abortion rhetoric in the United States.

One mechanism of understanding alterations to political trajectories and rhetorical landscapes is to is look to high level discourses that are attached to material changes in the world, a description which fits campaign rhetoric neatly. As a massive body of prior scholarship has detailed, interactions between political candidates both respond to, and reshape, the contours of how the public conceives of policy issues (Asen, 2002), perceptions of both candidates and their parties (Coker, 2017b), and the relationship of the government to the polity (Coker & Reed, 2021). Relevant to the present study, then, is how local debates can (re)shape the contours of a broader rhetorical landscape and alter extant rhetorical trajectories. As Coker (2017a, 2020) has argued in the study of state level abortion debates, states provide novel opportunities for the employment of strategies that, though situationally appropriate, may not translate clearly or cleanly onto the national stage. Given the difficulty in locating topoi capable of encompassing the multiplicity of perspectives and needs incumbent in abortion access and broader medical autonomy (Dubriwny & Siegfried, 2021), the 2022 midterms were one of the first opportunities for politicians to consider the (re)negotiation of abortion access as a political, cultural, and economic issue.

The relevance and timeliness of abortion rhetoric to the midterm was further magnified, by the surprisingly clear defeat of an anti-abortion ballot measure in Kansas in July prior to the November midterm. Kansans rejected an attempt to ban abortion in the state 59% to 41% in a special election featuring nearly

The Limits of Being "100% Pro-life"   **217**

triple the turnout of 2014 with no meaningful contested races to assist turnout (Jansing, 2022). As such, it is helpful to conceive of the Kansas ballot results as proof of concept for voters' interest in abortion access as a political appeal; that interest, previously unique to "single issue" voters who almost exclusively broke toward the Republican Party, facilitates the use of novel strategies capable of transcending extant gridlock and altering rhetorical trajectory.

Given this capacity for local debates to translate into rhetorical resources on the national stage, the study of abortion rhetoric in the American Southwest in the context of the 2022 midterms is desirable for at least three reasons. First, as CNN political analyst David Axelrod noted, "control of the Senate is going to be determined by Nevada and Arizona," a conclusion confirmed by the end of the midterm cycle (CNN, 2022, para. 25). Second, Arizona and Nevada feature increased numbers of Latinx individuals relative to the rest of the nation, a demographic difference that is relevant given projections of population change in the coming thirty years. Furthermore, even though abortion is often understood through the lens of both personal and political identity, *USA Today* reported the results of a poll from UnidosUS which found "76% of Latino voters agreed, including 59% who strongly agreed, that no matter their personal beliefs on abortion, it's wrong to outlaw abortion and take that choice away from others," thus making the states novel proving grounds for rhetorical invention regarding *Dobbs* (Gonzalez, 2022, para. 4). Finally, Arizona and Nevada had unique contexts for abortion access. At a minimum, both states were experiencing increased traffic of individuals moving to (Nevada) and from (Arizona) in pursuit of abortion access. Christine Vestal (2022) with *Stateline* noted that abortion access in Arizona hinged on the gubernatorial race, with Republican Kari Lake promising to enforce a 15-week ban from her predecessor, while in Nevada "Democratic losses in gubernatorial and legislative races could lay the groundwork for future restrictions" (para. 14). In both instances, the status of abortion rights post-*Dobbs* was precarious; as such, the potential for altering the rhetorical trajectory of abortion discourse in the U.S. was comparatively high.

The preceding section has detailed the contours of the rhetorical landscape of the abortion debate in the United States pre-*Dobbs* while isolating our animating theoretical perspective- rhetorical trajectory- to contextualize how comparatively unique local races can alter national rhetorical landscapes The subsequent analysis substantiates the novel use of two pre-existing tropes- treating anti-abortion politicians as condescending paternalists and conceiving of democratic forums like majority control as a bulwark against anti-abortion legislation and jurisprudence- against comparatively standard GOP candidates. The urgency afforded to these strategies by the overturn of *Dobbs* constitutes the conditions for altering the rhetorical trajectory of the broader U.S. abortion debate.

## Campaign Context

Beyond the above context of abortion access, the candidates' themselves informed the capacity for rhetorical invention. Compared to other contested Senate races (such as Pennsylvania's between a TV personality and a popular politician who suffered a stroke on the campaign trail), both Arizona and Nevada offered banal candidates. Consider, first, the Arizona race between incumbent Mark Kelly (D-AZ) and challenger Blake Masters. Like many politicians, Kelly's professional life was spent in the military; Kelly graduated from the United States Merchant Marine Academy before pursuing a M.S. in Aeronautical Engineering from the U.S. Naval School. Prior to the 2022 campaign, in both his 2020 race against former Senator Martha McSally (R-AZ) and as an elected official, Kelly presented himself as a Democratic version of John McCain emphasizing his strong record of public service, his ability to compromise, and his willingness to call out nonsense. Kelly hewed close to the perceived center of American politics by pushing back on the Biden administration's border policies while rejecting many of the most extreme rhetorical elements of both the Trump administration and the progressive left.

Blake Masters, comparatively, followed a relatively traditional path to politics. Following a 2008 bachelor's in political science from Stanford University, Masters became active in conservative politics through measured yet outspoken stances consonant with, though significantly more polished than, the firebrand rhetoric of the Trump administration. 2022 was Masters' first run for office, with a primary victory characterized by high campaign spending from, among others, billionaire Peter Theil (Swan & Kraushaar, 2022).

The Nevada Senate race between incumbent Catherine Cortez Masto (D-NV) and former Nevada Attorney General Adam Laxalt featured similarly standard political biographies. Cortez Masto was admitted to the State Bar of Nevada in 1991 and, after four years as a civil attorney and two as a criminal prosecutor, successfully ran for state Attorney General in 2006. Following former Senator Harry Reid's endorsement as his successor, Cortez Masto became the first Latina in the U.S. Senate in 2016. Her tenure has largely been free of significant controversy, except for the notion that her seat in 2022 was considered one of the most "at risk" for Democrats (Ball, 2022).

Like Masters, Adam Laxalt matriculated through comparatively standard educational venues: a Georgetown B.A. in 2002, followed by a J.D. in 2005. Laxalt then followed a traditional political path; in 2014, Laxalt won the election for Nevada Attorney General following Cortez Masto's move to the Senate, only to lose the Nevada gubernatorial election in 2016. His Senate race with Cortez Masto was identified as one of the most competitive in the country.

As these candidate biographies demonstrate, and the analysis will confirm, all four candidates followed relatively standard political scripts derived from national party platforms. On balance each ran a comparatively disciplined and standard campaign though there were idiosyncrasies, to be sure, such as billionaire Peter Thiel's personal interest in Masters (Swan & Kraushaar, 2022), Laxalt's flirtation with election denial (Girnus, 2022), and Kelly's comparative short stint as an incumbent. Considering these characteristics, the analysis suggest that Arizona and Nevada are of interest *because* the comparative normalcy of their races confirms that the localization of abortion politics in tandem with national context is not an oddity, but rather a portent of things to come.

Two elements of the landscape and trajectory of abortion rhetoric in the United States are relevant to the present project, and below demonstrate how these strategies were used to great effect, despite their relative ineffectiveness pre-*Dobbs*. The first is (rejecting) paternalistic rhetoric, as clarified in Women Protective Anti-Abortion Arguments (WPAA). WPAAs presume that individuals who seek abortions are victims of coercion or deception, and as such access to abortion should be heavily regulated (see Coker, 2020). The prevalence of WPAAs in the late 2000s constituted a moment of symbol stealing wherein women's well-being became an overriding frame in the justifications for new restrictions on abortion. Though these arguments demote women's status as political subjects and envisions them as incompetent and in need of protection, meaningful pushback occurred primarily on the local level with limited success (Coker, 2020; Coker & Coker, 2022). Gibson (2019) suggested that the skepticism displayed by the female justices in the oral arguments and eventual majority opinion of *Hellerstedt* was the beginning of rejecting paternalism inherent in both WPAAs and Targeted Regulation of Abortion Providers (TRAP) laws, but ultimately paternalism stems from the broader imperatives and lack of compromise inherent in the dominance of <life> as an organizing term for the anti-abortion movement.

The second element is imagining political actors and institutions as defenders of choice and women's political agency. Understandably, the overweighed nature of the abortion debate and dominance of neoliberal ideology in the United States has primarily located <choice> as stemming from the individual, a profoundly personal and complicated choice not warranting government intervention (Coker, 2023b; Dubriwny & Siegfried, 2021). At times, however, politicians supporting stable abortion access have mobilized a trope of a political "war on women" to suggest that the constellation of interests represented by the GOP are demonstrable of antagonistic and retrograde patriarchy (Lake & Pickering, 2015). That mobilization has had limited success on the national stage, with gender being an ancillary issue in 2012 (Coker, 2017b) and 2020 (Winfrey & Carlin, 2023) alongside overt sexism failing to meaningfully tip the electoral scale in the 2016 election (Cassese & Holman, 2019).

## Analysis

The analysis draws from existing literature detailing the analysis of political campaigns through the assemblage of textual fragments (Asen, 2002; Coker, 2017a, 2017b, 2020, McGee, 1990). Using news data bases, all relevant news articles from national and local outlets concerning either Senate race were downloaded. Additionally, political advertising for each race was compiled from publicly available sources. Finally, idiosyncratic elements of each race— for example, the Arizona Senatorial Debate—were assembled. In close reading, authors consume the corpus to texts multiple times to note the salience of particular themes, the (re)occurrence of particular rhetorical or argumentative lines or interactions, and the presence/absence of common discourses endemic to the sociopolitical sphere in which the texts are uttered. Following a method of close reading (Brummett, 2018), the authors engaged in an iterative and theory driven engagement combined with collaborative identification of core themes and argument interactions to substantiate the following argument. The analysis is divided into two parts, dealing with both campaigns in kind. First in Arizona, Kelly successfully portrayed Masters as paternalistic for his stance on abortion. Turning to Nevada, where despite existing state level protections of abortion rights, Cortez Masto suggested she was the solitary firewall against additional fallout post-*Dobbs.*

### *"We All Know Guys Like This"*

State level races feature idiosyncrasies because Senators are expected to speak to both national political priorities and issues intrinsic to their state. In Arizona, both Kelly and Masters emphasized a combination of national and local policy issues. Consistent with the broader strategy of the Republican Party in the 2022 midterm elections, Masters tied Kelly to President Biden by criticizing the current economic climate and emphasized the (in)stability of Arizona's southern border with Mexico. Kelly responded through political ads which emphasized helping working class families (Captain Mark Kelly, 2022b) and how his bipartisanship had achieved results (Mark Kelly, 2022a). Additionally, as Hilary Rosen noted for CNN, "Mark Kelly talked about the border a lot. People in Arizona were concerned about the border. And Mark Kelly called for more enforcement and was very aggressive there" (CNN, 2022, para. 54). This is to say that abortion was not immediately apparent as the defining issue of the election; instead, pundits and many political elites focused on the economy and rising inflation as the central concerns (Edwards-Levi, 2022).

Beyond the overturn of *Roe* and *Casey* which, themselves, altered the contours and rhetorical possibilities within the campaigns, abortion became an issue in Arizona for at least two reasons. First, access to abortion in

The Limits of Being "100% Pro-life"  **221**

Arizona was ambiguous following *Dobbs* as then-Governor Doug Ducey implemented a fifteen-week gestational ban on abortion following *Dobbs* and a subsequent Arizona Supreme Court ruling on abortion, and the persistence and enforcement of that ban hinged on both the gubernatorial and Secretary of State races in the state (Vestal, 2022). Second, after the leak of a draft opinion from the U.S. Supreme Court overturning *Roe* and *Casey,* Masters received widespread criticism for calling for those same overturns alongside *Griswold v. Connecticut,* the 1965 case protecting contraceptive access. In response, Masters' campaign claimed: "In Griswold, the justices wholesale—made up a constitutional right—to achieve a political outcome. I am opposed to judges making law. It's the job of the legislative branch to create laws, not the courts" (Steller, 2022, para. 9). Masters adopted a common talking point of anti-abortion activists: a wish to return decision making to the states while protecting the enumerated rights of the Constitution, rarely stating explicitly for states to outright ban abortion (Duffy, 2015). This strategy was even relevant in *Dobbs,* as Kavanaugh's concurrent opinion emphasized that the overturn of *Roe* and *Casey* was not a ban on abortion per se, but a return of the power to decide to the states.

This seemingly technical criticism of Masters' policy positions wasn't guaranteed to become a sticking point in the campaign; not every gaffe, inconsistency, or lie will manifest as a fully realized indictment of a politician or party. Coker (2017b) noted that one of ways campaign elements become persistent is in the integration of those fragments into broader campaign narratives. In Arizona, the Kelly campaign seized upon this inconsistency—a contorted defense of a publicly unpopular position—alongside the newfound rhetorical context of *Dobbs* to suggest that Masters was arrogant and paternalistic in his attempts to wrest healthcare decisions away from citizens. That articulation of paternalism breaks meaningfully from the broader rhetorical trajectory of the abortion debate in the United States in at least two ways. First, framing encroachment on women's rights as a "war on women" or other various discussions of paternalism is comparatively limited in its rhetorical purchase because it flattens the contours of Republican advocacies which, though retrograde, hold purchase under postfeminist frameworks (Coker, 2023b; Lake & Pickering, 2015). Second, Coker (2020) noted that advocates for even the most draconian restrictions on abortion access often present proposals as neutral, even beneficial for women, while rejecting accusations of paternalism and mockery. As such, Kelly's successful portrayal of Masters as a misleading paternalist constituted an alteration of rhetorical trajectory that could result in new forms of invention.

The clearest articulation of this vision of Masters occurred in the October debate between Kelly, Masters, and Marc Victor, an also ran libertarian

**222** Media Messages in the 2022 Midterm Election

candidate. Early in the debate, Kelly went on the offensive, coupling *Dobbs* to Masters' espoused preferences:

> Women have totally lost their right to make a decision about abortion. It is devastating. It is wrong. It is exactly what Blake Masters wants. Blake Masters has called abortion demonic. Religious sacrifice. He has even said that he wants to punish the doctors. He wants a national abortion ban that is so strict that even in the case when a woman is raped, she will not have the option to make this decision. ... He thinks that he should make these decisions for you. He thinks he gets to make these choices instead of you.
>
> *(Arizona U.S. Senate Debate, 2022)*

In a single statement, Kelly proposed a coherent rejection of Masters' ideology; he casted his opponent as both dangerously extreme and committed to taking decisions away from women. At first, Kelly's language appears hyperbolic; it is uncommon for abortion supporters to use the language of heresy to criticize their opponents, and contentions regarding "choice" are easily subsumed within neoliberal and conservative political frameworks (Coker, 2023b). However, the extremity of Masters language, and Kelly's propensity to call it out, fits within a burgeoning change in anti-abortion discourse. A subset of the anti-abortion movement had always featured retributive and extreme moral language concerning individuals who procure and have abortions, and that subset was offered high profile rhetorical resources and a champion in President Trump (Coker, 2023a). As such, Kelly's decision to highlight and criticize Masters' extreme language combined with the impacts of *Dobbs* removing healthcare decisions from women constituted a break from the longstanding rhetorical trajectory of abortion discourse in the United States.

In response, Masters repeated widespread anti-abortion talking points concerning gestational limits and curtailing abortion access. For example, he claimed: "I am pro-life, I believe in limits... I prefer limits at the federal level. Senator Graham has proposed a 15-week bill with common exceptions. And I support that" (Arizona U.S. Senate Debate, 2022). Coker (2023a) suggested that rhetorical focus on the technical elements of the abortion debate is a logical response to the uptake and purchase of arguments circulated in the mid-2000. Politicians and experts began to defend and regulate abortion on medical, rather than moral, grounds. However, Coker (2023a) noted that a creeping impatience of anti-abortion activists, combined with a small but vocal minority insistent on (re)casting abortion in moral terms animated by disgust and retribution, has reduced the general purchase and visibility of technocratic arguments. Indeed, Gibson (2019) argued that those technical arguments were increasingly met with skepticism from the Supreme Court, and as such the purchase of those arguments had begun to wane well before

*Dobbs* radically eschewed gradual or incremental adjustments to abortion rights.

The unpopularity of *Dobbs* allowed for a more robust discussion of public will be relative to past debates which emphasis the legitimacy and intractability of "both" sides of the abortion debate (see Lake, 1984). When Kelly claimed that Masters' positions were out of line with public opinion, Masters responded:

> Kelly believes in no limits at all. I understand why he wants to lie about my position because of his own. The record he sponsored that legislation up until birth. That is so truly radical 80% of Arizonans are disgusted by that. I'm going to represent the vast majority of Arizonans on this issue. He has proven that he can't.
>
> *(Arizona U. S. Senate Debate, 2022)*

It is not uncommon for politicians of both parties to appeal to a populist center; they articulate the will of the people, variously construed, as a legitimate basis for their actions, and in prior rhetorical contexts Masters' response may have been satisfactory. Public opinion data on the acceptability of abortion in the United States supports, partially, Masters' contention; only 1 in 5 citizens believe that unconditional, unrestricted abortion access is acceptable (*Pew Research Center*, 2022). Technocratic language regarding gestational limits allows Masters to imply his position is a reasonable compromise, even if his policies are not truly consonant with the plurality of U.S.-Americans who believe abortion is acceptable in some instances (*Pew Research Center*, 2022). His emphasis on populism and technical limits could, conceivably, diffuse Kelly's criticism.

However, Masters quickly gave up the game regarding technocratic language and confirmed Kelly's contentions. He continued:

> I think states should decide. Let the state legislature grapple with the tough question. Let planned parenthood go in and sever spinal cords and dismember babies. That what this policy would allow, unlimited abortion up until the moment of birth.
>
> *(Arizona U.S. Senate Debate, 2022)*

Where TRAP laws may practically result in the closure of clinics, defenders of those laws routinely steal the symbol of "women's health" as a justification for onerous and unnecessary restrictions. The language of disgust—specifically the emphasis on viscera and babies—betrays an extreme anti-abortion sentiment out of step with a plurality of the U.S.-American public (Coker, 2023a). Kelly capitalized on that sentiment to cast Masters as incapable of making a reasonable decision because of his retrograde ideology and desire to wrest the decision from women.

## 224 Media Messages in the 2022 Midterm Election

Kelly's strategy manifested in rejecting the ambiguous political language of his opponent and speaking to a visceral, intuitive truth regarding paternalistic politicians. When asked if he supported a federal personhood law because his website formerly stated he was "Unqualifiedly pro-life from conception." Masters replied, "I encourage people to read my website now." This non engagement allowed Kelly to respond:

> This is code—code for throwing women into jail. And that is what my opponent supports. Now, I think we all know guys like this. Guys that think they know better than everyone about everything. You know, you think you know better than women and doctors about abortion. ... We all know guys like this. And we cannot be letting them make decisions about us. Because it is just dangerous.
>
> *(Arizona U.S. Senate Debate, 2022)*

This emphasis on the material as evidence of damaging paternalism had been employed in the past to some effect. Coker's (2017a) analysis of the Colorado debate over a personhood amendment to the constitution focused on anticipated practical result. A routine theme of anti-abortion discourse in the 1990s and 2000s is the almost explicit disavowal of considering the logical implications of the implementation of their policy preferences, so much so that many activists who advocated for the illegality of abortion were shocked when posed with the question of how much jail time women or doctors should serve upon conviction (Packer, 2013). As such, Kelly's insistence on unmasking the programmatic implications of Masters' positions constituted a break in the broader rhetorical trajectory of U.S. abortion discourse, and in doing so afforded rhetorical resources to future activists and campaigns. When Kelly insisted, "I am protecting your constitutional rights that you have lost because of rhetoric like this," he effectively neutralized the masking effect of technocratic language by reminding citizens that Masters is not engaged in a philosophical exercise, but rather a promise to govern in a particular way (Arizona U.S. Senate Debate, 2022).

Additionally, the context of *Dobbs* furthered the alteration of abortion's rhetorical trajectory. The political fallout of the Supreme Court decision supported Kelly's contentions because, in effect, decisions concerning abortion *had already* been wrested from a plurality of pregnant people. Kelly suggested:

> I supported *Roe v. Wade*, went into effect in 1973. This is a hard decision for women. This decision should be up to the women with her doctor. Shouldn't be politicians like the guy to my left in Washington D.C. making these decisions for you.
>
> *(Arizona U.S. Senate Debate, 2022)*

The Limits of Being "100% Pro-life"   **225**

Kelly contextualized his support of abortion as "hard decisions" made for health, a frame noted by Dubriwny and Siegfried (2021) as narrow but powerful in defense of mothers and their autonomy. He continued,

> I mean, he thinks he knows better than you. He thinks he knows better than doctors and women about abortion. I mean folks, I think that's that is a really bad place for us to be in when my opponent, Blake Masters, is making these decisions for women.
>
> *(Arizona U.S. Senate Debate, 2022)*

This contention goes beyond the anemic frames of "war on women" to specifically isolate a singular unfit individual who is making claims to decision making prowess. When combined with the public opinion fallout of *Dobbs*, Kelly affords new rhetorical resources to reproductive rights activists by demonstrating the viability of strategies which unmask the technical and paternalistic justifications for rolling back abortion rights. In essence, Kelly is providing a foundation to arguments pertaining to paternalism and the centrality of medical autonomy. Where paternalism may feel as though it is an abstract concept or justification for behavior—"protection" from either presumed incompetence or imagined threats—Kelly's casting of Masters as the distinct human *responsible* for withholding medical autonomy underscores the stakes of this policy debate.

This section has detailed Kelly's contentions that Masters was a misleading paternalist, contentions which capitalized on the shifting rhetorical landscape of the abortion debate in the United States to implement novel and uncompromising rhetorical resources for abortion supporters. In the next section, we substantiate a similar but distinct strategy in the Cortez Masto-Laxalt campaign wherein the incumbent Senator successfully portrayed herself as the bulwark against retrograde policies.

### *"I Will Fight [...] Laxalt Won't"*

Where Arizona featured a volatile context for abortion access, Nevada was comparatively stable—arguably to the detriment of an incumbent trying to make restrictions on abortion access a looming threat. The state encountered an influx of patients seeking abortion services, largely because of Utah's and Arizona's unclear or restrictive policies, but beyond that there didn't appear to be a meaningful change to the outlook for abortion rights in the state (Vestal, 2022). Additionally, as mentioned above, one justification for *Dobbs* was that the overturn of *Roe* and *Casey* left the decision making up to the states; conceivably, Nevada's liberalized access to abortion would be honored under extant frameworks. As such, it may seem odd that Cortez Masto was able to present her position in the democratic process as a bulwark against encroaching

**226** Media Messages in the 2022 Midterm Election

anti-abortion legislation and jurisprudence, given that a.) the Democratic majority in the Senate could not prevent *Dobbs,* and b.) Nevada's abortion access did not seem tenuous circa October 2022. Nevada didn't seem, immediately, to be at risk, and historically political claims to protecting women had limited purchase when few worst-case scenarios materialized (Lake & Pickering, 2015). Given that Adam Laxalt had routinely characterized Nevada's abortion policy as "settled law," many pundits had presumed campaigns would focus primarily, if not exclusively, on the economy (Edwards-Levi, 2022).

At first glance, the Nevada campaign dynamics clearly demonstrate the nature of this problem. For example, Cortez Masto's campaign (2022) deployed an ad in which she said she would "fight for a woman's right to make our own health-care decisions," while Republican opponent "Adam Laxalt won't." In response, the National Republican Senatorial Committee launched an ad accusing Cortez Masto of scaremongering by contending:

> Over the last two years, Democrat politicians have done incredible damage to America. They changed our lives. But one thing hasn't changed: Abortion in Nevada. Why do Democrats like Catherine Cortez Masto only talk about something that hasn't changed? Because they can't defend everything that has.
>
> *(Merica & Wright, 2022)*

The notion that abortion "hasn't changed" relied on a very specific reading of *Dobbs,* one that presumes the proffered justification of the Majority and Concurrent opinions would be honored by a Republican Senate. Prior to *Dobbs, Roe* was understood in most centrist political circles as something of an inevitability; it had survived almost 50 years of borderline constant attacks, and its persistence was a testament to the durability of both American political institutions and the tendency of courts to lean on precedent. However, that persistence demobilized politicians who pushed back on the gradual encroachment against abortion rights on the state level. Even though many states were *essentially* post-*Roe* prior to 2020 because of clinic closures, onerous regulations, and escalating political attacks on providers like Planned Parenthood, framing elections in terms of abortion access was viewed as a niche issue, bordering on hysteria. As such, the changed context of *Dobbs* painted more clearly for citizens the stakes of allowing unalloyed Republican control of legislature and the courts.

It is in this changing context that Cortez Masto's arguments gained additional purchase. Specifically, Cortez Masto was able to parlay her tenuous position in the Senate—her seat was identified as one of the most at risk for conversion—into an explanation of how she was one of the last lines of defense against a Republican takeover and subsequent roll back of abortion rights. At a campaign event reported by *The Washington Post*, Cortez Masto claimed, "There is no

The Limits of Being "100% Pro-life"   **227**

doubt in my mind that the Republicans in the Senate right now—that some of them are writing a draft legislation to further restrict abortion in this country," while warning Laxalt could cast the decisive vote in the Senate. In response, Laxalt posted an online video showed asking "Where was Cortez Masto and her bullhorn when you couldn't find formula for your baby? When gas prices soared past $5/gallon? When Bidenflation hit a 40 year high?" (Scherer, 2022, para. 3). Republican politicians have routinely and deftly defused criticism of misogynistic or paternalistic policies by pointing not only to female Republican politicians and voters, but also in accusing their opponents of uncharitable hyperbole and overreaction. The rhetorical trajectory of the abortion debate has featured similar dynamics; pre-*Dobbs,* anti-abortion politicians who proposed invasive and unnecessary medical regulations were painted as "anti-woman" under narrow and highly partisan circumstances, with most legislation and politicians being given the benefit of the doubt outside of egregious verbal missteps or criminal allegations.

Post-*Dobbs,* however, two elements combined to increase the visibility and importance of abortion in Nevada and alter the rhetorical trajectory. First, despite rhetoric post-*Dobbs* centering state level decision making, Democratic strategists and activists had identified national debates as intensely important because of their cascading material impacts. Nayyera Haq on CNN noted that "Democrats managed to make national issues like inflation and abortion local economic issues and they managed to distance themselves from the politics figures and make it highly localized" (CNN, 2022). Additionally, *The Washington Post* noted that individuals on the ground in Nevada were spurred by political and rhetorical changes in the Trump administration to take nothing for granted, reporting one activist as saying, "'if we don't go Democratic, we are at risk to lose our rights, things we have been fighting for, for a long, long time,' specifically noting abortion rights. 'In the blink of an eye, things can turn different.'" (as cited in Balz, 2022, para. 20). This understanding of the political process goes well beyond the abstract stakes of the economy that Laxalt emphasized. Though, typically, abortion is understood as an abstract moral issue with little standing on the everyday lives of citizens relative to things like food and gas prices, Laxalt's attempts to center the economy ring hollow as Cortez Masto presented her candidacy as a final defense against tangibly encroaching anti-abortion legislation and jurisprudence.

This is the second change that allowed for increased relevance and visibility of abortion. *Dobbs* constituted a genuine threat to abortion access in a plurality of states, even if immediate changes were not triggered. In a May 2022 interview with *The Dallas Morning News*, Mo Elleithee, Executive Director of Georgetown's Institute of Politics and Public Service, stated:

> In areas that are purple, it forces a lot of women to live on a seesaw, where the
> law could change based on the whim of whatever political party is in charge

**228** Media Messages in the 2022 Midterm Election

at any given moment. That just puts women at the mercy of the political volatility of the state legislature.

*(As cited in Gromer, 2022 para. 6)*

Where prior arguments concerning abortion access had presumed the persistence of *Roe* outside the most extreme circumstances, *Dobbs* demonstrated the threat presented by anti-abortion politicians actualizing their goals. Ultimately, this context allowed Cortez Masto to leverage Laxalt's relatively standard policy preferences—such as supporting a 13 week ban on abortion—as genuine political liabilities. For instance, the Democratic Senatorial Campaign Committee ran an ad featured a Nevada woman criticizing Laxalt's position saying: "I take it incredibly personally that Adam Laxalt is working to take away the rights of my daughters." The Democratic-aligned Senate Majority PAC went even further in an ad that included audio of Laxalt saying that *"Roe v. Wade* was always a joke." When combined with on-the-ground anxiety regarding the creep of national politics, Cortez Masto in casting abortion as at-risk constituted a meaningful break from the general rhetorical trajectory of the abortion debate in the United States.

This section has detailed Cortez Masto's contentions that Adam Laxalt constituted a threat to women in Nevada, even as the state maintains its existing abortion regime, because of the genuine threat of federal encroachment. These contentions capitalized on the shifting material and rhetorical landscape of the abortion debate in the United States to increase the purchase for arguments concerning incrementalism and democracy in the face of seemingly abstract or banal rhetoric. The final section outlines the various implications of these two strategies.

## Discussion and Implications

The preceding analysis has substantiated the existence to two rhetorical strategies—accusations of paternalism and treating the political process as the final bulwark against the retrenchment of rights—which are novel in the way they are mobilized against comparatively standard GOP candidates. In closing, two possible implications of this framing are discussed. First, this chapter suggests the strategies invite an expansion of abortion rights in contravention of existing rhetorical trajectories. Second, it clarifies how these strategies' rhetorical purchase suggests that skepticism toward even perceptually centrist candidates may become more common, even expected, given the extremity of overturning *Roe*.

First, our analysis suggests that the overturn of *Roe* and *Casey* encouraged both voters and politicians to consider the significant deficits in the patchwork system of abortion regulation in the United States. Prior to *Dobbs, Roe* had been criticized for its paternalism (Gibson, 2008) and artificial frameworks based not in medical autonomy to citizenship, but instead as a part of a constellation of right(s) to privacy. Subsequent rulings in *Casey* and *Gonzales v. Carhart* affirmed *Roe,* but facilitated state level encroachment that led to, by 2015, many citizens living in states with nominal abortion access, at best (Coker, 2020). The political interactions isolated in the analysis suggest that the overturn of *Roe* and *Casey* may paradoxically lead to *expanded* abortion access in states that codify rights to medical autonomy while also affording individuals greater rhetorical purchase—and urgency—to push back on the near thirty years of unallayed contraction of reproductive rights.

Second, at risk of overgeneralizing from a small rhetorical sample, the realization of the longstanding goal of the anti-abortion movement and the politicians who court them may present opportunities to treat extremist, unpopular positions as such, a noteworthy break from the broader rhetorical gridlock endemic to the U.S. abortion debate. Both Kelly and Cortez Masto successfully portrayed their opponents as extreme idealogues due to their stances on abortion, a portrayal previously most successful when candidates were subject to embarrassing political gaffes (Coker, 2017b). In both races, that portrayal was consonant with both public opinion, and the actual implications of Masters' and Laxalt's policy positions, despite the relatively boilerplate nature of their advocacies. The skepticism toward proposals like fetal personhood or federal backstops is justified given the mendacity displayed by members of the Supreme Court (see Coker, 2023b), but that skepticism has not routinely been mobilized by members of the news media or politicians in their engagement with comparatively standard GOP candidates who maintain good standing regarding civil discourse and (seemingly) consensus conservative policy positions. Only recently has skepticism been featured at the highest level in abortion jurisprudence (see Gibson, 2019), and the rulings in which it is present (*Hellerstedt* and *June v. Russo*) are some of the first national level rejections of "reasonable" restrictions. To see rhetorics of skepticism mobilized against comparatively standard GOP candidates is fascinating, as it suggests that having caught the proverbial car (and causing a catastrophic pile up in the process), the dog is going to learn why people are so angry at it.

Put simply, the fringe of the anti-abortion movement has been informing everyone, in no uncertain terms, of their end goals in terms of banning abortion services at the overt expense of pregnant people's lives. Prior to *Dobbs,* meaningful cover had been afforded to that movement in the form of centrist politicians approaching what appeared to be a middle ground—policies like TRAP laws or creeping gestational limitations. Post-*Dobbs*, however, that cover is tenuous at best. Though it is far too early to say, initial backlash against both the Supreme Court and a Republican Party who gleefully pursued the end of *Roe* may finally convince a plurality of the public that the mask is fully off. The

**230** Media Messages in the 2022 Midterm Election

success of Kelly and Cortez Masto in, respectively, constructing their opponent as a retrograde paternalist or in presenting a defense against a seemingly unlikely further retrenchment of rights suggests that a plurality of voters may begin treating abortion rights not as a political football, but as a debate with serious and significant social ramifications.

## References

Arizona U. S. Senate Debate. (2022). *C-SPAN.* www.c-span.org/video/?522999-1/arizona-us-senate-debate

Asen, R. (2002). *Visions of poverty: Welfare policy and political imagination.* MSU Press.

Ball, M. (2022). How Democrats defied history in the midterms—And what it means for 2024. *Time.* https://time.com/6231733/midterms-2022-analysis/

Balz, D. (2022). The Latino vote shifted towards Republicans in 2020. Will it shift back? *The Washington Post.* www.washingtonpost.com/politics/interactive/2022/election-2022-latino-voters/

Brummett, B. (2018). *Techniques of close reading* (2nd ed.). SAGE Publications.

Captain Mark Kelley. (2022a). *Mark's bill to lower gas prices* [Video]. YouTube. www.youtube.com/watch?v=5AO7yig6Y68

Captain Mark Kelly. (2022b). Team Arizona [Video]. YouTube. www.youtube.com/watch?v=XStHiEVE50k

Cassese, E. C., & Holman, M. R. (2019). Playing the woman card: Ambivalent sexism in the 2016 U.S. presidential race. *Political Psychology, 40*(1), 55–74. https://doi.org/10.1111/pops.12492

Chu, H., Davis, W., Daugert, K., Gourlay, K., Knight, S., & Wroth, C. (2023). Here's where abortions are now banned or severely restricted. *NPR.* www.npr.org/sections/health-shots/2022/06/24/1107126432/abortion-bans-supreme-court-roe-v-wade

CNN. (2022, November 11). America's Choice 2022; Significant amount of votes expected from Arizona; Democrats extend leads in latest release of AZ vote totals. Aired 8-9p ET. CNN Live Event/Special.

Coker, C. R. (2017a). Murder, miscarriage, and women's choice: Prudence in the Colorado personhood debate. *Western Journal of Communication, 81*(3), 300–319. https://doi.org/10.1080/10570314.2016.1245439

Coker, C. R. (2017b). Romney, Obama, and the 47%: gaffes and representative anecdotes in the 2012 presidential campaign. *Argumentation and Advocacy, 53*(4), 327–343. https://doi.org/10.1080/00028533.2017.1375759

Coker, C. R. (2020). Absurdity in the statehouse: Burlesque legislation and the politics of rejection. *Communication Quarterly, 68*(1), 94–113. https://doi.org/10.1080/01463373.2019.1681486

Coker, C. R. (2023a). "Do you think this isn't happening?" Rhetorical laundering and the federal hearings over Planned Parenthood. *Women & Language, 46*(1), 225–254. https://doi.org/10.1080/01463373.2019.1681486

Coker, C. R. (2023b). Replacing Notorious: Barret, Ginsburg, and postfeminist positioning. *Rhetoric and Public Affairs, 26*(1), 101–130.

Coker, C. R., & Coker, R. A. (2022). On (not) seeing the chicken: Perdue, animal welfare, and the failure of transparency. *Communication Quarterly, 70*(2), 161–180. https://doi.org/10.1080/01463373.2022.2026993

Coker, C. R., & Reed, J. L. (2021). "This is a patriotism check": Political economy, corruption, and duty to America in the 2020 primary debates. *Argumentation and Advocacy, 57*(3-4), 200–217. https://doi.org/10.1080/10511431.2021.1949544

Condit, C. M. (1990). *Decoding abortion rhetoric: Communicating social change*. University of Illinois Press.

Cortez Masto, C. [@CortezMasto]. (2022, September 27). *I'm Catherine Cortez Masto and I'll always fight for a woman's right to make our own health care decisions — but @AdamLaxalt won't* [Video attached] [Post]. Twitter. https://twitter.com/CortezMasto/status/1574772096319705088

Dionisopoulos, G. N., Gallagher, V. J., Goldzwig, S. R., & Zarefsky, D. (1992). Martin Luther King, the American dream and Vietnam: A collision of rhetorical trajectories. *Western Journal of Communication, 56*(2), 91–107. https://doi.org/10.1080/105703 19209374405

*Dobbs v. Jackson Women's Health Organization*, 597 U.S. 215 (2022). www.supremecourt.gov/opinions/21pdf/597us1r58_gebh.pdf

Dubriwny, T. N., & Siegfried, K. (2021). Justifying abortion: The limits of maternal idealist rhetoric. *Quarterly Journal of Speech, 107*(2), 185–208. https://doi.org/10.1080/00335630.2021.1903538

Duffy, C. (2015). States' rights vs. women's rights: The populist argumentative frame in anti-abortion rhetoric. *International Journal of Communication, 9*. https://ijoc.org/index.php/ijoc/article/view/3324/1500

Edwards-Levi, A. (2022, November 5). Polling shows that most voters say economic concerns are top of mind. *CNN*. www.cnn.com/2022/11/05/politics/voters-issues-economy-midterms-2022/index.html

Gibson, K. L. (2008). The rhetoric of Roe v. Wade: When the (male) doctor knows best. *Southern Communication Journal, 73*(4), 312–331. https://doi.org/10.1080/104179 40802418825

Gibson, K. L. (2019). The women take over: Oral argument, rhetorical skepticism, and the performance of feminist jurisprudence in *Whole Women's Health v. Hellerstedt*. *Quarterly Journal of Speech, 105*(3), 319–340. https://doi.org/10.1080/00335 630.2019.1629002

Girnus, A. C. (2022). Adam Laxalt, Trumpism and the Big Lie: An (updated) chronology. *Nevada Current*. www.nevadacurrent.com/2022/10/19/adam-laxalt-trumpism-and-the-big-lie-an-updated-chronology/

Gonzalez, D. (2022, October 3). Many Catholic Latinos don't think abortion should be illegal, despite personal views. *USA Today*. www.usatoday.com/story/news/nation/2022/10/03/most-latinos-oppose-abortion-but-others-say-they-stand-with-it/816 8024001/

Griffin, L. M. (1984). When dreams collide: Rhetorical trajectories in the assassination of President Kennedy. *Quarterly Journal of Speech, 70*(2), 111–131. https://doi.org/10.1080/00335638409383683

Gromer, J., Jr. (2022, May 16). America's divide may deepen after pending Supreme Court *Roe v. Wade* ruling on abortion. *The Dallas Morning News*. www.dallasnews.com/news/politics/2022/05/16/americas-divide-may-deepen-after-pending-supreme-court-roe-v-wade-ruling-on-abortion/

Jansing, C. (2022, August 3). *Chris Jansing Reports*. https://archive.org/details/MSNBCW_20220803_170000_Chris_Jansing_Reports/start/45/end/105

Lake, R. A. (1984). Order and disorder in anti-abortion rhetoric: A logological view. *Quarterly Journal of Speech, 70*(4), 425–443. https://doi.org/10.1080/0033563840 9383708

Lake, R. A., & Pickering, B. A. (2015). Argumentative trajectories in the war on women. In C. H. Palczewski (Ed.), *Disturbing argument: Selected works from the 18th NCA/AFA conference on argumentation* (pp. 187–92). Routledge.

McGee, M. C. (1990). Text, context, and the fragmentation of contemporary culture. *Western Journal of Communication, 54*(3), 274–289. https://doi.org/10.1080/105703 19009374343

Merica, D., & Wright, D. (2022). Republicans largely stay away from abortion issue in their ads. But not all of them. *CNN.* www.cnn.com/2022/10/04/politics/republicans-abortion-ads-midterm-election/index.html

Packer, J. C. (2013). How much jail time? Returning women to the abortion debate. *Argumentation and Advocacy, 50*(2), 89–103. https://doi.org/10.1080/00028 533.2013.11821812

*Pew Research Center.* (2022). Majority of public disapproves of Supreme Court's decision to overturn *Roe v. Wade.* www.pewresearch.org/politics/2022/07/06/major ity-of-public-disapproves-of-supreme-courts-decision-to-overturn-roe-v-wade/

Rowland, A. L. (2017). Zoetropes: Turning fetuses into humans at the national memorial for the unborn. *Rhetoric Society Quarterly, 47*(1), 26–48. https://doi.org/10.1080/02773945.2016.1238105

Rowland, R. C., & Jones, J. A. (2001). Entelechial and reformative symbolic trajectories in contemporary conservatism: A case study of Reagan and Buchanan in Houston and beyond. *Rhetoric & Public Affairs, 4*(1), 55–84. https://doi.org/10.1353/rap.2001.0010

Scherer, M. (2022, June 29). After the overturning of *Roe,* many Republicans want to change the subject. *The Washington Post.* www.washingtonpost.com/politics/2022/06/29/republicans-abortion-midterms/

Steller, T. (2022, May 10). Contraception tied to abortion debate. *Arizona Daily Star.* https://tucson.com/news/local/subscriber/tim-stellers-column-contraception-tied-to-abortion-debate/article_a17425f0-d09c-11ec-9484-43b5752b9c24.html

Swan, J., & Kraushaar, J. (2022, October 12). Scoop: Peter Thiel offers to double down on Arizona Senate race. *Axios.* www.axios.com/2022/10/12/peter-thiel-arizona-blake-masters-mcconnell

Vestal, C. (2022, August 11). Abortion ballot measures seen as critical — but tricky — strategy. *Stateline.* https://stateline.org/2022/08/11/abortion-ballot-measures-seen-as-critical-but-tricky-strategy/

Winderman, E., & Hallsby, A. (2022). The Dobbs leak and reproductive justice. *Quarterly Journal of Speech, 108*(4), 421–425. https://doi.org/10.1080/00335630.2022.2128205

Winfrey, K. L., & Carlin, D. B. (2023). Have you come a long way, baby, since 2008?: One major step forward with missteps along the way. *Communication Studies, 74*(2), 131–146. https://doi.org/10.1080/10510974.2023.2177691

Ziegler, M. (2020). *Abortion and the law in America: Roe v. Wade to the present.* Cambridge University Press.

# 11

# FLORIDA'S 2022 SENATE RACE

## Social Media, Social Justice, and Partisanship

*David Lynn Painter, Tanja Vierrether, and Fiona Bown*

The predicted red tide of Republican victories in the 2022 U.S. midterm failed to materialize on a national scale, but there was nothing short of a crimson tsunami in Florida. Specifically, Republicans won supermajorities in both chambers of the state legislature, flipped four Congressional districts, and won every statewide election (Tawfik, 2022). Most notably, Senator Marco Rubio (R) and Governor Ron DeSantis (R) won reelection in double-digit landslides suggesting the largest swing state has become a Republican stronghold.

At the top of the 2022 Florida ballot, U.S. Senator Marco Rubio faced Val Demings (D), a central Florida Congressperson. Next, Governor Ron DeSantis faced Charlie Crist (D), another Congressperson who was also a former Republican governor. Compared to DeSantis, Rubio maintained a low profile, characteristic of his political persona since losing the 2016 Florida Republican presidential primary to Donald Trump (R), but winning Senate reelection later the same year (Everett, 2022). The Rubio-Demings contest was also more competitive than the DeSantis-Crist race, with polling indicating Demings was closing-in on Rubio even as DeSantis maintained a wide lead over Crist (Cowan, 2022).

The comparatively lower information but more competitive Rubio-Demings Senate race provides a compelling context for investigating the influence of campaign information on voters' attitudes toward the 2022 midterm candidates. Specifically, this experimental investigation explores the differential effects of social media content categorized according to Aristotle's Triad of Argumentation (Mshvenieradze, 2013) that promoted the candidates' (1) image traits (ethos); (2) issue positions (logos); or (3) negative attacks (pathos). Additionally, this study compares viewers' responses to social media information based on their

DOI: 10.4324/9781003440833-15

political party affiliations. Further, viewers' racial justice and gender equity attitudes may have influenced their candidate evaluations since Rubio is a first-generation Cuban American, Demings is a Black woman, and these issues were prominent during the campaign. Finally, this study finds its place in the literature through an exploration of the ways that different types of social media content may interact with participants' political attitudes to shape their candidate evaluations.

## Candidate Evaluations and Social Media in the 2022 Midterms

Scholars have analyzed the influence of campaign information on voters' attitudes toward the candidates at least since the groundbreaking research published in *The People's Choice* (Lazarsfeld et al., 1948) and *The American Voter* (Campbell et al., 1960). These studies suggested voters' political party affiliations and candidate evaluations were the best predictors of their voting preferences. Thus, candidate evaluations are conceptualized as summaries of voters' electoral judgments and proxies for their voting intentions (Arcuri et al., 2008; Miller et al., 1986).

During the 2022 midterm elections, more U.S. adults got their news from digital rather than traditional media sources and about half learned about current events on social media (Shearer, 2021). Moreover, political campaigns have used digital media to inform and influence voters at least since Howard Dean's (D) 2004 campaign (Bode et al., 2013). Subsequently, Barack Obama's (D) use of digital media was at least partly credited for his 2008 and 2012 electoral victories (Hendricks & Denton, 2010; Hendricks & Kaid, 2014).

When comparing the effects of different digital media channels, research indicates social media may exert significantly stronger positive influences on viewers' cognitions and attitudes than news or campaign websites (Kenski et al., 2022; Kim et al., 2013; Painter et al., 2014; Painter, 2015). Indeed, social media may powerfully influence users' attitudes toward political actors and policies. For example, about a quarter of U.S. social media users in 2020 reported changing their views on a policy issue or politician within the last year because of social media (Perrin, 2020).

While social media's ability to influence viewers' attitudes is relatively well-established, this current project's goal is to parse the differential effects of social media content classified according to Aristotle's typology of rhetorical appeals. This Triad of Argumentation classifies appeals dependent upon the content's focus on promoting the candidates' (1) image or character traits (ethos); (2) issue or policy positions (logos); or (3) negative attacks on opponents (pathos). These classifications have been used in analyses of both traditional (Triadafilopoulos, 1999) and online (Bronstein, 2013; English et al., 2011) political campaign communications. Indeed, scholars have categorized the persuasive appeals in campaign messages based on whether they focus on the candidates' image traits, their issue positions, or their negative attacks on opponents for decades (Benoit et al., 2011; Kaid & Johnston, 2001; Kaid et al., 2011).

Although classic democratic theory emphasizes issue positions as the most logical basis for electoral decision making, voters use more affective intelligence processes when deciding on candidate preferences (Marcus et al., 2000). Similarly, political campaigns use social media strategically based on their messaging goals and the electoral context. Thus, the verbal and visual content in each social media post is intentionally crafted to maximize its effectiveness. For instance, analyses of the 2008 and 2012 Obama campaign's use of Facebook suggested the posts largely appealed to viewers' emotions and emphasized the candidate's image qualities—but the different types of posts elicited distinct responses from viewers (Bronstein, 2013; Gerodimos & Justinussen, 2015). Based on this line of research, the first research question asks:

RQ1: How will the different types of social media content influence participants' candidate evaluations?

## Partisanship

Decades of research indicates political party affiliations may shape voters' attitudes toward the candidates as well as their responses to campaign information (Campbell et al., 1960; Greene, 2002). For example, Lau and Redlawsk's (2001) research suggests voters commonly use candidates' political party affiliations as heuristic cues or cognitive shortcuts that exert strong influences on their attitudes. Specifically, social identity theory predicts these cues will positively influence voters' affect toward in-group candidates from the same political party, but negatively influence their affect toward outgroup candidates from the other political party (West & Iyengar, 2020). Moreover, as the political environment has become hyper-polarized in recent years, political party affiliation has become more central to many Americans' social, if not ethnic, identities (Mason, 2018). This identity formation and expression is particularly powerful on social media (Kreiss et al., 2020; Lim, 2020).

Coinciding with the electorate's polarization, political campaigns have focused more on activating their base of support than appealing to moderate, swing, or independent voters in the last several decades (Hill, 2017; Panagopoulos, 2016). This focus on in-group voters is logical since research indicates independents are the least interested, the least knowledgeable, and the least likely to participate in politics compared to partisans (Laloggia, 2019; Magelby, 2011). Further, research indicates independents report the greatest changes in their cognitions, attitudes, and behavioral intentions when provided with campaign information (Holbrook and McClurg, 2005). Alternately,

**236** Media Messages in the 2022 Midterm Election

partisans are more likely to have more political knowledge as well as more stable attitudes and voting habits than independents, making them more resistant to campaign appeals (Achen, 1992). Thus, when parsing the influence of political party affiliation on viewers' responses to the campaigns' social media content, the first hypothesis predicts:

> H1: Independents will report the greatest changes in candidate evaluations compared to Republicans and Democrats.

## Electoral Context: Candidate Familiarity and Salient Issues

### *Marco Rubio*

Incumbent Florida Republican Senator Marco Rubio, a Miami-born Cuban American, served four terms in the State House in the early 2000s, then launched a successful, insurgent Tea Party candidacy against Charlie Crist (R), the establishment party pick in the state's 2010 Republican Senate primary. After Rubio defeated Crist, he won the general election with 49 percent of the vote because Crist ran as an independent, garnering 30 percent of votes, and Kendrick Meek (D) earned 20 percent. In the process of winning the general election, Rubio also flipped Miami Dade county from the Democrats, a surprising feat given that Obama won the county by a margin of 16% only 2 years prior (Election Results Archive, 2022). Next, in 2016, Rubio sought the Republican nomination for the presidency, and was famously nicknamed "Little Marco" by Donald Trump who ridiculed Rubio's stature in the 11th GOP primary debate. After he lost the Florida primary to Trump, Rubio dropped out of the presidential race, but easily won reelection to the Senate the same year (Bustos, 2016).

### *Val Demings*

Val Demings emphasized her 27-year law enforcement career, especially her tenure as Chief of the Orlando Police Department, throughout her campaign. After retiring from the force, Demings lost her 2012 bid to unseat Daniel Webster (R) in Florida's 10th Congressional district, but won a landslide victory in 2016 after redistricting flipped the district's partisan composition. Demings ran unopposed in 2018 and was reelected to the U.S. House of Representatives in 2020 in another landslide. Clearly, Demings was relatively well-known in central Florida, but as one of Florida's 27 U.S. Representatives, she was relatively unknown in the rest of the state. While this lack of name recognition was an obstacle with the voters, Demings's campaign raised $79.5 million, nearly doubling the Rubio campaign's $42.5 million (Dixon, 2022).

### Campaign Horserace

At the beginning of the campaign, Rubio enjoyed higher favorability and name recognition ratings than Demings. Indeed, early polls indicated Rubio had an 11-point lead, but by the end of October, only four points separated Demings and Rubio (FiveThirtyEight, 2022). However, a fifth of respondents indicated they had not heard of Demings, and another 22% reported that they had heard of her, but had not formed an opinion (Suffolk University, 2022). These survey results suggest voters' attitudes toward Demings would be more susceptible to campaign information compared to Rubio. Indeed, the literature has long indicated that campaign information exerts stronger effects on voters' attitudes toward lesser-known candidates compared to those with established reputations (Lodge et al., 1995). Thus, the second hypothesis predicts:

> H2: Participants will report greater changes in their evaluations of Val Demings than of Marco Rubio.

### Racial Justice Attitudes

In addition to voters' familiarity with the candidates, salient social justice issues could also influence their evaluations of the candidates. Specifically, the United States has been experiencing an ongoing racial reckoning triggered by viral videos showing Minneapolis police officers murdering George Floyd in 2020. Subsequently, a series of protests across the country also focused attention on police brutality in the cases of Breonna Taylor, Daunte Rice, Amir Locke, and countless others. Not surprisingly, these racial justice issues are also highly partisan, with more than three-quarters of Republicans feeling that only a little or nothing needs to be done to ensure equal rights for Americans, regardless of their racial or ethnic backgrounds. Alternatively, about three-quarters of Democrats feel that a lot more needs to be done to achieve racial equity (Pew Research Center, 2021).

These issues were prominent in the 2022 Florida Senate election not only because of their partisan appeals, but also because the incumbent was a first-generation Cuban American and his challenger was a Black woman. Moreover, both campaigns promoted their positions on opposite sides of the racial justice divide. For instance, Rubio repeatedly attacked Demings as a supporter of the Black Lives Matter and Defund the Police movements (Powers, 2022). Rubio also campaigned against the "radical Democrat's woke agenda," and promoted his endorsement from 55 of Florida's 67 sheriffs as well as the Florida Fraternal Order of Police (Harris, 2022).

Demings responded to these attacks with a simple message: "I am the police" (Harris, 2022). This response from a Democratic candidate who also happens to be a Black woman is particularly interesting in the context of her party's relationship with the Black Lives Matter movement and its focus on police brutality. Moreover, this combination of conditions suggests participants' racial justice attitudes may influence their candidate evaluations in ways independent of their political party affiliation. Thus, the second research question asks:

> RQ2: How will participants' racial justice attitudes influence their evaluations of the candidates?

### Gender Equity Attitudes

While inflation, racial justice, and the future of democracy may have been top-of-mind for voters in the 2022 midterm (Schaeffer & Van Green, 2022), the ongoing battle for women's rights was also a prominent contextual consideration (Axios, 2022). In particular, the Supreme Court's Dobbs decision, which effectively eliminated legal abortions in at least a dozen states including Florida, even in cases of rape and incest, elevated women's rights, healthcare, and abortion issues (Dixon, 2022). These issues were also emphasized in the campaigns' messaging. For instance, Demings attacked Rubio's anti-abortion stance, claiming he wanted to ban all abortions, even those terminating pregnancies resulting from rape or incest (Bohman, 2022). Rubio responded by citing his support of Senator Lindsey Graham's (R-S.C.) federal proposition to ban abortions after 15 weeks, except for pregnancies by rape or incest (Dixon, 2022). Rubio then attacked Demings' views, claiming she wanted to make abortions legal up until the moment of birth (Dixon, 2022). The Demings campaign responded that she supported abortion up to the moment of viability (Myers et al., 2022).

Although about 60% of Americans and 56% of Floridians support legal abortions in all or most cases, these views are also split along partisan lines (Gallup, 2023; Pew Research Center, 2023). Specifically, about 80% of Democrats, but only about 40% of Republicans support legal abortions in all or most cases (Hartig, 2022a). However, there are sizable variations in these views within the parties (Hartig, 2022b), which may result in these attitudes exerting independent influences on participants' candidate evaluations, particularly given that one of the candidates is a woman. Thus, research question three asks:

> RQ3: How will participants' gender equity attitudes influence their evaluations of the candidates?

## Interaction Effects

In addition to the direct effects of social media, political party affiliations, and contextual factors, this investigation also explores how these independent variables may interact to influence voters' candidate evaluations. Thus, the final research question asks:

> RQ4: How will the different types of social media content, participants' political party affiliations and social justice attitudes interact to influence their candidate evaluations?

## Method

To answer the research questions and test the hypothesis, this investigation used an online experiment with a pretest-posttest factorial design and three treatment conditions: image, issue, or negative social media campaign posts. Participants were 589 Florida residents who were registered to vote and recruited from a liberal arts college, as well as Prolific Academic, a widely used platform for recruiting high-quality research participants, for a more diverse sample of Florida voters. Participants completed the project on Qualtrics between October 21 and October 28, 2022. Fifty-one percent of participants were men, 49% were women, and their median age was 35 years old. Participants were 69% White, 20% African American, eight percent Hispanic, and three percent another ethnicity. Fifty-five percent of participants were Democrats (or Democrat-leaners), 26% Republicans (or Republican-leaners), and 19% Independents. Although this distribution represents an oversampling of Democrats, the goal of this experiment is test hypotheses aligned with Aristotle's rhetorical models rather than achieve strict representativeness of the population as would be required for a survey. Moreover, when the participants were randomly assigned to one of the three social media conditions, the distribution was equitable with no significant differences in demographic or partisanship variables among the conditions ($p > .05$).

## Procedure

Participants in all conditions completed a pretest questionnaire with items measuring demographics; partisanship; racial justice and gender equity attitudes; and candidate evaluations. Upon completion of the pretest, participants were randomly exposed to the social media posts curated for each condition. After indicating they had read each social media post (one per candidate per condition), participants were directed to the posttest questionnaire that included items reassessing their candidate evaluations.

## 240 Media Messages in the 2022 Midterm Election

### *Independent Variables*

*Manipulated.* This experiment tested the influence of social media content focused on the candidates' (1) image qualities (ethos), (2) issue positions (logos), or (3) negative attacks (pathos) on their opponents (Kaid & Johnston, 2001).. First, an exhaustive review of more than 120 Facebook, Instagram, and Twitter posts from each candidate that elicited the most engagement between August 1 and October 12, 2022, were classified into an ethos, logos, pathos, or other category. Then, the posts were reviewed to select the ones most accurately capturing each candidate's thematic focus on their individual characteristics (ethos), policy issues (logos), and opponent attacks (pathos). The order of the posts (Rubio or Demings campaign) presented to participants was also randomized.

Specifically, the image condition focused on patriotism with posts of Demings honoring her predecessors who sacrificed for the rights we enjoy in America today while Rubio reminded viewers that "In God We Trust" is the basis of our country. Next, in the issue condition, the Demings post defended voting rights, women's rights, and marriage equality while the Rubio post promoted health care for veterans. Finally, Demings' negative post attacked Rubio for wanting to take away a woman's right to choose, even in cases of rape and incest, while the Rubio post attacked Val Demings as a supporter of Black Lives Matter and Defund the Police. These posts were intentionally chosen to capture key themes in each candidates' rhetorical strategies, to reflect actual campaign messages, and to preserve some measure of external validity rather than a direct comparison of each campaign's statements on the same personal qualities (ethos), policy issues (logos), or opponent attacks (pathos).

*Measured.* First, the pretest questionnaire included five items measuring participants' racial justice attitudes ($\alpha$ =.93): (1) White people still have certain advantages because of the color of their skin; (2) Racial and ethnic minorities do not have the same opportunities as White people; (3) Racial problems in the U.S. are rare, isolated situations (reverse-coded); (4) Racism may have been a problem in the past, but it is not important today (reverse-coded); and, (5) It is important for political leaders to talk about racism so that we can solve it (Henry & Sears, 2002; McConahay, 1986).

Next, participants answered four items measuring their gender equity attitudes ($\alpha$ =.89): (1) Men still have some advantages over women in our society today; (2) Discrimination against women is rare these days (reverse-coded); (3) The mistreatment of women may have been a problem in the past, but it is not important today (reverse-coded); and, (4) It is important for political leaders to talk about gender inequalities so that we can solve them (Swim et al., 1995).

Finally, participants identified their political party affiliation by answering a single item: "Generally, how would you describe your identification with the political parties in the United States?" Participants identified as Republicans, Independents who leaned Republican, Democrats, Independents who leaned Democratic, or as Independents who did not lean toward either party. Participants identifying as Independents who leaned toward a political party were grouped with those who identified with that political party.

### Dependent Variable

*Candidate evaluation changes.* In both the pretest and posttest, a 100-point feeling thermometer scale (American National E lection Studies, 2020) was used to measure participants' evaluations of the candidates. Then, the aggregate pretest evaluations were subtracted from the posttest evaluations to create an evaluation change variable for each candidate.

## Results

To answer the research questions and test the hypotheses, a multivariate analysis of covariance (MANCOVA) test was performed. This MANCOVA model was constructed with the social media content condition (image, issue, or negative) and participants' political party affiliations (Republican, Democrat, Independent) entered as categorical independent variables; each candidates' evaluation change scores as continuous dependent variables; and participants' racial justice and gender equity attitudes as continuous covariates. Significant differences in candidate evaluations were found for social media content type, Wilks's $\Lambda = .92$, $F(2, 576) = 21.67$, $p < .01$, $\eta_p^2 = .07$; political party affiliation, Wilks's $\Lambda = .92$, $F(2, 576) = 13.25$, $p < .01$, $\eta_p^2 = .04$; racial justice attitudes, Wilks's $\Lambda = .92$, $F(2, 576) = 5.89$, $p < .02$, $\eta_p^2 = .02$; and gender equity attitudes, Wilks's $\Lambda = .92$, $F(4, 576) = 21.67$, $p < .06$, $\eta_p^2 = .06$. The interaction between social media content condition and political party affiliation was also significant, Wilks's $\Lambda = .92$, $F(2, 576) = 12.96$, $p < .01$, $\eta_p^2 = .08$. The model accounted for 29% ($R^2 = .29$) of Val Demings' evaluation changes and 25% ($R^2 = .25$) of Marco Rubio's evaluation changes.

### Main Effects

**Social Media Condition.** The first research question asked how the different types of social media content influenced viewers' candidate evaluations. The MANCOVA results indicate the changes in Val Demings' evaluations were significantly different across conditions, $F(2, 577) = 26.11$, $p < .00$, $\eta_p^2 = .08$. Specifically, as shown in Table 11.1, post-hoc Bonferroni tests indicated image content elicited the greatest changes in Demings' evaluations, followed by issue and then negative content, which were also significantly different from each

## 242 Media Messages in the 2022 Midterm Election

**TABLE 11.1** Candidate Evaluation Changes by Condition

| | Image (n = 205) | Issue (n = 196) | Negative (n = 188) | Total (N = 589) | df | F | p |
|---|---|---|---|---|---|---|---|
| Demings | 11.46** | 6.87** | 0.14** | 6.22 | 2 | 26.11 | .00 |
| | (3.98) | (2.76) | (1.39) | (3.17) | | | |
| Rubio | 2.41** | 8.16** | -3.71** | 2.21 | 2 | 26.02 | .00 |
| | (1.90) | (2.05) | (1.91) | (2.47) | | | |

Note: Table lists means with standard deviations in parentheses.
** significantly different, $p < .05$.

**TABLE 11.2** Candidate Evaluation Changes by Party

| | Republican (n = 152) | Independent (n = 113) | Democrat (n = 324) | df | F | p |
|---|---|---|---|---|---|---|
| Demings | 0.39** | 17.23** | 5.11** | 2 | 24.72 | .00 |
| | (1.63) | (3.44) | (2.32) | | | |
| Rubio | 0.33 | 10.30** | 0.27 | 2 | 8.04 | .00 |
| | (.22) | (1.10) | (.43) | | | |

Note: Table lists means with standard deviations in parentheses.
** significantly different, $p < .05$.

other, $p < .05$. Next, Marco Rubio's evaluation changes were also significantly different across conditions, $F(2, 577) = 26.02$, $p < .00$, $\eta_p^2 = .08$. In particular, post-hoc Bonferroni tests indicated issue content elicited the greatest changes in Rubio's evaluations, followed by negative and image content, which were also significantly different from each other, $p < .05$.

**Political Party Affiliation.** The first hypothesis predicted Independents would report greater changes in candidate evaluations than Republicans or Democrats. As shown in Table 11.2, the MANCOVA results indicated candidate evaluation changes were significantly different across political party affiliations for both Val Demings ($F(2, 577) = 24.72$, $p < .00$, $\eta^2 = .08$) and Marco Rubio ($F(2, 577) = 8.04$, $p < .00$, $\eta^2 = .03$). Moreover, the results of post-hoc Bonferroni tests indicated Independents reported significantly greater changes than Republicans or Democrats in their evaluations of both candidates, $p < .05$. These results support H1.

Interestingly, when we conducted follow-up paired-samples $t$-tests on the candidates' evaluations by participant partisanship, we found that the changes in Republicans' evaluations of both candidates, and Democrats' evaluations of Marco Rubio, were not significant, $p > .05$. However, Democrat's posttest ($M = 79.18$, $SD = 3.57$) evaluations of Val Demings were significantly greater

($t(323) = -7.92$, $p < .00$) than their pretest ($M = 74.08$, $SD = 3.59$) evaluations. Thus, while Independents reported greater evaluation changes than partisans (i.e., Republican or Democrat) for both candidates, Democrat's evaluations of Val Demings also improved significantly, $t(194) = 3.88$, $p < .00$.

**Candidate Familiarity**. The second hypothesis predicted that participants would report greater changes in their evaluations of Val Demings compared to Marco Rubio. To test this hypothesis, paired-samples t-tests were first conducted to determine whether the candidates' aggregate posttest evaluations were significantly different from their pretest evaluations. The results indicated Demings' posttest evaluations ($M = 60.57$, $SD = 6.57$) were significantly greater than her pretest ($M = 54.36$, $SD = 6.21$) evaluations, $t(588) = -9.53$, $p < .00$, $d = -.39$. Similarly, Rubio's posttest ($M = 34.00$, $SD = 6.62$) evaluations were significantly greater than his pretest ($M = 31.80$, $SD = 4.73$) evaluations, $t(588) = -3.11$, $p < .00$, $d = -.13$. Next, a paired-samples t-test was conducted to determine whether the changes in Demings' evaluations were greater than the changes in Rubio's evaluations. As shown in the fourth column of Table 11.1, the results indicate Demings' evaluation changes ($M = 6.22$, $SD = 3.17$) were significantly greater than Rubio's evaluation changes ($M = 2.21$, $SD = 2.47$), $t(588) = -5.56$, $p < .00$, $d = .23$. These results support the second hypothesis.

**Racial Justice and Gender Equity Attitudes.** Research questions two and three inquired about the influence of participants' racial justice and gender equity attitudes, respectively, on their changes in candidate evaluations. Since these attitudes were measured as continuous variables, they were entered into the MANCOVA model as covariates, and the results indicate participants' racial justice attitudes ($F(1, 577) = 4.90$, $p < .05$, $\eta^2 = .01$), and gender equity attitudes ($F(1, 577) = 36.0$, $p < .00$, $\eta^2 = .06$) were significantly and positively related to the changes in Val Deming's evaluations. However, neither of these attitudes were significantly related to changes in Marco Rubio's evaluations, $p > .05$.

### Interaction Effects

The fourth research question asked how the independent variables interacted to influence participants' candidate evaluations. Before analyzing these interactions, a closer examination of the relationships among participants' social justice attitudes and political party affiliations was necessary. This analysis was needed to determine whether collinearity issues would invalidate consideration of participants' social justice attitudes independent of their political party affiliations when probing for interaction effects. The results indicated participants' political party affiliations were strongly correlated with their racial justice, $r(588) = .71$, $p < .01$, and their gender equity, $r(588) = .69$, $p < .01$, attitudes. Moreover, there

**244** Media Messages in the 2022 Midterm Election

**TABLE 11.3** Evaluation Changes by Party and Condition

| | Republican (n = 152) | Democrat (n = 323) | Independent (n = 113) |
|---|---|---|---|
| Demings | | | |
| Image | 4.96 | 8.13 | 24.06[**] |
| | (2.34) | (2.31) | (6.11) |
| Issue | -1.66[**] | 8.84[**] | 17.71[**] |
| | (2.47) | (2.31) | (1.99) |
| Negative | -2.56 | 0.37 | 2.69 |
| | (1.25) | (1.85) | (2.90) |
| Rubio | | | |
| Image | -3.46 | -3.73 | 19.74[**] |
| | (2.28) | (1.67) | (6.41) |
| Issue | 1.85[**] | 10.58[**] | 13.65[**] |
| | (.74) | (3.72) | (1.83) |
| Negative | 3.11[**] | -3.69[**] | -13.31[**] |
| | (.64) | (2.55) | (2.70) |

Note: Table lists means with standard deviations in parentheses.
[**] significantly different, $p < .05$.

were too few Republicans with high scores on the racial justice ($M = 2.08$, $SD = .71$) and gender equity ($M = 2.26$, $SD = .63$) scales, and there were too few Democrats with low scores on the racial justice ($M = 3.67$, $SD = .48$) and the gender equity ($M = 3.59$, $SD = .38$) scales for valid statistical analyses. Thus, the interaction analysis focused on social media content and participants' political party affiliations.

**Condition and Political Party Interaction.** The results of the MANCOVA indicated the interaction between social media content type and participants' political party affiliations significantly influenced their evaluation changes for both Val Demings ($F(4, 577) = 7.96$, $p < .01$, $\eta^2 = .05$) and Marco Rubio ($F(4, 577) = 25.49$, $p < .00$, $\eta^2 = .15$). To specify the interaction effects for Val Demings, follow-up simple ANOVAs with post-hoc Bonferroni tests were conducted (see Table 11.3). The results of these tests indicated Independents ($M = 24.06$, $SD = 6.11$) responded significantly more positively ($F(2, 202) = 17.32$, $p > .00$) to image content than Republicans ($M = 4.96$, $SD = 2.34$) or Democrats ($M = 8.13$, $SD = 2.31$), whose evaluation changes were not significantly different from each other, $p > 05$. Next, in the image condition, Independents ($M = 17.71$, $SD = 1.99$) also reported the greatest gains in Demings' evaluations compared to Democrats ($M = 8.84$, $SD = 2.31$) and Republicans ($M = -1.66$, $SD = 2.47$), who were also significantly different from each other, $F(2, 185) = 31.27$, $p > .00$. In the negative condition, however, differences across parties were not significant, $p > .05$.

For Marco Rubio, the results of follow-up simple ANOVAs with post-hoc Bonferroni tests in the image condition indicated Independents' ($M = 19.74$, $SD = 6.41$) evaluation changes were significantly greater ($F(2, 202) = 32.68$, $p > .00$) than Republicans ($M = -3.46$, $SD = 2.28$) and Democrats ($M = -3.73$, $SD = 1.67$), whose evaluation changes were not significantly different from each other, $p > .05$. Next, in the issue condition, Republicans' ($M = 1.85$, $SD = .74$) evaluation changes were significantly smaller than Democrats ($M = 10.58$, $SD = 3.72$) and Independents ($M = 13.65$, $SD = 1.83$), whose evaluation changes were not significantly different from each other, $p > .05$. Finally, in the negative condition, Republicans' ($M = 3.11$, $SD = .64$) evaluation changes were greater than Democrats' ($M = -3.69$, $SD = 2.55$), or Independents' ($M = -13.31$, $SD = 2.70$), whose evaluation changes were also significantly different from each other, $F(2, 196) = 12.72$, $p > .00$.

## Discussion

Overall, the results of this study suggest social media may exert significant influences on viewers' attitudes toward political candidates. Moreover, the type of social media posts as well as the viewers' political party affiliations and familiarity with the candidates may shape their responses. For instance, aggregate evaluations of Val Demings, the relatively unfamiliar candidate, increased by about six percent. Specifically, negative content elicited only marginal changes, but issue content elicited nearly seven percent increases, and image content about 11% increases in Deming's evaluations. Alternately, changes in evaluations of Marco Rubio, the more familiar candidate, were significantly smaller. In particular, Rubio's aggregate evaluations increased by about two percent, closely matching the increase elicited by image content. In the issue condition, however, viewers reported about eight percent increases and the negative condition elicited about four percent decreases in Rubio's evaluations.

Next, when examining the influence of partisanship, we found that independents reported the greatest changes in candidate evaluations compared to Democrats and Republicans. This finding aligns with prior research suggesting independents have less knowledge and more fluid attitudes toward the candidates than partisans. Likewise, we found that participants reported greater changes in Val Demings' evaluations, likely due to her relative unfamiliarity compared to Marco Rubio. In fact, the combination of these factors resulted not only in independents reporting greater evaluation changes than partisans for both candidates, but also that Democrat's evaluations of Val Demings also improved significantly. However, Republicans' changes in evaluations of the candidates were only marginal across conditions.

Finally, when probing for the main effect of participants' social justice attitudes on their attitudes toward the candidates, we found they were positively related to

**246** Media Messages in the 2022 Midterm Election

evaluations of Val Demings, but unrelated to Marco Rubio's evaluations. In the context of the campaign, this finding is intuitive given that Black Lives Matter, police brutality, and abortion rights were salient issues, and Val Demings would have become the only Black woman serving in the U.S. Senate had she won the election. Thus, participants with strong racial justice and gender equity attitudes responded more positively to Val Demings than Marco Rubio. However, when testing for interaction effects among the independent variables, we were unable to use participants' racial justice and gender equity attitudes because too few Republicans reported high scores while too few Democrats reported low scores on these scales. This finding also aligns with research indicating these issues define the cleavage between the political parties (Pew Research Center, 2021).

When analyzing how social media content type interacted with participants' political party affiliations, we found that participants in the image condition reported increases in Demings' evaluations ranging from 24 to nearly five percent, depending on their political party affiliations. Moreover, independents responded significantly more positively to image content, but less negatively to negative content than partisans, which drove the main effect of social media condition and partisanship on Demings' evaluation changes. Alternately, for Marco Rubio, independents responded significantly more positively to image and issue content as well as more negatively to negative content than partisans. In particular, Democrats and independents in the issue condition reported about 10 and 13% increases in Rubio's evaluations, respectively, while Republicans' evaluations remained more stable. However, independents and Democrats' evaluations of Rubio decreased by about 13 to three percent, respectively, in the negative condition, while Republicans' evaluation changes increased about three percent. Alternatively, both Republicans and Democrats reported about three percent decreases while independents reported nearly 20% increases in Rubio's evaluations in the image condition, driving the main effect of social media condition and partisanship on his evaluation changes.

### Implications

These results have some important implications for the ways we conceptualize the public sphere as well as how political party identification may shape responses to political campaign communications on social media. First, finding that different types of social media posts exerted distinct responses from viewers not only aligns with prior research, but also illustrates how Aristotle's typology more comprehensively and accurately captures political speech than other theorists' normative ideals. Specifically, Habermas' (1996) model of the public sphere limits political speech to rational truth claims presented in public deliberations that lead rational consensus. However, Aristotle argues that political speech is not only logically based in issues and policies, but also "passionate, and reflective of the character of the speaker" (Triadafilopoulos, 1999, p. 742).

In practical terms, these results suggest relatively unknown political candidates may benefit the most from social media posts promoting their image traits while more familiar candidates may benefit most from messages specifying their issue positions. Additionally, negative or attack posts may have negligible or even negative effects on viewers' attitudes, suggesting their use should probably be limited. Moreover, finding that social media posts exerted much stronger influences on independents' evaluations suggests political campaigns should expand their appeals to target independent voters beyond their base of in-group supporters.

### Limitations and Future Research

While this study provides some interesting results implications, there are some general limitations of cross-sectional experiments related to their lack of insight into longitudinal changes and inability to control for every potential confounding variable external to the experiment that must be acknowledged. Additionally, participants in each condition were exposed to messages from both campaigns, so it is impossible disentangle the influences of the individual campaign messages. For example, in the negative condition, participants saw attack posts from both candidates, which may have neutralized their responses to the individual campaign posts. Further, the sample included more Democrats than Republicans or independents. Thus, having a larger and more equally distributed sample might lead to more variance in social justice attitude scores, allowing for more in-depth analysis of social justice attitudes' interactions with social media posts and political party affiliations. Future research with a larger sample and treatment conditions separated by candidate as well as content type might be able to provide more nuanced findings regarding these issues.

### References

Achen, C. H. (1992). Social psychology, demographic variables, and linear regression: Breaking the iron triangle in voting research. *Political Behavior*, *14*(3), 195–211. https://doi.org/10.1007/BF00991978

American National Election Studies. (2020). *2020 Time Series Study*. ANES. https://electionstudies.org/data-center/2020-time-series-study/

Arcuri, L., Castelli, L., Galdi, S., Zogmaiser, C., & Amadori, A. (2008). Predicting the vote: Implicit attitudes as predictors of the future behavior of decided and undecided voters. *Political Psychology, 29*(3), 369–387. https://doi.org/10.1111/j.1467-9221.2008.00635.x

Axios (2022). *Midterm elections 2022: The issues that matter to Americans.* www.axios.com/midterms-elections-2022-issues-americans-care

## 248 Media Messages in the 2022 Midterm Election

Benoit, W. L., Henson, J. R., & Sudbrock, L. A. (2011). A functional analysis of 2008 US presidential primary debates. *Argumentation and Advocacy, 48*(2), 97–110. https://doi.org/10.1080/00028533.2011.11821757

Bode, L., Edgerly, S., Sayre, B., Vraga, E. K., & Shah, D. V. (2013). Digital democracy: How the internet has changed politics. In A. N. Valdivia (Ed.), *The international encyclopedia of media studies* (pp. 505–524). Wiley-Blackwell. https://doi.org/10.1002/9781444361506.wbiems128

Bohman, D. (2022, November 1). Is Val Demings' ad attacking Sen. Marco Rubio on abortion accurate? *WPTV*. www.wptv.com/news/political/elections-local/is-val-demings-ad-attacking-sen-marco-rubio-on-abortion-accurate

Bronstein, J., Aharony, N. & Bar-Ilan, J. (2018). Politicians' use of Facebook during elections: Use of emotionally-based discourse, personalization, social media engagement and vividness. *Aslib Journal of Information Management, 70*(5), 551–572. https://doi.org/10.1108/AJIM-03-2018-0067

Bustos, S. (2016, 8 November). Rubio wins reelection in Florida. *Politico*. www.politico.com/story/2016/11/rubio-murphy-florida-senate-race-2016-election-results-230983

Campbell, A., Converse, P. E., Miller, W. E., & Stokes, D. E. (1960). *The American voter*. University of Chicago Press.

Cowan, R. (2022, September 26). Democratic ex-cop Demings closes in on Republican Rubio in Florida. *Reuters*. www.reuters.com/world/us/democratic-ex-cop-demings-closes-republican-rubio-florida-2022-09-26/

Dixon, M. (2022, August 24). Money isn't everything: Demings hauls in cash but Rubio holds firm. *Politico*. www.politico.com/news/2022/08/24/florida-senate-demings-cash-rubio-holds-firm-00053531

Election Results Archive. (2022). *Miami-Dade County Elections Department*. www.miamidade.gov/global/elections/election-results-archive.page

English, K., Sweetser, K. D., & Ancu, M. (2011). YouTube-ification of political talk: An examination of persuasion appeals in viral video. *American Behavioral Scientist, 55*(6), 733–748. https://doi.org/10.1177/000276421139809

Everett, B. (2022, June 13). Rubio embraces his low-key side. *Politico*. www.politico.com/news/2022/06/13/marco-rubio-demings-00038912

FiveThirtyEight. (2022, November 22). *Latest polls*. https://scri.siena.edu/2022/10/03/governor-desantis-49-crist-41us-senate-rubio-48-demings-41florida-ag-moody-41-ayala-34/

Gallup. (2023). *Abortion trends by party identification*. https://news.gallup.com/poll/246278/abortion-trends-party.aspx

Gerodimos, R., & Justinussen, J. (2015). Obama's 2012 Facebook campaign: Political communication in the age of the like button. *Journal of Information Technology & Politics, 12*(2), 113–132. https://doi.org/10.1080/19331681.2014.982266

Greene, S. (2002). Understanding party identification: A social identity approach. *Political Psychology, 20*(2), 393–403. https://doi.org/10.1111/0162-895X.00150

Habermas, J. (1996). *Between facts and norms: Contributions to a discourse theory of law and democracy*. MIT Press.

Harris, A. (2022, September 12). The Val Demings gamble. *The Atlantic*. www.theatlantic.com/politics/archive/2022/09/val-demings-midterms-2022-democratic-party/671327/

Hartig, H. (2022a, June 13). *About six-in-ten Americans say abortion should be legal in all or most cases.* Pew Research Center. www.pewresearch.org/fact-tank/2022/06/13/about-six-in-ten-americans-say-abortion-should-be-legal-in-all-or-most-cases-2/

Hartig, H. (2022b, May 6). *Wide partisan gaps in abortion attitudes, but opinions in both parties are complicated.* Pew Research Center. www.pewresearch.org/fact-tank/2022/05/06/wide-partisan-gaps-in-abortion-attitudes-but-opinions-in-both-parties-are-complicated/

Hendricks, J. A., & Denton, R. (Eds.). (2010). *Communicator-in-chief: How Barack Obama used new media technology to win the White House.* Lexington Books.

Hendricks, J. A., & Kaid, L. L. (Eds.). (2014). *Techno politics in presidential campaigning: New voices, new technologies, and new voters.* Routledge.

Henry, P. J., & Sears, D. O. (2002). The symbolic racism 2000 scale. *Political Psychology, 23*(2), 253–283. https://doi.org/10.1111/0162-895X.00281

Hill, S. J. (2017). Changing votes or changing voters? How candidates and election context swing voters and mobilize the base. *Electoral Studies, 48*, 131–148. https://doi.org/10.1016/j.electstud.2017.06.001

Holbrook, T. M., & McClurg, S. D. (2005). The mobilization of core supporters: Campaigns, turnout, and electoral composition in United States presidential elections. *American Journal of Political Science, 49*(4), 689–703. https://doi.org/10.1111/j.1540-5907.2005.00149.x

Kaid, L. L., Fernandes, J., & Painter, D. (2011). Effects of political advertising in the 2008 presidential campaign. *American Behavioral Scientist, 55*(4), 437–456. https://doi.org/10.1177/0002764211398071

Kaid, L. L., & Johnston, A. (2001). *Videostyle in presidential campaigns: Style and content of televised political advertising.* Greenwood Publishing Group.

Kenski, K., Kim, D. H., & Jones-Jang, S. M. (2022). Candidate evaluations and social media following during the 2020 presidential campaign. *Journal of Political Marketing, 21*(3-4), 272–283. https://doi.org/10.1080/15377857.2022.2099585

Kim, J. Y., Painter, D. L., & Miles, M. A. (2013). Campaign agenda-building online: Emotions, evaluations, and important perceptions. *Journal of Information Technology & Politics, 10*(3), 326–340. https://doi.org/10.1080/19331681.2013.807757

Kreiss, D., Lawrence, R. G., & McGregor, S. C. (2020). Political identity ownership: Symbolic contests to represent members of the public. *Social Media and Society, 6*(2), 1–5. https://doi.org/10.17615/kcmk-3r63

Laloggia, J. (2019, May 15). *6 facts about U. S. political independents.* Pew Research Center. www.pewresearch.org/politics/2019/03/14/political-independents-who-they-are-what-they-think/

Lau, R. R., & Redlawsk, D. P. (2001). Advantages and disadvantages of cognitive heuristics in political decision making. *American Journal of Political Science, 45*(4), 951–971. https://doi.org/10.2307/2669334

Lazarsfeld, P. F., Berelson, B., & Gaudet, H. (1948). *The people's choice: How the voter makes up his mind in a presidential campaign* (2nd ed.). Columbia University Press.

Lim, M. (2020). Algorithmic enclaves: Affective politics and algorithms in the neoliberal social media landscape. In M. Boler & E. Davis (Eds.), *Affective politics of digital media: Propaganda by other means* (pp. 186–203). Routledge.

Lodge, M., Steenbergen, M. R., & Brau, S. (1995). The responsive voter: Campaign information and the dynamics of candidate evaluation. *American Political Science Review, 89*(2), 309–326. https://doi.org/10.2307/2082427

Magleby, D. B., Nelson, C. J., & Westlye, M. C. (2011). The myth of the independent voter revisited. In P. Sniderman & B. Highton (Eds.), *Facing the challenge of democracy: Explorations in the analysis of public opinion and political participation* (pp. 238–266). Princeton University Press.

Marcus, G. E., Neuman, W. R., & MacKuen, M. (2000). *Affective intelligence and political judgment*. University of Chicago Press.

Mason, L. (2018). *Uncivil agreement: How politics became our identity*. University of Chicago Press.

McConahay, J. B. (1986). Modern racism, ambivalence, and the modern racism scale. In J. F. Dovidio & S. L. Gaertner (Eds.), *Prejudice, discrimination, and racism* (pp. 91–125). Academic Press.

Miller, A. H., Wattenberg, M. P., & Malanchuk, O. (1986). Schematic assessments of presidential candidates. *American Political Science Review, 40*(2), 521–540. https://doi.org/10.2307/1958272

Mshvenieradze, T. (2013). Logos ethos and pathos in political discourse. *Theory and Practice in Language Studies, 3*(11), 1939–1945. https://doi.org/10.4304/tpls.3.11.1939-1945

Myers, T., Allen, C., & Barrera, E. (2022, October 19). Rubio, Demings Tussle in Senate campaign's only debate but no knockouts. *WGCU*. https://news.wgcu.org/2022-10-19/rubio-demings-tussle-in-senate-campaigns-only-debate-but-no-knockouts

Painter, D. L. (2015). Online political public relations and trust: Differential source and interactivity effects in the 2012 presidential campaign. *Public Relations Review, 41*, 801–808. https://doi.org/10.1016/j.pubrev.2015.06.012

Painter, D. L., Fernandes, J., Mahone, J., & Al Nashmi, E. (2014). Social network sites andinteractivity in campaign 2012. In J. A. Hendricks, & D. Schill (Eds.), *Presidential campaigning and social media* (pp. 185–197). Oxford University Press.

Panagopoulos, C. (2016). All about that base: Changing campaign strategies in US presidential elections. *Party Politics, 22*(2), 179–190. https://doi.org/10.1177/1354068815605676

Perrin, A. (2020, October 15). *23% of users in U.S. say social media led them to change views on an issue; some cite Black Lives Matter*. Pew Research Center. www.pewresearch.org/fact-tank/2020/10/15/23-of-users-in-us-say-social-media-led-them-to-change-views-on-issue-some-cite-black-lives-matter/

Pew Research Center. (2021, August 12). *Deep divisions in Americans' views of nation's racial history – and how to address it*. www.pewresearch.org/politics/2021/08/12/deep-divisions-in-americans-views-of-nations-racial-history-and-how-to-address-it/

Pew Research Center. (2023). *Views about abortion among adults in Florida*. www.pewresearch.org/religion/religious-landscape-study/state/florida/views-about-abortion/

Powers, S. (2022, August 5). Counter-counter-counter punch: New Marco Rubio ad continues policing attack. *Florida Politics*. https://floridapolitics.com/archives/544243-counter-counter-counter-punch-new-marco-rubio-ad-continues-policing-attack/

Schaeffer, K. & Van Green, T. (2022, November 3). *Key facts about U.S. voter priorities ahead of the 2022 midterm elections*. Pew Research center. www.pewresearch.org/fact-tank/2022/11/03/key-facts-about-u-s-voter-priorities-ahead-of-the-2022-midterm-elections/

Shearer, E. (2021, January 12). *More than eight-in-ten Americans get news from digital devices.* Pew Research Center. www.pewresearch.org/fact-tank/2021/01/12/more-than-eight-in-ten-americans-get-news-from-digital-devices/

Suffolk University Political Research Center. (2022, September 21). *Poll: DeSantis leads governor's race as Rubio edges Demings in senate bid.* www.suffolk.edu/news-featu res/news/2022/09/21/17/28/2022-florida-poll

Swim, J. K., Aikin, K. J., Hall, W. S., & Hunter, B. A. (1995). Sexism and racism: Old-fashioned and modern prejudices. *Journal of Personality and Social Psychology, 68*(2), 199–214. https://doi.org/10.1037/0022-3514.68.2.199

Tawfik, N. (2022, November 11). Ron DeSantis: How the Republican governor conquered Florida. *BBC.* www.bbc.com/news/world-us-canada-63565224

Triadafilopoulos, T. (1999). Politics, speech and the art of persuasion: Toward an Aristotelian conception of the public sphere. *Journal of Politics, 61*(3), 741–757. https://doi.org/10.2307/2647826

West, E. A., & Iyengar, S. (2020). Partisanship as a social identity: Implications for polarization. *Political Behavior, 44*(2), 807–838. https://doi.org/10.1007/s11 109-020-09637-y

# 12

## THE CENTRALITY OF CITIZEN-AS-CONSUMER

A Study of the 2022 Texas Midterms and the Failing Concept of the Marketplace of Ideas in a Digital Era

*Zoë Hess Carney and Rita Kirk*

The Texas 2022 midterm campaign season was historic—in its spending and efforts, if not its outcome. Texas candidates for governor spent more money in the 2022 election cycle than ever—with Democrat Beto O'Rourke raising $50.21 million and Republican Greg Abbott spending $69.63 million (AdImpact, 2023). In Congressional races, funds were focused on South Texas, with almost $40 million spent on advertising in majority Hispanic Districts 15, 28, and 34 alone (Alvey, 2022). The results were unremarkable—neither a "Red Wave" nor a "Blue Wave" came to fruition in the Congressional profile, yet Texas Republicans held all statewide offices. At the same time, Democrats kept two necessary House seats in South Texas. The urban/rural divide continued as cities remained blue, while rural areas and most suburbs remained red. Why, then, would the campaign strategies of the 2022 Texas midterm elections beg a closer look? Because midterm elections are the proving grounds for techniques and strategies that may later be applied to national races. Running for office in Texas is akin to a national race with multiple media markets, a diverse landscape, and engrained and competing visions for the future. With Texas holding 59 electoral votes and two potential Republican presidential candidates, Governor Greg Abbott and Senator Ted Cruz, as well as a growing Democratic base, it is instructive to understand how these races differed from previous campaigns—the difference, in this case, being a shift of funds and focus to digital advertising, particularly on Facebook and Google. Between 2018 and 2022, there was an approximate 144% national increase in campaign spending, with digital spending making up 15% of that total (Edgerton, 2022).

DOI: 10.4324/9781003440833-16

This chapter focuses on digital advertising, using the 2022 midterm elections in Texas—and specifically the highly contentious gubernatorial campaign—to illuminate a gap in our understanding of how political persuasion works in the current climate. Considering how campaigns and citizens use online spaces to engage with campaign advertisements, this essay argues that in the digital market landscape, internet users are not viewed as citizens or even voters but rather as consumers within a "marketplace of ideas." The marketplace of ideas is an ideal that, since popularized in Justice Oliver Wendell Holmes Jr.'s dissent in *Abrams v. United States,* 250 U.S. 616 (1919), has captured the hearts and minds of many free speech advocates and helped extend speakers' rights in U.S. free speech law, as it relied on the logic that within a marketplace of ideas, good speech will win out.

We contend that this optimistic analogy fails within online political campaigns, where political ideas are commercialized and sold to technology platforms. Most citizens are targeted by advertisements, consuming what is shown to them—rarely weighing the merits of political ideas. The majority of Americans do not follow the news closely, and that number is trending down. According to a Gallup/Knight Foundation poll (Fioroni & Reinhart, 2021), 56% of Americans reported paying a great deal of attention to national news, whereas 33% reported paying attention in December of 2021. Those who do tune in are inclined to tune into highly polarized politics; and the majority of Americans—those who do not pay close attention to national news—come into contact with political news through social media or political ads. These political touchpoints that reach the non-engaged is often click-bait journalism meant to evoke outrage and fear (Mercieca, 2024). As Parsons (2020) aptly argues, the Supreme Court's insistence that good ideas prevail over bads ones does not align with reality.

This essay begins with an overview of the digital marketing landscape, including how campaigns approach advertising online and insights into the 2022 midterm election. It then examines the digital campaign ecosystem within U.S. political thought on free speech, drawing connections between the Supreme Court's guiding metaphor of the marketplace of ideas and contemporary campaign practices. This study indicates that the metaphor, when considered within a digital era, devalues speech while it purports to sustain it and weakens the role of the citizen within a democracy. Instead of garnering civic discourse and providing a competition of diverse ideas, it coalesces power, as Alphabet and Meta both rely heavily on publishing paid ads. In conclusion, this study highlights the need to rethink the role of digital media in political campaigns and to develop new strategies that prioritize active citizenship and democratic participation.

## The Digital Marketing Landscape

The landscape of digital marketing is vast, consisting of both paid and search advertisements that appear in many places online—including emails, search pages, banners on webpages, and social media news feeds. These advertisements target audiences in ways traditional television and radio do not, and they are almost ubiquitous in their placement. We know that advertisements work differently online and offline. For instance, television ads are more likely to attack opponents than Facebook ads; Facebook ads contain less issue content than television ads; and Facebook ads are more easily identifiable as partisan and are more ideologically polarized than television ads (Fowler et al., 2021). Each of these findings informs us of how candidates and citizens communicate and engage with one another. Technology companies are actively involved in U.S. electoral political processes because they reap revenue from advertisements and because their relationship to political processes increases the usage of their products (Kreiss & McGregor, 2016). In a rapidly changing campaign environment with a significant increase in digital campaigning, it is essential to understand how the move to online marketing alters our schema for politics, democratic practices, and citizenship.

Digital marketing includes two aspects: direct response and persuasive advertising. In direct response, campaigns seek immediate action from audience members, such as filling in their-contact information or donating their time or finances. In addition to providing campaigns with voter outreach and donor information, campaigns use data to refine campaign messaging and target outreach efforts. Per AdImpact (2022), in October 2022, almost half of the total digital campaign spending ($47.8 million) was directed to fundraising—building voter and donor lists online and requesting donations. Analyzing data from these lists helps campaigns identify critical issues that resonate with potential supporters to craft their messages. Later in the campaign season, strategists move their focus from direct response marketing to persuasive advertising. Where direct response advertising seeks and immediate response, persuasive advertising builds a case for the candidate or attacks the other candidates.

Nationally, according to AdImpact (2023), 980 million campaign dollars were spent on digital media in the 2022 midterm cycle, with most ads placed on Alphabet (which includes YouTube and Google search ads) and Meta (which includes Facebook and Instagram). Across the nation, gubernatorial races spent more than ever before, with the Texas Governor's race placing sixth in line as the most expensive gubernatorial races ever (AdImpact, 2023). When considering the digital campaign strategies Abbott and O'Rourke used in this election cycle, it would be impossible to uncover all the ways campaign messages were spread online or the effects of those messages. However, it is clear that Alphabet and

Meta were the most prominent players in digital campaign spending across the board (Fowler et al., 2023).

In 2018, both Google and Meta published ad libraries that archived every paid advertisement used on their sites. These libraries provide the most comprehensive view into the digital campaign landscape available. Google and Meta's respective libraries provide data alongside each ad in their libraries, such as how much the ads cost and how many times the advertisements were viewed alongside general demographic information such as where the ads were shown geographically and across which platforms, age categories of audience members, and, on Meta, also the gender of audience members. Mining these libraries is not without its difficulties. The libraries are uneven in the information they share, and neither Google nor Meta categorizes their advertisements by election or office, making it challenging to analyze advertisements across technology companies and platforms. Moreover, the information the libraries present is not easily interpreted. For instance, when filtering advertisements by the most viewed (or with the most impressions) at the top of the search, multiple entries of the same video will appear; it is unclear whether the audience total is the number presented in one ad description, or if each ad has a distinct audience that should be combined with the ad descriptions of identical ads. The same issue occurs when trying to find the amount spent per ad (always presented as a range). If there are multiple identical ads, it is unclear whether the candidate spent 125 thousand dollars or 150 thousand dollars for that particular ad or that amount times four. As imprecise as the data is, it is possible to access all paid advertisements published on Alphabet and Meta platforms, which provides insight into real-time campaign strategies. The fact that the data are difficult to ascertain, though, hints at the larger problem of how political persuasion is working.

Both Google and Meta have redefined how we interact with the internet, digital marketing, and data analytics. While Google's dominance in search and advertising is well-documented, Meta has emerged as a formidable challenger with its social media platform ecosystem and continues to lead the market in political campaign advertising. As such, political campaigns navigate the strengths and challenges of Alphabet and Meta to maximize their online presence and reach their target audiences. Campaigns use paid search marketing and search engine optimization to attract consumption of, or participation with, their product. In doing so, citizens navigate a new way to encounter campaign messages. These messages are sold like products but largely unregulated and protected by the Federal government like political speech. One way to understand and evaluate the burgeoning relationship between citizens and digital campaign advertising is through the legal thought that made it possible.

## The Marketplace of Ideas: The Supreme Court's Guiding Free Speech Metaphor

The law, legal and rhetorical scholar James Boyd White (1985) reminds us, is fluid and abstract—it is through the authoritative voice of the Supreme Court that the public understands its meaning; indeed, the judges' words constitute the community by which the law works. Rather than being an objective list of rules, the law is formed through judicial opinion, an interpretation of that law. In writing their opinions, judges bring life to the law and enact "a way of imagining and participating in the world," or at least in the community constituted by shared laws (White, 1989, p. 697). Political actors must accept or argue against the rulings of judges. Their opinions cannot be ignored because legal interpretations are central to how citizens function together as a society. For instance, the Constitution brought officials—the President, the Supreme Court, Congress—into existence, and their limits and powers, as well as their relationship to citizens, continue to be refined and reinterpreted through judges (White, 1992, p. 669). Because of this function of legal language, the free speech as a "marketplace of ideas" has become a heuristic for how American imagine free speech will function.

The idea that would later evolve into the "marketplace of ideas" can be traced to 1644 when John Milton wrote and distributed, *Areopagitica.* A response to an English ordinance that required authors to be granted a license from the government before their work could be published, Milton argued that such a law would not only fail in its effort to suppress "scandalous, seditious and libelous books," it would also cause immense harm, discouraging "all learning, and the stop of truth, not only by disexercising and blunting our abilities in what we know already, but by hindering and cropping the discovery that might be yet further made both in religious and civil wisdom" (Milton, 1644, para. 2). In other words, to Milton, the licensing requirement was profoundly anti-truth. Two centuries later, John Stuart Mill (1859) likened "silencing the expression of opinion" to evil against humanity (p. 31). Mill (1859) argued, similarly to Milton, that to deprive the public of a correct opinion disallows the opportunity of "exchanging error for truth" (p. 31). If a wrong opinion were to surface, according to Mill, this too is advantageous. Without its publication, the public would lose "the clearer perception and livelier impression of truth, produced by its collision with error" (Mill, 1859, p. 31). While Mill was more liberal in his interpretation of free speech than Milton, both thinkers promoted the idea that intellectual progress can only be made if people are allowed to express themselves and that it is through the testing of ideas that the ideas' worthiness can be upheld or rejected.

In the early twentieth century, Justice Oliver Wendell Holmes extended the ideas of Mill and Milton by transposing their concept into economic terms, creating the "marketplace of ideas." The marketplace of ideas functions as an analogy, drawing on the more familiar to explain the less apparent (Fahnestock, 2011). In this case, Holmes illuminated the somewhat abstract concept of "free speech" by contextualizing it within a capitalistic marketplace where public members select the most valuable ideas. In a dissenting opinion on the Supreme Court case *Abrams v. United States* (1919), Holmes argued that a "free trade in ideas" leads to the "ultimate good desired" and that "the best test of truth is the power of the thought to get itself accepted in the competition of the market" (p. 250 U.S. 630). That is, when ideas are tested against one another, the best ones will win; therefore, the government should not constrain political speech.

The metaphor of the marketplace of ideas, propelled by a consumerist society, has become the cornerstone of free speech in the United States. It has been invoked in numerous legal cases, demonstrating its continued relevance and importance. Hopkins (1996) wrote that justices had used the metaphor to "bolster free expression in virtually every area of First Amendment jurisprudence" (p. 41). Undergirding the analogy is the assumption that the market will, over time, self-correct in determining appropriate courses of action. Implicit in Holmes's argument are several assumptions: that everyone has access to the marketplace; that the marketplace is neutral, thus allowing truth to stand out among its competition; and that the public, within the marketplace, is capable not only of knowledgeable participation but also the ability to distinguish between truth and error. The marketplace of ideas, as conceived by Justice Oliver Wendell Holmes in the pre-digital era, helped form a national imaginary based on the ideal of a free and open exchange of ideas, where individuals could organize and discuss controversial ideas without fear of persecution or censorship by the Federal government.

In the digital age, the marketplace expands, offering the potential to reach a much wider audience and circulate an even greater range of voices and perspectives. Candidates could interact directly with citizens nationwide and create forums for meaningful dialogue. However, this potential has yet to be realized in contemporary political advertising. Candidates target their audiences, which results in a lack of exposure to diverse viewpoints. Dark-money groups produce untraceable advertisements. Citizen trust dwindles, and voting is suppressed. That was not its goal. In a legal history of the marketplace of ideas metaphor, Stanley Ingber (1984) noted that "in addition to its usefulness in the search for truth and knowledge, the marketplace came to be perceived by courts and scholars as essential to effective popular participation in government" (p. 3). In the digital campaign space, the analogy legitimizes the prioritization of campaign capital and citizen polarization over the idea of truth competing against falsehood or valuable ideas against lesser ideas. The competition is between the campaigns, with little room for discourse comparing the ideas presented within the campaigns. The voice of the candidate is valued at the expense of the citizen.

## 2022 Midterm Election Problem One: A Crowded, Outraged Mediascape

Between October 28 and November 1, 2022, an advertisement paid for by Greg Abbott reached between 300,000 and 350,000 people on Meta. The ad featured the caption "Beto O'Rourke wants to DEFUND & DISMANTLE the police. I signed a law defunding cities that defund our police. I will always PROTECT our law enforcement officers" (Texans for Greg Abbott, 2022). It included a video of O'Rourke praising Black Lives Matter and discussing plans to dismantle police forces.

At the same time, O'Rourke's campaign ran a separate ad reaching between 100,000 and 500,000 Meta users, which included the caption: "Greg Abbott is taking million dollar checks from corporate executives and special interests—the very people who have helped him implement his extreme, radical, and dangerous agenda" (Beto for Texas, 2022, para. 2). These examples represent a microcosm of the advertising landscape in this election: ads were driven by fear, rarely engaged with opposing viewpoints due to limited overlap in messaging, and were targeted using sophisticated algorithms, ensuring users were mostly exposed to content that aligned with their political preferences while avoiding ads from opposing candidates.

The metaphor of the marketplace of ideas is not a particularly practical guide for free speech because of the nature of the marketplace where much of this speech exists—the internet. The marketplace of ideas assumes that citizens will access different opinions and weigh them against one another, but it is a false assumption. On the one hand, citizens are bombarded with too much information to be able to grapple with any profound ideas. On the other hand, citizens lack agency in their campaign-consuming experience as technology companies make the rules about how their information will be shared and used, where ads will be placed and by whom, and how this speech will be regulated. Studies show that the Facebook ranking algorithm is biased toward the extremes (Jingnan & Bond, 2023). Only keen attention to how a user is interacting—being careful not to like, or use an angry emoji, or watch a video, and share a post—will protect users from being served political content meant to bait them (Mercieca, 2019). Because of technology biases, particularly in Google and Meta, the ideal presented by the marketplace metaphor in which citizens encounter multiple points of view and choose the most worthwhile is a phantom—albeit persuasive—driving decisions regarding internet regulation.

The mediascape is crowded, with messages fighting for attention. Estimates show that average consumers are exposed to many ads; according to Vangelovski (2022), that number ranges between 6,000 to 10,000 advertisements daily. It is impossible for citizens to absorb, much less critically weigh, even a fraction of the political messages. They likely do not even often focus on advertisements that come through on their screens with singular attention. According to Frank Maguire (2022), 64% of adults use a second device while watching TV, and approximately 75% of consumers watch video content on mute throughout their day (Kirkland, 2021). Relatedly, over half of the 16-to-34-year-olds who watch TV use captions while doing so, and on average, most people are more likely to consume videos on their phones, TVs, and computers if captions are enabled than if they are not (Kirkland, 2021). As such, campaigns must continue implementing new strategies to gain the attention of consumers.

Citizens' political ad consumption is at the whim of media technology companies whose design, algorithms, and policies influence the type of messages users encounter and how they encounter them. The variables within the media itself create multiple opportunities for the failure of the marketplace of ideas. For instance, Google advertising is powered due to its sheer company size and its primary identity as a search engine. Despite its vastness and the variety of its products and platforms, the word "Google" is often used interchangeably with the generic noun "search engine" and the verb "search." This means that while Google's advertising platform, with ads placed on Maps, Gmail, YouTube, and other services, as a primary source of revenue, users still widely trust Google as a search engine. This trust is critical to Google's power, as internet users approach it as a neutral platform. As noted by Schultheiß (2021), studies show that search engine users have a high level of trust in search engines in general and in Google. Trust in a search engine is a significant factor for campaign messaging, as it is through search engines that most Americans seek information (Robertson et al., 2019).

Public trust in a search engine does not, on its face, threaten the value of the marketplace of ideas as a guiding principle for legal decisions about how political speech be regulated. However, search engines are persuasive by design. For instance, the position of information on search engine results influences consumer behavior, as users pay more attention to higher-ranked results (Draws et al., 2021). This is particularly relevant for understanding campaign advertising because paid placements are usually ranked higher than organic campaign messages. It is a rare searcher who goes past one or two pages of results. While there are search engines that provide more robust results up front, they do not match Google's power as a name brand.

Moreover, studies indicate that not only do users engage with results that are positioned higher, but these results can also have a cognitive influence on users. If highly ranked results are biased toward a certain viewpoint, users shift their attitudes to align with the search results; a phenomenon coined the search engine manipulation effect (Draws et al., 2021). Furthermore, search engine bias extends past search result positions. According to Hu et al. (2019), the snippets that appear under Google Search results are also persuasive and somewhat manipulative. Google snippets tend to distort, by way of amplification, partisan views communicated in the web pages they represent, which could influence how Google searchers consume and understand political information (Hu et al., 2019). Search result positions and biased Google snippets are but two examples of ways that search engines complicate the concept of the marketplace of ideas. There are other areas of communication bias, such as predictive text in searching; placement of ads; the language used; search engine optimization, and so on. We are left with a highly trusted search engine working persuasively while it is widely understood as a neutral tool.

Facebook and Instagram, Meta's platforms that publish political ads, reveal other media biases. For instance, there is heightened trust among networked individuals with like-minded groups of friends on Facebook and Instagram, and ads are most persuasive when shared by friends. A study by the American Press Institute (2017, para. 4) revealed that

> people who see an article from a trusted sharer, but one written by an unknown media source, have much more trust in the information than people who see the same article that appears to come from a reputable media source shared by a person they do not trust.

That is, Facebook users care more about who shares the information than the creator of the information, and if they trust the sharer, they are more likely to recommend or follow the original content creator.

Meta can influence political messaging by microtargeting ads to users based on algorithmic interest classification (Thorson et al., 2021). Because of Meta's advertising policy, users are, in a very practical sense, unable to compare political messages against one another because they only receive political ads targeted to them. Meta also influences political messages in ways similar to Google search—it selects which stories show up on users' news feeds, which is biased toward a point of view. It also permits foreign and domestic trolls to encourage outrage on the left and right and encourage citizens not to vote (Kim, 2020). Foreign interference into the American marketplace of ideas and elections, Nunziato (2019) notes, is a uniquely modern problem. Social networking wields power over political advertising to such an extent that it weakens the notion that citizens are considering varying political ideas against each other to find the strongest one.

## Midterm 2022 Problem Two: Questionable Information

The month before the midterm election, U.S. Representative Joaquin Castro, alongside a coalition of Latino organizations, called on social media platforms to weed out electoral misinformation aimed at Latino communities (Downen, 2022). At the same meeting, Brenda Castillo, president and CEO of the National

Hispanic Media Association, spoke on behalf of Latinos, saying, "We are being lied to and discouraged to exercise our right to vote on a massive scale." Calling out Facebook, Castillo said, "people like Mark Zuckerberg are doing very little while they profit" (Downen, 2022, para. 3). It makes sense that citizens are concerned about transparency and truth. Other than the FEC's regulation that political ads use disclaimers and a few state regulations, mostly to do with disclosure requirements, internet service providers themselves function as regulatory boards (NCSL, 2024). That is, as private companies, Google and Meta have the right to take down (or keep up, as the case may be) false political advertising.

Internet users find it difficult to know what information to trust. According to a University of Texas poll conducted in the month prior to the election, 51% of those surveyed thought the misinformation was "extremely serious," with another 27% saying it was "somewhat serious" (The Texas Politics Project, 2022). These results cut across party lines and the urban-suburban-rural spectrum, revealing that the more strongly the citizens identified with the party, the more likely they held strong opinions concerning the seriousness of the problem. Not knowing whom to trust is not unique to the digital marketplace. In the Texas midterm gubernatorial election, for instance, O'Rourke's campaign steered clear of attack ads to motivate audience members to vote against Abbott; dark-money groups, on the other hand, did not. In a particularly hard-hitting series of attack ads, a group called *Coulda Been Worse LLC* skirted Texas state finance laws by registering as a Limited Liability Corporation under Delaware laws, and spent $25 million in advertisements against Abbott and $5.7 million against Texas Attorney General Ken Paxton (Morris, 2022). Unlike traditional PACs, the group was not required to disclose its donors immediately. The Texas Election Code defines a "political committee" quite broadly: "two or more persons acting in concert with a principal purpose of accepting political contributions or making political expenditures." These groups must register with the Texas Ethics Commission and follow the state's disclosure requirements. Questions raised about *Coulda Been Worse LLC* cannot be determined since there is insufficient information to determine whether it meets the state's definition.

Journalists likely assumed that since advertisements were produced, press conference footage used, and airtime was purchased, there would be a trail to find the identity of the financier. Reporters from around the state searched through those clues to no avail. The company, headed in Arlington, Virginia, only provided that Michael Waters was its executive director and Icon International, a Connecticut-based firm, was its media buyer (Morris, 2022). Neither of them took media inquiries. Some scorned Delaware as a state with lax corporate laws which became the source of online attacks by posters assuming that the funder was out of state. Thus, the rumors of "dark money" influence in the Texas political campaign raised the profile of the ads among online conspiracy sites.

**262** Media Messages in the 2022 Midterm Election

While *Coulda Been Worse LLC* bought TV ads, the internet provides an even richer ground for authorship to be hidden and facts obscured, as users have endless opportunities to generate content. The 2022 election did, in fact, showcase how dishonesty can affect elections. George Santos, elected as a U.S. Representative from New York, grossly distorted his biography during his campaign. In many instances, the facts of his life and career were simply fictitious. Still, Speaker of the House McCarthy appointed him to serve on committees, including the Science Committee. After all, the First Amendment widely protects political speech, even when it is false—though the Supreme Court has limited both defamation and fraud, in part on the basis of falsity (Congressional Research Service, 2022). Technology reporter Cecilia Kang (2022) reported that the effects of online posts generated three main fears among voters during the midterm elections, nationally: "continued falsehoods about rampant election fraud; threats of violence and citizen policing of elections; and divisive posts on health and social policies that have become central to political campaigns" (para. 4). The lack of transparency in digital spaces is unique, and it leads to confusion and distrust among the public.

### Conclusion: Is There Room for Citizenship within the Digital Marketplace?

In *Augustus*, a book by Adrian Goldsworthy (2014), the story is told of political life in Rome prior to the development of political parties, at least as currently conceived. The most important qualities a candidate could offer were ones of character. That man's past behavior became an indicator, but perceived behavior also factored into an office seeker's ethos. One mark of perceived character consisted of assessing who surrounded a candidate. Interestingly, an office seeker wore a whitened toga known as the *toga candidate,* thus marking himself as a candidate. Early in the morning, those supporting a candidate would gather to walk with him to the Forum. This very public expression of support enabled viewers to assess initial support and the growth or diminishment of supporters over time.

Then, as now, voters want to be a part of the winning coalition. Like the Romans, contemporary citizens trust whom their friends' trust. But there are key differences. In the digital marketplace, citizens are positioned as consumers. They are not interacting with the candidate and the candidate's ideas; they are liking and sharing. Sometimes they are outraged; sometimes, the outrage is created by trolls placing hyper-emotional misinformation on their newsfeeds, causing widespread confusion and increased polarization. The Texas 2022 midterm election was a microcosm of this phenomenon—20 million dollars were raised in the gubernatorial race alone, much of which was used on political advertising. But to what end?

The marketplace of ideas shapes our political and social landscape. It is also flawed. Justice Brandeis argued in the *Whitney v. California,* 274 U.S. 357 (1927) case that if there is time to expose falsehood and fallacies through discussion and education, more speech should be employed rather than enforced silence. In the digital marketplace, citizens are targeted with advertisements, thereby exposure to specific ideas and creating a situation where only a select few truly grapple with opposing viewpoints. While the digital marketplace values a free flow of information on the internet, it can reduce the ability of citizens to access competing political ideas and weigh them against each other. While the marketplace of ideas metaphor has been useful to help legal minds consider the role of speech, it does not offer a particularly useful heuristic for the citizen who must navigate a mediated political landscape.

## References

Abrams v. United States, 250 U.S. 616 (1919). *Oyez.* www.oyez.org/cases/1900-1940/250us616

AdImpact. (2022, October 10). Breakdown of digital political ad spending for the 2022 midterms. https://adimpact.com/blog/breakdown-of-digital-political-ad-spend-for-the-2022-midterms/

AdImpact. (2023, February 28). AdImpact's 2022 year in review. https://adimpact.com/2022-cycle-in-review/

Alvey, R. (2022, November 8). GOP focuses spending in South Texas as it vies for U.S. House control in 2022 midterms. *Dallas Morning News.* www.dallasnews.com/news/politics/2022/11/08/gop-focuses-spending-in-south-texas-as-it-vies-for-us-house-control-in-2022-midterms/

American Press Institute (2017, March 20). *'Who shared it?' How Americans decide what news to trust on social media.* www.americanpressinstitute.org/publications/reports/survey-research/trust-social-media/

Beto for Texas. (2022). *Meta ad library.* https://www.facebook.com/ads/library/?id=846521619858655

Congressional Research Service (2022, August 1). False speech and the first amendment: Constitutional limits on regulating misinformation. https://crsreports.congress.gov/product/pdf/IF/IF12180

Downen, R. (2022, October 13). U. S. Rep. Joaquin Castro, Latino groups warn about rampant misinformation targeting Spanish speakers ahead of the election. *The Texas Tribune.* www.texastribune.org/2022/10/13/spanish-latino-misinformation-2022-elections/

Draws, T., Tintarev, N., Gadiraju, U., Bozzon, A., & Timmermans, B. (2021). This is not what we ordered: exploring why biased search result rankings affect user attitudes on debated topics. In *Proceedings of the 44th International ACM SIGIR Conference on Research and Development in Information Retrieval* (pp. 295–305). Association for Computing Machinery https://doi.org/10.1145/3404835.3462851

Edgerton, A. (2022, October 5). Facebook is the only game in town for digital political ads. *Bloomberg.* www.bloomberg.com/news/articles/2022-10-05/facebook-is-politicians-last-resort-for-2022-election-ads

**264** Media Messages in the 2022 Midterm Election

Fahnestock, J. (2011). *Rhetorical style: The uses of language in persuasion.* Oxford University Press.

Fioroni, S., & Reinhart, R. J. (2022, February 17). *Americans' attention to national news lowest in four years.* Knight Foundation. https://knightfoundation.org/articles/americans-attention-to-national-news-lowest-in-four-years/

Fowler, E., Franz, M., Neumann, M., Ridout, T., & Yao, J. (2023, February 20). Digital advertising in the 2022 midterms. *The Forum.* https://doi.org/10.1515/for-2023-2006

Fowler, E. F., Franz, M. M., Martin, G. J., Peskowitz, Z., & Ridout, T. N. (2021). Political advertising online and offline. *American Political Science Review, 115*(1), 130–149. https://doi.org/10.1017/S0003055420000696

Goldsworthy, A. (2014). *Augustus: First Emperor of Rome.* Yale University Press.

Hopkins, W. W. (1996). The Supreme Court defines the marketplace of ideas. *Journalism & Mass Communication Quarterly, 73*(1), 40–52. https://doi.org/10.1177/1077699 09607300105

Hu, D., Jiang, S., E. Robertson, R., & Wilson, C. (2019). Auditing the partisanship of Google search snippets. *WWW '19: The World Wide Web Conference* (pp. 693–704). https://doi.org/10.1145/3308558.3313654

Ingber, S. (1984). The marketplace of ideas: A legitimizing myth. *Duke Law Journal, 1984*(1), 1–91. https://doi.org/10.2307/1372344

Jingnan, H., & Bond, S. (2023, January 27). New study shows just how Facebook's algorithm shapes conservative and liberal bubbles. *NPR.* www.npr.org/2023/07/27/1190383104/new-study-shows-just-how-facebooks-algorithm-shapes-conservative-and-liberal-bub

Kang, C. (2022, September 24). The most dominant toxic election narratives online. *The New York Times.* www.nytimes.com/2022/09/23/technology/midterm-elections-misinformation.html

Kim, Y. M. (2020, March 5). New evidence shows how Russia's election interference has gotten more brazen. *Brennan Center for Justice.* www.brennancenter.org/our-work/analysis-opinion/new-evidence-shows-how-russias-election-interference-has-gotten-more

Kirkland, C. (2021, November 4). Why captioning is becoming an integral part of video ad buys. *Digital News Daily.* www.mediapost.com/publications/article/368380/why-captioning-is-becoming-an-integral-part-of-vid.html

Kreiss, D., & McGregor, S. C. (2018). Technology firms shape political communication: the work of Microsoft, Facebook, Twitter, and Google with campaigns during the 2016 U.S. presidential cycle. *Political Communication, 35*(2), 155–177. https://doi.org/10.1080/10584609.2017.1364814

Maguire, F. (2022, February 10). New research: Understanding consumer behaviors during TV commercial breaks. *Sharethrough.* www.sharethrough.com/blog/new-research-understanding-consumer-behaviors-during-tv-commercial-breaks

Mercieca, J. (2019, June 5). Zocalo public square discussion on propaganda. *C-SPAN.* www.c-span.org/video/?460987-1/zocalo-public-square-discussion-propaganda

Mercieca, J. (2024, January 25). We, the political tune-outs and political junkies. *Resolute Square.* https://resolutesquare.com/articles/0GD7SJnOHO9SuWQiDW2gWC/tune-outs

Mill, J. S. (1859). *On liberty.* Project Gutenberg. www.gutenberg.org/files/34901/34901-h/34901-h.htm

Milton, J. (1644). *Areopagitica*. http://galileo.phys.virginia.edu/classes/inv_inn.usm/aero pag.htm

Morris, A. (2022, November 4). Ads against Abbott, other Texas Republicans by Coulda Been Worse test campaign ethics law. *The Dallas Morning News*. www.dallasnews. com/news/elections/2022/11/04/ads-against-abbott-other-texas-republicans-by-cou lda-been-worse-test-campaign-ethics-law/

NCSL. (2024). Digital political ads. www.ncsl.org/elections-and-campaigns/digital-politi cal-ads

Nunziato, D. C. (2019). The marketplace of ideas online. *Notre Dame Law Review*, *94*(4), 1519–1584. https://scholarship.law.nd.edu/ndlr/vol94/iss4/2/

Parsons, G. M. (2020). Fighting for attention: Democracy, free speech, and the marketplace of ideas. *Minnesota Law Review*, *104*(5), 2157–2256. https://minneso talawreview.org/article/fighting-for-attention-democracy-free-speech-and-the-mark etplace-of-ideas/

Robertson, R. E., Jiang, S., Lazer, D., & Wilson, C. (2019). Auditing autocomplete: Suggestion networks and recursive algorithm interrogation. *Proceedings of the 10th ACM conference on web science* (p. 235–244). https://doi.org/10.1145/3292 522.3326047

Schultheiß, S., & Lewandowski, D. (2021). Misplaced trust? The relationship between trust, ability to identify commercially influenced results, and search engine preference. *Journal of Information Science*. https://doi.org/10.1177/01655515211014157

Texans for Greg Abbott. (2022, November 1). *Meta ad library*. www.facebook.com/ads/ library/?id=651371079672060

The Texas Politics Project at the University of Texas at Austin. (2022, October). *2022 Election problems: Misinformation spread on social media*. The University of Texas at Austin. https://texaspolitics.utexas.edu/set/2022-election-problems-misinformat ion-spread-social-media-october-2022

Thorson, K., Cotter, K., Medeiros, M., & Pak, C. (2021). Algorithmic inference, political interest, and exposure to news and politics on Facebook. *Information, Communication & Society, 24*(2), 183–200. https://doi.org/10.1080/1369118X.2019.1642934

Vangelovski, S. (29 September 2022). *The billion dollar political ad problem*. Sharethrough. www.sharethrough.com/blog/2-strategies-to-grow-your-political-adve rtising-strategy-for-the-2022-election

White, J. B. (1985). Law as rhetoric, rhetoric as law: The arts of cultural and communal life. *The University of Chicago Law Review*, *52*(3), 684–702.

White, J. B. (1989). Judging the judges: three opinions. *West Virginia Law Review, 92*, 697–719.

White, J. B. (1992). "The Constitution as Literature." In L. W. Levy & K. L. Karst (Eds.), *Encyclopedia of the American Constitution* (pp. 105–107). Macmillan.

Whitney v. California. (n.d.). *Oyez*. 274 U.S. 357 (1927). www.oyez.org/cases/1900-1940/274us357

# 13

## GENDERED TREATMENT IN THE COMMUNICATION STRATEGY OF A FEMALE GUBERNATORIAL CANDIDATE

*Joyce H. Glasscock*

In 2022, Laura Kelly, a Democratic governor in the red state of Kansas, endeavored to hold the governor's office against a Trump-endorsed Republican who had been elected statewide three times as attorney general and boasted a record of handily winning in a state dominated by Republicans. Kelly was one of 25 women running for governor nationwide in the midterm but the only Democratic gubernatorial incumbent running in a state carried by Trump in 2020 (Glueck, 2022).

Citizens faced very serious issues during the 2022 midterm election such as the lingering effects of COVID, inflation-spiked prices, a reversal of the constitutional right to abortion, and a tug-of-war over social issues. For a gubernatorial candidate running as an incumbent, a multitude of problems and issues played out in the background. These topics influenced the communication environment and were subject to attacks leveled by an opponent.

For decades, researchers have studied the communication strategies of political candidates and, specifically, how women candidates manage their campaign communications relative to gender, with feminine approaches believed to impair their chances for success. Using a well-matched, nationally watched, and hotly contested race for governor, this study applies framing theory and Functional Theory of Political Campaign Discourse (Functional Theory) to analyze gendered communications in a female versus male race for Kansas governor between incumbent Laura Kelly and challenger Derek Schmidt.

This research was undertaken to better understand a female candidate's application of gendered traits and issues in her political communication and to what extent the male candidate attacked his opponent using feminine and masculine traits and issues. Two approaches were used for gathering materials for

DOI: 10.4324/9781003440833-17

study. First, a quantitative content analysis was conducted to assess the presence of gendered issues and traits in general election campaign communication in the form of tweets, TV ads, and debate statements of Kelly. Then, Schmidt's messages on the same platforms were examined for presence of attacks, acclaims, and defenses, with attention paid to his attacks of Kelly's traits and issues relative to gender. Similar treatment occurred for TV ads sponsored by political parties and top political action committees that collaborated with the candidates' campaigns. Materials collected for analysis were drawn from the general election campaign, beginning early August and ending on Election Day, November 8, 2022.

Second, qualitative research was conducted involving interviews during the general election campaign with the governor and Kelly's campaign staff. While the election was ongoing and the outcome of the election was yet unknown, interviews with the candidate explored how she viewed gendered issues and traits, as well as treatment of her by her opponent. From these interviews, the author witnessed the campaign execute on communications strategies in response to the polling environment and in response to attacks made by Kelly's opponent.

This research considers an election's campaign climate, candidates of opposite gender, and traits and issues unique to a gubernatorial race and arrives at several compelling takeaways concerning gendered treatment in campaign communications. Among those takeaways are the importance of maintaining message focus and aligning with the lessons of political theory.

## Campaign Climate

Leading up to the August, 2022, general election in Kansas, something unexpected occurred that set the stage for the general election. On June 24, the U.S. Supreme Court overturned *Roe v. Wade,* 410 U.S. 113 (1973), which for decades had guaranteed a constitutional right to abortion. On the August 2 primary ballot in Kansas, a Republican-backed measure proposed eliminating the state's constitutional right to an abortion. More voters turned out for the primary election than expected, with women constituting 56% of total ballots cast—exceeding the 2018 general election women's turnout of 52.5% of overall ballots (TargetSmart, 2022). The ballot measure was defeated.

Polling that had favored the likely Republican candidate in the race for governor shifted enough by the August 2 primary date to put candidates Kelly and Schmidt in a dead heat, with each having a 50–50 shot of prevailing (FiveThirtyEight, 2022). For its gubernatorial face-off, the media declared Kansas a state with a "consequential midterm race" (Todd et al., 2022) considering that the next governor would have power to sign or veto restrictive abortion legislation expected to pass the Republican supermajorities in the State Senate and House.

**268** Media Messages in the 2022 Midterm Election

Kelly, the state's 48th governor and third female in the role already had prevailed in a general election for this seat. She was now defending the title. In 2018, Kansans elected Democrat Kelly in a red state against male Republican candidate Kris Kobach who "styled [himself] in Trump's anti-immigrant image" (Davis & Shear, 2019, p. 343). A conservative Republican, Kobach had won statewide twice, but fell to Kelly in his bid for governor. That 2018 matchup for governor drew similar comparisons to this 2022 race against Schmidt. The newest challenger, Schmidt, was a male conservative Republican who voters had elected and reelected to statewide office and who, in this campaign, had secured Trump's "Complete and Total Endorsement!" (Tidd, 2022).

### Gender Considerations

Kelly and Schmidt each wore the mantle of their respective party's leadership in the state: Democrat Kelly as governor and Republican Schmidt as attorney general. Each had served their respective districts in the Kansas State Senate. Now, besides party affiliation, what most obviously distinguished the two candidates in the race for governor were their genders. The gender difference was expected to influence both the style of their political communication and how voters judged their qualifications.

Research on political campaigns through a lens of gender in female versus male candidate matchups has been a topic of study since the 1980s (Blankenship & Robson, 1995; Bystrom, 2019; Carroll, 1985; Huddy & Terkildsen, 1993; Jamieson, 1995; Sullivan, 1989; Winfrey & Schnoebelen, 2019; Witt et al., 1994). At that time, prevalent feminine traits of women were described as those tending toward compassion, whereas masculine traits describing men tended toward strength. On the issue front, it was common for women to concern themselves with topics such as health care and education, while men focused on economic-related issues (Bystrom, 2019). These concepts of feminine and masculine roles and traits were derived from traditional roles in society tied to "biological and evolutionary roles of women as denizens of the home and men as hunters outside the home" (Bauer, 2013, p. 27).

Perceptions of assigned gender roles also transferred to the political arena creating a mismatch between what people expected of women and what people expected of politicians. Jamieson (1995) described the problematic double bind in which expectations of femininity for women's success in traditional roles run counter to traits expected for succeeding in public life. In the femininity/competence bind, Jamieson explained, "by requiring both femininity and competence of women in the public sphere, and then defining femininity in a way that excludes competence, the bind creates unrealizable expectations" (p. 18).

Unfortunately, voters do not perceive women as having the characteristics "most valued in political leaders such as experience and knowledge" (Bauer,

2017, p. 279), and research continues to suggest that men persist in thinking of women as less capable relative to traits important for succeeding in traditionally male domains (Hentschel et al., 2019). Mendoza and DiMaria (2019) elaborated on existing research that suggested women are penalized in male-dominated disciplines with an outcome of receiving less support due to "a poor perceived prototypical fit between their gender and the job" (p. 2). Overcoming these stereotypes through which voters still judge candidates and which reinforce the double bind for female candidates "must be negotiated through communication" (Winfrey & Schnoebelen, 2019, p. 129).

### Gendered Traits and Issues

As applied to traits and issues, the terms feminine and masculine are considered "the social construction of gender rather than mere biological difference" (Blankenship & Robson, 1995, p. 356). Further, gender stereotypes can be thought of, generally, as what men are like and what women are like (Hentschel et al., 2019), and they "distinguish the appropriate roles and behaviors for women *relative* to men" (Bauer, 2013, p. 27).

Bauer (2013) defines gender stereotypes as having attributes that are either agentic or communal, with "agentic" describing traditionally masculine qualities and "communal" describing traditionally feminine qualities. Additional descriptors of feminine stereotypes or traits include those "promoting compromise and smooth interpersonal relationships" (Schneider et al., 2016, p. 526). Hentschel et al. (2019) offer agentic features as "assertiveness, independence, instrumental competence, [and] leadership competence" (p. 1) that describe attributes including ambitious, competent, competitive, logical, and strong. They offer communal stereotypes as "concern for others, sociability, and emotional sensitivity" (p. 1) that describe attributes including communicative, likable, sympathetic, and understanding. Their comprehensive list of 46 agentic (masculine) traits and 28 communal (feminine) traits were derived from past research on the topic.

Research also applies gender to issues commonly addressed in campaigns. Examples of issues considered feminine include education, poverty, equality, LGBTQ issues (Dubosar, 2022), reproductive health care, sexual harassment (Bauer, 2013), seniors, environment, drug use, women's issues (Banwart & McKinney, 2005), family (Schneider, 2014), childcare (Dolan, 2008), general children's issues, and welfare (Bauer & Santia, 2022). Examples of issues considered masculine include budget, economy, crime, military, government distrust (Dubosar, 2022), taxes, and immigration (Banwart & McKinney, 2005).

Bystrom (2019) found that compiled research over the past 35 years—which included TV ads from female versus male matchups for governor, for Congress, and for president—shows that candidates cross domains considered both feminine and masculine in an attempt to convey their strengths most relevant for the office. Even though women run and govern in a manner more consistent with goals that are communally-oriented rather than ambition-driven (Schneider et al., 2016), advice offered to women is to promote competence on issues that matter most to voters and display masculine stereotypes as needed.

To defeat Schmidt and to negotiate lingering effects of a double bind, the challenge for Kelly was to deliver in her communication those benefits derived from feminine traits, such as likability and collaboration. Kelly also needed to lean into masculine traits and issues to communicate her experience, leadership abilities, and competence as an executive—qualities considered important for the office.

## Framing and Functions

Framing occurs when a communicator structures and delivers a message in such a way as to influence an audience's opinion on a given subject. "It is through framing that political actors shape the texts that influence or prime the agendas and considerations that people think about" (Entman, 2007, p. 165). In the context of political campaigns, frames used by candidates are critical for influencing voters and the outcome of the election. Candidates for public office work to convince voters why they are best suited for the office in terms of the qualities they bring to the role and their perspectives on issues that matter most to their would-be constituency. Their campaign communications are key for framing their strengths, not only to voters, but also to the media who, in turn, message to voters through news coverage regarding characterizations of candidates' qualifications and positions on public policy.

Studying discourse apparent in campaign messaging helps explain candidates' strategies for influencing voters. Particularly pertinent to political communication, the Functional Theory of Political Campaign Discourse was first applied to the 1996 presidential campaign as a new methodology for examining strategic campaign messaging (Brooks, 1999). Since then, Functional Theory has been applied to all types of political messaging, including debates (Benoit et al., 2007; Benoit & Rill, 2013), TV ads (Airne & Benoit, 2005), and more recently, to campaign tweets (Stein & Benoit, 2021).

Functional Theory "investigates both the functions (acclaims, attacks, defenses) and topics (policy, character) of political campaign messages" (Benoit et al., 2007, p. 77). The theory posits that these political campaign functions are relevant for developing voter preferences and are used to enhance voters' perceptions of a candidate (via acclaims), lessen an opponent's desirability (via attacks), or refute and minimize perceived downsides of a candidate (via defenses). Topics (policy and character) as advanced by Functional Theory, for purposes of this study, aligned with issues and traits previously described. Candidate messaging of topics/policy (issues) are important for understanding what positions a successful candidate will support in office; and topics/character (traits) are important for understanding the type of leader that candidate could become if elected to office.

Informed by these theories, this study seeks to understand how Kelly framed traits and issues in her campaign communications, and how she came under attack from her opponent. This research prompts the following questions:

**RQ1:** In Kelly's campaign communication, were feminine traits or masculine traits more prevalent for promoting her candidacy?

**RQ2a:** Were feminine or masculine issues more prevalent in Kelly's campaign communication?

**RQ2b:** Which issues were most prevalent in Kelly's campaign communication?

**RQ3:** Did Schmidt's campaign communication contain more attacks, acclaims, or defenses?

**RQ4:** Of Schmidt's campaign attacks on Kelly, what traits—feminine or masculine—were more frequent in his attacks?

**RQ5a:** Of Schmidt's campaign attacks on Kelly, what issues did his attacks target?

**RQ5b:** Which issues were most prevalent in Schmidt's campaign attacks on Kelly?

**RQ6:** How did Kelly and her campaign treat the issue of abortion in gendered terms in a divisive election year?

## Methods

### Research Method and Population

Quantitative Analysis

This study's quantitative content analysis assessed the presence of frames relative to gendered traits and issues in campaign communications of Kansas gubernatorial candidates, Laura Kelly and Derek Schmidt. Campaign communications that constituted the sample population included the candidates' campaign tweets; TV ads from the two candidates and prominent third parties; and candidates' debate statements. Materials collected for analysis were produced or aired during the

**272** Media Messages in the 2022 Midterm Election

general election, a period between August 3 (the first day after the primary election) and November 8, 2022 (the date of the general election).

Tweets were collected manually during the campaign from campaign Twitter accounts @LauraKellyKS and @DerekSchmidtKS. In consultation with the Kelly campaign (Communications Director, personal communication, September 27, 2022) a decision was made not to collect Facebook or Instagram posts for evaluation, given that the Kelly campaign dedicated its social media focus primarily to Twitter. Further, Stein and Benoit (2021) offer that Trump's heavy reliance in 2016 on Twitter launched that medium to its prominence as a campaign communication tool. After eliminating retweets and tweets considered irrelevant to the study as duplicates, or generic fundraising or voting appeals, the number of tweets evaluated for study totaled 638 of which 274 were Kelly's tweets and 364 were Schmidt's. The unit of analysis was each tweet. Additionally, endorsements were removed from tweets under evaluation unless the candidate added, embellished, or repeated language in their own tweet. In tweets, coders did not take into consideration any links, images, or retweeted language. Coder analysis was limited to candidates' language only.

TV ads produced for the general election by each candidate's campaign were examined. Also examined—and contributing considerably to the negative tenor of the race—were prominent TV ads aired by campaign-aligned third parties. In particular, ads aired by the Kansas Values Institute (KVI) served up negative perspectives of Schmidt by tying him to a former conservative governor with low approval ratings. Ads aired by the Republican Governors Association (RGA) reinforced Schmidt's attacks of Kelly as a liberal politician out of step with Kansans. Due to close alignment with the respective campaigns, an RGA ad was treated as a Schmidt ad, and a KVI ad was treated as a Kelly ad. TV ads produced and aired by other political action committees with minimal expenditures in the race were eliminated from study. TV ads were secured online from Washburn University's collection of Kansas political ads (Kansas Institute for Politics, n.d.-b). A total of 44 TV ads were evaluated reflecting 23 ads aired in support of Kelly (including 13 from KVI) and 21 ads aired in support of Schmidt (including 10 from RGA). Of these, two ads dated August 1 (one from KVI and one from RGA) were included in the general election evaluation. Given that both Kelly and Schmidt were expected to easily win their respective primaries on August 2, an assumption was made that the two ads dated August 1 were produced for the general election getting underway the following day. The unit of analysis was each TV ad.

The two debates evaluated for quantitative content analysis were held on September 10 at the Kansas State Fair in Hutchinson and on October 5 in Overland Park at an event organized by the Johnson County Bar Association. Video recordings of debates were secured online from Washburn University's collected Kansas candidate debates (Kansas Institute for Politics, n.d.-a) and were transcribed by the author. From the transcripts a total of 110 debate statements were evaluated—54 from Kelly and 56 from Schmidt—each a unit of analysis.

## Coding Guidance

Codesheets were created to guide coders in recording the presence of gendered traits and issues in the collected communications. Codesheets contained protocols for recording traits and issues present in all TV ads, tweets, and debate statements of Kelly, and protocols for recording functions—acclaims, attacks, and defenses—made by Schmidt, as well as gendered treatment of traits and issues present in his attacks on Kelly. Traits were adapted from the existing feminine and masculine attributes listed in the appendix of Hentschel et al. (2019). The list was expanded or narrowed based on observations during the coding process. Issues were derived from the previously discussed sources (e.g., Banwart & McKinney, 2005; Bauer, 2013; Schneider, 2014) and additional issues referenced in the Kelly-Schmidt race.

Traits were coded as feminine or masculine based on communal and agentic descriptors provided in psychology research by Hentschel et al. (2019, p. 19). Communal terms were considered those that aligned more with feminine traits; and agentic terms considered those that aligned more with masculine traits. Examples of attributes consistent with feminine traits included collaborative, likable, modest, sincere, and understanding. Attributes consistent with masculine traits included analytical, competent, competitive, decisive, and direct. Through inductive analysis of Kelly and Schmidt communications, additional terms outside of Hentschel et al. (2019) included honesty as a feminine descriptor, and determined, experienced, and qualified as agentic descriptors.

Issue keywords searched in Kelly and Schmidt communications were derived from gendered political issues discussed in multiple scholarly articles (e.g., Banwart & McKinney, 2005; Bauer, 2013; Schneider, 2014). For the purposes of this study, issues more commonly expressed as feminine were: abortion, children/families, diversity/race, drug addiction/mental health, education, health/healthcare/Medicaid, LGBTQ/transgender, poverty, seniors/Medicare/Social Security, water/environment/climate, and women's rights. Issues more commonly expressed as masculine were: agriculture, business/industry/economy (including inflation), crime, death penalty, energy, government distrust, guns/Second Amendment, highways/transportation/infrastructure, housing, illegal drugs, immigration/border, jobs/labor/workforce, taxes/budgets (including deficits), unemployment, and veterans/military/first responders. Because housing and unemployment were differently classified in the referenced literature as masculine or feminine, these issues were coded according to their application and context.

Once all campaign communications were collected and organized, two coders (one of which was the author) undertook a period of training and test coding through which the coders reviewed and amended definitions, refined categories, and revised codebooks. For intercoder reliability, the two coders independently coded tweets and TV ads from the primary campaign. There being no primary debate samples available, testing for intercoder reliability of debates used statements from the state fair debate. Tests to control for agreement by chance used Cohen's kappa and were conducted for agreement on traits, issues, and functions (attacks, acclaims, and defenses). Results returned agreement of .75 or higher for these tests, indicating suitable intercoder reliability.

### Qualitative Analysis

Qualitative feedback was obtained from two interviews conducted with Laura Kelly during the general election; five interviews conducted between August 15 and October 24 with Kelly's campaign manager or campaign communications director; and two post-election interviews with campaign staff—one on November 17 with the campaign manager and one on November 18 with the campaign communications director. In-person interviews with Kelly ran 60–90 minutes long. Questions for Kelly were open-ended and prepared in advance. Kelly's first interview focused on her biography, perceived traits and strengths as governor, and challenges she faced in her reelection. In her second interview, Kelly discussed positioning on issues, her polling strength, and perceptions of her opponent, his campaign strategy, and his treatment of her in campaign communications. With campaign staff, interviews typically ran 30 minutes long. Questions were prepared in advance, were open-ended, and often focused on specific attacks on Kelly, the campaign's intended reaction to those attacks, how polling and the candidate's input advised campaign messaging, and on what topics campaign communications would focus. In these interviews, the author secured feedback that included the candidate's intended or passive use of gendered traits and issues, strategies around gendered topics, and perspectives on the opponent's campaign communications. Responses from interviews are included in the discussion section to provide insight and context to Kelly's campaign strategies. While research overall could have been enriched with similar engagement of Schmidt and his campaign staff, an express agreement was made with Kelly that this research be undertaken exclusively with her campaign and treated confidentially through the general election to ensure she and her staff could speak freely about internal decision making that advised Kelly's campaign strategy.

## Findings

### Kelly Traits and Issues

The first research question (RQ1) sought to determine whether feminine traits or masculine traits were more prevalent for promoting Kelly's candidacy. Among a total of 280 coded traits in Kelly's communications, the overall use of masculine traits ($n = 150$, 53.6%) exceeded the use of feminine traits

Gendered Treatment in the Communication Strategy **275**

**TABLE 13.1** Chi-square Test for Kelly Traits, Feminine and Masculine, by Platform

| Gender | Tweets | | TV ads | | Debate statements | |
|---|---|---|---|---|---|---|
| | n | column % | n | column % | n | column % |
| Feminine | 99 | 48.1 | 11 | 64.7 | 20 | 35.1 |
| Masculine | 107 | 51.9 | 6 | 35.3 | 37 | 64.9 |
| Total | 206 | 100.0 | 17 | 100.0 | 57 | 100.0 |

Note. Coded traits ($n = 280$): feminine ($n = 130$; 46.4%); masculine ($n = 150$; 53.6%).
$X^2(2, 280) = 5.45$, $p = .066$.

($n = 130$, 46.4%). Among tweets, masculine traits ($n = 107$; 51.9%) were more apparent than feminine traits ($n = 99$; 48.1%). Also, among debate statements, masculine traits prevailed ($n = 37$; 64.9%) over feminine ones ($n = 20$; 35.1%). TV ads for Kelly, however, contained fewer masculine attributes ($n = 6$; 35.3%) compared to feminine attributes ($n = 11$; 64.9%). Even with these differences, a chi-square test did not reach statistical significance at $p < .05$ in the relationship among the platforms relative to use of Kelly's masculine and feminine traits ($X^2(2, 280) = 5.45$, $p = .066$). However, these results are significant at $p < .10$, and these findings (summarized in Table 13.1) suggest the relationships are worth examining further.

A difference of proportions test resulted in a statistically significant finding for Kelly's feminine and masculine traits among debate statements in the two-tailed test ($z = -1.924$, $p = .054$). Kelly's use of masculine traits in debate statements ($n = 37$) were 24.7% of evaluated communications, while feminine traits were less prominent ($n = 20$) at 15.4% of evaluated communications. This test did not result in statistically significant relationships for tweets ($z = 0.912$, $p = .362$) or TV ads ($z = 1.559$, $p = .119$).

The next two research questions asked if feminine or masculine issues were more apparent in Kelly's campaign communications (RQ2a), and which issues were most prevalent (RQ2b). Descriptive analysis (Table 13.2) found that among 528 issue references in Kelly communications, masculine issues ($n = 303$; 57.4%) were more frequently referenced than feminine ones ($n = 225$; 42.6%). For this evaluation, masculine issues were more numerous in all platforms—tweets (masculine: $n = 174$ [57.2%] compared to feminine: $n = 130$ [42.8%]); TV ads (masculine: $n = 38$ [62.3%] compared to feminine: $n = 23$ [37.7%]); and debate statements (masculine: $n = 91$ [55.8%] compared to feminine: $n = 72$ [44.2%]). Still, a chi-square test did not indicate statistical significance in the relationship among the platforms relative to use of Kelly's masculine and feminine issues ($X^2(2, 528) = .77$, $p = .681$).

The analysis found, of Kelly's top five referenced feminine issues and masculine issues across all platforms, masculine issues ($n = 259$; 56.2%)

**276** Media Messages in the 2022 Midterm Election

**TABLE 13.2** Chi-square Test for Kelly Issues, Feminine and Masculine, by Platform

| Gender | Tweets | | TV ads | | Debate statements | |
|---|---|---|---|---|---|---|
| | n | column % | n | column % | n | column % |
| Feminine | 130 | 42.8 | 23 | 37.7 | 72 | 44.2 |
| Masculine | 174 | 57.2 | 38 | 62.3 | 91 | 55.8 |
| Total | 304 | 100.0 | 61 | 100.0 | 163 | 100.0 |

*Note.* Coded issues ($n = 528$): feminine ($n = 225$; 42.6%); masculine ($n = 303$; 57.4%). $X^2(2, 528) = .77, p = .681$.

**TABLE 13.3** Kelly's Top-Ranked Feminine and Masculine Issues, Platforms Combined

| Rank | Top feminine issues | | | Top masculine issues | | |
|---|---|---|---|---|---|---|
| | | n | col. % | | n | col. % |
| 1 | Education | 78 | 38.6 | Business/industry/ economy | 89 | 34.4 |
| 2 | Children/families | 64 | 31.7 | Jobs/labor/workforce | 58 | 22.4 |
| 3 | Health/healthcare/ Medicaid | 28 | 13.9 | Taxes/budgets | 57 | 22.0 |
| 4 | Drug addiction/ mental health | 17 | 8.4 | Highways/ transportation/ infrastructure | 29 | 11.2 |
| 5 | Women's rights | 15 | 7.4 | Veterans/military/first respond | 26 | 10.0 |
| Total | | 202 | 100.0 | | 259 | 100.0 |

*Note.* Among the 10 issues, feminine issues constituted 43.8%; masculine issues were 56.2%.

outnumbered feminine ones ($n = 202$; 43.8%). The top masculine issue of business/industry/economy had 89 references, while the top feminine issue of education had 78 (see Table 13.3).

### Schmidt's Attacks, Acclaims, and Defenses

The following research question (RQ3) asked if Schmidt's campaign communications contained more attacks, acclaims, or defenses. As seen in Table 13.4, an evaluation showed that the frequency of all attacks ($n = 237$; 53.0%) by Schmidt on Kelly and others—often President Biden—exceeded his acclaims ($n = 210$, 47.0%) and defenses ($n = 0$). Also, his attacks exceeded acclaims for each of the three platforms: tweets (attacks: $n = 169$ [53.1%] compared to acclaims: $n = 149$ [46.9%]); TV ads (attacks: $n = 21$ [58.3%]

# Gendered Treatment in the Communication Strategy  **277**

**TABLE 13.4** Schmidt Attacks, Acclaims, and Defenses by Platform

| Function | Tweets | | TV ads | | Debates | | Total | |
|---|---|---|---|---|---|---|---|---|
| | n | column % | n | column % | n | column % | n | column % |
| Attacks | 169 | 53.1 | 21 | 58.3 | 47 | 50.5 | 237 | 53.0 |
| Acclaims | 149 | 46.9 | 15 | 41.7 | 46 | 49.5 | 210 | 47.0 |
| Defenses | 0 | 0.0 | 0 | 0.0 | 0 | 0.0 | 0 | 0.0 |

**TABLE 13.5** Schmidt's Campaign Attacks on Kelly Traits by Gender and Platform

| Gender | Tweets | | TV ads | | Debate statements | |
|---|---|---|---|---|---|---|
| | n | column % | n | column % | n | column % |
| Feminine | 46 | 56.1 | 9 | 56.3 | 9 | 25.7 |
| Masculine | 36 | 43.9 | 7 | 43.8 | 26 | 74.3 |
| Total | 82 | 100.0 | 16 | 100.0 | 35 | 100.0 |

*Note.* Coded traits ($n = 133$): feminine ($n = 64$; 48.1%); masculine ($n = 69$; 51.9%).
$X^2(2, 133) = 9.55, p = .008$.

compared to acclaims: $n = 15$ [41.7%]); and debate statements (attacks: $n = 47$ [50.5%] compared to acclaims: $n = 46$ [49.5%]).

### Kelly Traits and Issues Attacked

The next research question (RQ4) asked whether Schmidt's messages that attacked Kelly were more frequent for feminine traits or for masculine traits (Table 13.5). Among all coded communications for Schmidt attacks on traits ($n = 133$), his total attacks on Kelly using masculine traits ($n = 69$; 51.9%) were slightly higher than those with feminine traits ($n = 64$; 48.1%). A chi-square test indicated statistical significance in the relationship among the platforms relative to Schmidt attacks on masculine and feminine traits ($X^2(2, 133) = 9.55, p = .008$). Among separate platforms, Schmidt's attacks in debate statements leaned much more heavily to masculine traits ($n = 26$; 74.3%) than feminine ($n = 9$; 25.7%). For tweets, feminine traits attacked ($n = 46$; 56.1%) exceeded attacks on masculine traits ($n = 36$; 43.9%). And, for TV ads, Schmidt attacks on feminine attributes ($n = 9$; 56.3%) exceeded attacks on masculine ones ($n = 7$; 43.8%).

When analyzed using difference of proportions tests, statistically significant relationships resulted for tweets ($z = 2.335, p = .020$) and debate statements ($z = -3.091, p = .002$) in a two-tailed test. Schmidt's tweet attacks on Kelly's feminine traits ($n = 46$) represented 71.9% of all feminine trait attacks, while

278 Media Messages in the 2022 Midterm Election

tweets attacking masculine traits ($n$ = 36) were only 52.2% of all masculine trait attacks. In this regard, Schmidt used tweets as a more common platform for attacking Kelly on feminine traits. Alternatively, Schmidt's attacks of Kelly traits in debate statements referenced masculine traits ($n$ = 26; 37.7%) more than feminine ones ($n$ = 9; 14.1%). Schmidt's attacks of Kelly traits in TV ads—while slightly higher using feminine traits ($n$ = 9; 14.1%) than masculine ones ($n$ = 7; 10.1%)—were not statistically significant, ($z$ = 0.694, $p$ =.488).

For the next research question (RQ5a) regarding issues Schmidt targeted when attacking Kelly, results showed a higher overall frequency of attacks on masculine ($n$ = 198; 57.4%) than feminine issues ($n$ = 147; 42.6%) as seen in Table 13.6. TV ads had more instances of attacks by Schmidt on feminine issues ($n$ = 27; 52.9%) than masculine issues ($n$ = 24; 47.1%). Among the other two platforms, however, masculine issues were attacked more frequently. Among tweets, attacks on masculine issues ($n$ = 107; 56.6%) exceeded those on feminine ones ($n$ = 82; 43.4%); and among debate statements, Schmidt attacked masculine issues at a much higher frequency ($n$ = 67; 63.8%) than he attacked feminine attributes ($n$ = 38; 36.2%). A chi-square test, however, did not result in a statistically significant result, ($X^2$(2, 345) = 4.04, $p$ =.133).

Spearman's rank order correlation was computed separately for tweets, TV ads, and debate statements to determine the relationship between top-ranked issues referenced by Kelly in her communications and Schmidt attacks on them (RQ5b). For tweets, a positive and strong correlation existed between the two variables, $r$(8) =.71, $p$ =.021, which was statistically significant using a two-tailed test. Nine of Kelly's top 10 referenced issues in tweets were issues attacked by Schmidt (see Table 13.7). For TV ads, there was a positive and moderate correlation, $r$(11) =.55, $p$ <.05, that was statistically significant with Schmidt attacking eight of Kelly's referenced issues (see Table 13.8). For debate statements, there was a positive and strong correlation, $r$(9) =.75, $p$ =.008, that was statistically significant with all of Kelly's top-ranked issue references drawing attacks from Schmidt (see Table 13.9). (Note that degrees of freedom for the tests differ. In tweets, the top 10 Kelly issues were tested; in debate

**TABLE 13.6** Schmidt's Campaign Attacks on Kelly Issues by Gender and Platform

| Gender | Tweets | | TV ads | | Debate statements | |
|---|---|---|---|---|---|---|
| | $n$ | column % | $n$ | column % | $n$ | column % |
| Feminine | 82 | 43.4 | 27 | 52.9 | 38 | 36.2 |
| Masculine | 107 | 56.6 | 24 | 47.1 | 67 | 63.8 |
| Total | 189 | 100.0 | 51 | 100.0 | 105 | 100.0 |

*Note.* Coded issues ($n$ = 345): feminine ($n$ = 147; 42.6%); masculine ($n$ = 198; 57.4%).
$X^2$(2, 345) = 4.04, $p$ =.133.

Gendered Treatment in the Communication Strategy **279**

**TABLE 13.7** Kelly Tweet Agenda Versus Schmidt Tweet Attack Agenda

| Issues | Kelly tweets | | | Schmidt tweet attacks | | |
|---|---|---|---|---|---|---|
| | n | % | Rank | n | % | Rank |
| Business/industry/economy | 61 | 21.6 | 1 | 28 | 19.3 | 3 |
| Education | 44 | 15.5 | 2 | 42 | 29.0 | 1 |
| Children/families | 43 | 15.2 | 3 | 15 | 10.3 | 5 |
| Jobs/labor/workforce | 40 | 14.1 | 4 | 18 | 12.4 | 4 |
| Highways/transp/infrastructure | 24 | 8.5 | 5 | 2 | 1.4 | 8 |
| Taxes/budgets | 21 | 7.4 | 6 | 29 | 20.0 | 2 |
| Health/healthcare/Medicaid | 14 | 4.9 | 7.5 | 0 | 0.0 | 10 |
| Veteran/military/first responder | 14 | 4.9 | 7.5 | 7 | 4.8 | 6 |
| Drug addiction/mental health | 11 | 3.9 | 9.5 | 2 | 1.4 | 8 |
| Women's rights | 11 | 3.9 | 9.5 | 2 | 1.4 | 8 |
| Total | 283 | 100.0 | - | 145 | 100.0 | - |

*Note.* Issues in italics denote feminine gender.
Top 10 Kelly tweets tested for Spearman's rank order $(r(8) = .71, p = .021)$, two-tailed test.

**TABLE 13.8** Kelly TV Ad Agenda Versus Schmidt TV Ad Agenda

| Issues | Kelly TV ads | | | Schmidt TV ad attacks | | |
|---|---|---|---|---|---|---|
| | n | % | Rank | n | % | Rank |
| Taxes/budgets | 20 | 32.8 | 1 | 6 | 15.8 | 3.5 |
| Education | 16 | 26.2 | 2 | 6 | 15.8 | 3.5 |
| Veteran/military/first responder | 5 | 8.2 | 3 | 8 | 21.1 | 1.5 |
| Children/families | 4 | 6.6 | 4.5 | 3 | 7.9 | 6 |
| Jobs/labor/workforce | 4 | 6.6 | 4.5 | 0 | 0.0 | 11 |
| Business/industry/economy | 3 | 4.9 | 6 | 2 | 5.3 | 7 |
| Agriculture | 2 | 3.3 | 7.5 | 1 | 2.6 | 8 |
| Crime | 2 | 3.3 | 7.5 | 4 | 10.5 | 5 |
| Health/healthcare/Medicaid | 1 | 1.6 | 11 | 0 | 0.0 | 11 |
| LGBTQ/transgender | 1 | 1.6 | 11 | 8 | 21.1 | 1.5 |
| Seniors/Medicare | 1 | 1.6 | 11 | 0 | 0.0 | 11 |
| Energy | 1 | 1.6 | 11 | 0 | 0.0 | 11 |
| Highways/transp/infrastructure | 1 | 1.6 | 11 | 0 | 0.0 | 11 |
| Total | 61 | 100.0 | - | 38 | 100.0 | - |

*Note.* Issues in italics denote feminine gender.
Kelly TV ads all issues named, Spearman's rank order $(r(11) = .55, p \leq .05)$, two-tailed test.

**280** Media Messages in the 2022 Midterm Election

**TABLE 13.9** Kelly Debate Statement Agenda Versus Schmidt Debate Statement Agenda

| Issues | Kelly debate statements | | | Schmidt debate attacks | | |
|---|---|---|---|---|---|---|
| | n | % | Rank | n | % | Rank |
| Business/industry/economy | 25 | 18.4 | 1 | 11 | 13.6 | 3 |
| Education | 18 | 13.2 | 2 | 12 | 14.8 | 2 |
| Children/families | 17 | 12.5 | 3 | 10 | 12.3 | 4 |
| Taxes/budgets | 16 | 11.8 | 4 | 16 | 19.8 | 1 |
| Jobs/labor/workforce | 14 | 10.3 | 5 | 7 | 8.6 | 5.5 |
| Health/healthcare/Medicaid | 13 | 9.6 | 6 | 3 | 3.7 | 9.5 |
| Water/environment/climate | 7 | 5.1 | 8 | 4 | 4.9 | 8 |
| Agriculture | 7 | 5.1 | 8 | 2 | 2.5 | 11 |
| Veterans/military/first responders | 7 | 5.1 | 8 | 7 | 8.6 | 5.5 |
| Drug addiction/mental health | 6 | 4.4 | 10.5 | 3 | 3.7 | 9.5 |
| Immigration/border | 6 | 4.4 | 10.5 | 6 | 7.4 | 7 |
| Total | 136 | 100.0 | - | 81 | 100.0 | - |

*Note.* Issues in italics denote feminine gender.
Top 11 issues tested for Spearman's rank order $(r(9) = .75, p = .008)$, two-tailed test.

statements, 11 issues were tested, since two issues tied at tenth place; and in TV ads, all 13 issues referenced by Kelly were tested, since five issues tied at tenth place.)

### Kelly's Treatment of Abortion Issue

Asked in the final question (RQ6) was how Kelly and her campaign treated the issue of abortion in gendered terms in a divisive election year. Kelly's references to abortion among the platforms was rare with only two references among tweets, four in debate statements, and none in her TV ads or those aired by KVI. In each case, Kelly teamed this feminine-coded issue with a masculine trait, expressing consistency in her record, firmness in her stance, and decisiveness in who should, or should not, be involved in decisions about this healthcare decision. In an interview with the author—and a nod to the feminine trait of collaboration—Kelly expressed concern that dwelling on abortion as a main campaign issue would only serve to divide and disaffect voters.

### Discussion and Conclusion

By a slim margin, Kelly prevailed in the Kansas race for governor with 49.5% of the vote to Schmidt's 47.3% (Kansas Secretary of State, 2022), and it stands to reason that her campaign communications were critical to this outcome. From research of these communications, two major takeaways were identified—one

## Kelly's Focus

Despite Schmidt's reliance on a variety of attacks, Kelly remained largely focused on her communications, reinforcing to voters her strengths for leading the state. In this race, Kelly was considered by a Washburn University political science professor and campaign authority to have run "one of the most disciplined campaigns I've ever seen" (Bahl & Tidd, 2022, para. 23).

A content analysis of tweets, TV ads, and debate statements suggested that Kelly employed a mix of feminine and masculine traits and issues. Among platforms—for both traits and issues—Kelly relied slightly more on masculine examples, except in her TV ads, which were coded with more feminine traits. Kelly's overall application of gender among all platforms was balanced, with traits being 46.4% feminine and 53.6% masculine, and issues being 42.6% feminine and 57.4% masculine.

When Kelly spoke about working with others, her messaging reinforced that she was collaborative, sincere, and likable—all feminine traits. Kelly's signature "middle of the road" slogan captured these feminine attributes, which appeared regularly in her campaign communications and was featured by name in three of her general election campaign ads: "Middle seat" (August 19, 2022), "Middle of the road 2: Tax cut" (September 30, 2022), and "Back in the middle of this road" (October 18, 2022).

Among masculine traits, surfacing regularly in Kelly's communications were descriptors of determined, competent, and consistent. Research suggests this trait-balancing behavior among women candidates is intended to maximize likability while communicating masculine qualities that voters perceive to be consistent with effective government leaders (Bauer & Santia, 2022). Research also suggests that "voters prefer their elected officials to exhibit such masculine characteristics as leadership, experience, and toughness but also want them to be honest, sincere, and, in more recent years, willing to cooperate with others" (Bystrom, 2019, p. xli). Kelly clearly aligned with this trait-balancing model.

In Kelly's issues strategy, masculine issues were more numerous—not only among her top 10 referenced issues, but among all issues for all platforms. With 89 references to business/industry/economy, and 58 and 57 references respectively to jobs/labor/workforce and taxes/budgets, Kelly reinforced her past wins and promised future successes. During the September 29 interview with the author, in a reference to bringing Panasonic and 4,000 jobs to Kansas, Kelly indicated her issue ownership of economic development and appropriating the typically Republican-advantaged topic. Regarding taxes/budgets, Kelly offered proof of her budget knowhow, reminding voters of her 14 years of experience on the budget committee in the State Senate. A tweet by Kelly pollster, Margie Omero (2022), reinforced that Kelly's work to secure tax cuts on food sales was tracking positively with voters in final polling.

Topping the feminine issues most named by Kelly overall, as well as in each platform, was education and children with 78 and 64 references, respectively. These mentions reflected Kelly's interest in being known as the "Education Governor." The topic of education was also featured in one of her general election TV spots: "Need fully funded schools" (September 13, 2022). In this TV ad, Kelly wove the feminine issue of education with the masculine topic of budgets and spoke to her commitment to restore funding to this policy priority.

What was not overtly present in Kelly communications was the topic of abortion. In Kelly's communications, she represented the topic as "private medical decisions" (Johnson County debate, October 5, 2022) and "a private matter between a woman and her physician" (Kelly, September 10, 2022). Given the unexpected outcome on the Kansas primary's abortion question and increased voter registrations among Kansas women, Kelly's limited treatment of the topic in tweets, TV ads, and debates seemed unusual.

An explanation ties back again to the discipline exercised by the Kelly campaign. Kelly's pollster offered that "abortion is not a top-of-mind topic when voters think of her" (M. Omero, personal communication, October 17, 2022). Abortion did not need to be front and center for Kelly, but rather "righting the ship" relative to state government. Kelly explained it this way: "I have a habit of not being vocal on divisive issues that don't bring us together" (L. Kelly, personal communication, October 11, 2022). Talking about abortion could distract from that focus, and Kelly's record on the topic spoke for itself. As governor, Kelly prevailed when a socially conservative state legislature tried to ban abortions in Kansas. In the October 5 debate, Kelly stood firm: "For 18 years I've had the same position on this issue. So I really don't have much more to say."

### Schmidt's Campaign Attacks

The second major takeaway of this research regarded the number and the nature of Schmidt's campaign attacks. The study found that Schmidt used all platforms for delivering both attacks to undermine Kelly and acclaims to bolster his own record and proposals. Schmidt's communications did not present defenses—not unusual, in that defenses constituted low frequencies among the three functions in past research using Functional Theory. Schmidt's attacks, however, exceeded acclaims on each of the three platforms. While studies using Functional Theory have suggested broadly that candidates attack more often than they acclaim, for challengers in gubernatorial races, this is not the case. Several studies returned findings that challengers in gubernatorial races, specifically, issued more acclaims than attacks in tweets (Stein & Benoit, 2021), TV ads (Airne & Benoit, 2005), and debates (Benoit et al., 2007).

Challengers typically use acclaims for introducing themselves to the electorate, building favorability ratings, and explaining their suitability for elective office in terms of character and policy. It appears that Schmidt's strategy deviated from this formula—at least among these platforms—by focusing more on driving negative perceptions of his opponent. By employing attacks on Kelly that exceeded his own acclaims in number, Schmidt potentially displaced opportunities to build and burnish his own qualifying traits or proposed policies. Further, although defenses are rarer and have their own drawbacks (Benoit, 2007), perhaps voters would have responded to a defense by Schmidt that refuted KVI and Kelly communications linking him to former Governor Brownback's unpopular cuts to education. What was never forthcoming from the Schmidt campaign, at least among these platforms, was such a defense.

Schmidt's attacks of Kelly's traits were higher in number overall for masculine attributes, but he employed attacks more on feminine traits in tweets and TV ads. Considered statistically significant in a difference of proportions test, his attacks in tweets indicated a much higher proportion of attacks on Kelly's feminine attributes. Feminine traits attacked by Schmidt were Kelly's honesty and skills at collaborating. Schmidt challenged Kelly's middle-of-the-road credentials around which Kelly built much of her campaign identity. In one tweet, Schmidt charged that "Laura Kelly has been telling Kansans for months that she is in the middle of the road. Truth is, on the issue of Fairness in Women's Sports and many others she is far from it" (Schmidt, September 2, 2022). On TV, Schmidt doubled down on this charge. One RGA TV ad closed with "she's not middle of the road, and she's not honest with Kansas" ("Kelly vetoed transgender ban," September 30, 2022). This accusation referred to Kelly in her own ad saying "of course, men should not play girls' sports." It was a statement Schmidt said contradicted her vetoes of legislation that would have limited transgender athletes' participation.

Among debate statements, notably higher counts of masculine traits and issues surfaced both for Kelly's references and for Schmidt's attacks. This outcome bears out an expectation that participants in debates employ more competitive (masculine) styles. Also, audiences at the two debates—geared to the agricultural community at the state fair and to legal professionals at the bar association—could have skewed topics to more masculine subject matter.

Among masculine traits, Schmidt attacked perceived shortcomings of Kelly that spoke to a failure of being competent, consistent, effective, and strong. For example, in debates, Schmidt criticized Kelly as an ineffective leader. When Kelly was asked if she sensed her opponent worked to define her leadership skills based on gender, Kelly offered that the attack by Schmidt on her effectiveness (a masculine trait) was apparent throughout the state fair debate (L. Kelly, personal communication, September 29, 2022). On the debate stage, however, Kelly anticipated the criticism and responded: "Maybe I'm not flashy, but I am effective." Kelly then pushed back by naming a list of agentic issues she

**284** Media Messages in the 2022 Midterm Election

led to success as governor, including new business investments in Kansas, jobs created, taxes cut, and budgets balanced.

Schmidt's attacks on issues leaned slightly more feminine for TV ads owing to his use of the medium to attack Kelly's position on education (for closing schools during COVID-19), LGBTQ/transgender issues (for supporting transgender women in sports), and diversity/racism (for supporting the recommendations of the Commission on Racial Equity and Justice). Totaled among all platforms, however, Schmidt's number of attacks were higher for masculine issues. In rank order, those top issues Schmidt criticized involved taxes/budgets; business/industry/economy; and jobs/labor/workforce. With these topics, Schmidt suggested that sales taxes on food would be lower if not for Kelly; that overall inflation and high gas prices were attributable to Kelly and Biden policies; and that actual statistics for job creation were not what Kelly's figures claimed.

Schmidt's attacks, while not consequential in turning enough voters against Kelly, may have worked against his own success. Rank correlation tests proved Schmidt directed attacks to the top issues on which Kelly also campaigned. But other issues on which he attacked focused on culture wars playing out nationally and in Republican party politics. While Kelly largely stuck to kitchen-table issues, Schmidt's attacks that included transgender bans in sports and drag shows in Kansas "risked ceding moderate Republicans and independents to Kelly" (Shorman & Bernard, 2022, para. 43).

### Limitations and Contributions to Theory

While other research regarding female candidate outcomes has examined the influence of party affiliation and treatment by earned media, this study did not consider those factors, which could add to overall understanding of communications strategies employed by candidates. Lost in the analysis of written communications are the non-verbal communications that display traits such as energy, emotion, or compassion. Such an analysis could present additional material for study and add nuance to the evaluations. Also, while the author had access to certain internal communications and polling of one candidate, this study could have benefited from access to the opponent's internal polling and campaign staff, and an understanding of circumstances and intentions that prompted his attacks.

Despite these limitations, this study makes a meaningful contribution to a vital body of knowledge in the field. Since the 1990s, researchers have applied Functional Theory to the study of candidates' use of attacks, acclaims, and defenses for political races at all levels, domestic and non-domestic, and have parsed data based on incumbents, challengers, and party affiliation. The current research contributed to Functional Theory for its examination of gendered treatment of campaign attacks. Further, this research considered the theory's application in the loss by the male challenger whose attacks were under study. The research also contributed to framing theory for its examination of how candidates for governor applied gendered treatment in political communications, specifically to what extent the female candidate employed gendered traits and issues, and to what extent the male challenger framed them in his attacks.

## References

Airne, D., & Benoit, W. L. (2005). Political television advertising in campaign 2000. *Communication Quarterly, 53*(4), 473–492. https://doi.org/10.1080/0146337050 0168765

Back in the middle of this road. (2022, October 18). Laura Kelly 2022 TV Ad #12. Kansas Institute for Politics at Washburn University. Kansas political ads. Kansas Governor. www.youtube.com/watch?v=_urP4UCUc5Q

Bahl, A., & Tidd, J. (2022, November 9). Laura Kelly leads Derek Schmidt by 14,255 votes with advanced mail ballots still coming in. *The Topeka Capital-Journal.* www. cjonline.com/story/news/politics/elections/2022/11/09/laura-kelly-derek-schmidt-loc ked-in-narrow-kansas-governors-race/69600462007/

Banwart, M. C., & McKinney, M. S. (2005). A gendered influence in campaign debates? Analysis of mixed-gender United States Senate and gubernatorial debates. *Communication Studies, 56*(4), 353–373. https://doi.org/10.1080/1051097050 0319443

Bauer, N. M. (2013). Rethinking stereotype reliance: Understanding the connection between female candidates and gender stereotypes. *Politics and the Life Sciences, 31*(1), 22–42. https://doi.org/10.2990/32_1_22

Bauer, N. M. (2017). The effects of counterstereotypic gender strategies on candidate evaluations. *Political Psychology, 38*(2), 279–295. https://doi.org/10.1111/pops.12351

Bauer, N. M., & Santia, M. (2022). Going feminine: Identifying how and when female candidates emphasize feminine and masculine traits on the campaign trail. *Political Research Quarterly, 75*(3), 691–705. https://doi.org/10.1177/106591 29211020257

Benoit, W. L. (2007). *Communication in political campaigns.* Peter Lang Publishing.

Benoit, W. L., Brazeal, L. M., & Airne, D. (2007). A functional analysis of televised U.S. senate and gubernatorial campaign debates. *Argumentation and Advocacy, 44*(2), 75–89. https://doi.org/10.1080/00028533.2007.11821679

Benoit, W. L., & Rill, L. A. (2013). A functional analysis of 2008 general election debates. *Argumentation and Advocacy, 50*(1), 34–46. https://doi.org/10.1080/00028 533.2013.11821808

Blankenship, J., & Robson, D. C. (1995). A "feminine style" in women's political discourse: An exploratory essay. *Communication Quarterly, 43*(3), 353–366. https://doi.org/10.1080/01463379509369982

Brooks, S. C. (1999). [Review of the book *Campaign '96: A functional analysis of acclaiming, attacking, and defending,* by W. L. Benoit, J. R. Blaney, & P. M. Pier]. *Congress & the Presidency, 26*(2), 209–210. www.proquest.com/scholarly-journals/campaign-96-functional-analysis-acclaiming/docview/205929750/se-2

Bystrom, D. G. (2019). Women as political candidates. In D. G. Bystrom, & B. Burrell (Eds.), *Women in the American political system: An encyclopedia of women as voters, candidates, and office holders* (Vol 1: A-M). ABC-CLIO.

Carroll, S. J. (1985). *Women as candidates in American politics.* Indiana University Press.

Davis, J. H., & Shear, M. D. (2019). *Border wars: Inside Trump's assault on immigration.* Simon & Schuster.

Dolan, K. (2008). Is there a "gender affinity effect" in American politics? *Political Research Quarterly, 61*(1), 79–89. https://doi.org/10.1177/1065912907307518

Dubosar, E. (2022). Assessing differences in the framing of Hillary Clinton and Donald Trump during the 2016 presidential election. *Society, 59,* 169–180. https://doi.org/10.1007/s12115-021-00659-8

Entman, R. M. (2007). Framing bias: Media in the distribution of power. *Journal of Communication, 57*(1), 163–173. https://doi.org/10.1111/j.1460-2466.2006.00336.x

FiveThirtyEight. (2022, August 2). How the governor's forecast has changed. https://projects.fivethirtyeight.com/2022-election-forecast/governor/kansas/

Glueck, K. (2022, October 17). In Kansas, a Democratic governor tests if any politics is still local. *The New York Times.* www.nytimes.com/2022/10/18/us/politics/laura-kelly-kansas-governor-democrats.html

Hentschel, T., Heilman, M. E., & Peus, C. V. (2019). The multiple dimensions of gender stereotypes: A current look at men's and women's characterizations of others and themselves. *Frontiers in Psychology, 10*(11), 1–19. https://doi.org/10.3389/fpsyg.2019.00011

Huddy, L., & Terkildsen, N. (1993). Gender stereotypes and the perception of male and female candidates. *American Journal of Political Science, 37*(1), 119–147. https://doi.org/10.2307/2111526

Jamieson, K. H. (1995). *Beyond the double bind: Women and leadership.* Oxford University Press.

Kansas Institute for Politics at Washburn University. (n.d.a). Kansas candidate debates. Governor debate #1 (September 10, 2022) and Governor debate #2 (October 5, 2022). www.washburn.edu/reference/cks/politics/debates.html

Kansas Institute for Politics at Washburn University. (n.d.b). Kansas political ads. Kansas Governor (2022). Laura Kelly, Derek Schmidt, Kansas Values Institute, and Republican Governors Association. www.washburn.edu/reference/cks/politics/ads.html.

Kansas Secretary of State. (2022). *2022 General election official vote totals.* https://sos.ks.gov/elections/22elec/2022-General-Official-Vote-Totals.pdf

Kelly, L. [@LauraKellyKS]. (2022, September 10). *Reproductive healthcare decisions should be a private matter between a woman and her physician. We must respect our fellow Kansans'* [Tweet]. Twitter. https://x.com/LauraKellyKS/status/1568641298567147522

Kelly vetoed transgender ban. (2022, September 30). Republican Gov Association PAC 2022 Kansas Governor TV Ad #8. Kansas Institute for Politics at Washburn University. Kansas political ads. Kansas Governor. Governor's race PAC ads. www.youtube.com/watch?v=Pyy7JCrYi3w

Mendoza, S. A., & DiMaria, M. G. (2019). Not "with her": How gendered political slogans affect conservative women's perceptions of female leaders. *Sex Roles, 80*(1-2), 1–10. https://doi.org/10.1007/s11199-018-0910-z

Middle of the road 2: Tax cut. (2022, September 30). Laura Kelly 2022 TV Ad #9. Kansas Institute for Politics at Washburn University. Kansas political ads. Kansas Governor. www.youtube.com/watch?v=reiRI4lBibU

Middle seat. (2022, August 19). Laura Kelly 2022 TV Ad #5. Kansas Institute for Politics at Washburn University. Kansas political ads. Kansas Governor. www.youtube.com/watch?v=L17_gMj6fSM

Need fully funded schools. (2022, September 13). Laura Kelly 2022 TV Ad #6. Kansas Institute for Politics at Washburn University. Kansas political ads. Kansas Governor. www.youtube.com/watch?v=xa6pwRvzUEk

Omero, M. [@MargieOmero]. (2022, November 11). *How did Laura Kelly win in a red state like Kansas? Here's the word cloud from our final tracking poll*. [Tweet]. Twitter. https://x.com/MargieOmero/status/1591064905427603456/photo/1

Schmidt, D. [@DerekSchmidtKS]. (2022, September 2). *Laura Kelly has been telling Kansans for months that she is in the middle of the road. Truth* is, on [Tweet]. Twitter. https://x.com/DerekSchmidtKS/status/1565675916834902018

Schneider, M. C. (2014). Gender-based strategies on candidate websites. *Journal of Political Marketing, 13*(4), 264–290. https://doi.org/10.1080/15377857.2014.958373

Schneider, M. C., Holman, M. R., Diekman, A. B., & McAndrew, T. (2016). Power, conflict, and community: How gendered views of political power influence women's political ambition. *Political Psychology, 37*(4), 515–531. https://doi.org/10.1111/pops.12268

Shorman, J., & Bernard, K. (2022, November 9). Kansas Gov. Laura Kelly defies history with narrow win over Republican Schmidt. *The Kansas City Star.* www.kansascity.com/news/politics-government/election/article267946082.html

Stein, K. A., & Benoit, W. L. (2021). A functional analysis of 2016 nonpresidential campaign tweets. *The American Behavioral Scientist, 65*(3), 432–447. http://doi.org/10.1177/0002764220975056

Sullivan, P. A. (1989). The 1984 vice-presidential debate: A case study of female and male framing in political campaigns. *Communication Quarterly, 37*(4), 329–343. https://doi.org/10.1080/01463378909385554

TargetSmart. (2022, September 16). *New data on Kansas abortion vote*. https://insights.targetsmart.com/new-data-on-kansas-abortion-vote.html

Tidd, J. (2022, October 24). Donald Trump touts 'somebody named Derek Schmidt' as Kansas governor's race heats up. *The Topeka Capita-Journal.* www.cjonline.com/story/news/politics/elections/2022/10/24/kansas-election-donald-trump-video-supports-derek-schmidt-kansas-governor/69586493007/

Todd, C., Murray, M., Kamisar, B., Bowman, B., & Marquez, A. (2022, September 26). Out of hundreds, here are 25 consequential midterm races to follow. *NBC News.* www.nbcnews.com/meet-the-press/first-read/hundreds-are-25-consequential-midterm-races-follow-rcna49382

Winfrey, K. L., & Schnoebelen, J. M. (2019). Running as a woman (or man): A review of research on political communicators and gender stereotypes. *Review of Communication Research, 7*, 109–138. https://rcommunicationr.org/index.php/rcr/article/view/29

Witt, L., Paget, K. M., & Matthews, G. (1994). *Running as a woman: Gender and power in American politics*. Macmillan.

# INDEX

*Note*: Figures and tables are denoted by *italic* and **bold** text respectively.

10DLC Rules 184–185, **186**
"100% pro-life" framing 213–230
*2000 Mules* 48–49, 63; audience for 60; confirmation bias in 58, 60; conspiracy and theory 50–51; detective story formula 58–59, 60; fact-checking of 50, 53, 61–63; first act of 51, 53–54; geo-tracking technology 55, 56; howcatchem configuration of 58–59; hypothesis of 53, 54–55; and inverted storytelling 58–61; mainstream responses to 61–63; recalculation of the 2020 election 57; recap of "what we know" 57; and scientific rationalism 53–58; second act of 51–52, 54, 55–56, 58; storied account of 51–53; and suspension of disbelief 59; third act of 52, 57–58, 60
2020 election 8, 49, 51, 53, 54, 57, 59, 61, 63, 94, 134
9/11 28, 35, **35**, 37, **37**, 50, 106

Abbott, Greg 19, 252, 254, 258, 261
*ABC News* 131
abortion 69–87, *76*, **79**, *83*, *85*; anti- *see* anti-abortion; and changed 2022 environment 84–85; framing of *see* framing, of abortion; and gender 70, 73, 74, 75, 77, 84, 85; and

incumbency 70, 71–72, 73, 74, 75, 84, 85–86; as owned issue 73, 74, 77, 84, 86; risk environment of 71, 73; as routine healthcare 84; *see also Dobbs v. Jackson Women's Health Organization*; rhetorical trajectory, and abortion debate
abortion access 214, 215, 216, 217, 218, 219, 221, 222, 223, 225, 226, 227, 228, 229
"abortion as healthcare" framing 82
abortion campaigning 76–86, *76*, **79**, *83*, *85*
abortion communication 70
abortion debate: campaign context of 218–219; and *Dobbs* decision 86, 213, 214; fetal rights versus women's rights 72; *"I Will Fight [...] Laxalt Won't"* 225–228; rhetorical invention in 214, 215, 217, 218; rhetorical trajectory of 213–230; *"We All Know Guys Like This"* 220–225
abortion discourse 217, 222, 224; in congressional campaigns 69–87, *76*, **79**, *83*, *85*
abortion framing 69–70, 71–73, 74–75, 76, 78–86, **79**, *83*, *85*; pro-choice 69, 72, 76, 81; pro-life 72, 75, 76, 80, 81, 82, 213–230

# Index  **289**

abortion legality 81, 224
abortion messaging 70, 73, 75–76, 77
abortion regulation 226, 227, 228–229;
  *see also* Targeted Regulation of
  Abortion Providers (TRAP)
abortion rhetoric 80, 86, 213, 214–217,
  219
abortion topic, in Congressional tweets
  125, 127, 128, 131, 132, 133,
  136–137, *136*
*Abrams v. United States* 253, 257
academictwitteR 131
acclaim advertisements 94, 108, 112, 282
accountability 11, 15, 70, **110**, 113, 182,
  183
AdImpact 252, 254
advertisements: acclaim 94, 108,
  112, 282; attack 94, 98, 116, 261;
  autobiographical 98; candidate video
  100; defense 94; video political 92, 94,
  99, 100, 116, 119
advertising: digital 6–7, 19, 94, 252, 253;
  persuasive 254; political 91–119, **101**,
  **102–103**, 107, **109–111**, **115**; targeted
  9, 21; television 6, 75, 94, 95, 254
aesthetics of science 53, 60–61
agenda building 129, 140, 141, 143
agenda fracturing 127, 142, 143
agenda inversion 126–128, 130, 141,
  143
agenda setting 15, 126, 128, 129, 140,
  142, 143, 193, 207
algorithms: digital 155, 158, 161,
  162; digital news *see* digital news
  algorithms; digital partisan news
  149–162, **157**, **159**, **160**; Facebook
  ranking 258; filtering of 16; ideological
  155, 156; polarized digital 155, 158;
  politically aligned 160, 161
Alphabet 253, 254–255
alternative media (alt-media) 27, 33, 36,
  37, **38**, 39, 41
*America is under existential threat* 102,
  **102–103**, 104, 105, 117
*America you knew is no longer
  recognizable, the* **102**, 104
American democracy 106, 162, 205
American Dream 15, 105, 117–118
*American dream is threatened, the* **102**,
  104, 108, 117
*American institutions have changed
  alarmingly* **111**, 114

American National Election Study
  (ANES) 73
American politics 1, 3, 14, 19, 49, 151,
  152, 162, 218
American Southwest, abortion in 213–230
American values 106
ANES (American National Election
  Study) 73
"annoying, but legal" media coverage
  178, 179–182, *182*
anti-abortion movement 72, 201, 214,
  215–216, 216–217, 219, 221, 222, 223,
  224, 226, 227, 228, 229–230; *see also*
  Women Protective Anti-Abortion
  Arguments (WPAA)
antisemitism 28, 29, 30, 50
anti-spam industry 17, **170**, **176**, 184,
  185–186
approval ratings, of President Biden 3,
  14–15, 91, 125, 142, 150–151, 204
*Areopagitica* 256
Aristotle 59, 60, 233, 234, 239, 246–247
Arizona: midterm communication
  17–20; Senate race 217, 218, 219,
  220–221, 222, 223, 224–225; vigilante
  activity 49, 61
*Associated Press, The* 52–53, 61–62, 131
attack advertisements 94, 98, 116, 261
authoritarian populism 27, 28, 30, 40–41;
  index of 35–36, 37, **37**, **38**, 39, **40**, 40
authoritarianism 30
autobiographical advertisements 98
autodialing **174**, 179, 180

ballots 11, 12, 29, 51–52, 53, 54, 56, 57;
  harvesting of 61, 62; security of 195,
  203
base strategy 70, 77–78, 86
*benefits campaigns* **171**, **175**, **176**, 180
*benefits democracy* **171**, **175**, 181
*benefits individuals* **171**
Biden, President Joe: approval ratings
  of 3, 14–15, 91, 125, 142, 150–151,
  204; cartoons of **198**, 200, 202, 204,
  206; in Congressional tweets 132, 133,
  134, 139–140, *140*, 142; effect of 149;
  GDELT Project Television Comparer
  Value **196**; and Seal Team 6 50; and
  *2000 Mules* 49; uncomfortable using
  word abortion 69–70; *will work across
  the aisle and hold President Biden
  accountable* **110**, 113

**290** Index

Big Lie 13, 27, 28, 29, 32, 33, 35, **35**, 36, 37, **37**, **38**, 39, **40**, 40–41, 59
Big Tech 58, 63
birther conspiracy 28, 29, 35, **35**, 37, **37**, 50
Brandwatch 15, 125–126, 130, 132–133, 144
Bush, George W. 192, 194

campaign fundraising 7, 8–9, 178
campaign messaging 92, 93, 254, 259, 270, 274
campaign participation 28, 33, 37
campaign spending 6, 7, 94–95, 252, 254, 255
campaign strategies 9, 11, 14, 16–17, 32, 214, 252, 254, 255, 274
campaign text messages 169, **171**, 184
campaign websites 14, 70, 74, 75–76, 77, 78, 80, 83, 234
candidate communication 12, 13–16
candidate quality 119, 191, 196, **196**, **198**, 199, 200, 201, 202, 203, 205
candidate video advertisements 100
Capitol attack on January 6th 33, 51, 59, 63
cartoons: of Barack Obama 193, 194, 205; of Democratic Party **198**, 199, 200, 202, 204; of Donald Trump **198**, 199, 200–201, 202, 203, 204; editorial 17, 191, 192, 193, 194–195, 197–198, *197*, 200, 204, 205, 206, 207; of election denialism 191, 195–196, **196**, 198, **198**, 199, 201, 202, 205; of inflation 191, 196, **198**, 199, 200, 202, 203, 204, 205, 206; of Joe Biden **198**, 200, 202, 204, 206; political 16, 17, 191–207, **196**, *197*, **198**; during presidential elections 192–193, 194, 206, 207; of red wave 191, 195, **196**, 198, **198**, 199, 200, 201, 204; of Republican Party **198**, 199, 200–201, 202, 203, 204; of *Roe v. Wade* 199; "voting is important" message in 206
Center for American Progress 11
citizen fatigue, with campaign season 195, 196, 202, 203
citizen-as-consumer, centrality of 252–263
citizenship 229, 253, 254, 262–263
climate change 8, 10
Clinton, Bill 82, 192

Clinton, Hillary 32, 193, 194
*CNN* 3, 36, 59, 131, 196, 217, 220, 227
coding 100, 102, 155–156, 195, 273–274; and SMS-based political communication 168–177, *168*, **170–174**, **175**, **176**, *176*, 181
cognition 92, 98, 126, 143, 201, 234, 235, 259
cognitive dissonance 63
collective action 17, 97
*Columbo*, and *2000 Mules* 59
commodification, of political communication 17, 182–185
communication: abortion 70; candidate 12, 13–16; and conspiracy theories 12–13; policy 70–71; political *see* political communication; SMS-based political *see* SMS-based political communication
communication dynamics 1–21, *2*, 127
communication strategies 12, 16; gendered 19–20, 266–285, **275**, **276**, **277**, **278**, **279**, **280**
communication theory 20–21
competitive districts 14, 15, 70, 77, 81, 91, 92, 99, 118
confirmation bias, in *2000 Mules* 58, 60
Congress: Democratic members of 130, 137, 138–139, 142; Republican members of 130, 133, 135–136, 142
Congressional Campaign Collection 75–76
congressional campaigns, abortion discourse in 69–87, *76*, *79*, *83*, *85*
Congressional tweets 130–133, **133**, 140–144; on abortion 136–137, *136*; on Donald Trump 131, 132, 134, 138–139, *139*, 140, 142; on economy 137–138, *138*; on immigration 135–136, *135*; on Joe Biden 139–140, *140*; topic volume of 133–134, *134*
conservative news algorithms 156, 157, 158, 160, 161
conservative websites 36
conspiracies 27–41, **35**, **37**, **38**, **40**; definition of 28; fringe 27, 28, 31, 32, 33, 35, 36–37, **37**, **38**, 39, **40**, 40–41; proliferation of 31–32; and theory 50–51
conspiracy culture 13, 49
conspiracy mentality *see* conspiratorial ideation

Index **291**

conspiracy rhetoric 30, 31, 51, 53
conspiracy theories 28–29; and
  communication 12–13; and echo-
  chamber media 50; and elections 32–33
conspiratorial beliefs 12, 13, 27, 30–31,
  41
conspiratorial ideation 13, 27, 28, 29–31,
  33, 36, 37, 40, 41
conspiratorial messaging 32
conspiratorial thinking 13, 28, 31, 40, 56,
  62
constructed narrative 92, 97, 101–102,
  117
content analysis 14, 20, 75, 155–156, 192,
  267, 271, 272, 281
co-occurrence relationships 175, **175–176**,
  177, 181
Cook Political Report Partisan Voting
  Index 77
Cortez Masto, Catherine 18, 213, 214,
  218, 220, 225–226, 226–227, 228, 229,
  230
*Coulda Been Worse LLC* 261, 262
COVID-19 pandemic 18, 29, 30, 50–51,
  56, 135, 178, 192, 194, 204, 206, 266,
  284
crime 4, 8, 15, 104, 125, 200, 203, 204,
  206, 269, 273, **279**; and *2000 Mules* 57,
  58, 59
Crist, Charlie 18, 233, 236
crowded and outraged mediascape
  258–260
culturally shared narratives 92, 95

*Daily Caller* 36, 131
"Deep State" cabal of satanic pedophile
  elites 32
*defending the American Dream that is
  under attack* 106, **107**, 117–118
defense advertisements 94
defunding: Planned Parenthood 78, 80,
  81; police 237, 240, 258
Demings, Val 19, 233–247, **242**, **244**
democracy 61, 125, **171**, **173**, **175**, 181,
  195, 203, 228; American 106, 162,
  205; citizen role in 253; future of 238;
  healthy 21, 70; participatory 177
Democratic Party 4, 149; and abortion
  84, 151; cartoons of **198**, 199, 200,
  202, 204; GDELT Project Television
  Comparer Value **196**; hero role of
  114; in House of Representatives
  150; members of Congress 130, 137,

138–139, 142; websites 77; and young
  voters 8
Democratic-leaning districts 100, **101**,
  106, **107**, 109–112, **109–111**, 114, 117,
  118
Democratic-preferred media **133**,
  135–136, 137, 138, 139
*Democrats are coming for you, the* **103**,
  104–105, 117
*Democrats are subverting America, the*
  **102**, 104
DeSantis, Ron 18, **103**, 135, 233
dialectical progression 215
digital advertising 6–7, 19, 94, 252, 253
digital algorithms 155, 158, 161, 162
digital era, marketplace of ideas in 19,
  252–263
digital marketing landscape 253, 254–255
digital media 4, 8, 9, 13, 16, 19, 96, 97,
  151, 234, 253, 254
digital news: aggregators 152, 153;
  algorithms 16, 149–150, 152, 153,
  154–155, 157, 160, 161, 162; articles
  156, 158, 160, 161
digital partisan news algorithms 149–162,
  **157**, **159**, **160**
digital partisan news consumers 153, 155,
  156, 161
digital partisan news framing 156–157,
  **157**
digital partisan news stories 153, 160
digital platforms 6, 7, 12, 16, 19, 20, 152
digital political polarization 154, 160
direct response 254
disinformation 11, 12, 62, **172**, 181, 182
*Dobbs v. Jackson Women's Health
  Organization* 14, 15, 18–19, 87, 141,
  205, 238; and abortion debate 213–214,
  215, 216, 217, 220, 221, 222, 223,
  224, 225–226, 227–228, 229–230; and
  abortion messaging 77; and abortion
  politics 86; and framing 70–75; leak of
  ruling 134, 136–137; and legal access
  to abortion and women's reproductive
  rights 69; and political communication
  dynamics 125, 127, 128
Dominion Voting Systems 48, 49, 52
D'Souza, Dinesh 13, 48–63

echo chambers 10, 16, 19, 20, 32, 50, 150
economy 3–4, 8, 15, 125, 127, 128, 132,
  134; in Congressional tweets 137–138,
  *138*, 141–142

editorial cartoons 17, 191, 192, 193, 194–195, 197–198, *197*, 200, 204, 205, 206, 207
election cycle 61, 94, 99, 169, 252, 254
election denialism 27, 29, 219; cartoons of 191, 195–196, **196**, 198, **198**, 199, 201, 202, 205
election fraud 29, 33, 51, 58, 262
election integrity 8, 11, 49, 58
election legitimacy 33
election truthers 60
electoral process 12, 16, 20, 203
elites 56, 63, 72–73, 126, 143, 152; and conspiratorial ideation 28–29, 30, 32, 35, **35**, 37, **37**; political 27, 58, 125, 127, 129, 213, 214, 220
emotional content: in narratives 92, 95, 98, 99, 104, 105, 106, 112, 113, 114, 116, 118; in political advertisements 16, 91, 92, 93–94; in social media 11
empathy 92, 98
employment 129; *see also* unemployment
*enacting policies to repair the damage opponents have done* **107**, 108
*endorsed by credible third parties* **110**, 113
engagement, of voters 21; and conspiratorial ideation 13, 27, 33
Engelbrecht, Catherine 54, 55, 56, 57
epistemic junk food 32
equal rights 81–82, 237
ethos 233, 234, 240
exceptions frame, of abortion 82, 83–84
extreme opponents **111**, 114, 118

Facebook 6, 9, 10, 36, 95, 128, 235, 240, 252, 254, 260; ranking algorithm 258
*FactCheck.org* 52, 61
fact-checking 12, 13, 50, 53, 62–63
family values 70, 85
*far right-wing danger lurks* 114, 117
far-right ideology 32, 36, 49, 53, 97, 114, 203
*fault of campaigns* **172**, **175**, **176**, 180
*fault of lawmakers* **172**, **175**, **176**, 180
*fault of regulators* **172**, **175**, **176**
Federal Election Commission 178, 180
female candidates 20, 74, 266, 269, 284, 285
female gubernatorial candidate, communication strategy of 266–285, **275**, **276**, **277**, **278**, **279**, **280**
fetal rights 72

Fetterman, John 17, 195, **196**, **198**, 201–202, 205
*fighting for you* 102, **103**, 105, 106, 117
*fighting the liberal agenda* **103**, 105
First Amendment **171**, 182, 257, 262
FiveThirtyEight.com 92, 100
Flipboard 155, 156
Florida Senate race 233–234, 245–247; campaign horserace 237; candidate evaluations 234–235; candidate familiarity 236, 243; electoral context 236–239; gender equality attitudes 238, 243; interaction effects 239, 243–244; method 239–241; partisanship 235–236; political party affiliation **242**, 242–243; political party interaction **244**, 244–245; racial justice attitudes 237–238, 243; results 241–245; social media 234–235, 241–242, **242**
*Fox News* 8–9, 36, 48, 49, 52, 59, 131, 152, 196
fractured agenda inversion 141
framing 13–16, 74, 266; issue 13–16, 143; media 12, 16, 17, 166, 167, 168, 181–182, 184, 185; partisan news 153–154, 156–157, **157**; of political texting 168, 182, 184; *see also* abortion framing
free speech 71, 253; guiding metaphor of Supreme Court 256–257, 258
fringe conspiracies 27, 28, 31, 32, 33, 35, 36–37, **37**, **38**, 39, **40**, 40–41
Fringe Index 37, **37**
*fringe opponent is not fit for office* **111**, 114
Functional Theory of Political Campaign Discourse 266, 270–271, 282, 284
fundraising 6–7, 178, 254, 272

Gates, Bill 29, 35, **35**, 37, **37**
GDELT Project 196, **196**
gender stereotypes 269
gendered communication 19–20, 266–285, **275**, **276**, **277**, **278**, **279**, **280**
gendered traits 20, 266, 269–270, 271, 273, 274, 285
*getting things done* **103**, 106
Golden Age of Conspiracies 41
Goodstein, Scott 178–179
Google 6, 94, 95, 252, 255, 258, 259–260, 261
Google News 152, 155, 156, 169

Index **293**

GOP (Grand Old Party) *see* Republican Party
government regulation *see* regulation
Grand Old Party (GOP) *see* Republican Party
grassroots
Great Awakening 32, 35
Great Replacement Theory 28
Greene, Marjorie Taylor 29, **111**, 114
guiding free speech metaphor, of Supreme Court 256–257, 258

Hall, Stuart 183
harassment 11–12, 48–49, 269
*harms campaigns* **172**, **176**, 181
*harms democracy* **173**, **175**
*harms individuals* **173**, **175**, **176**, 179, 181, 182, 183
hate speech 12
*have the personal background required to fix the mess created by opponents* **107**, 108
healthcare 8, 14; framing of abortion as 72, 74, 78, **79**, 82, 84, 85, 86
healthy democracy 21, 70
hero and villain binary 96, 105, 106, 108–109, 112, 113, 114, 116, 117
Holmes Jr., Justice Oliver Wendell 253, 256–257
House of Representatives 1, 4, 15, 91, 92, 94, 95, 99, 100, 125, 131, 150, 236

*"I Will Fight [...] Laxalt Won't"* 225–228
identity 181, 217, 235, 259, 261, 283; populist 115–116, **115**, 117; and winning stories 94, 96, 104, 105, 111, 118
ideology: algorithms of 155, 156; far-right 32, 36, 49, 53, 97, 114, 203; in news coverage of political texting 167–168, 181; theory of 167
*I'm one of you* **115**, 116
image traits 233, 234, 240
immigration 4, 8, 15, 18, 104, 125, 129; Congressional tweets on 131–132, 133, 134, 135–136, *135*
incumbency 14, 70, 71, 73, 74, 75, 84
individualism 55, 181, 183, 184
inflation 4, 6, 8, 15, 112–113, 125, 220, 227; cartoons of 191, 196, **198**, 199, 200, 202, 203, 204, 205, 206; Congressional tweets on 131, 132, 133;

GDELT Project Television Comparer Value **196**
Inflation Reduction Act 15, 138, 141, 142
influencers 9, 10, 29, 53, 55
information dissemination 9, 16
internet 50, 96, 253, 255, 258, 259, 261, 262, 263
Instagram 6, 9, 10, 12, 36, 94, 95, 240, 254, 260, 272
issue framing 13–16, 143
issue ownership 13, 14, 15, 73, 75, 126–127, 128, 129, 130, 141, 142, 143, 281
issue positions 233, 234, 240

January 6th, Capitol attack on 33, 51, 59, 63
JFK, Jr. fringe theory 29, 35, **35**, 37, **37**
judicial frame, of abortion 82

Kansas gubernatorial election 266–267, 280–285; campaign climate 267–268; findings 274; framing and functions 270–271; gender 268–269, 269–270; Kelly traits and issues 274–276, **275**, **276**, **277**, 277–280, **278**, **279**, **280**; Kelly's treatment of abortion issue 280; methods 271–274; Schmidt's attacks, acclaims, and defenses 276–280, **277**, **278**, **279**, **280**
*keeping you safe* **103**, 106
*keeping you safe when my opponent/ Democrats won't* **107**, 108
Kelly, Laura 19–20, 266–285, **275**, **276**, **277**, **278**, **279**, **280**
Kelly, Mark 18, 213, 214, 218, 220, 221–222, 223, 224–225, 229, 230

Lake, Kari 49, 195, **198**, 201, 202, 205, 217
Laxalt, Adam 18, 218, 219, 225, 226, 227, 228, 229
liberal digital news algorithms 157, 161
liberal political values 152
local values **109**, 112, 118
logos 233, 234, 240
Low-Threshold Activities Index 34

mainstream media 4, 10, 13, 27, 36, 39, 53, 55, 62, 63
male candidates 74, 266, 268
marketplace of ideas 19, 252–263

**294** Index

mass media 166–167, 168, 177, 182, 184, 185; framings of political texting 168, 182, 184

Masters, Blake 18, 70, 218, 220, 221–222, 223–224, 225, 229

media: alternative (alt-media) 27, 33, 36, 37, **38**, 39, 41; Democratic-preferred **133**, 135–136, 137, 138, 139; digital 4, 8, 9, 13, 16, 19, 96, 97, 151, 234, 253, 254; echo-chamber 50; mainstream 4, 10, 13, 27, 36, 39, 53, 55, 62, 63; mass 166–167, 168, 177, 182, 184, 185; news *see* news media; political 10, 126, 127; Republican-preferred **133**, 135–136, 137–138, 139–140, 141; social *see* social media; traditional 6, 10, 21, 36, 94, 128, 144, 234

media agendas 125, 126–127, 128, 129, 130, 144; social 125–144, **133**, *134*, *135*, *136*, *138*, *139*, *140*

media coverage: "annoying, but legal" 178, 179–182, *182*; polarization of 20–21; and public perception 16–17

media framing 12, 16, 17, 166, 167, 168, 181–182, 184, 185

media narratives 3, 4, 10, 17, 21, 194

media outlets retweeted and quoted by members of Congress 131, 132–140, **133**, *134*, *135*, *136*, *138*, *139*, *140*, 141, 143

media use, and proliferation of conspiracies 31–32

mediascape, crowded and outraged 258–260

medical autonomy 216, 225, 229

Meta 6, 7, 12, 94, 95, 253, 254, 255, 258, 260, 261

metanarratives 97, 104, 105, 108, 116

metaphor 104, 169, 180–181, 192, 253; guiding free speech 256–257; marketplace of ideas 19, 252–263; militaristic **173**, **175**, 181; natural disaster **173**, **175**, 181

midterm communication 17–20

midterm curse 3

midterm election cycle 94, 169

Mill, John Stuart 256–257

Milton, John 256–257

misinformation 9, 11, 12, 13, 20, 30, 31, 61, 260–261, 262

mobilization, of voters 13, 14, 178

moderate values 9

morality 14, 72, 78, **79**, 80, 81, 84, 85, 86, **102**, 104, **109**, 222, 227

Musk, Elon 126, 131, 143–144

narrative analysis 92, 101

narrative inquiry 98–99

narrative methodology 101, 117

narrative transportation 98

narrative turn, in humanities and social sciences 95

narratives: constructed 92, 97, 101–102, 117; culturally shared 92, 95; definition of 95; emotional content in 92, 95, 98, 99, 104, 105, 106, 112, 113, 114, 116, 118; media 3, 4, 10, 17, 21, 194; meta- 97, 104, 105, 108, 116; news 16–17; political 10, 16, 96–97, 98; in political advertisements 98–99; as political strategy 97–98; populist 116, 119; public 99, 117; strategic 92, 97–98, 117; winning 91–119, **101**, **102–103**, 107, **109–111**, **115**

national politics 19, 201, 228

*National Public Radio* (NPR) 131

*NBC News* 70, 131

negative attacks 233, 234, 240, 108

Nevada Senate race 218

*New York Post* 131

*New York Times, The* 4, 5, 69–70, 128, 131

news: digital *see* digital news; online 132, 149, 154, 155, 156; pink slime 10; television 36, 37, **38**, 39, 59, 196

news aggregators 16, 152, 155

News Break 155, 156

news coverage of political texting 168–177, *168*, **170–174**, **175–176**, *176*

news media 31, 58, 125, 130, 140, 142, 162, 178, 184, 229; and political communication 128–130

news narratives, and public perception 16–17

news producers 152, 153, 154

*Newsmax* 52, 59, 131

newspapers 8, 130, 194

niche social media platforms 32

9/11 28, 35, **35**, 37, **37**, 50, 106

NPR (*National Public Radio*) 131

Obama, Barack: birther conspiracy 28, **35**; campaign 177, 235; cartoons of 193, 194, 205; digital media use 234;

Facebook use 235; text messaging 177, 178; text-to-donate fundraising 178
online communities 10, 30
online news 132, 149, 154, 155, 156
Opera News 155, 156
*opponent is aligned with special interests* **115**, 116
O'Rourke, Beto 19, 252, 254, 258, 261
overperforming candidates 15, 92, 100, 118
Oz, Dr. Mehmet 17, 195, **196**, **198**, 201–202, 205

P2P texting 179, 180, 181, 182
pandemic, COVID-19 *see* COVID-19 pandemic
participatory democracy 177
partisan identification 36, 39
partisan lean 91, 92, 100, **101**
partisan news framing 153–154, 156–157, **157**
partisanship 19, 31, 86, 162, 235–236, 239, 242, 245, 246
party affiliation 14, 234, 235, 236, 238, 239, 240–241, 242–243, 243–244, 245, 246, 247, 268, 284
party identification 27, 28, 34, 36, 37, **38**, **40**, 40, 41, 246
paternalism 214, 217, 219, 220, 221, 224, 225, 227, 228, 229, 230
pathos 233, 234, 240, 108
Pennsylvania Senate race 201–202
*personal background as beacon* **109**, 112–113
*perspective of academics* **170**, **175**, **176**, 181
*perspective of anti-spam industry* **170**, **176**
*perspective of campaigns* **170**, **175**, **176**, 179, 181
*perspective of lawmakers* **170**, **175**
*perspective of marketing industry* **170**, **175**
*perspective of receivers* **171**, **175**, **176**
*perspective of regulators* **171**, **175**
persuasive advertising 254
Phillips, Gregg 54, 55–56, 57
pink slime news 10
*Plandemic* 50–51, 58
Planned Parenthood 78, 80, 81, 223, 226
*Planned Parenthood v. Casey* 213, 214, 215, 216, 220–221, 225, 228–229

plotted stories, in political advertisements 92, 116
polarization *see* political polarization
polarized digital algorithms 155, 158
policy communication 70–71
political advertising 91–119, **101**, **102–103**, 107, **109–111**, **115**
political agendas 3, 15, 16, 126, 127, 128, 129
political campaigns: advertising in 94, 119, 255; and base of support 235, 247; battle-oriented terminology in 181; "dark money" influence in 261; digital advertisement spending across 6; and digital media 234, 253; framing usage 270; and gender 268; harm of texting spam 181, 182, 185; issue framing in 13; and media 16; messaging for 92; online 253, 262; SMS marketing by 169, **171**, **172**, **173**, **174**; and social media 235, 247; text messaging for 166–167, 177, 178, 179, 180; and voting behavior 93
political cartoon research 192–194
political cartoons 16, 17, 191–207, **196**, *197*, **198**
political communication: and *Dobbs* decision 127; and news media 128–130; SMS-based *see* SMS-based political communication; and social media 128–130; and text messaging 177–179
political discourse 12, 13, 16, 19, 20, 160–161, 162, 181, 213
political elites 27, 58, 125, 127, 129, 213, 214, 220
political humor 191, 194
political ideologies 10, 27, 96, 155
political information 16, 32, 92, 95, 149, 151, 153, 260
political media 10, 126, 127
political narratives 10, 16, 96–97, 98
political participation 152, 166
political party affiliation *see* party affiliation
political polarization 16, 150, 151, 154–155, 161, 162; digital 154, 160; and digital partisan news algorithm paths 157–158
political polarization cultivator, and digital partisan news algorithm spheres 158–160, **159**, **160**

**296** Index

political spam *see* spam, political
political strategy, narratives as 97–98
political systems 96, 151, 152, 216
political texting 17; collecting and coding
    news coverage of 168–177, *168*,
    **170–174**, **175–176**, *176*; ideological
    rhetorical analysis of 167–168; mass
    media framings of 168, 182, 184;
    news coverage framing of 168, 178;
    regulation of 179–182, *182*
politically aligned algorithms 160, 161
*Politifact* 61
polling 5, 7, 21, 125, 180, 233, 267, 274,
    282, 284
popularity 3, 71, 87, 131, 150, 152, 223
populism 30–31, 96, 116, 119, 223;
    authoritarian *see* authoritarian populism
*populist identity makes it acceptable to*
    *vote for me* 115, **115**, 117
post-*Roe* politics 69–87, *76*, **79**, *83*, *85*
predictors, of midterm elections 3, 28, 39,
    40, 234
presidential elections: and Big Lie 13, 27,
    29, 35, **35**, 41, 48, 59, 125; cartoons
    produced during 192–193, 194, 206,
    207; and text messaging 178, 186
primaries 8, 11, 29, 74, 85, 86, 129, 130,
    178, 218, 233, 236, 267, 272, 273–274,
    282
priming 70–71, 73, 75, 85
pro-choice framing 69, 72, 76, 81
progressive values 9
pro-life framing 72, 75, 76, 80, 81, 82,
    213–230
proliferation of conspiracies 31–32
promissory responsiveness 70
public narratives 99, 117
public opinion 12, 20–21, 71, 86, 87, 154,
    155, 158, 160, 213, 223, 225, 229
public perception 16–17, 61, 126, 141
public safety 8, 71

QAnon conspiracies 13, 27, 28–29, 30,
    32, 33, 35, 40–41; and Donal
    Trump 50
QAnon Knowledge 35, 37, **38**, 39, **40**, 40

racism 28, 32, 240, 284
red wave 3, 4–5, 14–15, 21, 118; cartoons
    of 191, 195, **196**, 198, **198**, 199,
    200, 201, 204; high voter turnout 7;
    President Biden's low approval ratings

14, 91; suburban voters 9; Texas
    midterms 252; young voters 8
Reddit 9–10, 32, 132
redistricting 84, 236
referendum theory 149, 150–151
regulation: of abortion *see* abortion
    regulation; internet 258, 261; of
    political text messaging 178, 170–182,
    **172**, **174**, **175**, *182*, 184–185
religion, and abortion access 14, 72, 73,
    78, **79**, 80, 86, 222
religious elites conspiracy 28–29, **35**
reproductive freedom 81, 87, 127, 128,
    143
reproductive health 69–70, 82, 133, 269
reproductive rights 4, 6, 7, 10, 14, 75, 81,
    132, 213, 225, 229
Republican Party: and abortion access
    213, 214, 217, 229–230; cartoons of
    **198**, 199, 200–201, 202, 203, 204; and
    conspiracies 31; and Donald Trump 9;
    GDELT Project Television Comparer
    Value **196**; members of Congress 130,
    133, 135–136, 142; and 2022 midterm
    elections 5, 150; websites 78, 80, 83
Republican-leaning districts 100, **101**,
    102, **102–103**, 105, **115**, 119
Republican-preferred media **133**,
    135–136, 137–138, 139–140, 141
*results delivered* **110**, 112
rhetorical criticism 167, 177
rhetorical gridlock, and abortion debate
    215, 216, 229
rhetorical invention 214, 215, 217, 218
rhetorical trajectory, and abortion debate
    18–19, 213–230
rigged elections 11–12
*right personal background for the job, the*
    **103**, 105, 108
rights: to choose 70, 72, 115, 132, 240;
    equal 81–82, 237; fetal 72; reproductive
    4, 6, 7, 10, 14, 75, 81, 132, 213, 225,
    229; unborn 14, 78–79, **79**, 82, 84, 86;
    voting 8, 240; women's 14, 72, 74, 78,
    79, 81, 85, 86, 221, 238, 240, 273
right-wing politics 31, 32, 33, 36, 41, 48,
    49, 53, 55, 56, 61; see also *far right-*
    *wing danger lurks*
Robokiller 17, 184, 186
*Roe v. Wade* 8; and abortion regulation 14,
    80, 221, 225, 228–229; cartoons of 199;
    and issue framing 13–14; overturning

of 73, 142, 143, 213, 214, 216, 220–221, 267; and women's rights 82, 224; see also *Dobbs v. Jackson Women's Health Organization*; post-Roe politics
Rubin, Dave 51, 52, 53
Rubio, Marco 19, 233–247, **242**, **244**

safe districts 70, 73, 78
safeguards of rights 214
Salem Media 48, 49, 51, 52, 53, 57
satanic pedophile elites 28–29, 32, 35, **35**, 37, **37**
Schmidt, Derek 19, 20, 266, 267, 268, 270, 271, 272, 273; attacks, acclaims, and defenses of 276–280, **277**, **278**, **279**, **280**, 280–281, 282, 283–284
scientific method 53, 54, 55
scientific rationalism 53–58
search engines 255, 259–260
Senate race: Florida *see* Florida Senate race; Nevada 218; Pennsylvania 201–202
*service embedded in local values and local priorities* **109**, 112
*share your values* **109**, 111–112, 118
Smart News 155, 156
SMS political marketing 168–169; technology of **171–174**
SMS-based political communication: dominant media frames of 166–186, *168*, **170–174**, **175–176**, *176*, *182*; technology of 185–186
social justice 19, 237, 239, 243, 245–246, 247
social media: agendas 125–144, **133**, *134*, *135*, *136*, *138*, *139*, *140*; companies 11, 12; content 11, 19, 233, 234, 235, 236, 239, 240, 241, 244, 246; platforms 4, 6, 9, 10, 11, 13, 16, 27, 32, 36, 41, 255, 260; use 12, 37, 39, 136, 152, 234
*solution is campaigns* **173**
*solution is individual* **175**, 183
*solution is lawmaking* **174**, **175**
*solution is regulation* **174**, **175**
*solution is telecom companies* **174**
spam, political **173**, **174**, 179, *182*, 182; anti- 17, **170**, **176**, 185–186; solutions to 183–185, 185–186

spending, on campaigns 6, 7, 94–95, 252, 254, 255
*stark contrast with opponent* 106, **107**, 117–118
STM (structural topic models) 76, 78, 87
stories: digital partisan news 153, 160; plotted 92, 116; voter 98; winning 91–119, **101**, **102–103**, **107**, **109–111**, **115**
Storm, The 28, 32, 35
storytelling 13, 95; inverted 58–61
strategic narratives 92, 97–98, 117
structural topic models (STM) 76, 78, 87
suburban voters 9
Supreme Court 115, 135, 180, 229, 253, 262; guiding free speech metaphor of 256–257; see also *Dobbs v. Jackson Women's Health Organization*; *Whole Women's Health v. Hellerstedt*
surge and decline theory 149, 150, 151
swing voting 51, 78, 83, 86, 233, 235

*taking on Big Business* **111**, 113
target audiences 93, 152, 154, 254, 255
targeted advertising 9, 21
Targeted Regulation of Abortion Providers (TRAP) laws 219, 223, 229
telecom industry **174**, 179, 184–185, 186
television advertising 6, 75, 94, 95, 254
Television Explorer 196, 197, 199, 200, 201
television news 36, 37, **38**, 39, 59, 196
10DLC Rules 184–185, 186
testimonials 98
Texas midterms 252–254, 262–263; crowded, outraged mediascape 258–260; digital marketing landscape 254–255; marketplace of ideas 256–257; questionable information 260–262
text messaging, in U.S. political communication 177–179; *see also* political text messaging
text-to-donate fundraising 178
thematic analysis 101
*there is no solution* **174**, **175**, **176**, 182
TikTok 9, 10, 12, 36
toga candidate 262
topic modeling 75, 76
topic volume, of Congressional tweets 133–134, *134*

**298** Index

topical congruence 191, 193, 194, 195, 196, 198, 204, 205, 207
*Townhall* 131, 195
traditional media 6, 10, 21, 36, 94, 128, 144, 234
traditional values 72
TRAP (Targeted Regulation of Abortion Providers) laws 219, 223, 229
Triad of Argumentation 233, 234–235
True the Vote 51, 52, 54, 57
Trump, Donald: administration of 213, 218, 227; America First agenda 18; and authoritarian populism 30, 40–41; cartoons of **198**, 199, 200–201, 202, 203, 204; Congressional tweets about 131, 132, 134, 138–139, *139*, 140, 142; and conspiracy theories 50; effect of 149, 151; endorsements 17, 18, 119, 266, 268; GDELT Project Television Comparer Value **196**; on Marco Rubio 236; role in 2022 midterms of 8–9; supporters of 33, 48; and Twitter 49, 272; on *2000 Mules* 49, 52; *see also* Big Lie; Storm, The; True the Vote; Truth Social
Truth Social 36, 49, 52
TV news 36, 37, **38**, 39, 59, 196
2020 election 8, 49, 51, 53, 54, 57, 59, 61, 63, 94, 134
Twitter (X) 10, 11, 12, 49, 272; application programming interface (API) 15, 125, 126, 131, 143–144; use by sitting members of U.S. Congress during 2022 election 125–144, **133**, *134, 135, 136, 138, 139, 140*
*2000 Mules* 48–49, 63; audience for 60; confirmation bias in 58, 60; conspiracy and theory 50–51; detective denouement 60; detective story formula 58–59; fact-checking of 50, 53, 61–63; first act of 51, 53–54; geo-tracking technology 55, 56; howcatchem configuration of 58–59; hypothesis of 53, 54–55; and inverted storytelling 58–61; mainstream responses to 61–63; recalculation of the 2020 election 57; recap of "what we know" 57; and scientific rationalism 53–58; second act of 51–52, 54, 55–56, 58; storied account of 51–53; and suspension of disbelief 59; third act of 52, 57–58, 60

unborn rights 14, 78–79, **79**, 82, 84, 86
uncompetitive districts 75
unemployment 4, 273
unrecognizable institutions 118
U.S. Supreme Court *see* Supreme Court

values 95, **103**, 105; American 106; and authoritarianism as it relates to Trumpian populism 30; and destruction of American identity 104; family 70, 85; and hero stories 117; liberal political 152; local **109**, 112, 118; moderate 9; progressive 9; shared 15, **109**, 111–112, 118; traditional 72
video political advertisements 92, 94, 99, 100, 116, 119
vigilante activity 49, 61
visualization 92, 98, 175
voter behavior 9, 16, 19, 20, 93, 142, 143
voter choice 27–41, **35**, **37**, **38**, **40**
voter engagement 21; and conspiratorial ideation 13, 27, 33
voter fraud 11, 13, 29, 48, 49, 51, 52, 53, 54, 57, 60–61
voter mobilization 13, 14, 178
voter stories 98
voter turnout 7–8, 9, 21, 93, 143, 166, 206
"voting is important" message, in cartoons 206
voting rights 8, 240

Walker, Herschel 17–18, 195, **196**, 198, **198**, 201, 202, 204–205
*Wall Street Journal, The* 131
"war on women" 219, 221, 225
Warnock, Raphael 17
*Washington Examiner* 131
*Washington Post, The* 4, 60, 62, 128, 131, 226–227
wave elections 4, 83, 84
*"We All Know Guys Like This"* 220–225
websites 87; campaign 14, 70, 74, 75–76, 77, 78, 80, 83, 234; conservative 36; Democratic 77; far-right 36; Republican 78, 80, 83
White House 1, *2*, 3, 50, 63
*Whitney v. California* 263
*Whole Women's Health v. Hellerstedt* 216, 219, 229

*will work across the aisle and hold President Biden accountable* **110**, 113

winning stories 91–119, **101**, **102–103**, **107**, **109–111**, **115**

Women Protective Anti-Abortion Arguments (WPAA) 219

women's political agency 219

women's rights 14, 72, 74, 78, 79, 81, 85, 86, 221, 238, 240, 273

worldviews 30, 58, 96, 98, 167

WPAA (Women Protective Anti-Abortion Arguments) 219

X *see* Twitter (X)

*you can trust me* 109, **109–110**, 113, 114, 117, 118

young voters 6, 7–8, 9, 10, 177

YouTube 6, 9, 100